Unexplained
Phenomena

A ROUGH GUIDE SPECIAL

There are more than two hundred Rough Guide travel
titles, phrasebooks and reference books,
covering destinations from Amsterdam to Zimbabwe
and subjects from the Internet to Opera.

Forthcoming travel titles include
Alaska • Devon & Cornwall • Ibiza • Southeast Asia

Forthcoming reference titles include
Cuban Music • Hip-Hop • Latin Music: 100 Essential CD's
Personal Computers • Pregnancy

www.roughguides.com

Rough Guide Credits

Text Editor: Joe Staines
Design: Henry Iles and Helen Ostick
Typesetting: Helen Ostick
Production: Susanne Hillen and Julia Bovis
Proofreading: Russell Walton
Rough Guide Series Editor: Mark Ellingham

Acknowledgements

Bob Rickard and **John Michell** would like to thank the following for their assistance with illustrations, translations and information: Nicholas Allen, Larry E. Arnold, Denise Allison, Lionel Beer, Janet Bord, Brian Chapman, Mike Dash, Nigel Fairman, Peter Hough, Susan Lung, Michel Meurger, Steve Moore, Niall O'Mara, Brian Regal, David Shurville, Paul Sieveking, George Wingfield, Raspberry N. Zeigler and J.F. "Nosher" Neal. Plus special thanks to Joe Staines, our editor at Rough Guides.

To Sam whose support has enabled me to accomplish much – Bob.

Joe Staines would like to thank the following Rough Guide staff: Helen Ostick for typesetting, Henry Iles for design, Susanne Hillen, Michelle Draycott and Julia Bovis in production, Russell Walton for proofreading and Demelza Dallow for help with pictures. Thanks also to Naomi Pritchard at Thames and Hudson for all her help, and to Wim Van Klaveran for his assistance with translation.

Publishing details

This first edition published August 2000 by Rough Guides Ltd,
62–70 Shorts Gardens, London WC2H 9AB

Distributed by the Penguin Group:
Penguin Books Ltd, 27 Wrights Lane, London W8 5TZ
Penguin Putnam, Inc., 375 Hudson Street, New York, NY 10014
Pengin Books Australia Ltd, 487 Maroondah Highway, PO Box 257, Ringwood, Victoria 3134, Australia
Penguin Books Canada Ltd, 10 Alcorn Avenue, Toronto, Ontario, Canada M4V 1E4
Penguin Books (NZ) Ltd, 182–190 Wairau Road, Auckland 10, New Zealand

Typeset in Bembo and Helvetica to an original design by Henry Iles.
Printed in Spain by Graphy Cems.

Many of the pictures in this book first appeared in *Phenomena* (1977) and *Living Wonders* (1982), both published by Thames and Hudson.

All other photographs copyright of credited photographers and agencies.

400pp includes index

A catalogue record for this book is available from the British Library.
ISBN 1-85828-589-5

Unexplained
Phenomena

A ROUGH GUIDE SPECIAL

Written by

John Michell and Bob Rickard

ROUGH GUIDES

Contents

Introduction

The phenomenal world

Our first book on unexplained phenomena, *Phe-nomena: a book of wonders*, appeared in 1977; it was followed, five years later, by a companion volume, *Living Wonders*, which dealt mainly with anomalies in the animal world. *The Rough Guide to Unexplained Phenomena* combines selected chapters from both earlier books into a single volume, updating them with substantial new material.

Our purpose, as before, is to introduce readers to the rich variety of anomalous, and often bizarre phenomena, that people have experienced throughout the centuries. The world and our experience of it, are nothing like we have been taught. Things are far more interesting, humorous and wide-ranging than any rational science, religion or world-view can possibly accommodate. Too often, education enforces a standard view of things which dims individual perceptions and brings dullness to the world.

It is not our intention here to dispute anyone's beliefs or theories. But we should like to point out their limitations. There are things that happen in this world – and have occurred throughout the whole of human experience – for which there has never been a lasting, rational explanation. Explanations are temporary products, coming and going in response to fashions. Meanwhile, the happenings they are supposed to explain carry on as mysteriously as ever.

Yet mysterious phenomena are also to some extent influenced by fashion. For example, clusters of hibernating swallows and living toads encased in rocks, so regularly recorded by nineteenth-century naturalists, seem virtually to have died out; mariners today hardly ever witness sea-serpents; and rings of dancing fairies, once a commonly described part of country people's experience, are now very rare. To make up for these, perhaps temporary losses, other types of weird phenomena have flourished in modern times – UFOs for example, together with alien or demonic entities; rapes and abductions by "spacemen"; obscene mutilations of horses and cattle and – on a brighter note – the beautiful phenomenon of crop circles. At the same time, the standard mysteries, those which have puzzled humanity from the beginning, continue to do so. Creatures and artifacts fall, sometimes slowly, from unknown sources; poltergeists bring floods, fires and stone-showers to tormented households; people are levitated, walk over hot coals, are invisibly attacked, encounter monsters in lakes and mountains, are subject to amazing coincidences, and so on. You hear about these things in myths, legends and folklore, and you can read about their modern continuations in scientific journals and the daily press.

Charles Hoy Fort (1874–1932), pictured in 1930 with one of his diversions from collecting anomalies of science and natural history, the game of 'supercheckers' which he invented.

As authors we share a common interest in the writings, records and world-view of Charles Fort (1874–1932), the remarkable author and iconoclast who lived in the Bronx district of New York. Much of his life was spent in the New York Public Library, the British Museum Reading Room in London and other repositories of records. Sifting through back numbers of newspapers and science magazines he collected thousands of items referring to events, appearances, discoveries and types of phenomena which did not fit into any established theory or rational world-view. For that reason they were completely ignored and, as far as possible, forgotten. In Fort's view that was unfair and created a biased picture of life. The anomalous reports were often published in the same journals from which scientists derived the data behind their

respectable-sounding theories, but the theorists paid no attention to them. Their theories were therefore selective and prejudiced. They were held together by "exclusions" – by ignoring all data that contradicted them. To illustrate this, and to redress the balance, Fort used his collections of anomalies to create different pictures of reality. It is not that scientific orthodoxy is totally wrong, he said, for nothing in this world is ever totally anything, but he criticized it as being arbitrary. There are many different ways of perceiving and defining reality, and it seemed to Fort that much of the data which orthodox thinkers ignored gave a far more complete view of things than any of the established theories.

Fort called the anomalous items he collected "the damned facts" – damned by exclusion from the pale of scientific consideration. His first book, published in 1919, was called *The Book of the Damned,* and in the first twenty pages of it he outlined a picture of reality in which the damned facts were given equal rights with those accepted by science. The result was a world-view similar to that of traditional mysticism, in which there are no hard-and-fast laws, merely tendencies, and in which human imagination plays a significant part. In the course of time, he foresaw, the damned facts of the present would be accepted and made orthodox; new theories would be built upon them, and these in turn would then become exclusive, disregarding all evidence that challenged them. The situation, said Fort, is that nothing in our changing, fluctuating world is actually and permanently real, so our attempts to categorize and pin down nature are doomed to failure. The nearest thing to reality that he admitted was the universe itself. He saw it as a great, single organism, moving automatically, or perhaps even consciously, to satisfy its own desires and to direct whatever was needed to its various parts. As to the means by which this was done, Fort suggested an unknown force or mechanism which he called teleportation.

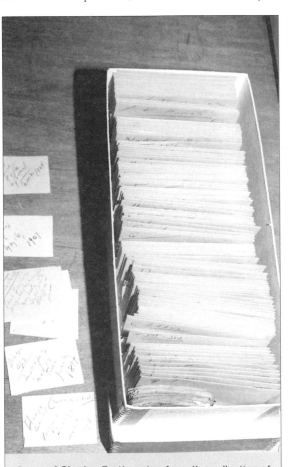

Some of Charles Fort's notes from the collection of over 40,000 in the Manuscript Section of New York Public Library.

disturbed young person; between unknown lights or objects in the sky and possible otherworldly intelligence; between outbreaks of hysteria or religious fervour and fires, earthquakes and other disasters. Of all his conceptions teleportation proved to be the most useful. One of his special interests was in the anomalies of animal distribution, whether it was the spontaneous appearance of life in newly-dug ponds, the mysteries of bird and insect migration or the strange ability of certain pet animals to find their owners, even when they have moved far away to unknown locations.

Together with these phenomena Fort collected cases of lost possessions miraculously rediscovered, modern artifacts excavated from ancient geological strata, and objects that manifest themselves at spiritualist sessions, at the behest of shamans and holy men, in response to prayer or intense desire or simply of their own accord. In connection with these and other mysteries Fort spoke of teleportation, not as a scientific theory to be proved or clamouring for precise explanations, which will never be forthcoming.

This is a humorous subject, but while laughing at it we are also somewhat respectful towards Fort's damned facts, and we are wholly respectful towards his inclusive attitude and world-view. There is nothing to be gained by worrying about or wilfully rejecting aspects of our human experience which can never be explained. The greatest of human pleasures (purer and more long-lasting than

Fort was among the first to draw attention to several types of phenomena which are now widely recognized, and he was also original in noticing connections between them – between poltergeist events and the presence of a distressed or mentally sex or any of the appetites) is to investigate the world, generally and in its various parts – and much more so if it is done honestly, without regard to prejudices, taboos, inhibitions and other people's conventions.

In this book we make all sorts of connections between the various types of mysteries and wonders described in it, but we do not ask readers to follow us, believe in us or accept any of our tentative conclusions. The most we hope for is to bring relief to those among us who have experienced strange happenings and have been told by their doctors, parents or contemporaries that this is unnatural and even perhaps a sign of madness. Our message of comfort to such readers is that you are not alone. As we carefully demonstrate in the following chapters, these things have always happened, they can happen to anyone, and at least some of them probably happen to everyone in the course of a lifetime. Our very existence in this world is an unexplained mystery, and that is something we have to accept and be happy with.

John Michell and Bob Rickard

1

Teleportation

1

Teleportation

Human teleportation

The idea behind "teleporting" is familiar to anyone who watches or reads science fiction: as demonstrated, for example, by the transport chambers in the *Star Trek* TV series, from which people and objects can be instantaneously "beamed" to a faraway location. Less well known is the fact that Charles Fort coined the word in 1931. Fort's hypothesis was of a mysterious force that could transport matter, objects and even living creatures between two points without seeming to travel the intervening distance; it could also manipulate them at a distance. If such a force exists, it could account for observations of such psychical phenomena as "apports" (the sudden appearance and disappearance of things in the presence of a medium), as well as provide a fundamental mechanism behind the more mysterious distributions of living creatures. By 1945, Fort's teleportation was being discussed by psychical researchers, such as Harry Price, as a reasonable hypothesis for poltergeist activity.

According to our present understanding of the laws of science, teleportation is not supposed to happen, but in later sections we quote cases where we conclude that it actually has. We are impressed by the evidence from centuries of human experience suggesting that living creatures and things are occasionally transported vast distances in the proverbial twinkling of an eye. But first let us consider the claims of human teleportation, of which we only have hints and images.

An old Spanish ghost story, suggestive of teleportation, has astonished people for four centuries and, as retold by the pioneer UFO writer M.K. Jessup, has influenced the modern generation of mystery writers. It is the tale of a soldier who was instantaneously transported from the Philippines to Mexico City (over nine thousand miles) in October 1593. The uniform that he was wearing, when he appeared in the city's main plaza, was unfamiliar to the inhabitants but later turned out to be that of a regiment stationed in the Philippines. Questioned by officers of the Inquisition, the soldier could only say that, moments before his appearance in Mexico, he had been on sentry duty at the Governor's palace in Manila – the Philippine capital. The Governor, he said, had recently been assassinated. How he came to be in Mexico he had no idea. Months later a ship from the Philippines confirmed the news of the assassination and other details of the soldier's story.

A simple experience of the teleportation effect is claimed by the respected mystic, Wellesley Tudor Pole, in his book, *The Silent Road* (1962): "On a wet and stormy night in December 1952, I found myself at a country station some mile and a half from my Sussex home. The train from London had arrived late, the bus had gone and no taxis were available. The rain was heavy and incessant.

'Transit of Venus': a satirical view of Mrs Guppy's teleportation across London.

that the exact time was 5.57 pm Three minutes to zero hour! What happened next I cannot say. When I came to myself I was standing in my hall at home, a good twenty minutes walk away, and the clock was striking six. My telephone call duly came through a few minutes later. Having finished my call, I awoke to the realization that something very strange had happened. Then much to my surprise, I found that my shoes were dry and free from mud, and that my clothes showed no sign of damp or damage."

The implication here is that Major Tudor Pole was instantly transported home in response to his strong desire to be there, but without any conscious magic on his part. Yet if it could so happen spontaneously, why not at the direction of the will? We think of witches and spiritualists and particularly of the incident – much satirized at the time – of the hefty psychic Mrs Guppy. In Harry Price's memorable account, in *Poltergeist Over England* (1945), on 3 June 1871, Mrs Guppy was "instantly precipitated from her home at Highbury (London) to a house in Lamb's Conduit Street, some three miles away, where she came down bump right in the middle of a séance" – dressed only in her underclothes.

An even more remarkable feat of teleportation, or bilocation, concerns the Venerable Mary Jesus of Agreda. Although she was never known to have left her Spanish convent, it was officially estimated that, between the years of 1620 and 1631, she made over five hundred trips to America to convert the Jumano Indians of New Mexico. This estimate was not arrived at lightly. At first, the Catholic authorities – made wary by the delusive claims of religious hysterics – put considerable pressure on Sister Mary to dissuade her from insisting on the

The time was 5.55pm and I was expecting an important trunk call from overseas at 6pm at home. The situation seemed desperate. To make matters worse, the station call box was out of order and some trouble on the line made access to the railway telephone impossible. In despair I sat down in the waiting-room and having nothing better to do, I compared my watch with the station clock. Allowing for the fact that this is always kept two minutes in advance, I was able to confirm the fact reality of her trans-Atlantic flights. Only the testimony of missionaries to the Mexican Indians persuaded them to authenticate her experiences. In 1622, Father Alonzo de Benavides, of the Isolita Mission in New Mexico, had written to Pope Urban VIII and to Philip IV of Spain asking who had pre-empted him in his mission to convert the Jumano Indians. The Jumanos themselves declared their knowledge of Christianity to have come from a "lady in blue", a European nun who had left with them crosses, rosaries and a chalice which they used for celebrating Mass. This chalice was believed to have come from Mary's convent at Agreda.

It was not until 1630, when Father Benavides returned to Spain, that he heard of Sister Mary and her fantastic belief that she had converted the Jumano Indians. He obtained leave to examine her and did so closely, receiving from her exact accounts of her visits to the Indians with details of their appearance and customs. She kept a diary of her experiences, but burnt it on the advice of her confessor. In it she described many details of her travels – including a vision of the planet earth as a sphere revolving on its poles. In his *Life of the Venerable Mary of Agreda* James A. Carrico concludes: "That Agreda really visited America many times, is attested to by the logs of the Spanish conquistadors, the French explorers, the identical accounts by different tribes of Indians a thousand miles apart. Every authentic history of the Southwest of the United States records this mystic phenomenon unparalleled in the entire history of the world."

There are unsatisfactory aspects to Father Benavides' 1631 account of the legend and his interview. It was a best-seller in its day and many people had a vested interest in the legend as a means of encouraging colonization of the New World. Benavides claims that Mary gave him many proofs of her flights to the Jumanos, carried by Saints Michael and Francis. In fact, in unpublished records, she never directly confirms her bodily transportation and later doubted it. She had narrowly escaped being condemned as a witch in her youth and was wary of official reprimands for her frequent ecstasies and levitations. She had to choose her words carefully and so, pressed to explain her undoubted visions of the faraway Indians, Mary supposed that angels had impersonated her while allowing her to witness their exploits. What further complicated the matter was that often while she was in an ecstatic state, or isolated in her cell, the nuns would tell visitors that she was "away with the Indians".

Mary of Agreda appears to the natives of New Mexico. A woodcut from Father Benavides' *Letter to the Friars* (1730 edition).

Nevertheless, Mary's dream-like impressions of travelling through the air accord with similar descriptions from mystics who levitated or bi-located. The coincidence of her clairvoyant visions of the Indians and their insistence on the physical presence of a nun cannot be dismissed completely. One of Mary's memoranda includes a detail that will delight all phenomenalists. Just as the folk traditions of all lands warn the traveller into fairyland against taking gifts from fairies, eating fairy food, or lusting after fairy women, so Mary says she was warned by God, "that neither by thought, word nor deed must I presume to long for or touch anything, unless it were God's express will that I should do so."

Involuntary teleportations often seem like the attacks of Invisible Assailants. A young Indian boy, the focus of unwelcome poltergeist attention in the famous and well-attested "Poona" case, was "levitated and transported on more than one occasion", according to Harry Price. In the period of a year (1928–29), Price and his colleague, Miss

H. Kohn, recorded hundreds of incidents of objects flying around (often in curved trajectories), moving, vanishing and reappearing in the boy's presence, all observed by reliable witnesses.

In another famous case that began in December 1761, the children of Richard Giles in Bristol suffered terribly at the "hands" of a violent poltergeist; they were struck, dragged, pelted, bitten, throttled, stuck with pins and slobbered over. On occasions, several men could not hold them down as they rose into the air. These events had many adult witnesses and were recorded in a diary each day by Henry Durbin, known as a pious and conscientious man. On Thursday, 16 September 1762, the youngest daughter, Dobby, vanished from the kitchen before five people. The household was mobilized to look for her, without success. An hour later she was found in a stupor, under a bed in an upper part of the house, behind a door that was locked. Like other cases we could cite, the afflicted girls blamed an apparition.

In recent years, some remarkable cases of involuntary teleportation have been reported, mostly within the UFO context, some of which are summarized in John Keel's *Our Haunted Planet* (1971). Another example, described in detail in *The Unidentified* (1975) by Jerome Clark and Loren Coleman, is that of José Antonio da Silva who turned up on 9 May 1969 near Vitoria, Brazil, shocked and dishevelled. He had vanished from near Bebedouro, some five hundred miles away, four and a half days earlier. His story – that he had been captured by creatures about four feet tall, taken by them to another planet and then returned to earth – sounds fantastic, but the case was thoroughly investigated and no one doubted that da Silva's account was sincerely given. The significant feature of the UFO-linked teleportation cases is that the victim reappears in a state of shock, trance or semi-amnesia, exactly as is reported of the abductees of an earlier generation.

Teleportation is usually spontaneous and unbidden, but in some cases it seems as though it is directed and purposeful. The man who was teleported from Goa to Portugal in 1655 was judged by the Inquisition to have procured the effect by

A boy is carried through the air to an upstairs room; an English case attributed to witchcraft. Detail of frontispiece to Joseph Glanvill, *Sadicismus triumphatus* (1681).

magic, and he was therefore burnt for the prohibited use of occult powers. No one then doubted the existence of such powers, and the further back into history we go – through times of witches and tribal shamans to the powerful state magicians of archaic civilizations – the more exact is the knowledge claimed of techniques of teleportation and magical flight.

Today, the phenomenon is largely unrecognized outside religious hagiographies, folklore and the annals of witchcraft, but can be observed as an occasional chance happening. Instead of the legendary feats of flying mystics – for example the aerial transport of great stone slabs by the builders of Stonehenge – we hear of ambiguous out-of-the-body journeys and the malicious pranks of poltergeists.

Materialization and flight of objects

In December 1894 a house on Lord Portman's estate at Durweston, Dorset, was the scene of inexplicable events. The residents told of objects rising into the air and being propelled toward their dwelling. The gamekeeper, Newman, investigated, and inside the house saw beads and a toy whistle come up and hit a window without breaking it. He decided to wait and see what developed, and later told his story to the Society for Psychical Research: "I sat down and was looking at the door opening into the garden; it was wide open leaving a space of fifteen inches between it and the inner walls when I saw, coming from behind the door, a quantity of little shells. They came round the door from a height of about five feet, one at a time at intervals varying from half a minute to a minute. They came very slowly and when they hit me I could hardly feel them. With the shells two thimbles came so slowly that in the ordinary way they would have dropped long before they reached me. Both thimbles struck my hat. Some missed my head and went just past and fell down slanting-wise (not as if they were dropped). Those that struck me fell straight down."

Similar accounts – with many detailed observations from reliable witnesses with no motive to distort or lie – abound in the literature of spiritualism and psychical phenomena, where they are put down to so-called "noisy spirits" or poltergeists. In using this word we do not commit ourselves to belief in the agency of a *geist* or spirit; though there sometimes appears to be intelligence or purpose behind such activity, we are inclined to see such occurrences as evidence of some unrecognized universal force rather than of wilful persecution by ghosts and demons.

There are two aspects of Newman's story which particularly interest us – the materialization of objects (presumably from somewhere else), and their strange, slow flights through the air. Both present an exciting challenge to science, because they appear to suspend what we think of as established laws of how matter should behave. The trajectory and force of the missiles that hit Newman defy our understanding of the laws of motion and of gravity, and yet his testimony is so honestly given that we have to wonder what happened here to normal inertia and mass.

We have many good reports of objects that fell or flew, either faster or slower than would normally be expected, often swerving to evade grasping hands. Professor Sir William Barrett addressed the Society for Psychical Research on this subject in 1911; and the Jesuit scholar Father Herbert Thurston gives many examples in his *Ghosts and Poltergeists* (1953) after a lifetime's study of the phenomenon. For instance, Thurston cites a case from Germany in 1718, in which "a large stone seemed to be falling perpendicularly and with great velocity right on the minister's head. One of the maids who was looking on shrieked in terror, but the stone turned aside in full career, though at the cost of a pane of glass through which it passed into the court outside."

Apart from the problems of authentication, what often makes such stories unpalatable to serious scientists is a sense of mischievous, frequently malicious, intent in the actions. For example, Thurston quotes a German pamphlet about a doctor whose house was effectively demolished in 1713 by a constant bombardment of missiles that became solid

PSYCHIC NEWS

Mrs Teresa Costa and her baby, terrorized by flying kitchen equipment in June 1955. The Costa family had gone to stay in a 14th-century cottage in the village of St-Jean-de-Maurienne on the French–Italian border, when, almost immediately, loud knocks were heard on doors and in walls, the furniture and the stove shook and objects took flight. After several days of disturbances, they were visited by reporters and one took this photograph. He stated that he saw the objects over an extended period, 'slide from their places, make a semicircle in the air and fall in different locations.'

and visible seconds before they hit anything. During this harassment the doctor took to swiping about him with his sword and once, upon re-sheathing it, found the scabbard stuffed full of dirt.

A lengthy disturbance in 1928–29, involving the eight-year-old adopted son of an Indian family at Poona, was reported in *Psychic Research* (May 1930) by Miss H. Kohn who, with her sister, lodged with the family. One day both sisters counted some eggs into several baskets and shut them in a cupboard. Almost immedi-

ately an egg shot past the girls from the direction of the cupboard to smash on the floor. Looking in the cupboard, they found one egg missing. As they cleaned up the mess, another egg smashed nearby, and again an egg was missing from the baskets. Three more eggs suffered the same fate, and then one basket containing forty-two eggs vanished out of the cupboard and was never seen again. Several times the girls saw coins fall: "At first we could not always see the coins in mid-air, but merely saw them fall, being startled by the contact of the coin with the floor. Soon, however, we were able to observe more closely, and actually saw the money appear in the air."

The term "apport" is applied by spiritualists to objects that move through the air or materialize at seances and hauntings. Guy Lyon Playfair gives an unusual example in *The Flying Cow* (1975). The famous Brazilian medium, Carlos Mirabelli, was asked to locate the missing remains of a woman who had died insane. A seance was held at which, according to the sworn testimony of Enrico de Goes, director of the São Paulo Municipal Library, there was a foul smell of decomposition as numerous human bones fell on the heads of those present along with a gruesome rain of hair and other remains. More pleasantly, we note many instances of the materialization of flowers and living plants, some out of season at the time. The phenomenon is, we know, a stock item in the repertoire of stage magicians as well as spiritualists but we are impressed by the record of a blue marshland flower, said to have materialized from heaven and given to the French explorer Alexandra David-Néel in mid-winter in Tibet, as recounted in *My Journey to Lhasa* (1927).

Universally regarded as a spirit of some kind, the "poltergeist" and its activities are commonly dealt with by exorcism. Sometimes this treatment is effective, yet the phenomenon is not always respectful of religious people and their rituals. Quite the reverse: the twelfth-century English saint,

This photograph - taken by Leon Isaacs in February 1939 - seems to show a heavy table and books in mid-flight during a seance. The London medium Jack Webber (centre) became well-known for manifestations of physical phenomena.

During Professor Zoellner's tests, at Leipzig University in 1877-78, on the American medium Henry Slade, these solid wooden rings, threaded on a sealed string, vanished to reappear on the central pillar of a table, apparently travelling through solid material.

Godric, was pelted by all the moveables in his hermitage, including his Mass utensils. In *Itinerarium Cambriae*, Giraldus Cambrensis recorded a case in Pembrokeshire in 1184 in which a "foul spirit" threw excrement at the exorcising priests and ripped their vestments. Church reformer Martin Luther was tormented by "poleter geister", and so was the preacher John Wesley.

Charles Fort was inclined to replace the notion of poltergeists, angels, etc with the less anthropomorphic concept of teleportation as a universal force responsible for many of the reported aberrations in normal reality. Here are a couple of examples that did not rely on supernatural entities. In about 1200, Gervase of Tilbury wrote in his *Otia imperialia* of a merchant from Bristol who lost his favourite knife over the side of his ship while on a far ocean. When he returned to port, his wife told him that one day, while she was sitting in her parlour, his knife fell in through the skylight and stuck in the table below. Both had kept a record of the disappearance and reappearance of the knife, and the times were found to be "simultaneous".

Harold T. Wilkins, in *Strange Mysteries of Time and Space* (1958), tells a modern knife story in which a man's need coincided with a discovery. The man was working on electric power-lines in a field at Brockworth, Gloucestershire, in February 1956. At lunchtime he found to his annoyance that he had forgotten to pack a knife in his lunchbox. Suddenly he noticed a knife at his feet. It was a brand new table-knife which was not his and which, he claimed, had not been there seconds before. The man kept the knife until his death, when it vanished forever.

Practical witchcraft

In his book *Lo!* (1931) Charles Fort presented some of his amazing collection of recorded phenomena which, he suggested, might be caused by teleportation. He began with the well-recorded cases of stones and liquids falling "out of the blue" – the sort of cases that are conventionally attributed to mischievous spirits or poltergeists. Psychologists have often succeeded in linking such happenings to repressed juvenile passions or mental disturbance in the people involved with them. No one, however, has been able to identify the mechanism behind the physical effects in "poltergeist" cases – the leaping pots and pans, the showers of stones and missiles and so on. If we attribute strange events to invisible spirits, we are merely personifying the agency behind the spontaneous movement of objects. **We prefer the more neutral term of teleportation, and having adopted it, we find that it fits a wide range of phenomena of the type that has previously eluded rational explanation.**

There is often something quite unusual about these falls that makes them hard to explain in terms of anything known. We agree with Fort in finding no apparent distinction between falls of living things and falls of stones and other inanimate objects, and in suggesting that the same notion of teleportation might be applied to both types of phenomena. For instance, in reports of showers of stones from many parts of the world, observers have noted that the objects fell slowly, or even floated down, as if under the influence of some anti-gravitational force. In this connection, Fort drew attention to the curious lack of injury to most falling creatures, as if they too had had the benefit of a slow descent.

If a force exists that acts to redistribute animals and objects about this Earth – a force transcending the currently known laws of physics – there is no reason why its influence should be limited to this planet. Fort's notion of teleportation derived from his view of the universe as a huge unified entity which was more like a vast organism than Newton's "great machine", and whose parts interacted with each other. He compared teleportation to the automatic process in the human or animal body which balances its energies and makes it self-healing and self-regulating. A deficiency in one part of a living body evokes responses from the organism as a whole, and the same, as Fort saw it, is true of the universe.

Although teleportation sometimes seems to act efficiently, sending fish to new ponds and predators to deal with insect swarms, it also has lapses, resulting in the appearance of strange animals in incongruous places. At other times it appears to over-compensate, as in the case of droughts broken by excessive downpours. Fort noted that these incidents often followed ceremonies or prayers for rain, and he suggested that the tribal rainmakers, by adding their own desires to the desires of nature, might have caused a violent response. Another of Fort's excuses for the whimsical or mischievous aspect of teleportation was that it was past its prime, senile even. As he put it: "The crash of falling islands – the humps of piling continents – and then the cosmic humor of it all – that the force that once heaped the peaks of the Rockies now slings pebbles at a couple of farmers near Trenton, New Jersey."

Fort was no mystic. He passed over the supernatural elements of occultism and spiritualism to focus on the practical phenomena of apports. He recognized that there are certain people who, particularly during adolescence, are more susceptible than others to teleportation. It is now well established that households which become victims of poltergeist disturbances – bombarded by stones for example – often contain a lonely or repressed teenager who seems to be related in some way to the troubles, usually as a victim or focus. Fort was one of the first to notice this. In his day, this "agent" was often a poorly-educated youth or servant girl attached to the disrupted family, who was commonly blamed, on little evidence, for creating the effects by trickery. In many cases the injustice of such accusations was plain; the unhappy suspect could hardly have manifested the reported phenomena single-handed or by intent.

Fort wondered whether the suspicions might be correct in a less-obvious way, that the "poltergeist" effects were produced unwittingly. "It may be that, if somebody, gifted with what we think we mean by 'agency', fiercely hates somebody else, he can, out of intense visualisations, direct, by teleportation, bombardments of stones upon his enemy."

If there are some people who can, unconsciously, set teleportation to work, it is likely that there are other people who have observed this and have studied how to manipulate the force by will. History provides many examples of a technology developed for practical use long before the processes involved were scientifically understood – gunpowder, medicines and electricity for example. In 1926, the French psychical researcher Gustave Geley proposed that "genuine" witches might simply be people with some control over their "powers", their "wild talents", as Fort called them. In a typical flight of fancy he imagined adolescent "poltergeist girls" employed in industry (to keep motors running) and, terrifyingly, in warfare: "The alarm – the enemy is advancing. Command to the poltergeist girls to concentrate – and under their chairs they stick their wads of chewing gum. A regiment bursts into flames, and the soldiers are torches. Horses snort smoke from the combustion of their entrails. Reinforcements are smashed under cliffs that are transported from the Rocky Mountains. The snatch of Niagara Falls – it pours upon the battlefield. The little poltergeist girls reach for their wads of chewing gum."

The record of involuntary teleportationists is long and varied if you accept the testimony about

A typical 'poltergeist girl' case. In March 1849, a young maid, Adolphine Benoît (seen in the background) is blamed for the objects flying around the baby's nursery in Guillonville, France.

the saints of Christianity, Buddhism and Islam who have been prone to unexpected levitations or materializations. As numerous are the secular reports of ordinary people subjected to mysterious forces (see LEVITATION AND SPONTANEOUS FLIGHT, p.81) or puzzling abductions and time lapses (see ENCOUNTERS WITH ALIENS, p.137). Three traditional explanations for such things are that they are caused by fairies, spirits or poltergeists, sometimes directed by witches, and today they are commonly blamed on extra-terrestrials.

Yet despite the variety of explanations, the phenomenon is essentially the same in all ages: people are unaccountably levitated, or hurled through the air, or made to disappear for a while. The experience usually has side-effects; those who experience teleportation are never quite the same afterwards. They develop sensitive or mediumistic qualities, and in modern societies their lives are often ruined thereby. John Keel's *UFOs: Operation Trojan Horse* (1970) has some sad accounts of "contactees" or "abductees" in alleged UFO cases who have been unable to reconcile themselves to their experience and have ended up in disgrace or madness or worse. Yet in traditional and tribal societies, according to anthropologist Mircea Eliade's *Shamanism* (1964), people who undergo spontaneous levitation – or abduction to another world or dimension – are marked out as potential shamans. One of his examples is of a man who became a noted prophet among the Basutos after he had been suddenly lifted up into the air in the company of a multitude of spirits.

In contrast to the "civilized" religions, which have always discouraged their levitating ecstatics from practicing or investigating their involuntary powers, shamanistic societies have encouraged levitators to cultivate the art. Thus the powers of shamans and witch doctors traditionally include the ability to ascend aloft in magical flight. Nor is the deliberate practice of teleportation confined to archaic societies; the Greeks knew of Abaris the "Sky-traveller", who "traversed rivers, seas and steeps as if walking on air". In Porphyry's *Life of Pythagoras* (third century AD) it is claimed that the sage addressed meetings at Metapontum and Tauromenium on the same day, even though these places are two hundred miles apart and separated by the sea.

Fort accepted that the wonders and miracles attributed to shamans, witches, magicians, saints and holy men could be real events brought about by the use of teleportation. He saw it, however, as an amoral, universal force, not confined to any particular religion or to religion in general, nor to the human race. If it exists, it must of necessity be an active principle throughout nature, a force which responds to desires in nature wherever located. It could procure a local rainfall for a needy tree in times of drought, just as, biblically, a people in a wilderness might receive "heaven-sent" manna in a time of need. In RAINS OF SEEDS AND ORGANIC MATTER (see p.47), we tell of showers of grain from the sky which hungry locals made into bread. Another of Fort's favourite examples was of newly-made ponds unaccountably found to be full of fish. This is a phenomenon that has puzzled country people for centuries; we recently came across a statement by the writer Michovius, to the effect that the Russians take the fish-teleportation effect for granted. They "do not stock their lakes and ponds with fish, as is done in other countries, but instead, when ponds are made, fish drop into them out of the heavenly dew without human intercession or effort." Fort's idea was that intense desire on the part of humans, animals, plants, ponds or any other natural entity was liable to set in motion the distributive, compensating energies of teleportation.

He also wondered whether the ability to use teleportation was one which people were gradually developing or losing. Eventually, he favoured the idea that it was more common in earlier stages of society. In ancient times a talent for teleporting fire, water and other necessities would have been a social asset to wandering tribes, but now "with political and economic mechanisms somewhat well established, or working, after a fashion" such talents are no longer so valued. They linger on, particularly among children, who are more atavistic than their elders and "may be in rapport with forces that mostly human beings have outgrown."

On the other hand, perhaps knowledge of teleportation belongs not so much to the past as to the future. In that case, said Fort lightly, it might be commercialized. "Cargoes, without ships, and freights, without trains, may be the traffics of the future. There may be teleportative voyages from planet to planet", he wrote around 1930, long before space travel was taken seriously. In fact, one of Fort's most appealing qualities was that he did not take his own ideas any more seriously than he took anyone else's. Of the social future of teleportation he wrote: "Here is an idea that may revolutionize industry, but just now I am too busy revolutionizing everything else, and I give this idea to the world, with the generosity of someone who bestows something that isn't any good to him."

Our reason for beginning this book with a summary of the concept of teleportation is that it provides a unified theory for so many of the natural wonders and enigmas described later in these pages. We are fascinated by the way in which the parameters of science keep expanding towards the point of embracing Fort's "unthinkable" notions, including that of teleportation. Modern physics recognizes so many instances of apparent bi-locations and instantaneous teleportations among particles, that phenomena, once regarded as irrational and impossible, now have good claims to be accepted as natural.

2

Strange Rains

2

Strange Rains

Falls of fishes and frogs

Rains of fishes or frogs sound biblical, but it would be wrong to dismiss the phenomenon simply because it seems as improbable as an Old Testament miracle. The hundreds of eyewitness accounts, collected by scientists and others, place the reality of such events beyond dispute. Works of early history and geography, and the memoirs of travellers, explorers and colonial administrators form the bulk of sources from antiquity until the nineteenth century; after this, accounts begin to be found in scientific journals as well as in newspapers. No one has yet tabulated all the known cases, so precise numbers and statistics must remain guesswork, even so, we suspect that the collected examples only really scratch the surface.

The quality of evidence for rains of fishes and frogs is good, with a canon of well-observed cases going back into antiquity. The *Deipnosophistae*, compiled by Athenaeus (c. 200 AD), summarizes the writings of around eight hundred authors that he read at the Library of Alexandria – most of which were lost when the Library was destroyed. Under the heading "De pluvius piscium" (Rains of Fishes), he wrote: "Phaenias, for example, says, in the second book of *The Rulers of Eresus* that in Chersonesus it rained fishes for three whole days. And Phylarcus in his fourth book says that certain persons have in many places seen it rain fishes, and the same thing often happens with tadpoles."

Conventional science has tended to be sceptical about the phenomenon. In an 1844 issue of the *Zoologist* the editor, Edward Newman, included an item about a shower of little frogs, "about the size of a horse-bean", that occurred at Selby in Yorkshire. Those witnessing the occurrence had convinced themselves that the frogs had come down with the rain by holding out their hats into which falling frogs landed. Newman, of course, knew better. "I am continually receiving similar accounts not only of frogs, but toads, white fish and eels," he wrote, before exhorting his correspondents to check their facts more rigorously. "Methinks it would be no difficult matter to trace the presence of the animals to more natural sources than the clouds." (For a further discussion of expert reactions, see THEORIES AND EXPLANATIONS, p.21.)

A more open-minded approach emerged in the late nineteenth century, when a small number of scientists began to discuss the anomalies of their chosen field. Among them were the English meteorologist D.P. Thompson, the naturalist George Buist, the French astronomer Camille Flammarion, the German naturalist G. Hartwig, and the American ichthyologist E.W.

DE   PISCIBVS

De lapſu Piſcium, Ranarum, Murium,
Vermium, & Lapidum.

CAP.   XXX.

A chapter-heading from Olaus Magnus' *Historia de gentibus* (1555) in which he discusses many falls of fishes, frogs and animals, events which have repeated in every age up to the present.

Gudger. The first popular article on creature showers appeared in 1917, when Waldo McAtee, a distinguished biologist with the US Bureau of Biological Survey, became intrigued by his father's tale of coming in from the rain to find earthworms on the brim of his hat. McAtee went on to compile a broad survey of showers of organic matter and animals that, in turn, inspired both E.W. Gudger and Charles Fort.

E.W. Gudger confined his data to falls of fish, but Fort's researches extended wider and further than even McAtee, to include falls of organic matter, liquids, ice, stones and even artifacts. Fort's work is particularly significant because his eclectic reading brought so many different citations together for the first time and he attempted a critique of conventional explanations which exposed the weaknesses of dogmatic authorities such as Newman.

One case that Fort looked into took place in the Aberdare valley in South Wales. On the morning of Friday, 11 February 1859, a storm broke over the village of Mountain Ash bringing "thousands" of living fish, between one and four inches in length. There were two falls about ten minutes apart. The local curate sent a report to the *Times* (2 March 1859) which stated that locals, seeking to preserve some living specimens, put some in salt water and others in freshwater; those in saline died. The greatest peculiarity is that the fall occurred only in the vicinity of a lumber yard; many were found on roofs in the area. Specimens were sent to the British Museum, where Dr John Gray, Keeper of Zoology, identified them as minnows and sticklebacks.

In his discussion of this case, Fort's sarcasm was fired by the reactions of narrow-minded scientists. After identifying the fish, Dr Gray expressed the opinion that they had come from a local stream, in a bucket of water which one citizen had playfully emptied over another. Or, as Fort summarized, "someone soused someone else with a pailful of water in which were thousands of fishes, some of which covered roofs of houses."

More modern examples include the following. On the morning of 23 October 1947, A.D. Bajkov, a biologist with the US Department of Wildlife and Fisheries, was in a restaurant in Marksville,

Louisiana. He was having breakfast with his wife "when the waitress informed us that fish were falling from the sky . . . We went immediately to collect some of the fish." Several people had been struck by the fish, which were two to nine inches long, and some said they were icy to the touch. Bajkov later identified them as freshwater bass and shad, fish native to local waters (*Science*, vol.109, p.482).

At West Ham in London, following a heavy rainfall on the night of 27 May 1984, a builder found nearly a dozen small fish on the roof of Ron Langton's house. When Bob Rickard visited the site, nine days later, the builder was still able to find some in the guttering – cats had got the rest. The fish were identified at the Natural History Museum as smelts and flounders. In the same night, fish also fell at three other locations in the same part of London. They were all of the kind you would expect to find in the nearby River Thames, leading to speculation that they were dropped by waterspouts or by regurgitating herons (*Fortean Times*, no.42, p.28).

In Fort Worth, Texas, Louis Castoreno thought someone was playing a trick on him when dozens of small fish flopped into his backyard on 8 May 1985. As he noticed a dark cloud passing above, he had to leap out of the way as "a whole bunch came down at one time. It scared me." A local spokesman for the National Weather Service confirmed that it had happened before in the past five years, usually just before a tornado or heavy storm (Fort Worth *Star Telegram*, 9 May 1985).

When it comes to frogs, both the number of recorded incidents and the quantity of falling creatures is larger. At Carnet-Plage, France, "thousands" of frogs fell "just prior" to a heavy storm

Ron Langton and some of the small fish that fell on the roof and path of his terrace house in West Ham, in east London, during the night of 27 May 1984.

A fall of frogs in Scandinavia, illustrated in the *Prodigiorum ac ostentorum* (1557) of Conrads Lycosthenes.

One of the band of little frogs found in the Bedford garden of Mrs Vida McWilliam in June 1979, believed to have fallen with rain the previous day. Tadpoles littered her lawn, and her bushes were found draped with frogspawn, making this one of the most unusual cases in our 'frogfall' records.

(*Journal of Meteorology*, 1977, p.300). On 23 September 1973, "tens of thousands" of small frogs fell during a storm at Brignoles France (*Times*, 24 September 1973). While, according to *Nature* (1915, p.378), "millions" of small frogs fell from the clouds during a storm over Gibraltar.

Writing in *English Mechanic* (1911, p.21), a witness describes how he was drenched during a violent thunderstorm in Bournemouth in 1891 and saw "small yellow frogs dashed on the ground all around me". When the rain stopped, he found hundreds around his shelter and "thousands impaled on the furze bushes on the common close by." The stench of their rotting corpses lasted for days afterwards.

Similar incidents abound in the literature, each with reliable witnesses. Mrs Sylvia Mowday, told us of her experience, on 12 June 1954, while crossing Birmingham's Sutton Park in a sudden downpour. "We tried to reach some trees. My four-year-old daughter put up her little red umbrella and we heard things thudding against it. To our amazement it was a shower of frogs, coming down from the sky, hundreds of them. We looked up and saw the frogs coming down like snowflakes. The ground was absolutely covered with them for about fifty square yards. We were afraid to tread on them, they were so tiny."

Before we move on to the scarcity of obser-vations of falling spawn or tadpoles, we must briefly touch on the case of the thumbnail-sized frogs reported from several locations in Gloucestershire in October 1987 (*Fortean Times*, no.51, p.14). A naturalist from the Gloucester-shire Trust for Nature Conservancy (GTNC) thought they might be a North African species, on account of their colouring, but was baffled as to how they could have reached the UK. Two reports helped suggest a solution: in the first, an unnamed woman told of "tiny rose-coloured frogs" coming down in torrential rain near Stroud. They were "bouncing off umbrellas and pavements and hopped off in their hundreds to nearby streams and gardens," she said (*Daily Mirror*, 24 October 1987). The *Fortean Times* (no.51, p.10) notes that parts of England – including the West Country – had experienced at least four falls of Sahara sand between May and September. At first we wondered whether the winds that lift sand into the stratosphere over the Sahara and blast it towards western Europe where it falls in "red rains" could also have transported the little frogs. However, Mark Nicholson of the GTNC later announced that the colourings fell within the normal and albino variations of the common frog (*Fortean Times*, no.76, p.8). So, if these frogs were local, were the red rains and Stroud frog fall coincidental? As in so many other fortean cases, we are left with more questions than answers.

Tadpoles are smaller and more numerous than frogs, and should, therefore, be more likely to be lifted up from ponds by waterspouts. Fort, however, could find no records of tadpole showers and in all our own researches, far and wide, we have had little more success. Only four reports have come to our notice, one more a matter of folklore than record. *Fate Magazine* (January 1958) tells of the Pueblo Indians of Acorna, New Mexico, whose explanation for the millions of tadpoles found in isolated pools of rainwater in the desert, is that they fall with the rain.

The second reference to tadpole showers is more specific, but still not very satisfactory as evidence. In *A Naturalist's Sojourn in Jamaica* (1851), Philip Gosse tells how he visited San Domingo on the island of Haiti in the West Indies. There, he learnt from his colleague, Richard Hill, of the local belief that a certain species of frog had first appeared on the island following a shower of tadpoles many years ago. Hill's words, as recorded by Gosse, were: "I was told that some frogs I used to hear croaking at night in the boggy ground about Port au Prince, in Haiti, were not known there till a shower of rain brought them to the island. The precise

period of this occurrence was mentioned to me, and I have a note of it somewhere. If I could be satisfied that what the historian Moreau de St-Méry likened to 'tetards' (bull-heads) were tadpoles, I should say it was the same shower as the one he commemorates on May 1786." Têtard is the French word for tadpole.

Our third instance is the recollection of eighty-year-old Leonard Burrough, the accuracy of whose memory we have no way of judging. In the Maidenhead *Advertiser* (4 December 1981), he tells of the day, in 1910, when his family relocated to the Berkshire town. It was shortly before a violent storm, "the worst in memory", when the sky became "darker than the darkest night" and the thunder and lightning terrified him. When young Leonard later went out onto the High Street, he was astonished to find it alive with thousands of tiny frogs and tadpoles.

In Moreau de St-Méry's *Description de St Domingue* (1796) there is an account of what may be one of the few showers of frog-spawn on record. It fell during a drought over the whole of San Domingo (now Haiti and the Dominican Republic) on 5 May 1786. De St-Méry wrote: "There fell, during a strong east wind, in several parts of the city of Port an Prince . . . a great quantity of black eggs, which hatched the following day . . . They shed their skins several times [and] resembled tadpoles."

Theories and explanations

By the end of the eighteenth century – when the first efforts were being made to fit Natural History into the straitjacket of scientific rationalism – the notion that frogs or any other creatures could fall from the sky had been officially banished. Gilbert White, in 1789, called it a "foolish opinion", and academics of the day dismissed it as "popular error". A striking example concerns the interpretation that pious locals gave to the shower of snails which fell on a farm near Bristol in July 1821. They believed that it was a divine punishment of the

farmer, who had been guilty of "disrespect to the virtues of our late Queen". We feel that this explanation is in a class of its own, but there are a number of serious and historical explanations of how creatures can rain from the skies which we review and assess below.

Under the date 23 May 1661, Samuel Pepys notes in his *Diary* his attendance at a dinner hosted by the Lord Mayor of London, where: "At table I had very good discourse with Mr Ashmole, where he did assure me that froggs and many other insects do often fall from the sky ready formed." Elias Ashmole was one of the most renowned alchemists and astrologers of

On *Wednefday* before *Eafter, Anno* 1666. a Pafture Field at *Cranftead* near *Wrotham* in *Kent,* about Two Acres, which is far from any part of the Sea or Branch of it, and a Place where are no Fifh Ponds, but a Scarcity of Water, was all overfpread with little Fifhes, conceived to be rained down, there having been at that time a great Tempeft of Thunder and Rain ; the Fifhes were about the Length of a Man's little Finger, and judged by all that faw them to be young Whitings, many of them were taken up and fhewed to feveral Perfons; the Field belonged to one *Ware* a Yeoman, who was at that *Eafter-Seffions* one of the Grand Inqueft, and carried fome of them to the Seffions at *Maidftone* in *Kent,* and he fhowed them, among others, to Mr. *Lake,* a Bencher of the *Middle-Temple,* who had One of them and brought it to *London,* the Truth of it was averr'd by many that faw the Fifhes lye fcattered all over that Field, and none in other the Fields thereto adjoining : The Quantity of them was eftimated to be about a Bufhel, being all together. Mr. *Lake* gave the Charge at thofe Seffions.

A letter from Dr Robert Conny to Dr Robert Plot, a fellow of the Royal Society, as recorded in the *Philosophical Transactions* (1698).

the day, a distinguished member of the Royal Society who gave his name to the Ashmolean Museum at Oxford. He was in town because, the previous day, the Royal Society had held a special debate on the subject of the spontaneous generation of insects.

The idea that desiccated frogspawn may be drawn or blown up into the clouds, where it hatches, causing showers of little frogs to fall to earth, is an ancient and well-debated one. Robert Plot in his *Natural History of Staffordshire* (1686) credits "spontaneous generation" theory to the Italian polymath, Jerome Cardan, whose encyclopaedia, *De subtilitate*, appeared in 1550. Plot gave two illustrations in support of the theory. The first one featured little frogs, all of the same size, which had sometimes been found on the roof of a "stately gate-house", to which they had no ordinary means of access. The second was of someone who, while walking through low marsh ground on a foggy morning "had his hat almost covered with little frogs that fell on it as he walked." If that story is true, says Plot, then Cardan's theory must also be true – in some cases

at least. To combat the objection that frogs from the clouds would probably be killed or damaged by the fall, Plot advocated a rival notion, that frogs found on house-tops had been generated from a special kind of dust blown there by the wind which "fermented" under the action of sun and rain to produce the creatures. He was not dogmatic about this latter theory and thought it only applied in some cases.

Pliny, in his *Natural History* of 77 AD, mentions the falls of a number of organic and inorganic substances, including fishes. Although he alludes to the spontaneous generation of some animals from dormant dust or slime which contains their "seeds", we find no discussion there of falling frogs. It was the natural philosopher Giovanni Battista Porta who first formally associated the idea of spontaneous generation with falling frogs. In *Natural Magick* (1678) he stated that: "Frogs are wonderfully generated of rotten dust and rain; for a summer shower, lighting upon the putrefied sands of the shore, and dust of the highways, engenders frogs . . . The generation of them is so easy, and sudden, that some write it hath rained frogs, as if they were gendered in the air."

The idea of spontaneous generation continued to be put forward, in all seriousness, as recently as 1915, with the publication of *The Ages of Ice and Creation* by George Prentiss. Prentiss was more radical than today's Scientific Creationists because he believed that Creation did not stop at a certain time, but is continuing at this very moment all around us. His most dramatic evidence was a number of tales from the southern United States of the sudden appearance of fish, found in fresh puddles of rainwater, between rows of cotton, just after storms. To Prentiss the fish had obviously just come into being; he did not even consider that they might have fallen with the rain.

The most favoured official explanation for the phenomenon is summarized in the magazine *Science* (7 June 1946) by the naturalist Dr E.W. Gudger. "The explanation is to be found in the action of whirlwinds and waterspouts and possibly of strong typhoon and monsoon winds. A 'twister' or whirlwind starts in front of an approaching storm and as it gains in size the 'snout' elongates and approaches the water. This, caught by the whirling wind, rises up in a cone. The two unite, and the swirling column moves along, picking up water, fishes and any other fairly light objects at or near the surface of the water . . . Everything moveable would be sucked up in the whirling vortex. Furthermore, whirlwinds, originating inland, will not only progress over land, picking up various objects, but over ponds and lakes, becoming waterspouts. As such they will there pick up frogs, fresh-water fishes, snails, etc. and carry them away over the land. Sometimes the fishes are found in a long narrow, fairly straight row over some distance, evidently having been dropped as the waterspout progressed over the country with lessening speed and carrying power. When the waterspout or

Dr E.W. Gudger of the North American Museum of Natural History had a special interest in nature's enigmas and wrote scientific articles on many of the subjects covered in this book. He was the great authority on fish rains, which he concluded were caused by waterspouts or whirlwinds.

whirlwind, with its load of fishes breaks, water and fishes will fall as a rain of fishes."

Charles Fort cited a case that demonstrated exactly what happens when a waterspout travels over a pond; things are not so much sucked up as violently raised and scattered about. There are also cases – to which Gudger alludes – in which fish have been found deposited in a straight line, but we venture to suggest that nothing so neat has ever been clearly witnessed by observers of whirlwinds. Fort protests: "It is so easy to say that small frogs that have fallen from the sky had been scooped up by a whirlwind . . . In the exclusionist imagination there is no regard for mud, debris from the bottom of a pond, floating vegetation, loose things from the shores [only] a precise picking out of frogs . . . A pond going up would be quite as interesting as frogs coming down. Whirlwinds we read of over and over – but where and what whirlwind? It seems to me that anybody who had lost a pond would be heard from."

A waterspout – the aquatic equivalent of a tornado – is created when the whirling column of air touches down on water and sucks up huge quantities of it. Any fish near the surface would be included. In Dr Gudger's third collection of accounts, in *Annals and Magazine of Natural History* (January 1929), he mentions a waterspout deluging an open boat in the Gulf of Mexico in 1921. The witness saw it form and then break, showering the boat with fish along with dangerous amounts of water. This was the only clear incident involving a whirlwind or waterspout in Gudger's total of seventy-one records.

In January 1975, a correspondence in the pages of the *East Anglian Magazine*, yielded a number of recollections of earlier instances, including one from an old farmhand who experienced a rain of frogs in direct association with a waterspout. Frogs from a waterspout, though, must be considered a rarer occurrence than frogs from clear skies or with light rain, to judge by the recorded observations. Fort said of his own data: "Of all the instances I have that attribute the fall of small frogs or toads to whirlwinds, only one definitely identifies or places the whirlwind."

With some reservations, whirling winds provide the most logical explanation for many falls, but there are many other cases – reported throughout this book – in which they are simply not relevant. For example, when he was a boy in

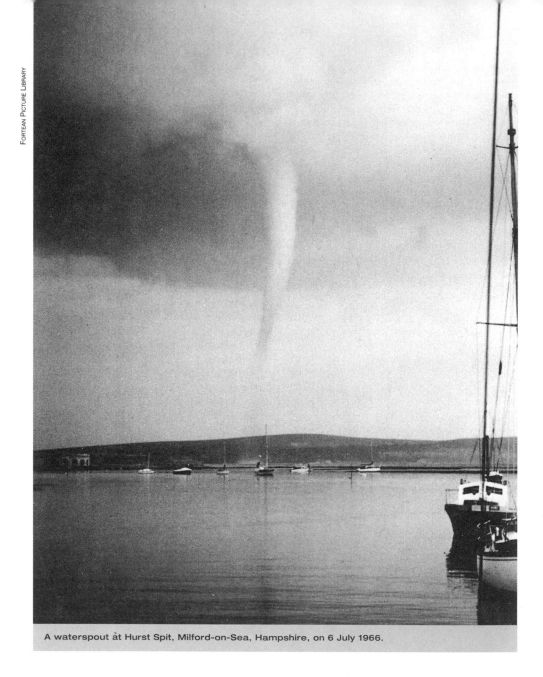

A waterspout at Hurst Spit, Milford-on-Sea, Hampshire, on 6 July 1966.

Montreal, Canada, in 1841, Sir George Gibb came across myriads of frogs on an isolated road. The road was wet in that part and, as he wrote in his booklet *Odd Showers* (1870), "We took it for granted there had been a shower of frogs." Rationalizing the event (which had happened to him 29 years earlier), Sir George opted for the waterspout theory, although his account reveals nothing more violent than "a smart rain just before we came up . . . on a beautiful summer's day."

One anomalous aspect of the evidence is voiced by Minnesota fortean, Robert Schadewald, who wonders why there are "so many fish falls from Great Britain but none whatsoever from Minnesota, the 'Land of Ten Thousand Lakes' which averages seventeen tornado touchdowns a year."

In 1771, the meteorologist, Raphael Eglini, was in the rare position of having friends who reported to him directly that they had observed fish falling when they were caught in a thunderstorm. They even provided him with specimens, which Eglini passed on for identification. Unmoved, he published a note of the event in the German scientific journal, *Wittenbergisches Wochenblatt*, with the comment that if they should turn out to be a local fish the explanation lay in an overflow from a neighbouring stream, or a waterspout. Later in the same journal it was stated that the fish were a species of "trout not found locally". Eglini's only comment was: "Incredible!"

Eglini favoured the theory that frogs and toads are flushed out of their hiding places by rainwater. The same opinion was put forward by the nature writer E.A. Ellis, in his column for the *Eastern Daily Press* (11 July 1975): "It is tempting to assume that these young creatures had arrived in a shower from the sky, but the explanation, at least in most cases of sudden swarming after rain, is that young amphibians, having migrated from the water where they developed as tadpoles, tend to remain under the cover of grass and other herbiage by day and move only at night, but are tempted out of cover at any time by a shower." Ellis doesn't use this to explain all fish and frog falls and indeed he expresses some faith in the whirlwind theory, adding: "I think it very unlikely that the alleged phenomenon occurs at all frequently but having myself seen a variety of objects sucked up in waterspouts and whirlwinds on several occasions and having also been at the receiving end of the material showered down afterwards, I can see no reason to discredit every tale of objects descending from the air."

Some fish, it seems, have organized their lives around periodic rains. In *Fortean Times* (no.106, p.1) Tony Healy and Paul Cropper describe several sudden appearances of numbers of "grunters" at Wellbourne Hills in the northern desert of South Australia coinciding with drought-breaking rains. There are other species of fish known to migrate across tracts of land, usually using pools of water made by recent rain or floods. This theory clearly does not apply to cases involving dead fish, species not known for migrating, or fish found in high inaccessible places.

We have referred above to the archaic theory of "spontaneous generation", but there is a natural phenomenon which, to an untutored observer, would appear to be similar. This is aestivation, the ability of some fish, amphibians and molluscs to survive periods of drought by hibernating in soft mud before a pond or stream dries up. It usually involves living eggs and young forms which are revived again, often with surprising rapidity, when rains or floods bring fresh water. When offered as an explanation for fish falls, it is assumed that the young fish are flushed out of their hiding places to appear suddenly, in great numbers, on the wet ground and in puddles. It fails to account for eye-witness accounts of fish falling, those found in high inaccessible places, or the fact that many "falls" involve fish that are not known to aestivate.

Large fish-eating birds, like herons, swallow fish whole or carry them off in their beaks or claws. Sometimes, when attacked in flight, they may drop or vomit their recent catch. While this could be a reasonable explanation of falls of single fishes (of which there are a significant number) it fails to explain falls involving great numbers of fish. Some authorities have sought to explain the fall of thousands of fish by supposing that a whole flock of birds must have disgorged simultaneously.

In our first chapter we describe teleportation, the concept introduced by Charles Fort in connection with mysterious comings and goings of creatures and objects. This unknown, hypothetical force, he suggested, has been active from the beginning of the world, piling up mountains, populating remote islands and bringing fish to isolated lakes. Regarding the universe as a single organism, a hermaphrodite satisfying its own wants, Fort identified teleportation as its means of self-regulation.

It is an old idea that nature has nerves or imagination that communicate the needs of each part to every other, producing compensatory reactions. It is inherent in the mystical view of the world and in the operations of ritual magic. There are more rational ways of explaining fish-falls than by teleportation and the imagination of nature; but none of them is entirely satisfactory and in many cases the mystical view seems more adequate than any of its rivals.

Fort frequently noted the tendency of authority figures to trot out explanations that sounded reasonable yet actually accounted for very little of the observed phenomenon. A prime example occurred on 30 May 1881, when great quantities of periwinkles and crabs fell on the English city of Worcester. The "official" response was to suggest that a mad fishmonger or practical joker must have travelled the byways of the city, unseen, shovelling thousands of periwinkles off the back of his cart.

Anomalies and questions

In the *Sourcebook Project*, an ongoing encyclopaedia of natural anomalies compiled by William Corliss, the phenomenon of fish falls is not rated as a "serious anomaly", meaning that there are many examples which can adequately be explained. While this is undoubtedly true generally, there are other well-observed aspects of the phenomenon that cannot be easily accounted for and which are consistently overlooked by those seeking to explain it away.

Among the most troublesome of these are the observations of some kind of selection process at work; not only are falling frogs and fish often separated from the mud, water, vegetation and debris of their normal environment, but there is a peculiar selectivity at work among the creatures themselves. Mixed showers do occur, but in nearly all cases only one species is involved. Also, the falling creatures are usually of about the same size and age, and frequently young or immature. The most strikingly "unreasonable" feature about such happenings, however, is that we rarely hear of falling creatures being crushed or damaged. One of the few cases we can recall occurred at Newcastle in the South African province of Natal, on the morning of 14 April 1909, when hundreds of fish of the species *Barbus gurneyi* were found on wet ground "some alive and unhurt, some dead, and some smashed to a pulp".

It is worth dwelling further on this point, but we must first mention the mixed fortunes of the fish that fell on Calcutta in 1839, as cited in Charles Tomlinson's *Raincloud and Snowstorm* (1864). Observers noted that the fish that landed on hard ground were killed, while those falling on grass survived. A curious feature of this case was that the fish fell in a straight line, indicating – according to some – the operation of a waterspout. Yet it was an upholder of the waterspout theory, W.H. Carey, who, in describing other Indian fishfalls in *Good Old Days of the Honourable John Company* (1907), wrote: "The fish are . . . swept up by whirlwinds from ponds and held suspended in the rain cloud until they are thrown down in showers. The curious part is, that the fishes are found on the ground alive and uninjured."

The idea that grass or other soft surfaces saved falling fish from smashing on impact was popular for a time. Fort commented: "The devotees of St Isaac [Newton] explain that they fall upon thick grass and so survive; but Sir James Tennant, in his *History of Ceylon*, tells of a fall of fishes upon gravel, by which they were seemingly uninjured." Fort's reference is to Tennant's *Natural History of Ceylon* (1861), in which the author describes seeing a short, torrential rainstorm and of finding at the spot "a multitude of small silvery fish . . . leaping on the gravel of the high road, numbers of which I collected and brought away."

Another anomaly is the falls of dead fish, in some cases dead so long that they are decomposing. A baffling fishfall occurred on 19 February 1830 at Jelalpur in India, detailed by James Prinsep with the affidavits of nine witnesses in the *Journal of the*

These panels, from Erasmus Francisci's book *Der wunder-reiche Überzug unserer Nider-Welt* (1680), depict various recorded showers of wheat, fish, frogs and worms.

Asiatic Society of Bengal (1833), in which thousands of dead fish fell on a factory; "some were fresh, others rotten and mutilated". Many of the fish were stinking and headless, which is difficult to attribute to the action of a whirlwind. Nine witnesses testified to being hit by them or finding them on roofs. Yet there was no storm. One said they were seen up in the sky "like a flock of birds descending rapidly to the ground." In contrast, in another Indian case, recorded by Major J. Harriett in his *Struggles Through Life* (1808), marching troops experienced a shower of fish so light and gentle, that the fish found in the soldiers' hats were shaken out and made into a curry for their general.

Robert Schadewald has calculated, from experiments, the terminal velocity of a small falling fish to be very nearly 32 miles per hour, yet Fort noted the singular lack of any account of fish being seriously damaged or killed by their fall. Summing up his notes in *Lo!* (1931) Fort wrote: "In all the hosts of stories that I have gathered . . . of showers of living things, the rarest of all statements is of injury to the falling creatures." With his theory of teleportation in mind, Fort wondered whether "the creatures may not have fallen all the way from the sky, but may have fallen from appearing-points not high above the ground – or may have fallen a considerable distance under a counter-gravitational influence."

In cases where the fish are not just dead or decaying we can suppose that the shock of aerial transition killed them, or they had been a long time in transit. In the case of fish found dried and stiff, we must ask how this could be accomplished in damp winds or the wet interiors of clouds? In the Natal case (discussed above), the mix of unhurt, intact but dead and "smashed" fish challenges every explanation.

Many fallen fish are reported to be unusually cold to the touch and some have been found frozen or mixed with hail. This is quite consistent with being held within a storm cloud, whose interior temperatures drop well below freezing. Severe cold of this sort may also allow fish to be transported great distances by keeping them in a state of suspended animation. We know of accounts of animals coming down with hail and snow, but we keep a special place by the fire of curiosity for those completely frozen into the ice. During a fall of frogs and fish at Derby, in 1841, lumps of half-melted ice fell with the creatures (*Atheneum*, 17 July 1841), while at Dubuque, Iowa, on 16 June 1882, small frogs were found inside hailstones, some still alive (*Monthly Weather Review*, 1882).

The most extreme note we have is of a six-by-eight-inch gopher turtle that came down with a hailstorm, entirely encased in ice, at Bovington, Mississippi – an event respectably recorded in the *Monthly Weather Review* for May 1894.

Also noticeable, in a number of cases, is the good marksmanship in the placing of falls. Instead of being scattered widely, as one would expect from a powerful, chaotic, whirling wind, the fall is frequently almost poured, or dropped, onto a location from a seemingly stable point above it. There are cases in which several falls have taken place over a few days. It seems highly unlikely that whirlwinds would follow the same track with such precision although, in the Aberdare case (see FALLS OF FROGS AND FISHES, p.17) the principal witnesses noted "two showers, with an interval of ten minutes and each shower lasted about two minutes." George Buist gives a case from near Calcutta, in 1839, in which a witness says: "The most strange thing which ever struck me . . . was that the fish did not fall helter-skelter . . . but in a straight line not more than a cubit in breadth."

Fort noticed a correlation between some falls and seismic phenomena. For example, the Count de Castelnau witnessed a fall in Singapore during a three-day rainstorm that immediately followed an earthquake. In Ecuador, in 1691, Baron Humboldt observed a shower of cooked fish, ejected from a steaming vent near a volcano. A possible explanation, according to the Canadian psychologists Michael Persinger and Gyslaine Lafreniere, is that subterranean stress may generate strange electromagnetic fields which, in turn, trigger events like fish falls.

Many historical instances of "jelly falls" (see RAINS OF SEEDS AND ORGANIC MATTER, p.47) occur in association with unexplained aerial lights. The German physicist Ernst Chladni (1756–1827) tells of a viscous mass that fell with a "luminous meteorite" in Italy in 1652, and of a "gelatinous matter" that fell with a globe of fire on Lethy Island, India in 1718.

It is hard to avoid the conclusion that, in a great many falls, some sort of selection seems to have taken place; the creatures are typically all of one species, or at the same stage of development. Schadewald's experiments allowed him to predict that fish in the updraft of a waterspout would rise at different speeds, according to their weight and aerodynamic qualities. Further segregations could be performed by cross winds . . . so some form of "selection" seems logical at first glance. However, if this were the case, one might reasonably expect

Waterspouts are the commonest scientific explanation for the mysterious transportation of marine creatures from sea to dry land.

all manner of pond or aquatic debris of similar weight or shape to accompany fish falls and this is generally absent from witnessed descriptions.

We now have a great many more cases than those McAtee considered and we can say that, for the most part, falling animals are living, young specimens which are undamaged by the fall and quickly disperse after landing. Just two years after McAtee, Fort wrote: "If living things have landed alive on this earth, in spite of all we think we know of the accelerative velocity of falling bodies, and have propagated. . . the exotic becomes the indigenous." Or to put it another way: "If hosts of living frogs have come from somewhere else, every living thing upon this earth may, ancestrally, have come from somewhere else."

Fort himself never insisted that teleportation was the true or only answer to the problem of falls of creatures. Some – perhaps all – the theories we have mentioned (whirlwinds, waterspouts, fish-vomiting birds, practical jokers, etc.) might adequately explain some aspects of certain cases, but, from our own investigations, we have found that they are useless in many others. The existence of this variety of explanations is an indication that nothing has really been fully explained over the centuries. Certainly, in cases of frog and fish falls, as we have seen, there are features of some reports that no scientific or "rational" theory has yet accounted for satisfactorily. You'll find this is true generally, as we extend our discussion into some of the other varieties of falls.

Insect showers

One of England's earliest newspapers, the Exeter *Flying Post*, reported on 27 August 1789 that "London and its environs were, on Thursday, covered with a black insect in an astonishing manner. They seem to have been engendered in the atmosphere at a considerable distance from the earth." Countless numbers of this insect fell into the streets barely alive.

This unexpected arrival of a cloud of insects may well have something to do with migration or swarming but, at this remove, it is difficult to determine precisely what happened. While it seems reasonable to suppose that a swarm of insects encountering a region of cold air might fall to ground numbed and lethargic, we are struck by the attempt to explain their *sudden* appearance. Like the falls of toads that baffled Pliny, Plot and Ashmole (see Theories and Explanations, p.21) is is suggested that they are spontaneously generated in the upper atmosphere. It is also possible to consider them in the light of Fort's notion of teleportation.

In the annals of falling creatures, records of insect falls are as numerous as those of frogs and fishes but in recent years less frequent than they were. The most recent report in our files – a cloud of unidentified insects that littered the French town of Luçon, in Vendée, on 24 April 1977 (*Le Progrès*, 27 April 1977) – hardly does justice to the exotic accounts of earlier times in which great numbers of insects are found in circumstances which suggest that they fell recently from the sky.

Entomologists who study the dispersal of insects tend to scorn the notion of falls. Canadian forestry naturalist W.R. Henson and his colleagues often discussed, in the pages of entomology journals, the theory that insects could be carried into the upper atmosphere by strong winds and carried great distances before plummeting to earth with rain or snow. Then in 1951, while in the Banff National Park, Alberta, Henson experienced a shower of ice crystals, one of which contained the body of a midge. The crystal was perfectly developed and completely enclosed the insect, suggesting it had been suspended for a while in a high, ice-forming air layer (*Nature*, 5 January 1952). We shall come across other ice-encrusted falls in later sections.

Other entomologists and meteorologists hold the opinion that was summarized by Waldo McAtee in one of the first collections of data on anomalous falls of living creatures and organic matter. McAtee declared: "The rains of insect larvae that have been investigated have proved to be merely the

The case of the coach travelling from Gournay to Gisors in France, turned back by an inpenetrable cloud of cockchafer beetles in May 1832, was treated by Flammarion as an insect fall. It is now believed to have been a mass migration.

Snow-worms on a small patch of snow, some of the vast number 'thickly strewn' over more than a quarter of a mile in a pass on Mount Olympus, Washington State. They were photographed on 1 June 1907.

appearance in large numbers on the surface of the ground, or upon snow, of the larvae of soldier beetles, or sometimes caterpillars, which have been driven from their hibernating quarters by the saturation of the soil by heavy rains or melting snow" (*Monthly Weather Review*, May 1917). We need not be too impressed with this appearance of certainty, since a few pages further on McAtee himself presents cases of witnessed falls of insects. Somewhat taken aback, he admits "but there have been apparently a few real rains of insects."

Certainly not every discovery of masses of insects lying on the snow can be explained by the "forced-out-of-hibernation" theory. In December 1855, a "strange rainstorm", which turned to snow, fell on Alexandria, Virginia. The next morning residents found that the snow for several miles "resembled a vast field of dark velvet". The cause was an unimaginable number of tiny black bugs, "each slightly larger than a grain of gunpowder". The unidentified "bugs" were stiffened by the cold and in no condition to have burrowed upwards. When thawed out by firesides they were quite lively, but of a kind unfamiliar to the locals. Henry

Splitter, who cites this incident in his collection of curious North American falls (*Fate*, October 1953) also mentions a shower of angleworms on Virginia City, Nevada, in April 1879. There had been a rainstorm during the night and in the morning the whole town lay under a blanket of wriggling worms. They were not indigenous and could not have come out of hibernation, since they were found on the streets, sidewalks and on roofs.

In 1946 the butler of the Cope family, in Philadelphia, took advantage of a lull in a torrential rainstorm to take out some refuse and, to his great surprise, found "thousands of tiny worms, none larger than one third of an inch, blanketing the yard, the fence and the highway." As reported the next year in *Doubt* (the journal of the original Fortean Society) this was in July, so snow could hardly be blamed. The creatures eluded identification. Unlike more familiar worms, these had "almost microscopic legs and walked like caterpillars."

According to the London *Evening Standard* (3 January 1924) red worms snowed at Halmstad, in Sweden. They ranged from one to four inches long and were seen coming down with snowflakes.

At Pakroff, in Russia, immense numbers of an unidentified black insect fell during a snowstorm in 1827 (*Scientific American*, vol. 30). Also in Russia, in December 1830, a snowstorm was peppered with multitudes of gnat-like insects (*American Journal of Science*, vol.1, p.22). At Bramford Speke, in Devon, large numbers of three-quarter-inch worms came down with snow (*Times*, 14 April 1837). In May 1955, the residents of Kinomacki, in Finland, were horrified by a torrent of worms from the sky, with no accompanying rain or snow. A Reuter's report at the time blamed the event on "a violent wind whipping them up from a wet meadow". From Charles Fort's data, we note: Silesia, Germany, 1806, "snowing larvae"; Eifel, Germany, 1847, snow and larvae "fell together"; Switzerland, 1890, falls of "incalculable numbers" of two distinct kinds of insect larvae.

Further records reveal more detailed observations. In 1869, French naturalist, Rey de Morande, reported two remarkable cases to the Association Scientifique de France. The first, occurring near Turin in November 1854, involved a Monsieur Tissot who witnessed several thousand living insects "thrown down by a violent wind . . . some were larvae and some adult . . . of a species of hemiptera that had never before been collected [outside] Sardinia".

Rey de Morande himself investigated a combined shower of a great quantity of insect larvae and spiders at Arache, in the French Alps (and we can't help noting that Arachne is the Greek word for a spider). It happened in the early hours of 30 January 1869 – the same year that saw the remarkable insect appearances in England. For days the temperature had been very cold, so there was little possibility they had hatched out there. The spiders were of a species more commonly found on old trees in the forests of southern France than on Italian mountains and, although Rey de Morande favours the "violent wind" mode of transport, he does not venture a guess as to how so many insects could have been collected together by a wind in such a way that only creatures of two species were selected and, futhermore, distinguished from woodland debris of the same size or weight.

The well-known characteristic of some spiders of spinning a web and sailing off on a breeze can hardly apply to insect larvae; besides, these particular spiders do not have that characteristic. We mention many unusual gatherings of animals in this book; perhaps some creatures occasionally congregate in the open in expectation of windy transport, as was suggested in the case of the Finnish worms.

Another example of mixed rain of insects, this time in Switzerland in March 1922, was summarized by Charles Fort from reports in the international press. One bulletin read: "During a heavy snowstorm in the Alps recently thousands of exotic insects resembling spiders, caterpillars and huge ants fell on the slopes and quickly died. Local naturalists are unable to explain the phenomenon, but one theory is that the insects were blown in on the wind from a warmer climate." The use of the word "resembling" probably implies they were unfamiliar species. In commenting upon this case, Fort suggested that the important thing was not the fall of unknown insects during a snowstorm (of which he had found many examples) but the segregational powers of a wind capable of lifting small objects from a faraway place, keeping them in the air together over great distances, and yet ensuring that a variety of different insects of different specific gravities could fall together in the same place. We shall encounter this mysterious selecting process with other phenomena in this book.

Strange and ominous clouds have been associated with some well-observed falls. On 25 July 1872, Bucharest, Romania, was threatened by a small dark cloud that approached from the horizon on a generally cloudless and stiflingly hot day. At 9.15pm, the lurking cloud discharged its contents on the city below. According to *Nature* (1872) the townsfolk were filled with horror as, not rain, but small, fat, black worms or grubs covered most of the streets. In a similar case the *Meteorolgische Zeitschrift* (1901) describes a deep, black cloud that appeared in the evening sky over Szentes, in Hungary, on 14 August 1901. A heavy downpour began, "not of rain, but of winged insects, which in a few minutes covered the ground a foot deep". The insects are not identified, but only a few days before, another Hungarian village suffered similar rains, composed partly of winged ants and partly of four-winged *Neuroptera*.

At Bath, in Somerset, on 22 April 1871, there occurred what was described as "a storm of insects". During a heavy thunderstorm, a large number of glutinous drops fell near the city's railway station, where a boy first noticed them falling on his coat. Soon the whole platform was covered with jelly. According to Symons' *Meteorological Magazine* (1871), the egg masses hatched quickly into annelid-like worms. The event was investigated by the Reverend L. Jenyns, who sent his conclusion to the *Zoologist* and the Entomological Society of London. The culprit, said Jenyns,

In July 1903, during a voyage between islands off Normandy, a fishing vessel steamed through a blizzard of white butterflies which lasted for the best part of two days.

was a whirlwind "acting in a gyratory manner" that had scooped up a shallow pond, or one that was almost dried up, in which the eggs were concentrated into a small area. This explanation satisfied the savants because it exorcised the numerous difficult questions.

Curiously, another helping of jelly fell on Bath a few years later, in August 1894. It was described in *Notes and Queries* (8 September 1894) as consisting of thousands of shilling-sized jellyfish. Fort wondered if this was not misidentified frogspawn because, he notes, on the same day many small frogs fell at Wigan in Lancashire.

More recently it was the turn of Eton, Buckinghamshire, to be pelted with masses of jelly on 24 June 1911. They were insect eggs in clusters the size of peas and found covering the ground after a heavy rainfall. Once again we read of a rapid development, as if according to some cosmic restocking schedule, they had arrived just in time to hatch. It was reported in *Nature* (6 July 1911) that they yielded larvae of a species of midge.

Holinshed, in his *Chronicles* (1577) mentions a rain of blood-like matter in England, "during the rule of Rinall, which began fifteen years before the building of Rome". The foul rain lasted three days, "after which raine ensued such an exceeding number and multitude of flies, so noisome and contagious that much people died by reason thereof." Although this was long before microscopes could be used to identify micro-organisms, it was clear in Holinshed's mind, and those of his sources, that the plague, the flies and the evil rain were all connected. So many of the more famous "red rains" or "blood rains" (see RAINS OF SEEDS AND ORGANIC MATTER, p.47) have been found to consist of "insect excreta", infusoria and other organisms such as algae, that we wonder how many of the red rains mentioned frequently in historical chronicles might not be falls of insect eggs.

Rats, mice and lemmings

Captain J. Ben Jones, of Pwllheli, was fishing off the north coast of Wales, when a live rat dropped into his boat from a clear sky. Recounting the story in the *Liverpool Echo* (6 July 1954), Captain Jones says he chased it around the boat until he killed it and tossed it overboard. As he watched, a gull swooped on the rat's carcass. Pressed to explain the event, Captain Jones supposed the gull must have dropped the rat in the first place. Perhaps – or it fell from an appearing point above his boat. That was a single rat and so the gull explanation seems perfectly likely, but huge flocks of rat-carrying birds seem quite improbable in the following stories.

From the Indonesian island of Lombok comes a story of rats from the sky which threatened the islanders' precarious rice crop. It was told in the sober *Wall Street Journal* (25 August 1969). The reporter writes: "On the outskirts of Batudjai, a half dozen farmers are squatting in a ricefield . . . 'The rats came six months ago, before the rains stopped,' says [a] farmer. How did they come? 'They fell from the sky.' From the sky? 'Yes, in bunches of seven, and then they spread out across the land,' the farmer adds matter-of-factly. 'They are led by a great white rat as large as a cat,' says [another] farmer. 'The white rat is very smart. It knows when we plan to harvest. If we plan to harvest a field the day after tomorrow the rats will eat the field tomorrow night. If we plan, in secret, to harvest the field tomorrow then the rats will eat it tonight.' A visit

to the village chief, the only fat man to be seen in Batudjai ('He is of a higher caste,' explains a villager) repeats the farmers' story. Led by a white 'king of rats as large as a dog', the rats appeared last December, falling from the sky in bunches of seven, he says. As they landed the rats separated and spread in seven different directions, he says. Some farmers saw this happen, says the chief, and several farmers nearby nod."

The sceptical will interpret this story as the superstition of country yokels, but in his discussion of it (*Pursuit*, October 1969), the late Ivan Sanderson thought that a pest which could plunge already poor farmers into famine would not be made light of. Besides, he said, "The farmers of Lombok are not nearly as superstitious as one might suppose, and they know their local animal life very well indeed. The 'falling from the sky' is directly contrary to the normal behaviour of rats which pop out of the ground."

Beyond that, we are impressed with the mythical quality of the story, which seems of a kind more likely to be collected by a folklorist or cultural anthropologist than by a naturalist, meteorologist or agricultural scientist. These mythic elements include: the mystic number seven (prevalent in East Indies folklore); the geomantic connotation of the seven directions as a terrestrial mandala; the magical mode of transportation; an

De Hermelinis, quos fecundum Plinium mures Ponticos opinor.

CAP.   XX.

In his great history of the northern nations, Olaus Magnus illustrated the occasional falls of lemmings in parts of Norway. Many of these animals were devoured by ermines, whose especially luxurious fur was attributed directly to this unusual diet and caused them to be much sought after by trappers.

abnormal happening in nature preceding some disaster; and the vanishing crops (see also RAINS OF SEEDS AND ORGANIC MATTER, p.47). They also include the distinctive leader or "king", larger and more cunning than the other animals, who in true fairytale tradition grows larger with each re-telling of the story. If there had indeed been a disastrous fall of rats on an illiterate community, this is how the account of it might have been preserved.

A plague of mice in Inverness-shire in May 1832 has features in common with the Lombok story, even though no one claimed to have seen

mice falling from the sky. The mice appeared suddenly and in such huge numbers that the foxes reformed, giving up chickens for easier meat (in the same way the wolves of Alaska ignore their usual prey, caribou, when the lemming population explodes). In its account of the Inverness mouse plague the *Magazine of Natural History* (vol. 7) said that the mice were quite unlike any local species known to naturalists. They had brown bodies with white in a band around the neck and on the tip of the tail. Even if a few foreign mice had escaped from somewhere, they could hardly have multiplied into such vast numbers without their appearance and increase being noticed earlier. The sudden arrival of this alien horde of mice has the hallmark of an animal shower or teleportation.

Most people have heard of the periodic suicidal dash of lemmings (a kind of vole) in Norway, attributed to a frenzy engendered by over-population. A few lemmings, we are told, resist the death-urge and survive to rebuild their tribe. Regional traditions, from the earliest times, however, suggest that their numbers may be restocked by more periodic aerial drop-shipments.

In a book about the wonders of this Earth's atmosphere (*Der wunderreiche Überzug unserer Nider-welt*, 1680), Erasmus Francisci has a long, learned discussion about falls of rodents, frogs, snakes, fish, grain, stones and other things, mostly in the northern countries of Europe. He cites contemporary reports and also gives the views of many ancient and mediaeval writers on the subject. Chief among them was the geographer Olaus Magnus (1490–1557), who believed that falls of rodents were most common in the far north, particularly in Norway and the districts of Helsing and Uppsala, where rains of lemmings were said to occur during storms.

Two popular theories were current in the sixteenth century about where the creatures came from: some believed that they had been carried by winds from distant islands, others that they dropped out of thick mists and clouds. Olaus favoured the latter theory and so did Francisci, who argued reasonably

In his compendium of wonders, published in 1680, Erasmus Francisci elaborated on Olaus Magnus's brief mention of showers of rodents and included this illustration of falling shrew-mice.

that "If showers of stones can fall from the atmosphere why should it also not rain rats and mice?"

Francisci presents some interesting details about falling rodents, from people who had dissected them: that fresh, undigested grass is found in their stomachs; that every green thing they gnaw or touch withers, producing famines; and that they eventually die in great heaps, poisoning both land and people. Francisci was particularly convinced by the observation that, following rain or dense fog, hordes of lemmings had been discovered on the tops of mountains, even when the mountains were covered by deep snow. It could not be said that they had been driven by the weather out of their holes, because these were frozen up and blocked by the snow.

A similar phenomenon was noted in Alaska by the remarkable explorer-naturalist, Sally Carrighar. While staying in Nome in the hope of catching a few lemmings to take back to California, she was told by Eskimos that the creatures often drifted down slowly from the skies. Proof of this was that their tracks began abruptly in the snow. She did not take the stories seriously until, one day in April 1952, the Eskimo post-master at Unalakleet informed her that a few of the little creatures had that day touched down, appropriately, at the end of the town's airstrip. What happened next is worth citing in full, from Carrighar's *Wild Voice of the North* (1959): "The blacktop was covered with less than an inch of new, light, soft snow too shallow for any lemming to tunnel under it without thrusting up a ridge on the surface. And there, indeed, were the mysterious little trails, just as the Eskimos had described them. In fifteen places a track began rather faintly for a couple of inches, as if an animal had come down and gently coasted onto the snow. The tracks then continued more deeply, the individual footprints showing clearly, and also the slight brush marks between the footprints where the hairs on the lemmings' feet dragged. They were not mouse tracks, for then there would have been a tail mark between the footprints . . . In each case the tracks led off the blacktop to a clump of grass, where the lemmings evidently had burrowed down among the roots.

"And how could those tracks just begin suddenly, out there on the smooth white surface? I have no idea. Lemmings cannot jump even a fraction as far. They have no membranes between their forelegs and hind legs, as bats have, and therefore they cannot fly. They do have long, soft, thick fur, and briefly I wondered if the wind could have picked up the fluffy little creatures and set them down on the airstrip. That possibility would have been reasonable, perhaps, if the wind had been strong enough on that day to have drifted the snow. It wasn't; the snow was as light as eiderdown and it lay as level as it had fallen. That owls did not pick up the lemmings as they were venturing out on the surface is obvious because the tracks led to the clumps of grass, not away from them. An owl . . . might have dropped one squirming lemming – but hardly fifteen in a space about twenty yards square."

No scientist has yet given a convincing explanation of the migrations of the lemmings, not even of whether their "mass suicides" by drowning are a side-effect or the purpose of the migrations. In fact, we should like zoologists to explain how it is that this supposedly genetically-based instinct has not been bred out of the stock that resisted or survived it? Of course, the traditional belief that new breeding stock drops from the sky from time to time partly answers that

Lemmings on the run. People in many Arctic countries believe that they fall to earth from a distant star, thus accounting for their sudden proliferation.

objection, but no orthodox zoologist would express it openly. Sally Carrighar asserts that all the native peoples living near or within the Arctic Circle call the lemmings "mice from the sky". She continues:

"The Eskimo word is *kay-loong-meu-tuk*. Several serious-minded Eskimos told me of seeing the lemmings come down, 'falling in bigger and bigger circles that turned same way as sun' or, as we would say, clockwise. Eskimos who had not seen the lemmings descend, could all describe lemming tracks that 'start where the lemmings landed, without any footprints going out to that place'. The late Reggie Joule, an Eskimo bush pilot and son of native teachers, said that the familiar spurs of lemming tracks are often found on the roofs of the Eskimo cabins at Point Hope, where he grew up, 'and there weren't any tracks outside the cabins.' He concluded, 'I think lemmings fly.'" The more commonly held Eskimo explanation is that lemmings float down to the earth from some distant star.

Falls of other animals

In the Pacific, a Soviet ship spots a capsized boat. Its only survivor tells his rescuers an astounding story: "A cow fell into our boat!" The poor man is packed off to a mental institution but one official investigates further. He finds that a supply plane was smuggling a cow when the beast broke free in the cargo bay. After attempts to restrain it failed, the crew unceremoniously dumped the cow out of the hatch and into the sea . . . or so they thought.

When we first heard this story, we were suspicious about the absence of corroborating detail. Since then, we have noted a number of repetitions of the same story, each with its own appropriate details of location, date and people. The evidence of falls of larger animals is widespread but always circumstantial. Here are just a few items from our collections of news clippings, beginning with humble crustaceans and working up to something very strange indeed.

The German city of Paderborn was afflicted with a shower of living pond mussels on 9 August 1892, as reported in *Das Wetter* (December 1802). This was witnessed by a meteorological observer who sent an account to the Berlin Museum. A strange yellowish cloud had attracted the attention of onlookers "because of its colour and the rapidity of its motion; when it suddenly burst, a torrential rain fell with a rattling sound, and immediately after- wards the pavement was found to be covered with hundreds of the mussels." Dozens more living mussels fell within the walled confines of the Pittsburgh Gaol on 9 August 1834. The inmates were quick to seize the opportunity and most of the mussels were soon opened, salted and swallowed. The *Times* (30 September 1834) reported that the remaining mussels, some frogs and a number of largish stones (which all fell with the mussels during a storm) were put on exhibition.

On 24 April 1985, the Minneapolis *Star Tribune* reported that starfish – another rarity in the annals of falling creatures – had fallen on parts of St Cloud, Minnesota three days earlier. It was supposed that students from the nearby State University had thrown them off a high building, a mile away, into the wind, but they turned out to be a type found only hundreds of miles to the south, off Florida.

From Fort's collection we select the follow- ing examples of snake falls. The *Scientific American*, in 1860 tells of a man walking in the rain down a street in South Granville, New York, who, hearing a sound at his feet, looks down and sees a stunned snake which quickly revives and wriggles off. *Pearson's Weekly* (June 1900) reports a shower of "poisonous young rattlesnakes" dropping from the sky onto a party of Irish immigrants in Arizona, some thirty-five years previously. Conventionalists argued that they were there hidden on the ground in the first place, and were woken by the rain. Rather harder to explain are the "many thousands" of dark brown snakes found squirming on side-walks, in backyards and along streets after a violent storm in Memphis, Tennessee on 15 January 1877. Conventionalists again offered an explanation – this time a whirlwind. But there is a difficulty, that even *Scientific American* acknowledged: "In what locality snakes exist in such abundance is yet a mystery." It seems the snakes were so numerous that some were in tangled clumps.

The *San Francisco Chronicle* (27 October 1956) tells of the mystery of the Philippine monkey in the back-yard of Mrs Faye Swanson of San Mateo, California. On the morning of 26 October, Mrs Swanson stepped into her yard to find the dead monkey in a position, which suggested it had fallen from above, striking her clothes-line, splintering its solid post. Assuming it had fallen from a plane, the police and Civil Aviation Authority made an investigation but failed to find a culprit. There had been no planes over the area that day, leaving the official spokesman at a loss to account for a falling monkey.

Frank Edwards reports a very similar occurrence, also involving a backyard in California. In his *Strange World* (1964) he tells how the Trucker family heard a heavy thump outside their Long Beach home, one day in the autumn of 1960. The noise was followed by a loud, pained grunt and, stepping into the yard to investigate, they found a surly five-foot alligator.

In an inspirational tract of 1489, the religious scholar Franciscus de Reza illustrated a case reported by Albertus Magnus of a calf raised into the sky by the drawing power of the sun's rays.

The Truckers were convinced the saurian had just dropped in.

Perhaps a similar fall accounts for the alligator found frozen to death, in 1892, in Wisconsin, hundreds of miles north of its usual habitat in the south-eastern USA. Among other cases we could mention, we note a fall of young alligators in South Carolina reported in the *New York Times* (26 December 1877) with no mention of a storm or a whirlwind: "Dr J.L. Smith, of Silverton Township, while opening up a new turpentine farm, noticed something fall to the ground and commence to crawl toward the tent where he was sitting. On examining the object he found it to be an alligator. In the course of a few moments a second one made its appearance. This so excited the curiosity of the Doctor that he looked around to see if he could discover any more, and found six others within a space of two hundred yards. The animals were all quite lively and about twelve inches in length. The place whereon they fell is situated on high sandy ground about six miles north of the Savannah River."

The most astounding record of a falling – or teleporting – alligator we know of occurs in John Toland's sober history of dirigibles, *Ships in the Sky* (1957). In 1934, the US Navy airship *Macon* was on its way westwards after successfully participating in Caribbean manoeuvres as an strange creature "like a beaver" dropped into a street in Norrkoping during a thunderstorm in August 1708. Its startling appearance terrified the townsfolk, who took it for a troll.

After the publication of an earlier version of this book, we were contacted by Swedish fortean Sven Rosén who had traced the story to an even earlier source – Gustaf Otto Bilberg's *Almanackia* (1709). Bilberg wrote: "on the night between August 8 and 9, a great thunderstorm with continuous lightning raged over the country and set many villages on fire, causing much

After a violent hailstorm one September night in 1981, Cliff Davies of Killay, Swansea, found dozens of crabs on his lawn.

experimental lookout under the command of Leading Chief Robert "Shaky" Davis. "The return trip was a quiet, uneventful one," writes Toland, "and throughout Shaky Davis wandered about the ship in contented unease. Just as the ship was crossing into California, late in the afternoon of May 17, he heard a loud splashing over his head from one of the ballast bags. Suspecting a major casualty, he climbed into the rigging. The splashing was louder. He opened the ballast bag and looked in. Swimming around excitedly was a two-foot alligator."

According to Toland, the presence of the interloper was never explained. The incident occurred several days into the flight and it seems inconceivable that the restless captain could not have detected its noisy presence before. The circumstances are strongly suggestive of teleportation and it is acceptable to us that if the ballast bag of water, or the airship, had not surrounded the errant alligator's appearing point at the right moment, it would have been a case of "Look out, below!"

Our prize exhibit is the following account of a completely unknown type of animal. In his *Brontologia theologico-historia* (1721), Rhyzelius, Bishop of Linkoping in Sweden reports that a

damage. Then, according to testimonies by trustworthy men, it so happened that in Norrkoping, just as the lightning flashed and the thunder and rain seemed heaviest, a strange animal fell from the sky into a street not far away from the chemist's shop. It somewhat resembled a beaver, but its body was a little smaller than that of a full grown beaver, although its head was a bit larger, and its lower jaw a little longer than its upper jaw. It had rather small eyes, short hind legs and a tail, and rough brownish fur."

According to Rosén, the astronomer and mathematician Bilberg (who was in Norrkoping at the time but didn't see the creature) scorned as ridiculous the rumour that the thing was a troll. It was spread, he said, by the gossip of people who had not seen the carcass. Bishop Rhyzelius refers to the view of a local scholar, that a leather worker had poured into the street a barrel of seal lard that had gone bad. This is far from being a valid conclusion as the bishop and his informants assume that the barrel contained the body of a flayed or bald young seal, revealed by the heavy rain; and the description given by Bilberg is not very seal-like. All Bilberg could suggest was that the animal had been transported by a whirlwind, but what it was and where it came from he was unable to say.

Missiles from upper regions

Pierre Gassendi (1592–1655) and Antoine Lavoisier (1743–94) are just two of the pioneering scientists who investigated reports of stones dropping out of the sky. Having touched them, probed them, and cross-examined witnesses, neither could face the implications of the evidence they had unearthed. "There are no stones in the sky," Lavoisier, infamously, told the Academy of Sciences in Paris, "therefore stones cannot fall from the sky." On 13 September 1768, a meteorite weighing 7and a half pounds dropped, with a loud explosion, near Luce, in Maine, France. Lavoisier made his investigations once more, but concluded the stone must be of terrestrial origin, probably unearthed by being struck by lightning. "In spite of the belief of the ancients," he wrote, "true physicists have always been doubtful about the existence of these stones."

The existence of meteorites is so obvious to us now that it seems incredible that intelligent minds could so stubbornly hold onto opinions in the face of overwhelming data to the contrary.

Both believers and sceptics use this stick to beat each other with. Non-scientists can often be forgiven their ignorance, but Lavoisier's obstinate stand against meteorites – like Voltaire's against fossils and Sir Richard Owen's against Darwinism – shows how the narrow-mindedness of scientists can actually hinder the development of science. The existence of meteorites was finally accepted in 1803, but falls of a non-meteoric character, which often occur in odd circumstances or in connection with other phenomena, still raise some interesting questions. For instance, it is a little known fact that the famous Dhurmsalla meteorite, which fell in India on 28 July 1860, was not only covered with ice but preceeded several unusual occurrences.

Dhurmsalla's Deputy Commissioner reported, in the *Canadian Institute Proceedings* (vol.2, no.7, p.98) that within months of its descent there was a fall of fishes at Benares, a fall of red matter at Furruckabad, an earthquake, a dark spot on the sun's disc, an "unnatural darkness of some duration" and peculiar auroral displays. The evening after the event, he himself saw many lights in the sky that, today, would probably be called UFOs. The first great catalogue of meteorites, compiled by R.P.

HARROW OBSERVER

A car with its bonnet smashed by a massive ice-block at Pinner, Middlesex, on 25 March 1974.

HARROW OBSERVER

A fragment of the Pinner ice-block.

testimony of the editor, who had himself witnessed two further showers of warm stones at 7.30am and 1.30pm on the same day. He noticed that the missiles seemed to come from a point overhead and were, strangely, confined to an area of about 75 square feet.

The *Rand Daily Mail* (29 May 1922) carries an even stranger story. For several months a chemist's shop in Johannesburg, South Africa, was bombarded with stones. The phenomenon was thought to centre on a Hottentot girl employed there, so the police staked out the garden and the girl was sent into the shop. Stones were seen to fall in quantities vertically all around her. The police noted this verticality because they were hoping to trace an accomplice by the trajectory. They searched the vicinity, nevertheless, while the stones continued to fall around the girl. Weeks of fruitless investigation followed and, all the while, the girl was persecuted by showers of large stones, even as the police watched.

A disturbing case of a personalized stone fall was reported in the *Journal* of the International Fortean Organization (INFO). On the evening of 27 October 1973, two men fishing in a lake at Skaneatles, New York, were disturbed by a large stone splashing into the water near them. It was followed by a second and third stone, each progressively larger. They searched the area with their torches but saw nothing. Then a rain of small pebbles around them forced them to pack up. The pebble shower seemed to follow them as they ran to their car. They drove off in a hurry but, later, when they stopped to change their clothes, stones fell on them again. They stopped for a drink and were bombarded once more as they emerged from the bar; and again when they parted company outside one of their homes. The only comment from orthodoxy was the analysis on samples (grabbed by the men) by the Geology Department of Syracuse University; they iden-

Greg describes the Dhurmsalla object as "so intensely cold as to benumb the fingers and hands" (*Report of the British Association*, 1860). In any conventional sense, the Dhurmsalla phenomenon does not seem to have been meteoric in origin.

The most interesting and unusual falls of stones are those that fall slowly; those associated with a particular person; and those which seem to have some kind of portentous significance. We pick a few stories at random. The *Times* (1 May 1821) reports showers of stones falling upon a house in Truro, Cornwall, during many days of guarding and investigation by the mayor, soldiers and others.

In Charleston, South Carolina, on 4 September 1886, stones bounced off the pavement outside the offices of the *Charleston News and Courier*. It was 2.30am, and no one could see any likely perpetrator, but the stones were found to be warm. Two days later the edition of the paper carried the tified the pebbles as local rock-types (*INFO Journal*, n.14).

That story seems to us to have more in common with a poltergeist or "magic" curse than with a natural phenomenon. Indeed, this association is strongest with falls within enclosed spaces (see MATERIALIZATION AND FLIGHT OF OBJECTS, p.7). It is worth dwelling on the series of striking examples that occurred in Australia, investigated by Tony Healy and Paul Cropper for an article in *Fortean Times* (no. 116, November 1998).

A stone-throwing poltergeist had first manifested itself at a farm at Mayanup in 1955. Cyril Penny , a young Aborigine farm worker, went to see the phenomenon with many others. Two years later stones began raining around Cyril at Pumphrey in Western Australia. Conventionalists explained it away as due to "freak winds", but there seems to have been a lot more to it than that. Two witnesses swore that, while they were in a closed tent with the young man, stones fell at their feet. There had been no trickery, they said, and no holes in the tent material from either stones or freak winds (*Daily Express*, 22 March 1957). Fed up with the persecution at Pumphrey, Penny relocated to a new camp 16km away, but stones fell on him there too, so he was advised by tribal elders to move out of the district entirely. That worked but, as the phenomenon died away at Pumphrey, it started up on the Dickson farm fourteen kilometres away.

Like Cyril Penny, Mr Dickson had made the trip to Mayanup to gawp at the phantom stone-

A Turkish painting showing an incident in which a rain of stones, dropped by birds, saved Mecca from the attacking Yemenite army.

thrower and it seemed to have followed him home. The phenomenon seemed to concentrate on Dickson's son Harvey – just eleven years old at the time – but never hurt him. On one occasion a storm of stones raged around Harvey as he sat in his father's car with the windows up. According to Healy and Cropper, the phenomenon was not confined to stones. "Stones fell indoors and outdoors or rose from the ground to the roof. Shovels jumped and a four-gallon drum soared into the air, circling three times before landing. Visitors saw half-bricks, potatoes, bottles, stones, a spade and a broom fall out of thin air." The Haunted Farm, as it is called, has ever since been visited by such disturbances.

Healy and Cropper go on to detail two other older cases, at Cooyal in 1887 and Guyra in 1921, both of which mixed stone falls with classic poltergeist phenomena. Blows would be felt on the sides of houses, strong enough to shake the buildings, yet little damage was done. Stones that should have hurt people, by virtue of their size or speed, struck them gently and harmlessly. Finally Healy and Cropper tell of their personal investigation of the "haunting" at Humpty Doo, near Darwin in the Northern Territory. Once more they found a baffled community, a variety of flying and falling objects, and (despite close vigils) no detectable culprit or method.

One detail – possibly unique in the annals of falls – occurred in February, when residents noticed long, shallow troughs in the gravel driveway,

Steve Clark and some of the dozens of red and blue stones that fell outside his house in Kings Road, Radpole in Dorset over a weekend in December 1994. He was alerted by a man who saw them fall as he sat in his car. 'There are too many of them to have been thrown by children,' he said, adding that he didn't recognize them as anything local.

shortly after being showered with gravel. One evening, a visitor said he saw a small, black, spherical object, flying from the driveway, through the porch and away at high speed. It was trailing a long stream of gravel behind it. "He may have caught a glimpse of a polt reloading," remarked Healy and Cropper.

By far the largest category of falls in our files is that of ice, in particular large jagged chunks of ice. Various theories have been put forward to account for them: that they are fragments of ice comets; that they were created in storm clouds by strong winds or by super-lightning in the upper atmosphere; that they formed from leakage from aircraft toilets. None of these satisfy every occurrence and we must warn against excessive reliance on the apparently rational explanation that they drop off aircraft, by pointing to the abundance of cases from before the advent of powered flight.

The astronomer Camille Flammarion refers to a huge mass – 15 feet long, 6 feet wide and 11 feet thick – falling at the time of Charlemagne (*L'Atmosphere*, 1888). The *Times* (14 August 1849) reported that the previous evening an irregular shaped mass of ice had fallen at Ord, Ross-shire, after an extraordinary peal of thunder. It was about twenty feet in circumference and must have weighed nearly half a ton. According to Dr George Buist, a number of massive "hailstones" have fallen in India, including one at Candeish, in 1826, which was apparently a yard wide, and at Seringapatam, around the year 1800, which was said to have been "the size of an elephant. It took three days to melt."

Cases continue to be reported to this day and there have been some spectacular incidents. In November 1950, a farm on Exmoor, in Devon, was found littered with lumps of ice the "size of dinner-plates". Among them was a dead sheep, its neck cleanly slashed by the fourteen-pound chunk embedded in the ground by its shoulder (London *Evening News*, 9 November 1950). But this hardly compares with the thousands of sheep killed by ice bombardment in Texas, as reported in *Monthly Weather Review* (May 1877); nor with the bizarre death of a carpenter on the roof of his house near Dusseldorf, Germany, on 10 January 1951, skewered by a spear of ice six inches in diameter and six feet long.

Falls of artifacts

The largest category of artifact falls are stones that have apparently been worked. Ancient flints and shaped stones – called variously "thunder-stones", "thunderbolts", "sky-axes" and "lightning arrows" – are universally prized as talismans against lightning. We read in C. Blinkenberg's *Thunder Weapons* (1911) that the natives of Burma, China and Japan believed these objects to be manufactured in the sky. Tallius, writing in 1649, alluded to the belief that thunder-stones "are generated in the sky by fulgurous exhalation conglobed in a cloud by the circumfused humour". An impressive explanation for those who understood it, and certainly ahead of its time. Several centuries were to pass before scientific orthodoxy was ready to accept that stones could fall from the sky.

Fort was particularly interested in the number of accounts in which "axe-shaped" stones were found near lightning strikes or were embedded in trees struck by lightning. Blinkenberg says that, as far and wide as Jamaica, Norway, Malaya and the British Isles, it is popularly believed that these "axes" come down with the lightning. To these Fort adds the similar beliefs of the Indians of North America and South America.

When we see the term "sky weapons", we immediately think of the numerous cultural traditions of gods or spirits with supernatural weapons – Jove with his thunderbolts or Thor and his thunder-hammer. The Anglo-Saxons believed that fairies manufactured and threw tiny, enchanted missiles they called "elf-shot" or "fairy arrows" (see THE LITTLE PEOPLE, p.117). These were regarded as particularly terrifying, since to be struck by one meant being knocked senseless and was followed by bad luck, disaster and illness. (Some etymologists think this may be the origin of the usage of the word "stroke" to mean a paralytic seizure following brain haemorrhage; others say it refers to a stroke or touch of God's hand.)

A fine, modern account of "elf-shot" is related in A.A. MacGregor's book, *The Haunted Isles* (1933): "A specimen of these fairy arrows was picked up at Loch Maddy some years ago by a young girl, who on going out into the darkness for an armful of peats, heard something whizz through the air and drop at her feet." When we come upon data repeating in different countries and times, we think of folk-memories that may once have been founded on real incidents and vice versa; what was once a fiction has a way of becoming fact.

One of the strangest Christian traditions holds that the "Pillar of Saragossa" was carried to that place by angels in the company of the Virgin Mary (during her lifetime), and that from the top of it she gave instruction to the Apostle St James. The traditions of cultures all over the world include artifacts, like the Pillar, that are alleged to have fallen from the sky. They used to be held sacred, preserved in temples or put to magical use; nowadays they languish in museum basements, or in some forgotten display, labelled "Stone Age Ritual Object" or something similar. We note with interest that R.P. Greg's great meteorite catalogue in the *Report of the British Association* (1860) lists a pillar-like worked stone that fell from the sky in Constantinople in about 416 AD.

A disc of worked stone, "très régulier", fell at Tarbes, France, in June 1887. The *Comptes rendus* (1887) suggested a whirlwind was responsible, but the stone came down without attendant debris and was covered in ice. Data like this directly challenges the orthodox definition of "meteorite" as merely fragments of nickel-iron asteroids. Another challenge is posed by the 1910 controversy, which raged in the pages of *Scientific American*, when Charles F. Holder announced that he had deciphered a deeply incised inscription on "a strange stone resembling a meteorite" which had fallen into the Yaqui Valley, Mexico. Holder's assertion that the signs were Mayan was easy to discredit, and the matter was conveniently dropped, leaving uninvestigated the original claim that a stone bearing inscriptions had descended to the earth.

All kinds of balls – big and small, metal and plastic – have dropped since the early nineteenth century. At Bijori, India, beads of many colours, holed ready to string, have apparently fallen regularly for nearly a hundred years. At times they are so plentiful that

A rain of crosses in 1503 as recorded by Lycosthenes in *Prodigiorum ac ostentorum* (1557).

A red-hot chain fell on a bulldozer at Rockhill, Missouri, on 14 May 1959.

you can scoop them up by the handful. According to *Fate* (January 1955) all efforts to trace the source have failed. Similarly, a police investigation failed to account for the rain of golf balls that occurred during a storm at Punta Gorda, Florida on 3 September 1969.

Police were similarly baffled by a "small, egg-shaped canister" that fell from the sky onto a farm near Muchea, Western Australia. The canister disintegrated, but the farmer collected a sample of the liquid oozing from it. He described it as "green bubbling fluid". This reminds us of the Chinese folk-tale about Lei Kung, the Duke of Thunder, in which the god drops a bottle of healing lotion down from heaven to help a woman who had been struck by lightning (see E.T.C. Werner's *Myths and Legends of China*, 1922). Parallels could be found in modern accounts of the sky-gods, the extra-terrestrials (see ENCOUNTERS WITH ALIENS, P.137).

Fortean archives contain a huge catalogue of artifact falls. Four times during 1968 a mix of mud, wood-chunks, stones, broken glass and pottery fell during storms on the Cuban town of Piñar del Rio (*Beyond* magazine, October 1969). On the night of 12 October 1888, a great quantity of nails dropped out of the night sky onto the wife of the lighthouse keeper at Point Isabel, Texas. The *St Louis Globe-Democrat* (16 October 1888) said the nail-shower was repeated the next night but, this time, accompanied by clods of earth and oyster shells. The report attracted crowds of sightseers, many of whom later testified to seeing nails plummeting down near the lighthouse.

The periodic rains of airplane parts tend to have a reasonable explanation, but we collect them nonetheless. For example, in 1969, a wheel dropped out of the sky and badly damaged the roof of a car travelling along a road in Palm Springs, California. According to the *New York Times* (17 April 1969), investigating authorities could find no report of any plane with a missing wheel.

A particular favourite with us are falls inside rooms, for they seem doubly damned. A rain of buckshot fell at intervals over several days inside an office at Newton, New Jersey. *The San Francisco Chronicle* (3 March 1929), called it the greatest mystery in the history of the town; and there was no apparent means by which the shot could have entered the building. After a similar case was reported in the *Religio-Philosophical Journal*, its issue for 24 April 1880 carried a correspondent's description of bullets that fell at intervals in broad daylight in every room of his house in 1867. The falls of "large birdshot" increased to last an hour or more and yet, whenever he went to gather them up, he could never find more than half a dozen. The rest had vanished as mysteriously as they came.

Particularly well observed, among indoor falls, were the pieces of furnace-made brick that kept up a regular rain inside various rooms of the Sri Aurobindo Ashram at Pondicherry, India, in December 1921. The *Bulletin of the Sri Aurobindo International Centre of Education* (February 1974) has a lengthy recollection by an eyewitness to continuous falls in the courtyard, kitchen and stairwell, although searches revealed no culprit or cause. Observers reported that the bricks were visible only a little distance below the level of the roof, as though they simply came into being at that height, falling as soon as they materialized. Some of the residents noticed that the phenomenon seemed associated with a young boy, assistant to the cook. They locked him in a room with no apertures, and bricks still fell around him, wounding him. Forty-one years earlier, in a schoolroom near Government House in Madras, bricks had also fallen, and had continued to fall in the presence of thirty investigators for at least five days. *The Madras Mail* (5 March 1888), says that the clergy advised marking a brick with a white cross and placing it in the centre of the room. To their utter astonishment, "a brick of a corresponding size, but bearing a black

E. TWEEDY

An unusual 'meteorite', thought to be a 12-inch cylinder of marble that fell in Ohio in August 1910.

cross, dropped out of the air onto the top of the first brick", so precisely that it stayed balanced there.

In the section on RAINS OF SEEDS AND ORGANIC MATTER (see p.49), we cite an eighth-century Irish record of a rain of silver. To many modern minds, a rain of money would be the equivalent of a rain of manna in the concrete wilderness. Most of these seem to occur during "poltergeist" hauntings: e.g. pennies fell with pieces of soda and lumps of coal during the famous 1927–28 disturbance at Battersea, London, investigated and recorded by Harry Price in *Poltergeist Over England* (1945). One of the most devastating poltergeists of all time is that which completely demolished a house near the Sorbonne, Paris, in 1849. The continuous bombardment of building materials every night for three weeks is recorded in the official French police magazine, the *Gazette des tribunaux* (2 February 1849). The account includes an undated allusion to similar excitement in Paris, when "a rain of pieces of small money drew together the loungers of Paris every evening in the Rue de Montesquieu".

Fort mentioned a fall of coins in Trafalgar Square, London, but did not give details; however, we can report that pennies and half-pennies dropped around children going home from school in Hanham, Bristol, according to the *London People* (30 September 1956). At Meshehera, Russia, silver coins fell "all over the district" during a storm (*Daily Express*, 5 August 1940). The *People* (17 February 1957) reported that a woman at Gateshead in County Durham was in her yard when "two objects whizzed past her head" which turned out to be halfpennies. About forty to fifty pennies came down in short bursts over fifteen minutes at Ramsgate, Kent. According to the *Daily Mirror* (10 December 1968), "You could not see them falling. All you heard was the sound of them bouncing off the pavement." Curiously, they were all bent.

Rains of seeds and organic matter

Rains of blood are among the oldest prodigies known to man yet, despite many modern recurrences and ancient allusions (e.g. Homer and Plutarch), the phenomenon is still regarded as mythical. On 15 May 1890, a blood-like substance fell at Messignadi, Calabria. *Science News* (vol.35, p.104), reported that the Italian Meteorological Bureau identified it as bird blood. They suggested that a flock of birds had been torn apart by a violent wind – but their own records contained no mention of such a wind, nor could they explain why no carcases fell with the blood.

On 17 August 1841, workers in a tobacco field in Tennessee were startled by the rattle of large drops on the leaves. Looking closer they saw that the drops looked like blood, and that they fell perpendicularly from a peculiar red cloud overhead. They fetched the owner and a certain Professor Troost who, on arrival, saw the field strewn with foul-smelling bits of matter. The *American Journal of Science* (October 1841) carried a report from Professor Troost in which he declared that the stuff was animal fat and muscle tissue, though he would venture no opinion on the "blood". No one bothered to take statements from the workers; instead, the learned journal seemed to accuse them of perpetrating a hoax and, for reasons never explained, scattering a decayed hog over the field. In contrast, an account of flakes of meat drifting

A rain of blood at Lisbon in 1551, pictured by Lycosthenes in *Prodigiorum ac ostentorum* (1557).

down from a clear sky into a field in Kentucky had many credible witnesses. According to the *Scientific American* (March 1876), the fall was strangely confined to the oblong field, occurring nowhere outside it. One investigator found that the meat-flakes (one was 3–4 inches square) were "perfectly fresh" and ate some. He said they tasted like "mutton or venison".

The phenomenon seems to happen far less frequently now; the most recent occurrence in our files comes from the *Flying Saucer Review* (November 1968, quoting from Brazilian papers). For more than five minutes on 27 August in that year, meat and blood fell on an area, one kilometre square, between Cocpava and São José dos Campos.

Rain can be coloured red for a number of reasons. For example, *La Nature* (28 September 1880) relates that Professor Brun of Geneva investigated reports of a blood-rain in Morocco, and found rocks and vegetation covered in dried red scales, which he identified as the remains of colonies of the minute organism *Protococcus fluvialis*. He believed that they had been deposited there by a whirlwind, but confessed he was puzzled by the extraordinary selection involved. The colonies were uniformly made up of young organisms. Other rains – red, black, yellow, etc. – have been found to be coloured by varieties of dust (e.g. sand from the Sahara), or colonies of blue-green algae, or infusoria, or pollen, or the exudations or eggs of insects.

Other falls of organic matter are more enigmatic, such as the jelly-like substance believed by rural folk to have fallen from the stars in association with a light. According to the *Scientific American* (vol.2, p.79), a bright object, four feet in diameter, was seen to fall, at Loweville, New York, 11 November 1846, and subsequently became – or left behind – a mass of "foetid jelly". More recently, the Dublin *Evening Herald*, 7 February 1958, reported a strange light passing over West Meath and landing in a field. It was thought to be a UFO, but investigators rushing to the spot found only a mass of what they called "bog butter".

The continuity of this phenomenon is well documented. For example, the Bishop of Cloyne, writing in 1696 (quoted in *Philosophical Transactions*, vol.19, p.224) spoke of many such falls in his lifetime in Ireland, and said that this "bog butter", whatever it is, was highly prized by the local people as a treatment for scalds. Professor McKenny Hughes, in *Nature* (23 June 1910), wrote that the notion of falling stars turning into jelly was very common; he claimed he had seen "the rot of the stars" for himself and that the Welsh called it *Pwdre Ser*. Attempts to explain it as the gelatinous fungus *Tremella mesenterica* are inconclusive.

Fort advanced the idea that, just as nourishment is supplied to the developing parts of an egg, perhaps these organic and vegetable falls are attempts by our existence to nourish itself, or a vestige of the processes that originally prepared our environment for our arrival. Eccentric though this sounds, it is quite in accordance with the evidence: for, as we hope we have shown, things do fall from the heavens, and many of them are alive and edible. There was, after all, a positive response to the Israelites' prayers for quails and manna, and, as far as we know, showers of edible lichen still occur in Asia Minor to this day.

The seeds that rained into the streets of Kirkmanshaws, Persia, in 1913, were thought to be manna, but they were later identified (London *Daily Mail*, 13 August 1913) as "like Indian corn". *INFO Journal* (no.8, 1972), tells of a rain of West African beans on a farm in north-west Brazil in the summer of 1971. In these cases and others, we note how predictable it is that the whirlwind explanation is brought in, often without regard for the circum-

FORTEAN PICTURE LIBRARY

Roland Moody with some of the broadbeans and other seeds that deluged his home in Southampton in 1979.

stances. Consider the torrent of an incalculable number of strange seeds upon several towns in the Italian province of Macerata in 1897. In *Notes and Queries* (18 September 1897) they are identified as fruit of the Judas tree, a native of Central Africa, and most were in the first stage of germination. What kind of whirlwind can pick up *only* these seeds in such quantity (no twigs, leaves, etc.) and transport them to Italy, keeping them together in the air without dropping any in between?

Records of seed falls in medieval chronicles are more numerous than those of frog falls. A good example is in the *Annals of Clonmacnoise*, which exists only as a sixteenth-century English translation of the lost Irish original. Niall Frosach began his reign as a king in Ireland, in 759 AD, while a severe famine gripped the land. He made

A shower of wheat, one of a number of 'strange signs' in the year 1680, which the writer and illustrator of a contemporary broadside hoped would make the sinful repent.

a public appeal to God, praying, in the company of "seven godly bishops", on a hill at Ard-Uilline. Three strange rains followed; first silver, then honey and finally wheat. The record says it was "pure wheat, which covered all the fields over that the like was never seen before, soe that there was such plenty & aboundance of wheat that it was thought that it was able to maintaine many kingdoms." Even if the first two rains seem fanciful, the account of the third comes across as one of honest astonishment.

In 1749, Dr Thomas Short of Sheffield published his *General Chronological History of the Air*, which compiled meteorological data from old histories. Although modern historians regard his methodology as unreliable and often unreferenced, it is worth noting some of his entries on this topic. In Campania, in 722, there was a fall of wheat and barley; in Saxony, in 987, something like wheat came down; and near Oxford, in 1656, a further fall of wheat occurred.

Fortunately the phenomenon has continued and reliable reports can be found; for example, the *Philosophical Transactions* (vol.16, p.281) states that grains of wheat fell in Wiltshire in 1686 but contained in hailstones. In our own time it rained rice on Mandalay, Burma, where, according to the *Daily Telegraph* (10 January 1952), people in the streets gathered handfuls. In 1950 men working high on New York's Empire State Building were stung by an odd-looking hail that turned out to be grains of barley (*Fate*, April 1951).

Nuts have rained, too. On the night of 9 May 1867 a number of streets in Dublin were peppered with hardened berries, "like a very small orange . . . and when cut across seem as if made of some hard, aromatic dark brown wood." Further accounts of them were published in Symons' *Meteorological Magazine* (June 1867): one said they had fallen "in great quantities and with great force", driving even policemen with protective helmets to take shelter; another declared them to be hazelnuts which had been "preserved in a bog for centuries." The author of that last opinion never revealed how he arrived at this conclusion or suggested how they might have been plucked from the bog by a whirlwind.

According to Charles Fort's notes, the following year (1868) saw nearly simultaneous rains of small black stones in Italy, Hungary, Switzerland and Birmingham, England. What if they were not stones but shriveled hazelnuts? We raise the question because Birmingham had seen a number of frog and stone falls. In 1868 hazelnut husks came down with stones in a prodigious shower (Birmingham *Daily Post*, 1 June 1868).

On 13 March 1977 hazelnuts dropped into a Bristol street beside Alfred Wilson Osborne and his wife, making clicking sounds on the pavement. Mr Osborne, a chess correspondent for a local newspaper, thought, at first, that buttons had come off his coat, but quickly realized something had fallen from the clear sky. Suddenly, hundreds more nuts fell around them. Another person experienced a nut shower on the same spot a few minutes later. Mr Osborne bit into one and said it was "fresh and sweet" but not only were there no nut trees in the vicinity, the hazelnut season is much later in the year. "I have thought that a vortex [might have] sucked them up, but I don't know where you suck up hazelnuts in March," he said.

The experience of Roland Moody, in 1979, is even stranger. The conservatory at the back of his Southampton house was the target for many different kinds of falling seed. On the morning of 12 February he heard a "whoosh" on the glass roof. It was snowing so he took no notice until, nearly an hour later, the sound came again. He found the entire roof covered with many thousands of tiny mustard and cress seeds. "The cress seeds were coated in jelly," he said. There were five or six more batches through the day covering Mr Moody's entire garden.

The next day, he consulted his neighbours. One, Mrs Stockley, had some in her garden and then made a startling confession to Mr Moody. The previous year, she said, the same seeds had fallen to cover her front garden and it had taken all year to get rid of them. The phenomenon did

A whirlwind lifts straw at Beckhampton Down, Wiltshire, in July 1989.

FORTEAN PICTURE LIBRARY

not end there. The following day down came peas, maize and haricot beans, while his neighbours on both sides were pelted with bean and pea seeds. Mrs Stockley, interviewed for Arthur C. Clarke's TV series *Mysterious World* in 1980, said "I got masses of broad beans every time I opened my front door. They travelled right up the hall into the kitchen, which is some ten yards." Police were called but no obvious source could be found. Eventually the phenomenon, which targeted only these three houses in the road, faded away, but not before ten pounds of beans had been collected from at least twenty-five showers. Mr Moody gathered eight bucketfuls of cress seeds from his garden alone. The victims were baffled but appreciative: when we spoke to him, Mr Moody said all the seeds they collected grew healthily and the crops were "excellent".

Erasmus Francisci, in *Der wunder-reich* (1680) has a discussion on whether seeds that fall from the sky should be eaten. He answers by citing a rain of grain in Carinthia, in 1558, that fell for two hours over an area of two square miles and yielded good bread when baked. He also referred to rains of wheat in Alsace, that occurred when the harvest failed, as evidence of God's Providence. We could add the fall of oranges near Naples in July 1833, or the young peaches at Shreveport, Louisiana in July 1961.

Within a few years of the mighty eruption of the Indonesian volcano Krakatoa (on 28 August 1883) its remaining terrain had been recolonized by plant and even insect life. Of course we are not suggesting that they arrived by teleportation – the distributive powers of winds, ocean currents and birds are well known and sufficient – but we do wonder if falls of seeds play an inconspicuous part in such recoveries.

Mysterious flows and oozings

Before leaving behind this summary look at the voluminous records of strange falls, we want to mention another category of teleportation in which liquids appear from "nowhere" and ooze or flow from objects or drop down from mid-air. It was only when Charles Fort collated his notes on falls that he spotted such localized repetitions as the remarkable series at Geneva. The *Comptes rendus* (vol.5, p.549) carried a report that large, well-separated drops of warm water fell on Geneva from a clear zenith at 9am on 9 August 1837. This was repeated on 31 May the following year and twice on 11 May 1842 (*Comptes rendus*, vol.15, p.290). During a series of quakes at Inverness in June 1817 hot water fell on the 30th of that month (*Report of the British Association*, 1854, p.112).

Intense localized rain is called by meteorologists "point rainfall". As an example, *Symons' Meteorological Magazine* (vol.47, p.140) records a "cascade" of water and hail upon an area of London of no more than 200 acres on 9 June 1809.

The *Toronto Globe* (3 June 1889) described the townsfolk of Coburg, Ontario, looking up to see a vast bag-like body of water crossing the town and flopping down two miles away. It was explained away as a "waterspout".

As well as such cloudbursts, there also exist more steady flows. According to the *Comptes rendus* (vol.14, p.664) a steady stream of water fell from a stationary point in the sky over Noirfontaine, France, for at least two days in April 1842. The *New York Sun* (24 October 1886) reported that water had been falling steadily for fourteen days out of a cloudless sky onto the same piece of ground in Chesterfield County, South Carolina. About the same time a similar fall at Aitken was confined to an area of ten square feet. The following month a fall at Dawson, Georgia, concentrated on a spot 25 feet wide. In each case it was as if an invisible, stationary tap had been left running in the sky.

In North Carolina the *Charlotte Chronicle* (21 October 1886) reported: "Citizens in the southeastern portion of the city have witnessed for three weeks or more a very strange phenomenon. Every afternoon at 3 o'clock there is a rainfall in one particular spot, which lasts for half an hour. Between two trees at the hour named there falls a gentle rain while the sun is shining, and this has been witnessed every day during the past three weeks." A Signal Service observer later sent a report on this to the *Monthly Weather Review* (October 1887), saying he had seen it himself over several days. The trees were red oaks and "sometimes the precipitation falls over an area of half an acre, but always appears to centre at these two trees, and when lightest, there only".

At Brownsville, Pennsylvania, it was a peach tree that received this watery manna. According to the *St Louis Globe-Democrat* (19 November 1892), witnesses saw the water falling from a little way above the tree and covering an area round it of about fourteen feet square. Could these trees, Fort wondered, act like mediums and make this happen?

Other mysterious manifestations of liquids are called, conventionally, "poltergeist flows". In early February 1873, the Bank House at Eccleston, Lancashire, was the scene of an extraordinary series of events. Torrents of water rained down inside the rooms, soaking the elderly inhabitants and ruining their furniture. There was no question of imposture; everyone who investigated the case was impressed by the genuine misery the phenomenon caused. The water did not appear to come from leaking domestic pipes; a report in the *Chorley Standard* (15 February) noted that "the most singular feature of the affair is that the ceilings themselves were quite dry." Again, on 9 September 1880, a reporter from the *Toronto Globe* described his investigations of improbable occurrences at a farm near Wellesley, Ontario, where windows were broken by unlocatable missiles and furniture moved about of its own volition. He told of such volumes of water falling inside the house – often while the rooms were full of sightseers – that the family's effects were ruined. Yet neither walls nor ceilings bore any trace of the water's passage.

A liquid poltergeist that plagued the (appropriately named) Waterman family of Windsor, Vermont, is recorded by Frank Edwards in *Strange World* (1964). It began one morning in September 1955, when beads of moisture appeared on their furniture as though a heavy mist had settled on it. They sponged off the strange dew, but it repeatedly returned, sometimes copiously. Checks made by service engineers found all the pipes tight and dry but the water appeared relentlessly. One day, says Edwards, as Dr Waterman "transferred a shallow dish of grapes from one room to another, it filled with water during the transit."

An article on mysterious flows of all kinds in the American paper *Grit* (26 July 1970), mentioned a watery persecution that drove the Martin family from their house in Methuen, Massachusetts, in 1963, and resumed its harassments in their new home in another city. Water was described as "spurting" from different points throughout the house, as well as seeping from the walls and ceilings. We know from studies of poltergeist cases that the activity can transfer to the new home, but we also know of cases where the disturbances have remained with the house to plague the next occupants.

The case of nine-year-old Eugenio Rossi is reminiscent of other "persecution" cases. Eugenio was in hospital in Nuoro, Sardinia, for a liver complaint, when, according to the *Sun* (30 November 1972) large quantities of water began to seep through the floorboards around his bed. He was moved five times, each time for the same reason – water came through, or appeared on, the floor around his bed. Again we read of baffled officials and service engineers failing, despite a thorough search, to find any acceptable cause. People who, even unwillingly, possess this natural affinity with water must surely have been the water-finders and rainmakers of ancient societies.

Possibly the classic case of a "liquid poltergeist" occurred at the Rectory at Swanton Novers, Norfolk, and was chronicled in most of the leading English papers of the day. On 30 August 1919, an oily substance was noticed seeping through the ceilings of some rooms, or rather collecting in patches on the ceilings. Over the next few days these seepings became constant flows, sometimes, as witnesses described, spurting from the walls. It was suggested the house was built over an oil well, but it was not crude oil that was flowing, but paraffin (kerosene) and petrol (gasoline). It arrived at the rate of a quart every ten minutes, and a report dated 2 September said that about fifty gallons had been caught in receptacles. Of the thirteen indoor showers on 1 September, two were of water while the others consisted of methylated spirits (alcohol) and sandalwood oil.

Everything in the house was ruined and the vapours became so dangerous that evacuation became necessary. Walls were torn open and the ceilings probed and exposed, but no clue to the flows' origin was ever found. The rector, the Reverend Hugh Guy, employed a young housemaid, and attempts were made to implicate her. The *Times* (9 September) reported that an "illusionist", Oswald Williams, while investigating the mystery

CEILING BROKEN TO INVESTIGATE SOURCE OF TROUBLE

OIL DRIPPING FROM SCULLERY CEILING

OIL DRIPPING FROM KITCHEN CEILING

The ceilings at Swanton Novers Rectory, from the *Daily Mail*, 3 September 1919. The rector, the Reverend Hugh Guy, said to a reporter who noticed drops of paraffin, 'Next time it will be methylated spirit, or just water. I'm sorry you can't see it gushing . . . gallons of water came from that ceiling . . . the queer part is that the ceiling, the paper, and the laths are quite dry.'

had witnessed the girl throwing water on the ceiling. On 12 September the *Times* printed an interview with the girl; she had gone into the house with Williams, and when water appeared on the ceiling Williams accused her. He gave her one minute to admit it or he would see she was sent to prison. Later she brought a charge against Williams and his wife, claiming that they had beaten her. The case was dismissed. It was never explained why the girl should spend her low wages on exotic liquids, where she could have obtained them, or how she could transport fifty gallons of oils onto a ceiling in the midst of investigations without being detected.

Liquid poltergeists remain fairly rare occurrences, but a recent example, which occurred in Rochdale, Lancashire, attracted the attention of investigator Peter Hough. Water dripping inside a house, occupied by the Gardner family, was investigated by the local council without the cause being identified. As chairman of the Northern Anomalies Research Organisation (NARO), Hough, with a small team of fellow investigators,

visited the Gardners' house on 31 August 1995; it was a hot day during a near-drought and a hose-pipe ban was in force.

The Gardners told the NARO team that the drip of water from walls and ceilings had completely disrupted their lives for the last ten months. The flow would move from room to room. "It would start dripping in one place then shoot from corner to corner", said Mrs Vera Gardner. Supposing that condensation was to blame, the council installed extraction fans, but dripping ceilings and sodden bedding continued to plague the family. Besides, as Jim Gardner pointed out, "You don't get condensation in summer."

Hough found the attic side of the ceiling, adjacent to a seeping patch in the room below, to be "bone dry". Alicia Leigh, one of the team, saw the kitchen door become wet: "I noticed the bottom of the door was wet and was about to alert the others when thousands of tiny droplets instantaneously covered the entire door. It happened right before my eyes." Stephen Mera, another NARO member, saw water flash across a bedroom ceiling as the Gardners were being questioned in another room. "It was as if the ceiling was a floor and someone had thrown a cupful of water across it." Hough said: "It had defied gravity!"

These phenomena were accompanied by the usual poltergeistery: household objects hovered and flew around, sometimes hitting the family; objects would appear and disappear; there were strange sounds and smells, and a mark appeared on Stephen's back where he felt sure a "phantom" had "flicked" him. The investigation was concluded with no one any the wiser. No source for the indoor rain could be found, and neither the NARO team's cameras nor analysis of water samples yielded anything useful. The council fobbed off the Gardners with a facile explanation; the best that Hough was able to come up with was a "poltergeist".

All these phenomena, in different combinations, echo through this book; they indicate to us that teleportation, or something very like it, must be considered as a connecting link between them.

3

Wild Talents

3

Wild Talents

Fire-walking and fire-immunity

No reasonable person would attempt to walk barefoot across a pit of fiery coals or hot stones, so we can only suppose that those who do so are not in their right minds but in some other state. How is it possible for people to so delude themselves as to the nature of physical reality that they voluntarily undertake such a feat? And yet the fact is that they do – universally and with impunity. Fire-walking is one of the last remaining tokens of the power over nature attributed to the ancient magicians; and, according to Professor Mircea Eliade, modern shamans especially value it for that reason.

In *The Miracle Hunters* (1959), George Sandwith gives several detailed accounts of the Hindu fire-walks that he witnessed while a government surveyor on the island of Suva, Fiji. After one dramatic ceremony he returned to his hotel with another spectator, a banker, who was obviously deeply disturbed by the experience. "Very grudgingly he admitted the fire-walking was genuine, for he had thrown something on the pit and it caught fire at once, but he was strongly of the opinion that the Government ought to stop it! When asked why, he became very annoyed replying that it does not conform with modern

scientific discoveries. When I suggested that something of value might be learned from the fire-walkers, he was so furious he turned on his heel and left me." This turning on the heel and leaving is a not uncommon reaction among people confronted with the types of phenomena described in this book.

One of the first "scientifically controlled" fire-walks was held at Carshalton, Surrey, in September 1935 under the auspices of the University of London. The walker was a young Indian Muslim, Kuda Bux, who strode across the twenty-foot trench four times without signs of burning. It was described in *Fifty Years of Psychical Research* (1939) by Harry Price who rationalized that the secret lay in brief contact and the low thermal conductivity of the burning wood. We recently saw some unpublished notes on the incident, made at the time by Harold S.W. Chibbett, which include many of the rationalizations that he overheard that day. One doctor loudly pronounced that anyone could do it, as, despite appearances, the temperature was only that of a cup of tea (it was over 800°F). He was invited to try it if he was so sure of his theory, but declined, saying he was not suitably dressed for the occasion.

Andrew Lang, the great folklorist, was one of the first to point out the ubiquity of the fire-walking ritual. He collected many modern instances from widely separated countries but the practice was already old when it was recorded by

Chief Terrii Pao. a Hawaiian kahuna (shaman), clutching sacred leaves, walks calmly across white-hot stones.

Plato, Virgil and Strabo. Eliade pushes its antiquity back to the very origins of shamanism, and in *The Forge and the Crucible* (1979) he has much to say on fire-immunity rituals. These are practised in different forms by many people, from the fire-dancing Navajo Indians of North America to the Hindus, and even occur within a nominally Christian tradition in Europe. To this day, on the feasts of St Constantine and his mother St Helen, the villagers of Langadas in Greece dance on glowing coals, clutching icons of these saints.

Many earlier examples of fire immunity among devout Christians are given in Father Thurston's *The Physical Phenomena of Mysticism* (1952). Olivier Leroy's key work on the subject, *Les Hommes sala-mandres* (1931), gives even more cases; for example it is reliably recorded that when St Polycarp of Smyrna was put to the stake in about 155 AD, the flames formed an arch over him, and he was unscathed until a soldier stabbed him with a spear. The Protestants are also reported to have had their fire heroes. Vincent Gaddis in *Mysterious Fires and Lights* says that during the Huguenot revolts in seventeenth-century France, Claris, a Camisard leader, was condemned to be burnt yet continued unsinged and still talking in the midst of the flames.

When the fire died down, "not only was he unhurt, but there was no mark of fire on his clothes". The Camisard general, Jean Cavalier, and other witnesses confirmed the story when they were later exiled to England.

Behind the universal demonstrations of the fact of fire-immunity lies a bewildering variety of methods by which it is achieved. Trance and religious ecstasy seem to be a vital prerequisite in the Hindu rituals (whether in India, Ceylon or Fiji), nearby temple where the priest sprinkled salt over his head. Professor Stephenson later described, in the *Journal of Borderland Research* (vols. 2 and 5), how he walked, in quite a leisurely way, over the fire and felt only a tingling in his feet. He mentions one interesting detail, that during his crossing he felt a pain in one foot and later found a small cut, evidently made by a sharp stone. Dr Harry B. Wright wrote in *True* (March 1950) of a firewalk he witnessed on Viti Levu, Fiji, over a twenty-

Saints Cosmas and Damien, two early martyrs, were brother doctors whose ministrations to the poor were unpopular with the authorities. Legend says that they were, unsuccessfully, drowned, crucified, stoned and burnt (as in this painting by Fra Angelico).

yet Kuda Bux and many others have reproduced the effect without trance. Sometimes there are elaborate preliminaries involving chanting, dancing and sexual abstinence, yet there are many other cases in which the walking has been performed without preparation or after a merely perfunctory ritual. E.G. Stephenson, a professor of English Literature, attended a Shinto ceremony in Tokyo and was seized by the urge to cross the ninety-foot charcoal trench himself. An officiating priest insisted that he must be "prepared" and took him to the five-foot pit of heated stones. He imagined the walkers to be in a pain-suppressing state of ecstasy, but when he examined their feet before and immediately afterwards, he found them ordinarily sensitive to prodding with a pin or his lighted cigarette.

The majority of fire-walks are over beds of coals – though Dr Brigham, whose adventures in Hawaii are described later, walked on lava; and Mircea Eliade refers to the Lolo shamans of China whose speciality was a walk over glowing ploughshares, recalling the medieval Christian "trial by ordeal". Dr B. Glanvill Corney, chief medical officer of the Fiji Islands, wrote in *Notes and Queries* (21 February 1914) that he had seen five mass walks over red-hot stones and had found no burnt feet among the walkers.

Now we come to two of the central mysteries of fire-immunity: the apparent selectivity of the fire in the matter of what it will or will not burn; and the ability of certain people to bring this selectivity under their own control.

Leroy's "Human Salamander" was the sobriquet of Marie Sonet, one of the *convulsionnaires de Saint-Médard* in Paris in the 1750s (of whom a good account is given by Dr E.J. Dingwall in *Some Human Oddities*, 1947). She would lie rigid over a roaring fire for long periods of time, supported at head and feet by stools and wrapped in a sheet. She would thrust her shod and stockinged feet into a brazier of coals and withdraw them only when the hosiery was completely burnt away. Just why the shoes and stockings should burn when the sheet did not remains a mystery, but we do know that something similar happens in a fire-walk. Max Freedom Long, in *The Secret Science Behind Miracles* (1948) quotes the account by Dr John G. Hill of a walk over red-hot stones on a Tahitian island, in which a white man took part. The pit was so hot that his face peeled, yet the glowing rocks made no impression on his leather boots.

Leroy's *Les Hommes salamandres* is also the source for what is probably the classic fire-walk, which took place near Madras in 1921 in the presence of the Catholic Bishop of Mysore (who sent the account to Leroy) and the local Maharajah. The proceedings were conducted by a Muslim, who never went into the fire himself, but conferred immunity on those who did. Many went through voluntarily; others were literally pushed into the fire by the Muslim, and the bishop tells how their looks of terror gave way to astonished smiles as they completed the walk. The Maharajah's brass band (all Christians) were induced to march through the flames, and they were so thrilled at their success that they went through a second time, trumpets blowing, cymbals clashing, etc – a performance we would have gone far to attend. According to the bishop, the flames rose up, licking their instruments and faces, yet their boots, uniforms and even sheet-music were all unscathed.

Wings of Fire is a US organization which uses fire-walking as a transformational tool for personal growth. Here instructor Ariel Frager undergoes a fire-walk near Sonora in California. The temperature of the red-hot embers can be anything between 900 and 1200 degrees Fahrenheit.

Max Freedom Long gives a detailed account of how his mentor, Dr W.T. Brigham of the British Museum, was taken onto fresh boiling lava near a volcano on Kona island by three Kahunas – local magicians. They instructed him to take his boots off as they would not be covered by the Kahuna protection, but he refused. As he watched one of the three walk calmly onto the lava flow, the other two suddenly pushed him and finding himself on the hot lava, he had no choice but to keep on running to the other side. In the course of the 150-foot dash, his boots and socks were burned off. The three Kahunas, still strolling barefoot on the lava, burst into laughter as they pointed out the trail of bits of burning leather.

What does go on in a fire-walk? Dr White expresses the widely held view that the walkers are in an exalted state of mind which suppresses pain. Yet there are fire-walks without trance or ecstasy. Neither is there any evidence to suggest that damaged tissues heal up so rapidly that they are not noticed (a process sometimes observed among Dervish, Hindu, Balinese and other body-piercing devotees). In *The Crack in the Cosmic Egg* (1973) by J.C. Pearce, the author suggests that the firewalk is a classic illustration of the creation of a new reality (albeit temporary and local) in which fire does not burn in the familiar way. As long as this reality is maintained all is well, but the history of the fire-walk contains many accounts of gruesome fatalities and shocking damage to those whose faith snapped so that they were plunged back into the world where fire burns. The magical state of affairs in which flesh, and sometimes other material, is immune to fire is created, it seems, by the person who officiates at fire-walking ceremonies. Leroy's Muslim writhed on the ground in agony as soon as the Maharajah announced the end of the proceedings. It was explained to the bishop that the man had taken the burning upon himself. In *Women Called Wild*, Mrs Rosita Forbes describes a fire-dance ceremony in Surinam, presided over by a virgin priestess, among descendants of African slaves who had intermarried with the local Indians. The priestess was in a trance for the duration of the fire-dance, and if she had emerged from it unexpectedly, the dancers would no longer have been immune from the flames. We have to agree with Dr Corney that psychical and psychological theories alone do not account for what happens, and that some physical phenomenon takes place which has not been understood or explained.

Pearce's theory of fire-immunity as a product of a state of temporary reality invoked by a magician explains why the fire-walk has so shocked and offended those who depend on using the reality they have grown accustomed to as a bulwark against the apparition which Freud called "the black tide of occult mud". In recent years, however, fire-walking has been used in the West as a motivational tool in the more extreme types of leadership training as well as in courses for personal growth and development. The successful fire-walker achieves a "natural high" through the conquest of his or her rational fear, a triumph of "mind over matter" that sets them apart as a kind of shaman and enables them to believe that they are capable of achieving anything.

Fire-proof people and fire starters

From *Time* magazine (7 April 1947) comes this brief story: "In Woodstock, Vermont, a fire broke out in the basement of the Walker home on Sunday; the staircase caught fire on Monday; an upstairs partition blazed on Tuesday; the jittery Walkers moved out on Wednesday; the house burned down on Thursday." We know a few briefer ones. Twenty-eight fires of unknown origin in one day forced the Hackler family to flee their Oclon, Indiana, farm (*Collier's*, April 1941); and about forty fires in a few hours drove the Hoyt family from their home in Woodstock (another Woodstock), New Brunswick.

What interests us here is the notion that some people are fireprone, or somehow act as catalysts for a process that causes outbreaks of fire in their vicinity. Charles Fort called such a person a fire genius: "By genius I mean one who can't avoid knowledge of fire, because he can't avoid setting things afire." These genii, he thought, might have been very useful in the days before men knew how to make fire artificially. In this section we examine some of the evidence which suggests that human beings possess both a capacity to project

Bradley Shell, one of the 'Saints' of the Pentecostal Holiness Church of Kentucky who demonstrate their faith by drinking strychnine, handling snakes and placing their limbs in fire, holds a flaming torch to his feet.

fiery heat and also something called – for lack of any better description – fire-immunity, one aspect of which we illustrate in connection with the firewalk.

As an example of fire-immunity the case of Nathan Coker, a blacksmith of Easton, Maryland, is of great interest because, unlike some other famous fire-handlers, he needed no trance or preparation to demonstrate his powers. Three authorities, Vincent Gaddis, Fodor and Father Herbert Thurston, accepted the validity of the account, in the *New York Herald* (7 September 1871) of Coker being tested before many prominent local officials. A shovel was heated to a white glow, and when all was ready, Coker "pulled off his boots and placed the hot shovel on the soles of his feet, and kept it there until the shovel became black". Coker also swilled molten leadshot around in his mouth until it solidified; held glowing coals in his hands; and took a red-hot iron out of the fire with his hands. He told them: "It don't burn. Since I was a little boy, I've

never been afraid to handle fire." This talent may be more common than we think. In *Mysterious Fires and Lights* (1967) Gaddis mentions the report of a New York physician, Dr K.R. Wissen, who met a shy backwoods boy while on a hunting trip in the Tennessee mountains in 1927, and found that he could pick up and hold firebrands without injury. The boy told him that he had discovered the ability by accidentally picking up a red-hot horseshoe in his uncle's smithy.

In *The Physical Phenomena of Mysticism* (1952) Father Thurston tells the story of a Canon charged with investigating reports of the immunity to fire of St Francis of Paola, who died in 1507. The Canon witnessed St Francis's performance but made light of it, saying that it was easy for him to bear the heat because he was not of "gentle blood" but a peasant "used to hardship". St Francis replied that that was quite true. "He bent down to the fire, which was a big one and burning fiercely. Filling his hands with the brands and live coals, he held them there while he turned to the Canon and remarked: 'You see, I could not do this if I were not a peasant.'"

Whatever the explanation, the phenomenon of fire-immunity is ancient and universal. Mircea Eliade in *Shamanism* (1972) says that it is a common practice for the smiths of the Dogon tribe to handle red-hot metal "to re-enact the practices of the first smiths". Nor do we doubt that there are some genuine performances among professional entertainers, such as that recorded by Max Freedom Long in *The Secret Science Behind Miracles* (1948). Long was so astonished by the fiery conjurings of a magician that he obtained a private performance and brought along with him a dentist to examine the man's mouth, for as part of his fire-handling repertoire, the magician would play the hottest flame of a welding torch over the inside of his mouth, keeping his jaws wide open to allow close inspection. He also heated an iron bar to red heat and, gripping the glowing part with his hands and teeth, bent the bar up and down.

We think that the historical evidence demands reconsideration, not only the many tales of the fire exploits of holy men, but also the sort of incident recorded by John Evelyn in his *Diary* on 8 October 1672. Evelyn, who had a scholarly interest in the curious, had been invited to dine with Lady Sunderland, who afterwards sent for the entertainer Richardson, well known throughout Europe. According to Evelyn, Richardson "devoured brimstone on glowing coales before us, chewing

Josephine Giraldelli, billed around 1819 as 'The Original Salamander', holds her arm in flames while standing on a red-hot shovel.

and swallowing them, he melted a beareglasse and eate it quite up; then taking a live coale on his tongue, he put upon it a raw oyster, the coale was blown on with bellows till it flamed and sparkled in his mouth, and so remained until the oyster gaped and was quite boiled; then he melted pitch and wax with sulphur, which he drank down as it flamed; I saw it flaming in his mouth a good while; he also took up a thick piece of yron, such as laundresses use in their smoothing boxes, when it was fiery hot, held it between his teeth, then in his hand . . . with divers other prodigious feates."

Further testimony to Richardson's abilities is quoted in Olivier Leroy's *Les Hommes salamandres* (1931) from the *Journal des savants* of 1677. During a test he held "a red-hot iron in his hands for a long time without any mark being left upon it afterwards".

In the nineteenth century Daniel Dunglas Home performed similar feats on demand and in clear light under scientific scrutiny. Sir William Crookes wrote in the *Quarterly Journal of Science* (1 July 1871) of seeing about thirteen different types of phenomena, including some astonishing displays of fire-handling, which proved to him the existence of an unknown "Psychic Force". When his full "Notes on Seances with D. D. Home" finally appeared in the *Proceedings of the Society for Psychical Research* in 1889, he had "nothing to retract or alter", despite eighteen years of merciless ridicule from his colleagues. Lord Adare in his *Experiences with D.D. Home* (1924) bears witness to many of these events and says that Home would allow other people to hold coals without injury, after making "passes" over their hands.

At the opposite pole to people who are immune to fire are those who, willingly or not,

attract it or project it. In reviewing some of these cases we are reminded of the old belief that combustion depends on the presence of latent "seeds of fire", and that there is a magic by which they can be made to blossom. There is the celebrated case of A.W. Underwood, of Paw Paw, Michigan, about whom Dr L.C. Woodman wrote in the *New York Sun* (1 December 1882): "He will take anybody's handkerchief, hold it to his mouth, rub it vigorously, while breathing on it, and immediately it bursts into flames and burns until consumed." Underwood would strip, rinse his mouth out and set any cloth or paper alight by his breath. It was most useful, he said, when he was out hunting; he could have his camp fire going in seconds.

If that sounds far-fetched, consider the fate of a young West Indian woman, Lily White, of Liberta, Antigua, whose clothes would suddenly burst into flames. Fire attacked her garments when she was at home and also in the streets, leaving her naked. The *New York Times* (25 August 1929) reported that she had become dependent on neighbours for things to wear, and that even as she slept her sheets burnt up and yet she herself was never harmed by the fires that consumed all around her. Consider also the strange story in the *Daily Mail* (13 December 1921) of the boy who, with his mother, was driven from their home in Budapest by "alarmed" neighbours who claimed that some of them had seen flames flicker over him as he slept, singeing his pillow. It was said that since the boy's thirteenth birthday

In *Man, Myth and Magic* (1970) Kenneth Grant tells how a disciple of Anandamayi Ma asked her to show her power and burn him to ashes. As she joined him under a sunshade he felt a fierce heat beat down upon his head. It grew so intense that he begged her to stop. Grant says that the sunshade was quite burnt in parts.

R. LANNOY

furniture had moved and fires had repeatedly broken out in his presence.

The Soviet parapsychologist Dr Genady Sergeyev referred in an interview in the *Sunday People* (14 March 1976) to the powerful telekinetic medium Nina Kulagina: "She can draw energy somehow from all around her, electrical instruments can prove it. On several occasions, the force rushing into her body left four-inch-long burnmarks on her arms and hands . . . I was with her once when her clothing caught fire from this energy flow, it literally flamed up. I helped put out the flames and saved some of the burned clothing as an exhibit." (For more on Mrs Kulagina and others manifesting strange paraelectrical forces, see ELECTRIC PEOPLE, p.69.)

There is also evidence to suggest that the tendency to attract or be immune to fire can be brought under human control. Max Freedom Long's exotic magician (see p.63) said that, although he was of white parentage, he was orphaned in India and adopted by local fire-walkers, who trained him from an early age. He was taught to meditate on a burning lamp, to "sense the God behind the flame" and thus enjoy his protection. The power to confer fire-immunity is attributed to many gods. The Hindu invokes the protection of Agni, the Kahuna calls on Pele, and the Greek villagers dance on fires clutching icons of St Constantine and St Helen. All their different invocations are effective, but so also were those of Home and Richardson who asked no favours of any god.

Human glow-worms

Our subject here is light emanating from human bodies. As with many of our phenomena, examples can be given from antiquity to the present day. The data comes mostly from three types of source; from medicine, religion and folklore. The effect, however, is the same throughout – people are lit up.

In May 1934, the "Luminous Woman of Pirano" was a sensation that spilled out from the squabbles of the Italian medical press into newspapers across the world. Signora Anna Monaro was an asthma patient, and over a period of several weeks she would emit a blue glow from her breasts as she slept. Many doctors came to witness the phenomenon, which was visible for several seconds at a time. One psychiatrist said it was caused by "electrical and magnetic organisms in the woman's body developed in eminent degree", which is one way of saying you don't know. Another doctor suggested "electromagnetic radiation from certain compounds in her skin". This was a reference to theories, then current, of bioluminescence, as found, for example, in E.N. Harvey's *The Nature of Animal Light* (1920). Dr Protti, who made a long statement on his observations of Signora Monaro, postulated that her weak condition, together with her fasting and religious zeal, increased the amount of sulphides in her blood, and that since the normal radiant power of human blood is in the ultraviolet range, and that sulphides can be stimulated into luminescence by ultraviolet radiation, here was a reasonable explanation (see the *Times*, 5 May 1934).

Clearly this did not explain the strange periodicity or localization of the blue flashes, and the embarrassed investigators fell silent. Harvey himself talks of luminous bacteria that feed on nutrients in sweat, but by Protti's own testimony Anna Monaro would break into a heavy sweat only *after* the light emissions, during which her heart rate doubled. Numerous toxicology textbooks discuss "luminous wounds", some in terms of bacteria, and others in terms of the modern view that the secretions contain the biochemicals, luciferin and luciferase, and a substance called ATP (adenosine triphosphate), which are normally kept apart, but when brought together give off a faint luminescence. The identical process lights up the glowworm and firefly. Yet, if this theory were applicable the Signora would have glowed all over.

In *Death: Its Causes and Phenomena* (1911) Hereward Carrington tells of a child who died of acute indigestion. As neighbours prepared the shroud they noticed the body surrounded by a blue glow and radiating heat. The body appeared to be on fire; efforts to extinguish the luminescence failed, but eventually it faded away. Medical records of the human glow-worm effect are almost always in reference to pathological cases. For instance, Gould and Pyle in their monumental *Anomalies and Curiosities of Medicine* (1937) tell of a woman with cancer of the breast: the light from the sore could illuminate the hands of a watch several feet away.

The only occurrence of light emission from an otherwise healthy person that we have on file (apart from saints) is in a letter to the *English Mechanic* (24 September 1869): "An American lady, on going to bed, found that a light was issuing from the upper side of the fourth toe on her right foot. Rubbing increased the phosphorescent glow and it spread up her foot. Fumes were also given off, making the room disagreeable; and both light and fumes continued when the foot was held in a basin of water. Even washing with soap could not dim the toe. It lasted for three quarters of an hour before fading away, and was witnessed by her husband."

Sometimes human radiance seems to be connected with inexplicable electro-magnetic phenomena, and in ELECTRIC PEOPLE (see, p.69) we give several accounts of luminous infants. But no amount of disease-based cases can match the show of luminosity put on by the mystics. The halo or shining aura is everywhere the attribute of the spiritual man; and we can only suppose that this universal symbol is derived from a universal phenomenon of common experience. Holy men glow, sometimes blazingly. Even in everyday speech we refer to faces "shining" or "beaming" with happiness. That this is not always simply a

In the art of most cultures holiness or sacred power has been represented by bodily light known as an aura or halo. In this manuscript illustration from *The Apostle's Biography* (c.1368), the Prophet Mohammed is shown wrapped in a golden flame during his vision of the angel Gabriel.

figure of speech is warily accepted by the Church. Prosper Lambertini (1675–1758) – later Pope Benedict XIV – was responsible for formulating the process of beatification. In *De beatificatione* he wrote: "It seems to be a fact that there are natural flames which at times visibly encircle the human head, and that also from a man's whole person fire may on occasion radiate naturally, not however like a flame which streams upwards, but rather in the form of sparks which are given off all around."

As one of many examples we can quote the biography of St Lidwina by Thomas à Kempis (1379–1471). "And although she always lay in darkness, and material light was unbearable to her eyes, nevertheless the divine light was very agreeable to her, whereby her cell was often so wondrously flooded by night that to the beholders the cell itself appeared full of material lamps or fires. Nor is it strange if she overflowed even in the body with divine brightness."

Father Herbert Thurston admitted: "There are so many stories of holy priests who lit up a dark cell or whole chapel by the light which streamed from them or upon them, that I am strongly inclined to adhere to the more literal interpretation . . . It is unquestionably true that there are hundreds of such

St Francis of Paola (d.1507) is one of many saints whose bodily radiance has been well-documented. He is also credited with possessing the power of fire-immunity.

examples to be found in our hagiographical records, and although a great number of these rest upon quite insufficient testimony, there are others which cannot lightly be set aside. . . There can, therefore, be no adequate reason for refusing credence to the report of similar phenomena when they are recorded of those whose eminent holiness and marvellous gifts of grace are universally recognized."(*Physical Phenomena of Mysticism*, 1952.)

Perhaps the most interesting thing in Father Thurston's statement is the reference to light streaming "from them or upon them". Both kinds of light are clearly implied in the passage about St Lidwina. Thurston goes on to relate the following story about the Spanish theologian, Father Francis Suarez, at the Jesuit College at Coimbra in Portugal. An elderly lay-brother, Jerome da Silva, came to tell the Father of the arrival of a distinguished visitor. The outer room of his quarters was in darkness, shuttered against the afternoon heat.

Suarez's biographer Father R. de Scorraille records da Silva's account of the incident:

"I called the Father but he made no answer. As the curtain which shut off his working room was drawn, I saw, through the space between the jambs of the door and the curtain, a very great brightness. I pushed aside the curtain and entered the inner apartment. Then I noticed that the blinding light was coming from the crucifix, so intense that it was like the reflexion of the sun from glass windows, and I felt that I could not have remained looking at it without being completely dazzled. This light streamed from the crucifix upon the face and breast of Father Suarez, and in this brightness I saw him in a kneeling position in front of the crucifix, his head uncovered, his hands joined, and his body in the air five palms [about three feet] above the floor on a level with the table on which the crucifix stood. On seeing this I withdrew . . . as it were beside myself . . . my hair standing on end like the bristles on a brush, and I waited, hardly knowing what I did."

About a quarter of an hour later, the Father came out, surprised to see the Brother waiting. "When the Father heard that I had entered the inner room, he seized me by the arm . . . then, clasping his hands and with eyes full of tears, he implored me to say nothing of what I had seen, at any rate, as long as he lived." They shared the same confessor, who suggested da Silva write his account and seal it with the endorsement that it should not be opened and read until after the death of Father Suarez. All three parties were well-known for their piety – they had nothing to gain by deception – and the account has a ring of honesty.

In the same manner, St Francis of Assisi was lifted (see LEVITATION AND SPONTANEOUS FLIGHT, p.81) and illuminated, and the radiance of Saints Philip Neri, Catherine de Ricci, Francis of Paola, Alphonsus Liguori, and many others who were holy but never beatified, shines out of their biographies. Some legends might not, then, be as mythical as it is comfortable to suppose. When

Modern photographic techniques have revived interest in the aura: a finger-tip seen with the Kirlian high-voltage method.

D. A. KENTZ

Moses came down from Sinai (Exodus ch.34, vv.29–35) it is written that "the skin of his face shone" so brightly that all who beheld it were afraid to go near him. For some time after, in the presence of others, he had to wear a veil.

The idea of the aura as a physical manifestation of the energy field which surrounds each living thing gained wider currency with the advent of Theosophy at the end of the nineteenth century. Though the Theosophists believed that human auras were only visible to clairvoyants, this did not prevent several enterprising photographers from attempting to capture the phenomena on film (see Thelma Moss *The Probability of the Impossible*, 1974). The most successful of these attempts was made by the Russian Semyon Kirlian and his wife who, in 1939, experimented with film exposed to the electrical discharges from selected objects (including humans) placed on a special apparatus. Kirlian photographs of human auras, with their rich and varied colours, have subsequently been used as a diagnostic tool – mainly by alternative therapists – although critics remain unconvinced that they show anything other than colourful discharges of static electricity.

Electric people

One of the earliest scientifically investigated cases of an "electric person" was that of Angélique Cottin of La Perrière, France, whose strange condition began on 15 January 1846 (when she was fourteen) and lasted ten weeks. Whenever she went near objects they retreated from her. The slightest touch of her hand or dress was enough to send heavy furniture spinning away or jumping up and down; and no one could hold an object she also was holding without it writhing from their grasp. A study group was appointed by the Academy of Sciences, and a famous physicist, François Arago, published a report in the *Journal des débats* (February 1846). He noted that her power seemed to be like electro-magnetism – compasses went wild in her proximity – that it was stronger in the evening, and seemed to emanate from her left side, particularly her left wrist and elbow. Poor Angélique would often convulse while the phenomenon was active, her heartbeat rising to 120 a minute, and she was so frightened by it that she repeatedly fled from the scene.

Angélique Cottin causing furniture to move.

We have no way of knowing just how many historical poltergeist cases were in fact instances of the high-voltage syndrome. Dr E.J. Dingwall presents a collection of accounts of compass deflection and movements in furniture, etc. in his four-volume history of *Abnormal Hypnotic Phenomena* (1967), the earliest case referred to occurring in 1786.

Cases are reported throughout the nineteenth century. Seventeen-year-old Caroline Clare of London, Ontario, became ill in 1877. Her weight dropped to ninety pounds and she would suffer dramatic fits, describing faraway places she had never seen. When she recovered about a year and a half later, her life was made a misery by strong discharges of electricity. Objects in contact with her became magnetized. Cutlery would stick to her skin and had to be pulled off by another person. She was the subject of an investigation and report by the Ontario Medical Association in the summer of 1879. In the 1890s, another teenager, Jennie Morgan of Sedalia, Missouri, became similarly highly charged; sparks would fly from her to nearby objects, animals would avoid her, and those people forgetful enough to shake her hand or touch her were often knocked unconscious.

Frank McKinstry of Joplin, Missouri, was the subject of study in 1889. When he felt charged he had to keep moving, because if he stopped his feet became glued to the spot and he had to ask passers-by to lift his feet and release the charge. Similarly, sixteen-year-old Louis Hamburger was studied by the Maryland College of Pharmacy in 1890. He too was a "human magnet" and could make metal objects dangle from his skin. With the tips of three fingers he could lift a glass jar full of iron-filings weighing about five pounds. These cases and those of a few other electric people have been briefly chronicled by Frank Edwards, Vincent Gaddis and

A row of matchsticks is moved by Nina Kulagina, apparently without touching them. From a Russian film made in 1967.

others. Drs Gould and Pyle in their monumental *Anomalies and Curiosities of Medicine* (1896) also deal with electric humans.

In 1938 the Universal Council for Psychic Research met in New York to offer a prize of $10,000 for demonstrations of psychic phenomena not reproducible by trickery. An elderly lady, Mrs Antoine Timmer, showed how cutlery stuck to her hands as if her skin were magnetized – but her case was dismissed because the chairman, the illusionist Joseph Dunninger, said he could do the same himself with a concealed thread. Thus another opportunity for research was lost for ever.

Perhaps the most famous case from that astonishing period was that of Lulu Hurst, who, between 1883 and 1885, made a stage career as "The Georgia Wonder" before quitting to marry her manager. The phenomena began, as in a classical "poltergeist" case, shortly after she was fourteen. China would smash in her presence, and at night there would be knocking sounds and frighteningly heavy thumps in the bedroom she shared with a younger sister. Soon it was discovered that questions spoken in the room were answered by raps for "yes" and "no". The day after the noises started, Lulu handed a relative a chair. As the chair twisted in Lulu's grasp four men tried to hold it, but the forces were too great, the chair broke into pieces and they were flung violently backwards. Lulu, like Angélique, ran screaming from the house.

Within two weeks her parents had persuaded Lulu to turn her affliction into an act. In it she presented variations on the theme of a little girl thwarting several grown men. She would hold one end of a billiard cue while two men struggled and failed to force the other end to the ground. She could also lift three men sitting on each other's laps on the same chair, merely resting her open palms on its back. She would then lightly touch the chair while five men tried in vain to budge it from the spot. Frank Edwards in *Strange People* (1961) quotes from many contemporary accounts. Investigators, who were allowed to get as close as they wished, consistently found no evidence of strain or trickery in the girl. Fort mentions two other "immovables" from that period: Mrs Annie Abbott demonstrated her powers in London, November 1891, and Mrs Mary Richardson in Liverpool, September 1921. Holms investigated both cases for his *Facts of Psychic Science* and concluded that the ladies did not resist pressure, but that in some inexplicable way pressure against them did not reach or touch them.

Forces without reaction seem to crop up in most "poltergeist" cases, yet we urge caution in explaining away these effects as products of unusual bio-electrical fields. In many cases of poltergeist activity there is no known human agency. Every attempt to establish a constant factor in our phenomena can be countered by contrary cases, as though the phenomena delighted in teasing us. It is astonishing that little serious research, if any, has been done on the pathological causes of para-electrical effects. Scientists seem to have been scared

BELFAST TELEGRAPH

Some people are so highly charged with static that they can light up some kinds of bulbs merely by holding them. For example, 12-year-old Vyvyan Jones of Henbury, Bristol, became unaccountably electric after breaking his arm in February 1976. For two days his hair was permanently on end and he shocked people with powerful discharges whenever touched: TV and lights flickered in his presence and watches stopped. A doctor treating him at Southmead Hospital, Bristol, said it was not unusual and that he had seen people with magnetic fields strong enough to lift iron bars.

off by the "occult" or "poltergeist" element in the phenomenon. The only analogies for the appearance and discharge of such high voltages are in the bio-electric processes of animals like eels. Each cell in our body can generate a small charge. Dr Mayne R. Coe (*Fate*, July 1959) believed that a cubic inch of human muscle cells could (in theory) generate 400,000 volts of very low amperage, but it would need a high amperage to cause the effects that we have mentioned, and they are still unexplained.

The phenomenon of electric peoples is not only associated with adolescents; Gould and Pyle mention a six-year-old Zulu boy who gave off intense shocks and was exhibited in Edinburgh in 1882. Fodor, in his *Encyclopaedia of Psychic Science* tells of a baby born at Saint-Urbain, France, in 1869, who badly shocked all who touched him. Luminous rays would shoot from his fingers, and when he died, just nine months old, a radiance was observed around his body for several minutes. Douglas Hunt, writing in *Prediction*, (January 1953) gives two other cases of high-voltage infants: one was able to charge up a Leyden jar, and the other caused "vibrations" in objects held near him, and was also seen to be surrounded by a soft, white radiance.

Another curious piece of the jigsaw appeared in the *Electrical Experimenter* (June 1920) in which Dr J.B. Ransom, chief physician at Clinton Prison, New York, reported on thirty-four convicts suffering from botulinus poisoning. One had tried to throw away a piece of paper and found it stuck to his hand. Soon all the afflicted were in the same highly-charged condition, varying in intensity with the severity of the poisoning. Compasses went wild in their vicinity and metal objects were deflected from their grasp; but the effects faded as they recovered.

The history of the poltergeist shows many electro-magnetic interferences, from dimming lights to gadgets running without power, as seen in a famous case at Rosenheim, Bavaria, in 1967. Translations of the investigation by Professor H. Bender, Dr Andreas Resch and others can be found in *The Journal of Paraphysics* (vols. 3 and 4). Interferences with telephones, electric power and lights were centred on a girl, Annemarie Schneider, and the phenomena stimulated by her presence included many of the "normal" mechanical tricks of the poltergeist repertoire, like bulbs unscrewing themselves from sockets, drawers opening, pictures rotating on the wall, etc. From this case alone, with its mass of documentary and even filmed evidence, it is clear that the "electric people" phenomenon exists, whatever the explanation.

Projected thought-forms

The idea of a reciprocal relationship between the subjective world of thoughts and the "real" world of objective events and objects is as old as philosophy itself. It can be seen operating in all forms of magic and ritual, and is the basis of many artistic and literary metaphors. Throughout the history of ideas recurs the belief that events and objects may be as ephemeral as thoughts, while thoughts can occasionally become concrete and objective realities.

With the rise of modern science such a notion became heresy, yet it has always persisted, and the latest findings from both para–physics and sub-atomic physics have given it some degree of respectability. Previously forbidden but now generally recognized are such concepts as the transmutation of matter and the relativity of the so-called "laws" of space, time, matter and energy. We are told that an electron can travel between two points in space without physically traversing the distance between them, just as objects in our own mundane world have been observed to disappear and reappear elsewhere. When solid objects spontaneously change their structure, colour or motion, these effects might be logical consequences of the inexplicable randomness that Heisenberg showed to exist in the motions of the sub-atomic particles. In the world of particle physics, anything conceivable can happen, and our evidence suggests that the same is true in the world of physical objects.

In the 1960s, Dr Jule Eisenbud studied the claims of Ted Serios to project mental images onto sealed film. Eisenbud found no evidence of trickery during his long investigation. The clearer picture of Westminster Abbey is the 'target' image, while the blurred image is Serios's projection.

The discovery of telekinetic forces was the main motivation behind the experiments of Dr J.B. Rhine at Duke University, who began research into what is now called psychokinesis in the 1930s. Psychokinesis, or PK, is the enigmatic process more popularly described as "mind over matter", and in 1945, Dr Rhine announced that he had conclusive evidence of PK effects in influencing the way in which dice fall. Rhine divides the subject into PK influences on "moving targets", like the dice; "living targets" which might imply anything from levitation and spontaneous flight to influencing the growth of plants; and "static targets" which include the "thoughtography" associated with Ted Serios.

The projection of an image onto sealed film, apparently by PK or some other mysterious means, gives results that are more accessible to analysis. It is interesting to note that with Serios and the small number of others who can repeat this effect, their "hits" are far outnumbered by "wild" images or complete disruption of normal optical processes, "overexposing" the film. The ability to affect, consciously or unconsciously, unexposed film may be more widespread than most people realize, judging from the number of accounts we can find of "wild images" turning up on photographs taken by ordinary people.

We are particularly interested in cases where a desired effect has been achieved purely through the exercise of imagination. In 1935, Mrs Gertrude Smith of York, Pennsylvania, discovered she could mentally coax her hens to lay eggs bearing images. The *York Gazette and Daily* (4 April 1940) quoted her as saying: "I would stand near the hen yard and visualize sunflower petals along with my initials. In a few days my father came into the house all excited and said: "Here is the sunflower egg". The pattern of a sunflower was incised into the shell on the flattened part." Soon Mrs Smith obtained more patterned eggs, one of them marked with the reversed letters of her initials: "When I broke one open, the design appeared raised on the inner surface of the shell." A later edition of the *Gazette and Daily* testified to the genuineness of the patterned eggs and referred to a sworn deposition by other witnesses. Mrs Smith said she tried visualizing an egg with a triangular cross-section, and when one arrived she became so frightened by her power that she never tried again.

In several of our sections we tell of objects or images that appeared in response to conscious or unconscious demand, and observe their synchronous nature (see COINCIDENCES, p.201). Catherine Crowe gives an example in *The Night Side of Nature* (1854) of a girl who dreamt she was offered two roses, one red and one white, and chose the red one. She woke with a pain in her arm, on which by degrees "there arose the perfect figure of a rose, perfect in form and colour. It was

Eusapia Palladino, at the height of her powers in the 1890s, could impress her features into putty in sealed containers, supposedly by an effort of will.

rather raised above the skin". It took a fortnight to fade away. The case of Mrs L. Forbes, of Thornton Heath, near London, was often quoted by Dr Nandor Fodor to support his opinion that poltergeists are genuine psychological phenomena, or as he put it, "bundles of projected repressions" (*On the Trail of the Poltergeist*, 1958). One night in 1938 Mrs Forbes dreamt of being pulled in two directions by her dead father and her husband. Her father then drew a cross on her left breast with a finger. In the morning Mrs Forbes discovered on that spot an inflamed mark. An examination by a doctor disclosed a previously unsuspected cancer in that position, necessitating an operation.

There are many other examples of "skin writing" in response to unspoken thoughts as well as to hypnotic suggestion. In his study *Stigmata* (1998), Ted Harrison says the phenomenon has been widely discussed in medical literature. He refers to the cases of Domenica Lo Bianco (see STIGMATA, p.76) and an unnamed man brought to a London teaching hospital in the 1950s. He

was in a terrible state, reliving a traumatic episode in his past in which he had been tied up with ropes. Under the gaze of doctors the unmistakeable marks of tightly bound rope would appear on his arms.

To this we would add the remarkable story of the Romanian peasant girl Eleonore Zugun. In 1923, when she was about eleven, she became the focus of poltergeist activity. Small objects around her would move, seemingly on their own account, and bite-like marks would appear on the skin of her face and arms; many impeccable accounts of these well-observed phenomena exist in the literature. Harry Price, who brought Eleonore to England for study in 1926, witnessed "time and time again" marks appearing on her arms as indentations which puffed up into weals which lasted "a few minutes and rapidly disappeared". When asked, the girl said the Devil ("Dracu") was attacking her. Price never found any sign that the girl might be biting or scratching herself.

An independent report on Eleonore was commissioned by Price from a Captain Seton-Karr,

FRGS., which gives the following account of how it all began. "When the so-called poltergeist phenomena became first apparent, the simple peasants so threatened her with Dracu and what he would do to her that her subconscious mind became obsessed with the idea of whippings, bitings, etc, which the ignorant peasants said would be her lot." Seton-Karr concluded, "Remove the Dracu complex and the girl would probably be troubled no further with stigmatic markings." (*Proceedings of the National Laboratory of Psychical Research*, January 1927). In fact Eleonore's phenomena ceased about this time anyway, coincident with her fourteenth birthday and the onset of menstruation.

In the entry on "Dermography" in the second edition of *The Encyclopedia of Occultism and Parapsychology* (1984), editor Leslie Shepard refers to the hyper-sensitivity of the skin in some hysterical patients, such that the slightest brush against it would raise a mark. Even he admits that this theory fails to account for the remarkable pictographic power of a girl in the service of a Lewis Burtis of New England in the 1860s. She seems to have been a living sketchpad with all sorts of images and words appearing on her skin as she went about her daily work. In a well-witnessed account, reported in Emma Hardinge's *Modern American Spiritualism* (1870), red lines on one arm formed "a distinct and beautifully represented picture of a kneeling man, with a woolly head and African cast of features, a chain around his waist terminating in two balls which were ingeniously fitted into the veins . . . above was written in fine character the words 'A poor old slave'." Even more remarkable is that the girl was acknowledged to be "nearly illiterate". It seems likely then that she had, by means unknown, reproduced something she had once seen.

The whimsical, and sometimes sinister character of PK projection is indicated by a series of disturbances that occurred in the house of Dr E.E. Phelps, a Presbyterian minister of Stratford, Connecticut in March 1850. The *New Haven Journal and Courier* (19 April 1850) quotes a witness to the disturbances, Dr Webster. "When the Phelps family returned from church, they found the furniture strewn about the rooms, and curious figures constructed of clothing arranged in one of them, constituting a sort of tableau, depicting a scene of worship. There were eleven figures, arranged in life-like attitudes. All but one were female figures; all were in postures of extreme devotion, some with their foreheads nearly touching the floor; others kneeling about the room with open Bibles

before them, which indicated different passages sanctioning the phenomena then going on. In the centre of the group there was a figure suspended as though flying through the air." Other figures were later found. The clothing they were made from came from all parts of the house. A close watch was kept, but no one ever saw the images being formed. One figure, made from Mrs Phelps's dress, looked so convincing that her young son was moved to say, "Be still, Ma is saying prayers". A good account of this, drawn from Dr Phelps's own records, can be found in E.W. Capron's *Modern Spiritualism: its Facts and Fanaticisms* (1855). Weird though this episode is, it is not unique. In *Poltergeists Over England* (1945) Harry Price quotes from a pamphlet of 1695 a story of similar clothing-figures during a haunting at Ringcroft, Galloway.

The many reports of "mind over matter" in both mythology and daily experience, suggest that the only limit may be human imagination itself. Dr W.Y. Evans-Wentz and the remarkable Alexandra David-Néel, both highly credible scholars and explorers of Tibet, spoke of the power of the *dubthab* rite by which Tibetan adepts materialize a human apparition called a *tulpa*. This power is claimed by many kinds of occultists and magicians. David-Néel attempted to manifest a *tulpa* of her own, using the prescribed meditation and visualizing exercises. How she succeeded is told in chapter eight of her *Magic and Mystery in Tibet* (1931). This was no subjective fancy, for the little monk-like figure she dreamt up was seen on many occasions by others. She tells how the *tulpa* slipped away from her control, acting independently and becoming more and more tiresome. Reflecting her fears, the *tulpa*'s placid features turned sly, mocking and malignant. In the end, she had to dematerialize it by an exhausting reversal of the whole process.

As with many of the phenomena in this book, the spontaneous occurrences outshine the feeble performances of exceptional human beings, and both of them pale before the controlled displays of power put on by the great mystics. In his life of Milarepa (*Tibet's Great Yogi*, 1928) Evans-Wentz says that the sage, while dying at the Red Rock, projected numerous *tulpas* of himself. Similar tales are told of Jesus after his Resurrection, of Pythagoras and of many saintly people, such as Padré Pio – that they were seen in several places at the same time. One example, the transatlantic bi-location of Mary of Agreda, is outlined in the section on HUMAN TELEPORTATION (see p.4).

Humans have the collective "wild talent" of seeing what they want or need to see – or rather, interpreting a visual experience in terms of a shared iconography (see SHARED VISIONS, see p.106). Can processes like these, that seem to project perceptible images, account for such phenomena as ghosts, fairies and UFOs? We simply don't know.

We are conditioned to think it rational to divide the world into subjective and objective phenomena. Living experience tells us this is arbitrary, as the basis of perception itself is to bridge both realms. And in such transitional processes, as Fort reminds us, where does one end and the other begin?

Stigmata

Strange marks and rashes can appear on any person's body but, when that person is an intensely religious Catholic and the marks seem to reproduce the nail and spear wounds believed to have been inflicted on Jesus at his Crucifixion, they are called *stigmata* and the person who displays them is generally considered a saint. The earliest recorded stigmatic was St Francis of Assisi, who received his marks during an ecstatic vision in September 1224, two years before his death, although the notion of stigmata seems implicit in St Paul's words: "I bear in my body the marks of the Lord Jesus." (Galatians 6:17).

The arguments about stigmata are voluminous and complex, but there is no doubt that the phenomenon exists. A.R.G. Owen's summary article for the encyclopaedia *Man, Myth and Magic* (1970) suggested there have been at least three hundred cases. Father Herbert Thurston, the soundest authority, isolates about fifty cases as having adequate documentation and presents them in his *Physical Phenomena of Mysticism* (1952). Ted Harrison, former religious affairs correspondent for the BBC, states in *Stigmata* (1998) that in the eight hundred or so years since the death of St Francis of Assisi there are records of around 406 stigmatics: of these 276 were members of established religious orders; 352 were female; and 25 were alive in the last twenty years.

While St Francis's experience created the stereotype for all subsequent manifestations, the wounds in his hands were extreme and largely unrivalled in the annals of hagiography. They were described in the *Tractatus de miraculis* (ascribed to Thomas de Celano, and written not later than

four years after St Francis died) as having the appearance of black nails which protruded considerably, as though a real nail pierced the hand with its point and head projecting on either side. Celano says that they were visible long after death, and he gives a bizarre description of pilgrims filing past the radiant and still pliant body of the saint (see also THE INCORRUPTIBLES, p.86).

Celano then describes an extraordinary detail; the marks were not just "the prints of the nails, but the nails themselves formed out of his flesh and retaining the blackness of iron . . . marvellously wrought by the power of God, indeed implanted in the flesh itself, in such wise that if they were pressed in on either side they straightway, as if they were one piece of sinew, projected on the other". St Bonaventure's *Legenda minor* (pre 1274) gives further details of the projecting points, saying that they were clinched over, and projected so far that the soles of the feet could hardly be placed on the ground. We would be inclined to doubt this phenomenon if we did not also know of Domenica Lazzari's hard, black, nail-like formations – though these did not project as far.

This might involve psychogenic processes similar to the less well-known phenomenon of the "Divine token of espousal", a "wedding ring" around the appropriate finger. The effect here obviously relates to the status of the devout man or woman as a "bride of Christ" and manifests variously as a vivid red line circling the finger, a thick ridge on the skin or a depression completely around as if made by an invisible ring. This is only one of many bizarre phenomena associated with stigmata.

In 1837 the *Annali universali di medicina* (vol. 84) published a study by Dr Dei Cloche of a girl, Domenica Lazzari, who had developed an astonishing degree of hyper-aesthesia after a traumatic shock. All her senses were heightened so that she was in constant pain, dazzled by lights, and deafened by sound. For the rest of her life she took no nourishment at all and remained bedridden till her death in 1848. When, in the year his paper appeared, Dr Cloche revisited Domenica, he discovered that she had developed stigmata.

He saw wounds in her hands, feet and side, and a row of punctures across her forehead. Her hands were tightly clasped all the time, and on their backs he saw, between the middle and fourth fingers, a black, domed lump, perfectly circular, like a blackened nail about an inch across. The palms had deep incisions in the corresponding places, from which blood flowed copiously. Lord Shrewsbury stated in his *Letters* (1842) that he had no doubt that the wounds perforated her hands. Overcoming Domenica's reluctance to reveal the sources of her constant pain, he "distinctly saw the wounds and the blood and serum, quite fresh and flowing down over the wrist". Examining her feet he noticed something equally remarkable. "Instead of taking its normal course, the blood flowed upwards over the toes, as it would do were she suspended on a cross". This curious, gravity-defying effect was corroborated many times. T.W. Allies's *Journey into France and Italy* (1849) records the author's visit to Domenica with two friends. One of them, J.H. Wynne, wrote: "The Doctor has seen her feet a hundred times which are marked like the hands, but the blood runs up towards the toes, as it does up [to the tip of] the nose, as we saw."

E. TWEEDY

The first major stigmatic was St Francis of Assisi, who received the marks of Christ's crucifixion in 1224 during a vision of a seraph. This woodcut depicting the event is by Albrecht Dürer.

Like many other stigmatics, Domenica bled every Friday – the day Christ was believed to have been executed – and in the eleven years during which she bore her stigmata there was never any suggestion of trickery. On the contrary, all who visited her took away impressions of great suffering. Her hypersensitivity continued, and Lord Shrewsbury once saw her face covered in blood that flowed from the punctures in her forehead, as though from an invisible crown of thorns. He wrote that her face was never washed because she could not bear the sensations of water and wiping, and that the blood seemed to disappear "of itself".

The records of many famous stigmatics disagree with the opinion of D.H. Rawcliffe (*Psychology of the Occult*, 1952) that the only "true" stigmata are what he calls "topoalgic hallucinations" (ie. localized pain without visible injury), and that all else is a mixture of imposture, gullibility and delusion or "purposive self-mutilation during hystero-epileptic attacks followed by amnesia". The impeccable accounts of the sufferings of St Teresa of Avila (1515–82), the recently canonized Padre Pio (1887–1968), and other stigmatics show no overt symptoms of hysteria yet plainly illustrate that so-called suggestion neuroses are not incompatible with lives of the deepest sanctity. Furthermore, Father Thurston has shown that, as with Domenica and Palma Matarrelli (1825–88), stigmata are not always the product of excessive

Padre Pio Forgione (1887–1968) is probably the most famous modern stigmatic, having born the marks since he had an intense experience of Christ in September 1918. He is credited with bi-location, levitation and healing miracles and was beatified by Pope John Paul II on 2 May 1999.

that its connotations of violent and uncontrolled emotional outbursts are misleading. In a clinical sense hysterical disorders are not confined to the overtly neurotic, the unbalanced, the weak-minded, or pathological liars. Ted Harrison, who studied six modern stigmatics over a seventeen-year period, found that they had lived "difficult lives", sometimes involving sexual or physical abuse (both as a victim and self-administered), Münchausen's Syndrome and "extremely low self-esteem bordering on self-hatred" (*Fortean Times*, no.96, p.37). It is a neurotic profile that is repeated among many of those who claim they were experimented upon by aliens (see ENCOUNTERS WITH ALIENS, p.137).

Even so, every theory of stigmatization that we know of breaks down when tested against the wide variation of the actual cases. There is strong evidence that some kind of psychogenic process is involved and this has led to experimental attempts to reproduce stigmata by hypnosis. For example, in 1933, Dr Alfred Lechler published *Das Rätsel von Konnersreuth,* in which he ventured to explain the stigmata of Theresa Neumann (1898-1962) with reference to his experiments on a young Austrian girl. Dr Lechler induced all the classic stigmata on her by suggestion during hypnosis, including sweating blood, tears of blood, the "crown of thorns", and an inflamed shoulder caused by her imaginary carrying of the cross. But despite this result and numerous other less dramatic experiments, induced stigmata cannot compare in intensity, persistence and strange detail with the genuine, spontaneous cases.

Stigmatization seems to involve a degree of selection in its imagery that suggests some subjective involvement in the process. The wounds themselves range from small red patches that never bleed to deep and completely penetrating holes. Straight cuts, square, oval and oblong shapes have also been recorded. In some cases the "nail-heads" are said to be in the palms; in others they appear on the back of the hand or on a foot. "Lance-wounds" have been found on right sides and left, and also assume different shapes, from deep slashes and holes to the cross-shaped scar that bled at its edges on Padre Pio's left side.

The role of suggestion is clear in some cases, even if the mechanism remains mysterious. St Francis was stigmatized on the feast day called Exaltation of the Holy Cross as he passed into an ecstasy in which he begged God to let him share the burden of Christ's suffering on the Cross. The unique Y-shaped cross on the breast of Catherine

devotion or morbid brooding on the sufferings of Christ. For modern examples, we could point to the ten-year-old Californian Cloretta Robertson and the case of Eleonore Zugun (see PROJECTED THOUGHT-FORMS, p.74).

Father Thurston is cautious of using the term "hysteria" in connection with stigmata suggesting

Nineteen days before before Easter 1972, Cloretta Robertson, of Oakland, California, was the first black, and the first non-Catholic stigmatic. Doctors found that the blood appeared through her skin for a few minutes several times a day. It ceased that Good Friday and never reappeared.

suggested that wounds might be teleported on to both bodies and statues (see IMAGES THAT WEEP AND BLEED, p.251).

Whether such a theory is acceptable, some process analogous to Fort's teleportation is suggested by the effects. Gemma Galgani's stigmata began as red marks; then a fissure would open slowly, visible beneath the skin, until finally the skin tore, revealing the cavity filled with congealed and flowing blood. This happened every Friday, and the hole would be healed by the Sunday. Could a similar process explain the scare in Japan, in 1890, in which inch-long slashes appeared on people's necks in broad daylight (see *The Religio-Philosophical Journal*, 17 May 1890).

Another variation of the stigmata effect has wounds appearing *inside* the body. In 1659 Caterina Savelli was stigmatized during communion by, she told her confessor, five rays that shot from the host. After her death in 1691, two surgeons performed an autopsy before many clergy, and found a deep wound "of old date" on her heart. Similarly, the heart of the Blessed Charles of Sezze (d. 1670), examined by a post-mortem under papal orders, was found to be completely pierced by a wound and bore a facsimile of a crucifix on its surface, and of a nail, four or five inches long, buried within it. These cases are given by Thurston and in Dr Imbert-Gourbeyre's *La Stigmatisation* (1894) which quotes from affidavits signed by the doctors and surgeons involved.

The "purity" of such older cases has been replaced in more recent instances by a kind of cross-pollination with phenomenologically similar categories of mystical experience. Nowhere is this more dramatic than in the case of Giorgio Bongiovanni who was stigmatized during a pilgrimage to Fátima in 1989 with deep cross-shaped wounds on his hands, feet, side and forehead. Prior to this he had, for eleven years, been a protégé of Eugene Siragusa, Italy's most famous UFO contactee. Siragusa claimed contact with space beings lasting nearly twenty years and taught that angels and

Emmerich (1744–1824) resembled the unusual cross in the church at Coesfeld where she meditated as a child. Gemma Galgani (1878–1903) manifested bleeding "scourge-marks" identical to those depicted on a large crucifix before which she often prayed.

Ted Harrison actually filmed this process of imprinting, or something very like it, for a TV documentary. It involved the modern Italian stigmatic, Domenica Lo Bianco, on whose arms would appear, every Good Friday, raised red marks in the shape of a rosary and a cross. As physician and psychotherapist Dr Marco Margnelli hypnotized her, and convinced her that it was the appointed time for her stigmata to appear. Harrison reported: "Under laboratory conditions . . . and over a period of an hour, during which time she was closely monitored and videoed, the religious images on her arm reappeared" (*Fortean Times*, no.96, p.37).

We suggest that this mysterious process is related to other phenomena in this book and may simply be a different manifestation of the same force. One correlation, noticed by Fort, is with records of liquids oozing from invisible sources (see MYSTERIOUS FLOWS AND OOZINGS, p.51); he

A photograph of Theresa Neumann (d.1962) 'weeping blood'. She lost nearly a pint of blood from hands, feet, side and forehead, and eight pounds in weight, every Friday in an re-enactment of Christ's suffering. Her stigmata conformed to the description of St Francis's wounds.

The Italian stigmatic and UFO contactee Giorgio Bongiovanni.

aliens were synonymous. Bongiovanni is often to be found at UFO conventions describing his visions of Jesus and Mary arriving in and descending from UFOs accompanied by "luminous beings" (who, he says, are responsible for some crop circles).

According to George Wingfield, who interviewed him for the *Cerealogist* in 1995, Bongiovanni also claims to be the reincarnation of Francisco Marta, one of the original child visionaries of Fátima (see SHARED VISIONS, p.108). But perhaps of greater relevance to this chapter is the independent testimony of doctors who have examined his stigmatic wounds. Wingfield records their astonishment at the rapidity with which the fresh blood coagulates (ten seconds), the absence of infection (to be expected in any large wound open for some time), and Bongiovanni's lack of anaemia (to be expected in anyone who bleeds as regularly and as copiously as he does).

Levitation and spontaneous flight

No modern historian of witchcraft has taken seriously the claims of witches that they could levitate and fly, yet there is impressive evidence that passages through the air (transvection) are not purely flights of fancy. We draw our data from several different categories, for the subject is bedevilled by exclusionism. Christians cherish their own levitating saints but with no regard for flying mystics of other persuasions. Collectors of folklore delight in stories of people who have ridden off with fairies, but show no enthusiasm for levitations by modern spirit mediums. Orthodox science has no interest in any of them.

There is no doubt in our minds that the phenomenon of human flight does, on occasion, take place. In most modern instances it is involuntary and hardly ever premeditated. Clearly, there is some natural force, unknown to our present science, by which people can achieve levitation. The further we move away in time and culture from the rationalistic world-view of modern times,

the more evidence we find that this force has been recognized, studied and made use of.

Father Herbert Thurston's two chapters on levitation, in his *Physical Phenomena of Mysticism* (1952), are the most impressive we have read, containing detailed and often startling evidence, much of it given under solemn oath and the threat of eternal damnation. For example, Thurston quotes from the process of canonization of St Bernardino Realino, who died in 1616. Questioned by senior clerics, a minor noble told how he saw "a certain glow or radiance" streaming around the slightly ajar door of the saint's room in 1608. Concerned that there might be a fire in the room he peeped in and saw the saint in a kneeling posture, face turned upwards, hovering two and a half feet in the air. His feelings of awe and fear gave way to a sense that he was intruding on something intensely private and so he crept away. The ecclesiastical court admonished the man several times during his testimony to think whether or not the scene was an hallucination and the glow a reflection of sunlight; but the man stood firm, saying: "The thing was so clear, unmistakable and real, that not only do I seem to see it still but I am as certain of it as I am speaking now." He said he had noticed

The levitations of medium Colin Evans took place at packed London seances in the 1930s. He preferred to perform in darkness with luminous bands on his arms and feet, claiming that flashlights interfered with the 'power of the spirits'.

the strange glow at least four times before he wondered about the danger of a fire, "and so I stood up on purpose and pushing open the door I saw with my own eyes Father Bernardino raised from the ground as unmistakably as I now see your Illustrious Lordship."

Records of levitation in a religious context are extremely common. Olivier-Gilbert Leroy's *La Lévitation* contains the legends of some 230 Catholic saints to whom this feat is attributed and a similar number are listed in *La Stigmatisation* (1894) by Dr. A. Imbert-Gourbeyre. Father Thurston provides another 20 less well-known but well-attested cases that Dr Imbert-Gourbeyre had overlooked. They include St Ignatius Loyola who was known to hover just above the ground while meditating; St Adolphus Liguori who was raised into the air in front of a whole congregation in 1777; and, in the nineteenth century, the Syrian Carmelite, Sister Mary of Jesus Crucified, who would sometimes be levitated into the treetops of the garden of her Bethlehem nunnery. Some levitators, like Passitea Crogi, a Sienese nun who died in 1615, are seen traveling a considerable distance just above the ground; others hover in an attitude of prayer; while St Joseph of Cupertino (d.1663) rose in great swoops to the ceiling of his chapel.

The public and involuntary flights of St Joseph were something of an embarrassment to him and his superiors. He would suddenly cry out and fly up in the air, and so disrupted church services that he was barred from public worship. Once, according to a witness, "he rose into space and, from the middle of the church, flew like a bird on to the high altar, where he embraced the tabernacle." On another occasion he flew into an olive tree, "and he remained kneeling for half an hour on a branch, which was seen to sway as if a bird had perched on it." Eventually the authorities moved him from one Franciscan house to another in an attempt to avoid publicity.

While the "divine" radiance is mentioned in some cases most levitations seem to occur while the levitator is in a trance or ecstasy. Father Thurston was particularly impressed by the illuminated levitation of Father Francis Suarez, a Spanish Jesuit theologian (see also HUMAN GLOW-WORMS, p.65) as recorded by the monk who had been sent to wake him: "I noticed that the blinding light was coming from the crucifix . . . and in this brightness I saw him in a kneeling position in front of the crucifix. . . his body lifted above the floor." The witness was, understandably, stunned: "Bewildered and as it were beside myself . . . I went out, my hair standing on end like the bristles of a brush."

In the fourth century, the Roman historian Palladius saw the levitation of a child with his own eyes. The child, thought to be possessed, had been brought to St Macarius, an Egyptian hermit, for exorcism. Palladius says that the boy rose and remained suspended in the air for some time while the saint prayed. The phenomenon is not, of course, exclusive to Catholic saints. Muslim levitators include the twelfth-century

There are many eye-witness accounts of the ecstatic flights of St Joseph of Cupertino, including one by the High Admiral of Castile who noted the Saint's 'customary shrill cry' as he took off.

Iranian dervish, Haydar, noted for his sudden flights to treetops and roofs of houses. The French official and travel-writer in India, Louis Jacolliot, claims to have witnessed two levitations of a fakir called Covindasamy. As recorded in his *Occult Science in India* (1884), they were in broad daylight and one, on the terrace of his home, lasted ten minutes.

In Europe, where spontaneous levitation outside the Christian context is either unrecognized or classified in terms of diabolism and the supernatural, its occurrence is unwelcome and often painful to the person affected by it. When such things happen in traditionalist communities, it is usually taken as marking out a future shaman. Many instances are given in Mircea Eliade's *Shamanism* (1964) of the levitations of witch-doctors, shamans and Eastern mystics, which cannot all be dismissed as imagination or figures of speech. Thus, in Sumatra, "he who is destined to be a prophet-priest suddenly disappears, carried off by spirits; he returns to the village three or four days later; if not, a search is made for him and he is usually found in the top of a tree, conversing with spirits. He seems to have lost his mind, and sacrifices must be offered to restore him to sanity."

An interesting English example of this is the account of a series of violent psychical assaults on a young man, recorded in a letter from a Devon clergyman and printed in John Aubrey's *Miscellanies* (1696). Francis Fry, a servant at a farm in the parish of Spreyton, became the target of flying missiles and blows that seemingly came out of thin air; the whole house became so disturbed that a young girl living there had to be sent away for safety (see also INVISIBLE ASSAILANTS, p.143). On Easter Eve, 1682, Fry disappeared and was searched for; much later he was found half-naked in a bog, whistling and singing and quite out of his senses.

Joseph Glanvill, author of *Saducismus Triumphatus* (1681), knew of levitation during psychic disturbances, but associated it with witchcraft.

FORTEAN PICTURE LIBRARY

His shoes were scattered one each side of the farmhouse and his wig was found at the top of a tree. "Coming to himself an hour after, he solemnly protested that the daemon carried him so high that he saw his master's house underneath him no bigger than a hay-cock, that he was in perfect sense, and prayed God not to suffer the Devil to destroy him; that he was suddenly set down in the quagmire."

The records of the Society for Psychical Research contain similar stories of people being raised into the air, thrown across the room, and so on, by unseen forces, but they are interpreted as the action of poltergeists. Had Francis Fry experienced this involuntary levitation in tribal society, it would have distinguished him as a seer and spirit medium; at the height of the witchcraft persecutions he might have been burnt. By Aubrey's time, he was able to record the curious phenomena he delighted in (like any true scholar) without the necessity for moralistic comment. The huge literature on UFOs, likewise, has cases involving descriptions of levitation (often associated with a beam of light), sudden teleportation, and dream-like encounters with entities who appear to be engineering the incident.

In the heyday of Victorian spiritualism there were many demonstrations of levitation – the most famous being that of the celebrated medium Daniel Douglas Home. In July 1871, Lord Adare and two other nobles claimed they saw Home float out of one window of a London flat and come in through another. Regrettably, the story does not hold up and many critics, including Father Thurston, have shown convincingly how Home fooled his credulous witnesses.

One explanation of the transports of witches is that the sensation of flight was brought about by drugs, trances and the power of suggestion. While

The levitation of medium D.D. Home in 1871 before a group of eminent observers in London is probably the most famous incident in Victorian spiritualism. Unfortunately, none of the accounts by those present suggest anything other than an accomplished feat of trickery on Home's part.

it is certain that shamans use such aids in their ecstatic journeys, this does not explain many well-documented observations of levitation. Leroy believed that the levitations of psychics – indeed of anyone who wasn't an approved saint – were tricks of the Devil to confuse the faithful. Of the pioneering psychical investigators, Sir Oliver Lodge suggested it was by the action of spirits, while Professor Charles Richet thought there might actually be an undiscovered anti-gravitational force involved.

There is another hypothesis; that reality itself is restructured by the intense imaginings of the mystics. After all, levitation is the perfect metaphor for being lifted in spirit just as the strange accompanying light is for spiritual illumination. St Teresa of Ávila (d.1582) gives a valuable first-hand account of the experience in her autobiography: "It comes as a shock, quick and sharp, before you can collect your thoughts or help yourself in any way and you see and feel it as a cloud or as a strong eagle rising upward and carrying you away on its wings." On another occasion she was calm enough to take note of what was happening: "It seemed to me . . . as if a great force beneath my feet lifted me up . . . I confess that it threw me into a great fear, for in seeing one's body thus lifted up from the earth, though the spirit draws it upwards after itself (and that with great sweetness if unresisted) the senses are not lost; at least I . . . was able to see that I was being lifted up . . . after the rapture was over, my body seemed frequently to be buoyant, as if all weight had departed from it."

St Teresa would try to resist the levitations, wanting the ecstasy but fearing the bodily rising would engender in her delusions of grandeur and might distract her nuns from their proper devotions. Once, feeling it come upon her, she clutched at mats but rose into the air still clutching them; on another occasion the effort made her vomit blood. She writes of being worn out "like a person who had been contending with a strong giant; at other times it was impossible to resist at all; my soul was carried away, and almost always my head with it – I had no power over it – and now and then the whole body as well, so that it was lifted up from the ground." Anyone reading her accounts cannot fail to be impressed by them: they challenge us to accept their reality however mysterious that reality may seem.

The incorruptibles

A French historian once commented that the true religion of the Middle Ages was the worship of relics. We now examine a subject that extends beyond the usual definition of a relic as a preserved piece – usually a body part – of a saint, to examples of the "miraculous" preservation of entire bodies. Although much of the documentation of such cases comes from religious sources, not every example of the phenomenon is confined to the ecclesiastical or the "holy".

One of the earliest cases with a convincing narrative is the story of the early Roman saints Gervase and Protase who were martyred in 64 AD, during the reign of Nero. Over three hundred years later, Ambrose, Bishop of Milan, had a "presentiment" (his student St Augustine later called it a dream) in which St Paul revealed the location of their long-missing bodies. "I then called together the bishops of the cities thereabouts . . . and we went together to the place indicated", wrote Ambrose in his *Epistle 22*. "I was the first to ply the mattock and throw up the earth, but the rest helped me, and at length we came upon a stone chest (twelve feet underground) in which was found the bodies of the two martyrs whole and perfectly sound, as if they had been laid there only that very day."

The assembled clergymen were intrigued and examined the bodies closely. After performing various tests, they concluded, "Their limbs were entire, their blood fresh, and the bodies emitted a sweet odour which spread through the city." Ambrose was in no doubt about the identity of the bodies: the spot had been revealed to him in a dream by an authority he would not dare question and, as also foretold in the dream, at their heads was a book containing an account of their lives and martyrdom. Ambrose built a church on the spot, located as many early churches were by similar dream revelation or divination.

While modern historians are unconvinced by the identification of the two bodies, we are left with the simple narrative of the finding of remains that had defied corruption for over three hundred years. It is a story that is consistently repeated and so often well-observed by many authoritative witnesses. The usual processes of mummification – drying out, using preservatives, petrification or saponification (literally, turning to soap) – seem hardly to apply in such well-documented circumstances. Also, in many instances, the incorruptible corpses are surrounded by other unremarkable bodies or graves.

Consider the fate of St Isidore who died in Madrid in 1130. A farm labourer, Isidore was buried directly in the earth, without the benefit of a tomb or coffin. Forty years later, prompted by a parishioner's dream, the local church dug up his body for a more worthy resting place. A his-

torian of the day recorded: "It was found to be perfect as if it had but just died although it had been lying in the earth for forty years. Not only was no sign of decay perceptible but a sweet ravishing odour proceeded from it, an odour which all extolled."

In 1622, Isidore was canonized and his body exhumed for a second time, before many witnesses, for removal to a splendid new tomb. The history of his canonization, printed by order of King Philip III of Castile, says: "Not only was the body sound and fresh but there issued from it a heavenly odour." The document was signed by Philip's minister, de Groote, on 18 June 1625. In May 1969, St Isidore's body was transferred to Madrid's cathedral, where it was exposed for ten days. Many thousands filed past the "darkened, rigid, but perfect" 800-year-old body.

Other cases abound in Christian archives and hagiographies. *The Incorruptibles* (1977), by Joan Carroll Cruz, details 102 cases and refers to a great

The body of St Bernadette of Lourdes, preserved in the Saint Gildard convent at Nevers. She died in April 1879 and was exhumed thirty years later before a small crowd of church officials, all of whom attested to the lack of decay, even though her clothes were damp. She was washed, reclothed and reburied in a sealed, double casket. A second exhumation took place ten years later and the body, although intact, was slightly discoloured. A thin coating of wax was applied to the face before the body was placed in a glass coffin for viewing.

When Reverend Father Paul of Moll, in Belgium, was exhumed on 24 July 1899 , three years after his death, his preservation was said to be 'perfect'.

many more little-known and unpublicized reports. One of the most impressive cases she cites is of "the perfectly preserved and bleeding body" of the Lebanese saint Charbel Makhlouf. This Maronite monk died on 24 December 1898, eight days after having a seizure while conducting Mass. During his life he practised a severe corporeal discipline: he wore a hair shirt, slept on the ground and ate only one meal a day. According to the custom of his monastery in Annaya, Lebanon, St Charbel was buried in his daily robes, unembalmed and without a coffin. It is acknowledged that he would probably have been forgotten but for an extraordinary phenomenon; for forty-five nights following the interment (reckoned to be the usual period of decomposition) a bright light surrounded his grave. The monastery officials requested permission from the superiors of their Order to exhume the body and this was done, three months later, in their presence with a crowd of villagers in attendance.

Because of the regular, heavy rains which had inundated the cemetery, St Charbel was found almost floating in a grave full of muddy water.

After the body was washed and reclothed a curious fluid seeped from its pores. Described as a mixture of perspiration and blood, it had the smell of blood and was regarded as such by the faithful. The flow increased, necessitating a change of clothing twice a week; portions of the soaked clothing were distributed as relics and were credited with cures. This continued until July 1927, when the body was placed in a wooden coffin lined with zinc, along with a sealed zinc tube containing notarized testimonies of the phenomena from some very senior Catholic officials. For the next twenty-three years the coffin was sealed in a special crypt in the oratory wall, raised on stones to protect it from moisture.

The piety of St Charbel gained a huge following, causing a flow of pilgrims to Annaya which continues on an even greater scale today. In February 1950, pilgrims noticed liquid seeping through the oratory wall onto the floor. Fearing damage to St Charbel's tomb, it was opened up in April and his body was again found to be "flexible and lifelike" and free of any corruption. As Cruz reports: "The sweat of liquid and blood continued to exude from the body, and the garments were found stained with blood, the white content of the fluid having collected on the body in an almost solidified condition." Following this news, the flow of pilgrims reached five thousand a day. His body is examined each year (on which occasion around three inches of "blood" are found) but has not been on public display since 1950.

While people generally take such phenomena as levitation, stigmata, visions and incorruption as miracles and tokens of sanctity, the Church's Congregation of Rites (which decides on canonization and beatification) itself warns that "alleged charismata and supernatural favours are common to good and bad alike". In our researches, we have had many occasions to admire the Congregation of Rites discerning, and at times quite scientific, attitude towards the evidence for miracles. Contrary to what is claimed by skeptics, miracles alone do not make a saint. On the other hand, the more simple among the faithful frequently take "miraculous" phenomena – including incorruption – to be tangible signs of sainthood. They are the first to be shocked when the remains of people who were definitely not saints during their lives, are found to be incorrupt.

When the body of Cardinal Schuster of Milan was discovered to be incorrupt in 1985, nearly thirty-one years after his death, the mood of the Roman clergy was one of dismay. Schuster was remembered as a friend of Mussolini and an open supporter of fascism and of Italy's war in Abbysinia. One religious writer called it "the most embarassing discovery since Eve noticed her nakedness." Nevertheless, supporters of Schuster began a campaign for his beatification which

Julia Buccola Petta died during childbirth in Chicago in 1921. The photograph shows her exhumation seven years later in the Mount Carmel cemetery, following her mother's persistent dream of Julia asking to be reburied. There have been apparitions of 'the Italian bride' (as she is known locally) and reports of a smell of flowers at the grave in winter.

was instantly countered with allegations that "injection marks" had been found where he had been injected with preservatives.

An interesting non-Christian case involved the famous yogi Paramahansa Yogananda (1893–1952), who settled in Los Angeles in 1920, where he taught classical yoga techniques and philosophy and founded the Self-Realization Fellowship. Part of his teaching included the idea that an advanced yogi could induce a state of suspended animation in which the vital functions were undetectable and which enabled the body's ageing processes to be controlled. In other words he could simulate death for long periods and extend his lifetime.

The biographies of Yogananda record that he predicted that his death would occur on 7 March 1952, and that his body would reveal a sign that he was a true yogi. Although seeming in perfect health, he died on the appointed day of a heart attack. According to his instructions, his body was not to be embalmed but placed in a glass-topped coffin for twenty days. When it was finally buried, the body was said to be without any sign of decay and exuding a pleasant fragrance. This "perfect preservation" was confirmed by Harry T. Rowen of the Forest Lawn Memorial Park in Glendale, California, in a notarized statement. It was, he said, "unparalleled in mortuary annals" (*Grit*, 2 July 1972).

However useful it may be to assume that highly developed yogic control over biological processes may be a factor in the mystery of incorruptible corpses, it clearly played no part in the case of two-year-old Nadja Mattei, who died in Rome in 1965. Her mother told reporters that for the following twelve years her daughter's voice would come to her in dreams, asking to be brought out of her coffin. When the girl's body was exhumed in 1977 it was found to be quite undecayed (*News of the World*, 8 May 1977).

The most recent case known to us is that of Maria Regina Tobon Restrepo of Medelin, Colombia, whose body was exhumed four years after she died in a diabetic coma, aged 33. Martha Valencia, a mortician with eighteen years' experience, said Maria Regina's eyes were intact, there was no sign of fungus, nor any smell of decay. Even her dress was preserved. "She looked like a precious doll," said Valencia (*El Tiempo*, 8 October 1998). It has been suggested that Maria may have been preserved by the large doses of insulin she needed. Instead of creating an object of veneration, the family decided the body should go to the University of Antioquia for research purposes.

There is a strong tradition of prescient dreams (containing messages from the deceased) associated with this topic but our last story shows that this is not always a reliable indicator. In 1976 a 33-year-old German girl, Anneliese Michel, died during an exorcism ordered by the Bishop of Wurzburg. The circumstances of her death were shocking: believing her to be possessed by demons (including the spirit of Hitler), the exorcists starved her during their protracted rites and were subsequently tried for criminal neglect.

After her death a feeling grew that a great injustice had been done to the girl. In 1977 a nun told the girl's parents that Anneliese had visited her repeatedly in dreams, saying: "Let my coffin be opened for all to see. They will find my body untouched by mortal decay, as you see me now, with the nail wounds of Christ on my hands and feet." Subjected to mounting pressure from the family, priests and the public, the local authorities agreed to exhume the body. On 26 February 1978 a crowd of many thousands gathered and overflowed the cemetery near Klingenberg in expectation of seeing a double miracle – the stigmatized and uncorrupted body of a saint.

The police tried in vain to control the crowds as they scaled walls and stood on graves and monuments for a better view. In the *News of the World* (12 March 1978), reporter George Edwards gives a first-hand account of the scene. As the earth-covered coffin was lifted and taken to the mortuary to be opened, the crowd spontaneously (and prematurely) shouted, "It's a miracle! She looks as if she's alive!" In the mortuary it was a different story. The coffin was opened before the Bavarian State prosecutor and the Mayor of Klingenberg to reveal the body in an advanced state of decomposition. According to Edwards, the crowd was stunned with dismay and dispersed "feeling they had been cheated".

Miraculous provisions

In his article, "Miracles", in the encyclopaedia *Man, Myth and Magic* (1970) A.R.G. Owen writes that Christ's miraculous feeding of the five thousand tends to be interpreted today as a parable of "spiritual feeding" rather than as a factual record of a multitude of people dining off five loaves and two fishes divided between the lot of them. The story may seem more rational that way, but St Mark in the sixth chapter of his Gospel, described it as a contemporary, eye-witnessed event. If Jesus actually performed such a miracle, he is by no means the only holy man to have done so. The feeding of very many on very little is called theologically a "miracle of abundance" and merits a whole chapter in Pope Benedict XIV's definitive guide to mystical phenomena, *De servorum Dei beatificatione et canonizatione*. Father Herbert Thurston re-examines a number of these in *The Physical Phenomena of Mysticism* (1952) and concludes that the phenomenon of multiplication cannot be lightly dismissed as belonging solely to the domain of legend.

It is claimed that such miracles of abundance are performed today by the Indian holy man Sai Baba. In *Sai Baba: Man of Miracles* (1971) Howard Murphet gives an account of a party after a religious ceremony at the house of Mr and Mrs Ramachandran, near Poona. A hundred guests had been catered for, but about a thousand turned up. Sai Baba was present and saved the day by miraculously multiplying the food tenfold during its serving so that all were fully satisfied. At other times, Murphet writes, the saint could instantly produce sweets still hot from cooking. These and other miracles are still witnessed by pilgrims to Sai Baba's sanctuary in India.

Prolific feats of edible magic were attributed to St Angiolo Paoli (d.1720), who delighted in multiplying small quantities of food to distribute to the poor of Rome and rarely refused any genuine request. According to his biographer, he was often sent on picnics arranged by the sponsors of some of the Carmelite missions. On one hot June day the saint took a group to a garden party where he provided lettuces and radishes for a salad, a tart, and a basket of strawberries for

Mosaic of loaves and fishes on the altar of the Church of the Multiplication which stands on the site where Jesus worked the miracle of the feeding of the five thousand.

Among well-documented angelic transportations of the Host (or communion bread) to the communicant's mouth is that of St Catherine of Siena (d.1380).

corn in their granary and no money to buy more. After admonishing their lack of faith in a sermon about Christ's multiplication miracle, St Andrew bade them gather what corn they could find into two heaps, around which he walked in prayer. Subsequently, the sister in charge of the granary drew enough to feed some two hundred sisters daily, and for the next two and a half months the heaps did not diminish at all. According to the *Summarium* for his beatification, St Andrew performed this miracle on several occasions and kept the house in cornflour from July to December.

Auffray's *Life of the Blessed John Bosco* also quotes from beatification documents in evidence of this saint's power to perform the miracle of abundance. One day in 1860 Don Bosco was informed there was nothing for breakfast in the Salesian house in Turin in which he was staying. The eyes of three hundred hungry boys were on him as he asked for all the scraps of bread of any size to be brought to him. Everybody there could see there were only fifteen or twenty small pieces of bread in the basket he held as he walked among them yet each person received a piece.

In some of these accounts the miracle takes place in the dough while the bread is still being made. For example, in the hard winter of 1845 the Bon Pasteur convent at Bourges was faced with supplying the daily needs of 116 people from a depleted granary. Blessed Mother Pelletier instructed the nuns to pray for the intercession of St Germaine Cousin, confident that the small supply would be replenished. The cooking sisters were urged to use about a third of the customary amount of flour; and, sure enough, within minutes the dough had swollen to overflow the kneading trough with enough for twice the usual number of loaves. This was repeated many times between November 1845 and February 1846, during which time the nuns did not have to buy any more flour. The documentation of these wonders was thorough enough to be cited for the canonization of St Germaine in 1854, and the beatification of Mother Pelletier.

It is interesting to note that traditional folklore stories of Christ's and St Peter's wanderings on earth include variants of this phenomenon. One story, in G.W. Dasent's *Popular Tales from the Norse* (1903), tells of how the two came to a baker's house and begged some bread from his wife.

dessert, all of which were very scarce because of drought.

One of the most authoritative cases of multiplication procured the beatification of St Andrew Fournet (d.1834), founder of Les Filles de la Croix, a house for educating the poor at La Puye, in Poitou. One year, about 1824, the sisters at La Puye were in despair because they had very little

Believing them to be mere ordinary beggars, she took a small piece of dough which then expanded to cover the whole griddle. Not wanting to give away so much, she broke off another small piece but this also expanded and she decided not to give it away at all. Christ angrily turned her into a woodpecker.

Miracles of abundance go back to well before Christian times. They can be found, all over the world, in legends of magic cauldrons and fairy cups that can never be drained and which provide everybody they serve with whatever they wish to eat or drink. Legends of the ever-full cups of the fairies are continuous with stories of miraculous draughts of wine in the lives of the saints. It is said that St Dominic, who died in 1221, blessed a cup of wine from which 26 people drank. It was then carried to a convent, where 104 nuns each swallowed a mouthful. It was returned to the saint still full. At the risk of being thought literal minded, we imagine that there may be some truth in these tales, but we also believe that such miraculous provisions must have come from somewhere. Being aware of the teleportation effect, and suspecting that it may sometimes be used by saints and magicians, we look around for corresponding stories of missing provisions and, indeed, could fill this book with accounts of food and other objects which vanish from one place and appear in another.

The supply of provisions to people who desperately need them sometimes takes place without the intervention of a holy man. In *Fortean Times* (no.48, p.16), Bob Skinner quotes an example of answered prayers from Increase Mather's *Remarkable Providences* (1684). Twelve people in a small boat were adrift for five weeks in the North Atlantic after their ship sank off New England. "God sent relief to them by causing some flying fish to fall into the boat which they ate raw and were well pleased therewith." Even better is the account of three fishermen from the island of Kiribati in the Pacific. In April 1986 the engine of their boat failed and they were adrift for 119 days before being rescued. They had survived by catching sharks with their bare hands, drinking their blood and eating their raw flesh. When sick of this diet, they prayed for a change, and while they were praying something fell into the boat. It was a rare blackfish. Police sergeant Paul Aingilia of Naurui, the island off which the men were rescued, was amazed by this. The blackfish, he said, never comes to the surface. "It lives about 620 feet down and cannot be caught by trawling."

In Malory's *Morte d'Arthur* (1485), the materialization of the Holy Grail brought each of the knights of the Round Table generous helpings of their favourite food and drink. Similar beliefs were held about the magical cups and cauldrons of fairies and witches.

In RAINS OF SEEDS AND ORGANIC MATTER (see p.47) we mention cases of seeds, all of one kind, falling from the sky onto a specific area of

BOTTOMLESS

Mrs. J. TIDMARSH, Hunton Bridge, Kings Langley, Herts, writes:

I WONDER if you or your readers can solve a creepy problem. My husband is fond of curries and makes them quite regularly.

About five years ago he bought a tin of ground coriander and each time he makes a curry he puts one heaped teaspoon of coriander in it.

Yet the next time he gets the tin out, it is packed tight under the lid.

In other words, although he has been using the coriander for five years, the tin is still full !

We can't understand it.

A modern Grail-style miracle of 1975.

land. These falls were seen and recorded. Imagine a fallow field that lies waiting for seed, like the empty ponds that yearn for fish (see FALLS OF FISHES AND FROGS, p.17), and an unobserved fall of seed which later sprouts. In 1919 there were two recorded instances of the mysterious appearance of wheatfields: the *Cardiff Evening News* (1 July 1919), said that in a field in Lincolnshire, which had been fallow since its last crop of barley ten years before, there appeared a crop of wheat said to be finer than that in surrounding fields; and the London *Sunday Express* (24 August 1920) tells that after a drought had killed off a field of wheat near Ormskirk, Lancashire, the previous year, "one of the best crops of vigorous young wheat" the farmer had ever seen appeared without his re-seeding the field. A more modern, tale of wheat appearing unexpectedly took place near Milan where a farmer noticed a fine crop in a 21-acre field. According to the *Daily Mirror* (29 April 1968) this had happened several times in preceding years, but as soon as the crop ripened it vanished overnight despite careful observation. We wonder if the grain ever materialized in some destitute convent's granary.

Records of vanishing seeds are less common, since this is a subject that is hardly likely to excite the interest of newspaper reporters, and few cases have been recorded. One that we have discovered took place in 1974 when farmers in Worcestershire and Shropshire were faced with a bill for £2000 when their sugar-beet seeds inexplicably vanished from the fields. Blaming a plague of mice, they took elaborate preventative measures – flattening the furrows and laying poison – but the seeds continued to vanish. According to the *Sunday Mercury* (26 May 1974) experts tried all that they could think of but remained baffled as to a possible explanation.

4

The Madness of Crowds

The Madness
of Crowds

Plagues, poisons and panics

What makes a person ill? Today, doctors know a lot about the actions of organisms but there are times when that knowledge seems of little use. In 1906 members of several families in New York were stricken with typhoid. Investigations revealed that a girl named Mary had worked in all these households as a cook, and the authorities branded her a carrier of typhoid germs even though she herself was immune. After three years in hospital, she was finally certified "free of germs", but was banned from food-handling jobs and required to report for regular check-ups. Instead she absconded.

About five years later, 25 cases of typhoid occurred at a New York maternity home. Once the health authorities learned that "Typhoid Mary" was working in the kitchens they looked no further, and she was detained again. What is less obvious is where, if she was free of germs, did she get re-infected? And why were no cases traceable to her either during the five years she used aliases to get kitchen-work, or before 1906?

We have an idea that mysterious outbreaks of disease overlap with some of our other sections. In STIGMATA (see p.76) and INVISIBLE ASSAILANTS (see p.143) we mention cases where marks and wounds have appeared on bodies, producing effects

that are "medically impossible". But if wounds can be teleported, why not germs? We suspect that "Typhoid Mary" was one of those unfortunates, mentioned in some of our other sections, who are somehow the focus of unexplained fires, accidents, lightning strikes, bombardments of stones, etc.

But if some people seem to be the focal point of contagious diseases, others appear to have a level of immunity that defies medical science. The germ theory that damned "Typhoid Mary" should have killed John Peck; but brought medical theory near to farce. In New York City in 1916, Dr Arthur Waite attempted to kill his father-in-law, a man named Peck, by feeding the old man on diphtheria germs and by giving him a nasal spray doctored with tuberculosis. When Peck survived this, Waite weakened him with calomel, loosed typhoid on him and then influenza. In the end he gave up and poisoned him with arsenic.

We can only speculate on what Waite, a professional bacteriologist, must have thought about germ theory. He had plenty of time to brood on it in prison. But even poison does not always work. Peck eventually died, but the Russian priest Rasputin, confidante of the Tsarina Alexandra at the beginning of the twentieth century, lived on after eating enough poisoned cake to kill a regiment. His assassins had to finish him off by shooting him twice, beating him with an iron bar and pushing him through a hole in the ice into a freezing river. He was found to have drowned.

In Mattoon, Illinois, Mrs Aline Kearney and daughter Dorothy re-enact the moment when they were overcome by a mysterious gas attack through the open window.

If some people fail to die when they ought to, others have died when there seemed no reason why they should. Marjory Quick, daughter of the Bishop of Sheffield, drank what she believed to be medicinal paraffin, vomited and died immediately. The report in the *Daily Express* (3 October 1911) says that no trace of paraffin could be found in the cup, her throat or her mouth. To the authorities it seemed obvious that she was in a suicidal state – whatever that may mean. An Associated Press report, which appeared in most American newspapers in January 1968, said that the wife of army Sergeant Robert Rush woke him up at 6am, screamed out and died instantly. The inquest disclosed that her sister had expired in a similar fashion five years earlier, having climbed out of a swimming-pool, looked around her with a horrified expression, screamed and dropped dead. Autopsies on both sisters failed to find the cause of death. Referred to today as SUNDS (sudden

unexplained death syndrome) instances continue to be reported in the papers. Some of these may have a relationship with the disturbing phenomenon of "cot deaths" and are, even now, largely unexplained.

When the Massachusetts State Commissioner of Health, Dr G.H. Bigelow, spoke after a supper at the Harvard Medical School, Boston, thirty students and doctors fell ill. Food poisoning was suspected but no cause could be discovered. The experts declared it was paratyphoid; then another twenty people were struck down. The circumstances were strange yet no evidence of any communication of the disease could be found. We note with some amusement that the subject of Dr Bigelow's speech was "Food-poisoning", a fact which did not go unnoticed by the headline writers of the *New York Herald Tribune* (30 January 1932). While real mass poisonings occur and are quickly identified there are also growing numbers of cases (eg swimmers breaking out in rashes, field workers having trouble breathing, cinema audiences feeling nauseous) in which all obvious causes have been eliminated leaving only mystery.

Unidentified fumes are a particularly common complaint. The magazine *Human Behaviour* (January 1975) admits that "accounts of victims gassed by undetectable vapours dot the annals of psychology", and details one case in March 1972 when 39 women at a data-processing centre in Kansas became dizzy, swooned and vomited. Analyses of air, blood and urine failed to find any trace of the "gas" they said made them "feel hot", their eyes sting and their heads reel. The next day they again dropped like flies. On the third day the management, under advice from psychologists, announced that the cause had been located; it was only "atmospheric inversion". The trick worked and the trouble ceased; or the trouble ceased despite the trick, for our records show that these attacks may repeat but rarely last more than a few days. The psychologists concluded that these cases were "examples of mass hysteria" which they defined as "a sort of psychic contagion".

The classic case of this sort occurred in the Illinois town of Mattoon in September 1944. It began when a woman complained to police that someone had opened her bedroom window and sprayed her with "a sickish sweet-smelling gas". She felt ill and her legs were paralyzed for a while. The headline in the local paper the next day shouted: "ANAESTHETIC PROWLER ON THE LOOSE". As others came forward to say they too had been attacked by this maniac, many residents armed themselves and lay in wait for any suspicious prowler. Despite further "attacks" and immediate police responses, no "phantom anaesthetist" was ever caught.

Loren Coleman, in his *Mysterious America* (1983), presents many other American examples of "mass hysteria" and particularly likens the "Mad Gasser of Mattoon" to the panic engendered in

Large communities can be gripped suddenly by irrational fears about real and imaginary illnesses, alien invasion or invisible wizards and assassins. We suspect the same process also creates or governs the expectations of large crowds. For example, thousands of the faithful gathered on a hillside at Pescara, on Italy's Adriatic coast, on 28 February 1988, to see an apparition of the Virgin Mary, prophesied by a local Catholic visionary. When the apparition failed to materialize, people were disappointed yet their faith was not dented in the slightest.

This bizarre drawing, dated 1564 and once ascribed to Pieter Brueghel the Elder, is entitled *The Epileptic Women of Meulebeek*. The explanatory text along the bottom states that 'These are the pilgrims who on St John's day had to dance outside Meulebeek and when they leapt over a bridge then they are cured for a whole year of St John's disease.' The women may have been suffering from convulsive ergotism.

London by "Springheel Jack" who continued to be sighted from 1837 to 1877. A better parallel with Mattoon is Halifax, West Yorkshire. Ten years before the panic at Mattoon, in November 1938, the town was brought to a standstill by its collective fear of a supposed razor-wielding maniac who stepped out of shadows at night to slash at solitary pedestrians. As folklorist Michael Goss points out, the wounds on the Slasher's first victims were all too real but a corporeal culprit was never caught (*The Halifax Slasher*, 1987). As at Mattoon, the longer the case went unsolved the more the press capitalized upon it, publicizing further claims. As at Mattoon, intense police and vigilante activity failed to stem the claims of further attacks. In the end the Halifax police, faced with an uncatchable perpetrator and increasingly dubious testimony from self-confessed "victims", were forced to put

much of it down to "imagination". In time, the "Halifax Slasher" became just another example of mass hysteria.

Perhaps there is something to the notion of "psychic contagion", not as those glib psychologists used it but as some human equivalent of, for example, the great sheep panic of 3 November 1888. On this morning, according to accounts in British papers shortly after the event, thousands of sheep throughout an area measuring 25 by 8 miles near Reading, Berkshire, were found scattered far and wide, panting with terror. What spooked them during the night was never ascertained.

Psychic contagion works like an imitation of pathological contagion; it doesn't matter how absurd the circumstances, it spreads through panic and anxiety – or, sometimes, through excitement and expectation – wherever large numbers of like-minded people interact. In America in June 1899, doctors across America were alarmed by thousands of new patients seeking medical attention for their lips, swollen and with tiny punctures. A fruitless search for the "kissing bug" drew criticism from senior medical authorities. Writing at the height of the scare, in *Popular Science Monthly*, Dr L.O. Howard noted that only six species of insect in the country could give such bites, and since this was the work of none of them, he dismissed the whole affair as "a senseless scare" and likened it to the tarantula bite scares that gripped southern Europe in medieval times (see SOCIAL ANXIETY ATTACKS, p.110).

The phenomenon of mass hysteria was certainly known of old; we refer readers to the curious records of many such scares in Charles Mackay's famous *Extraordinary Popular Delusions and the Madness of Crowds* (1852). For example, he details the almost incredible extent of the "poison manias" that swept Italy and France in the sixteenth and seventeenth centuries, in which hundreds of people believed themselves victims of a colourless, tasteless,

In Southern Italy there was a tradition that the bite of the tarantula spider could only be cured by wild dancing. The dance, the Tarantella, later became formalized by Neapolitan composers.

odourless poison. In response to this panic, the authorities carried out a vigorous campaign of executing alleged poisoners. It's highly likely – in the light of what we now know about such epidemics – that many, if not all, of the condemned were quite innocent.

Similarly, dancing manias raged like forest fires throughout Europe between the fourteenth and fifteenth centuries. It seems as if almost anything could set one off – the sound of music, the sight of pointed shoes, or a fiery preacher – and once the dancers hove into view, many found themselves compelled to join the line. They pranced or convulsed until exhaustion or restraining friends finally stopped them (in much the same way as was said about dancing in a fairy ring). An early example of compulsive dancing comes from the German town of Aachen in July 1374; within a short time the mania had spread to Liège in Belgium and Utrecht in Holland.

Some of these dance manias may have had an underlying medical cause. The condition now called Sydenham's chorea in which the victim is prone to making involuntary jerky and spasmodic movements was known in the Middle Ages as St Vitus's Dance. A not dissimilar condition was the, now uncommon, disease known as convulsive ergotism. Ergot is a fungal growth that sometimes appears on cereal crops, in particular rye. If accidentally harvested with the grain and consumed, ergot can produce two serious and unpleasant diseases: gangrenous ergotism (known as St Anthony's Fire) in which the limbs shrivel up, and convulsive ergotism in which the limbs twitch and shake in a violent and uncontrollable fashion. There were many recorded epidemics of ergotism from the end of the sixteenth century to the beginning of the eighteenth. Ergot also has medicinal qualities and was prescribed from the Middle Ages as a means of quickening childbirth.

The "tarantism" referred to by Dr Howard persisted from the fourteenth to the eighteenth centuries and was popularly believed to be caused by the bite of the southern European wolf spider or tarantula (named after the Italian city of Taranto). In reality the bite was only slightly toxic but, such was the power of communal belief that victims were made to dance frenetically in order to rouse them from the lethargy and inertia which the bite was thought to cause. The melodies which they danced to were called "tarantellas" and the cure was achieved when the patient collapsed in a convulsive crisis or exhaustion. Athanasius Kircher included several songs for curing the tarantula bite in his *Magnes sive de arte magnetica* (1641).

The element of compulsive behaviour here recalls the automatisms of the hypnotic state and this can be very significant in collective religious experiences. Gerald de Barry (Giraldus Cambrensis) describes a dancing mania he witnessed in Wales in 1188. An annual feast at the beginning of August at the church of St Eluned in Breconshire became famous for its procession of penitents; males and females would dance, sing or, "on a sudden falling on the ground as in a trance", would act out "in a frenzy with their hands and feet whatever work they have unlawfully done on feast days". Helpers take them into the church where, after prayers, "you will see them suddenly awakened and coming to themselves" (*Itinierarium Cambriae*, 1191). Similar phenomena are commonplace in Pentecostal and Charismatic Christian services today, especially those involving the so-called "Toronto blessing" in which rapt members of the congregation collapse laughing, crying or barking.

Wars of the worlds

Orson Welles's radio version of *The War of the Worlds* terrified millions of listeners when it was first aired on the evening of 30 October 1938. Welles and his script writer, Howard Koch, updated H.G. Wells's 1898 novel, transplanting the action from Surrey to New Jersey and presenting part of the narrative as a live news event. It began with an observation of explosions on the surface of Mars, followed by the landing on the US of huge Martian machines that strode over the landscape destroying people and property with their heat rays. The play ended with an announcer on the roof of the New York radio station, describing the advance of the Martian tripods towards Manhattan. The final silence was as powerful as the mounting panic in the voice-overs delivering news of the casualties and the mobilization of military battalions.

Reactions to the play were most intense in New Jersey and New York. Joseph Bulgatz devotes a chapter to the incident in his analysis of panics and mass hysteria, *Ponzi Schemes, Invaders from Mars and More* (1992), providing a comprehensive account of what happened that night. People rang friends and family, the police, radio stations, hospitals, newspapers, bus stations, etc, asking for more information, volunteering their help, or simply to warn others. The congestion of the phone system only added to the general anxiety, as did the fact that no one was sure in which direction safety lay.

All of this was reinforced by newspaper headlines the following day; wire messages spread around the world stories of "weeping, hysterical women", people "gathering in groups and praying", and chaos in the streets. "Probably never before have so many people in all walks of life and in all parts of the country become so suddenly and so intensely disturbed as they did on this night," wrote Hadley Cantril, a psychologist at Princeton.

Ironically, most of Welles's colleagues, including CBS executives, had thought the play "too fantastic" and "just not believable" before it was broadcast. So what made it so effective? Welles and his Mercury Theater Company had been engaged by CBS for a series of one-hour plays. Eager to experiment, Welles realized the dramatic potential of the "front line" news reports from Europe which was then on the verge of war with Germany. As Bulgatz notes, people "had become accustomed to news bulletins that interrupted the regular programming."

When the broadcast was condemned as "irresponsible" many writers and celebrities sprang to Welles's defence. Influential columnist Dorothy Thompson praised him for exposing the failure of popular education. Where Hitler used armies to terrify Europe, she added, Welles had demoralized a nation with a single microphone. That, at least, is the legend, but was the reaction really that extreme? Recent studies suggest the influence of the broadcast has been greatly exaggerated but the incident provides a remarkable perspective into the psychology of collective imagination and "mass hysteria".

This was the heyday of Flash Gordon, massive popular interest in Mars and its "canals" and growing political tensions in Europe and the Far East which, within a few months, dragged Britain and America into World War II. The grave tones of Welles's fake announcers and reporters – however fantastic their words – seemed utterly convincing in the general context. The records show that several public notices were given before and during the play, broadcast at Halloween. At one point Welles declares that the play is "the Mercury Theatre's own radio version of dressing up in a sheet and jumping out of a bush and saying boo." Many other signs of the fictional nature of the broadcast were present – eg compression of the action of days, even months, into less than an hour. The least-fooled were young people who rec-

Orson Welles in the CBS studios at the time of his historic broadcast.

ognized Welles's distinctive voice as that of the hero of another drama series, *The Shadow*.

Almost immediately after the broadcast, Hadley Cantril had the brilliant idea of collecting stories of the panic for a study that was eventually published in 1940 as *The Invasion from Mars*. His material was widely cited as an academic

Welles' Martians landed at Grover's Mill, NJ, where the real inhabitants looked far from panicky.

endorsement of almost all the extreme claims of what happened that night. Since then, several scholars of epidemic hysteria have criticized Cantril's sweeping generalizations from what was, in reality, a very small and localized sample (135 people from New Jersey). Dr Robert Bartholomew of Queensland's James Cook University, writing in *Skeptical Inquirer* (November 1998), suggests that panic had been the exception and not the rule. "There is little doubt that many Americans were genuinely frightened and some did try to flee the Martians," Bartholomew notes, "[Nevertheless] there is a growing consensus among sociologists that the extent of the panic, as described by Cantril, was greatly exaggerated."

When British ufologists John and Anne Spencer looked for evidence of the scale of the panic in the files of civil authorities in New Jersey and New York, they found very little. They confirm the picture of a minority of panicked individuals who, they argue in their *Encyclopedia of the World's Greatest Unsolved Mysteries* (1995), would surely have encountered, sooner or later, someone who knew the broadcast had been just a play.

The evidence, then, is that more people enjoyed or ignored Welles's broadcast than were alarmed by it. The real scare-mongering followed later when newspapers blew it out of all proportion creating, in the collective imagination, the stereotype of the full-out, chaotic urban panic beloved by Hollywood movies. As Bartholomew said in a BBC interview on the sixtieth anniversary (October 1998) of the Welles broadcast: "The supposed panic was put down to the power of the media. The fact that many believe a panic took place when it did not is also testimony to the power of the media."

The result of the gradual mythologizing of the incident has been far-reaching. The potential for mass panic was the main reason the US government kept quiet their knowledge about UFOs from the public – evidently envisaging a level of civil catastrophe based on the mis-reported reactions to Welles broadcast. By 1947 the growth of interest in "flying saucers" was a major concern to senior echelons of the US military and here was the perfect, plausible excuse for secrecy.

In January 1948 – just six months after the Kenneth Arnold sighting of flying disks skipping along like "flying saucers" – the US Air Force initiated Project Sign to study reported sightings. By August 1948, their infamous "top secret" report – *Estimate of the Situation* – was delivered to the Chief of Staff, General Hoyt Vandenberg. It pre-

sented the conclusion of many Sign consultants that "UFOs are interplanetary devices systematically observing the Earth." Many officers were opposed to the continuing policy of cover-up and denial, arguing that it was politically dangerous. Some of them urged Vandenberg to publicly acknowledge the presence of UFOs in US airspace. Vandenberg refused.

A further significant influence on military thinking was the report commissioned in 1960 by NASA from the Brookings Institution, a Washington think-tank, on the possible social consequences of public confirmation of a genuine extra-terrestrial (ET) artifact or contact. Citing many historical examples of cultures that "have disintegrated when confronted by a [technologically] superior society," they concluded, gravely, that any contact with ETs could cause "the downfall of civilisation on Earth". Richard Hoagland of the Enterprise Mission, has argued that the Brookings Report, coming as it did at the height of Cold War paranoia, set the seal on military secrecy and assured that many discoveries concerning the Moon, Mars and deep space are reserved for military eyes only.

And so the cover-up continued for decades. In a memo dated 24 September 1952, H. Marshall Chadwell, Assistant Director for Scientific Intelligence wrote to his CIA boss, Walter Smith, that: "A fair proportion of our population is mentally conditioned to the acceptance of the incredible. In this fact lies the potential for the touching-off of mass hysteria and panic." Even the notorious Condon Report (*Scientific Study of Unidentified Flying Objects*, 1968) – which described the Welles broadcast as "a coast-to-coast state of panic" – expressed the high-level opinion that there was more danger from a stampeding public than from the UFOs themselves. Worse, in the words of the Robertson Panel report (1953), the public was now vulnerable to "enemy psychological warfare".

Hadley Cantril has often been asked whether modern society has become too sophisticated for a panic, of the type precipitated by Welles's broadcast, to happen again. "Unfortunately, I have always had to reply that of course it could happen again and on a much more extensive scale," he wrote in the 1966 edition of *Invasion from Mars*. To some extent he is right. Many radio stations around the world have tried to re-create the hysteria of the original broadcast – usually on its anniversary. *Fortean Times* (no.120, p.42) lists nine of them; the most famous taking place in Quito, Ecuador, on 12 February 1949, was followed by

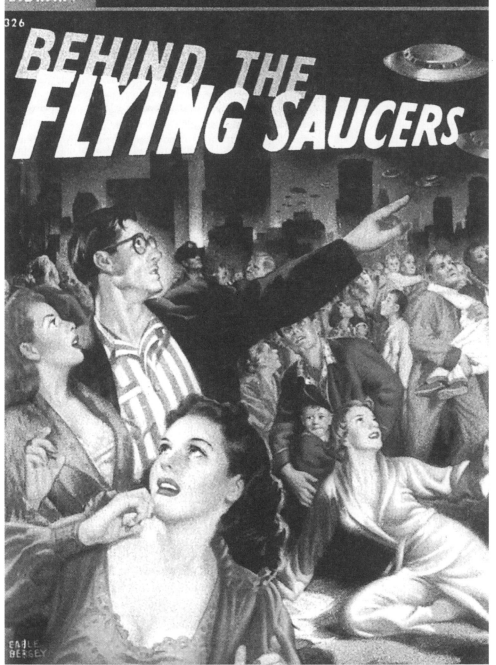

POPULAR
LIBRARY

The Book Everyone Is Talking About

326

BEHIND THE FLYING SAUCERS

EARLE
BERGEY

The cover of Frank Scully's *Behind the Flying Saucers* (1951), the first explicit, if credulous, discussion of crashed UFOs, recovered bodies, government conspiracy and mass panic.

widespread, genuine panic when listeners believed the country was being attacked by Peru or the Russians. The station's director deliberately did not announce the play was fictional. By the time he apologized it was too late; an angry mob besieged the station building and torched it. In the ensuing battle with troops six people were killed, fifteen were injured, some actors were arrested and the director fled the country. More recently, on 30 October 1998, when Radio Antena 3, a subsidiary of Portuguese National Radio (RDP), ended their re-enactment by planting a story in a later news bulletin, saying Martians were heading for the capital, Lisbon, hundreds panicked.

But, while academics argue over the scale of the *War of the Worlds* panics, the concern of the military has been exonerated. There can be no doubt about the power of collective imagination – which we examine further in the next two sections – to create predicaments which are damaging personally or socially. We are brought up to trust authority and we do not expect governments, priests, scientists or newsreaders to mislead us. We know how to react, it seems, when real newsreaders are used in spoof newscasts on comedy shows, but calamity can follow if the usual signals of "authority" are confused, misread or deliberately exploited. The military complex fears that malicious foreign agents could use a nation's credulity and anxiety against itself but, historically, the only signs of social manipulation on this scale are the lies many governments, dictators and tyrants have told their own peoples.

Shared visions

People see visions. It is a recurring feature of human experience and one on which rationalism has made little impact. In fact visions seem to be on the increase if our records are anything to go by, as almost weekly we learn of some new sighting of a phantom animal, an unidentified flying object (UFO), or the Virgin Mary. A wide range of explanations is available, from psychology and pathology to the occult. Our interest here is in those visions which are perceived by more than one person.

E. Parrish in *Hallucinations and Illusions* (1897) discusses an incident which began with the death of a ship's cook. Several days later the form of the cook was clearly seen and identified by all on board the ship, limping (he had one leg shorter than the other) across the waters towards them. As the vision drew nearer it suddenly resolved itself into a piece of floating wreckage. Parrish suggests that initially one person, brooding on the loss of a friend, thought he saw the cook and in telling the others planted the suggestion in their minds. This, he says, may be the genesis of all ghosts. We have our doubts – things are not always so conveniently explicable.

A vision was shared by the Abbé Caucanas and thirty of his congregation at Castelnau-de-Guers, France, at Easter 1974 and reported in many papers. The Abbé was rising from kneeling at the altar when he saw "the face of Our Lord" on the white napkin covering the ciborium containing the Eucharistic bread. He cried out, the congregation surged forward to help him and they too saw the face. The Abbé said he saw "the right eye closed, the left open. The nose was bruised and swollen and bore an expression of pain." Others saw tears flowing, and some a crown of thorns. After fifteen minutes the Abbé lifted the napkin to continue the service and the image disappeared.

Professor E.R. Jaensch (*Eidetic Imagery*, 1930) explained away, in a brief footnote, hundreds of accounts by people who saw statues and paintings come to life. They were persistent images generated in the eye and superimposed on normal vision, he said – eidetic images. By now we are used to explanations that explain nothing or even need explaining themselves. Taking a panoramic view of strange phenomena we can point to many accounts of groups of people who see previously inanimate objects move or speak, shed tears or bleed. The consistency of these accounts demands our respect and we have given them their own sections – IMAGES THAT WEEP AND BLEED (see p.251) and STATUES THAT COME TO LIFE (see p.255).

To account for mass visions which occur without any apparent element of suggestion, modern writers have proposed some kind of telepathic exchange. An earlier version of this theory, given by Catherine Crowe in *The Night-Side of Nature* (1854) is that a seer, by touching or otherwise spell-binding other members of a group, can induce them to share his or her vision. In FIRE-WALKING AND FIRE-IMMUNITY (see p.57) we have noticed the similar role of an officiating magician who creates temporarily the spell of a different order of reality. In *This Baffling World* (1968) John Godwin states his belief that the Indian rope trick is just that – a trick, and he suggests how it could be worked as a conjuring illusion. Against this is

a dog run off with an arm or leg, and this has to be recovered.

The psychologists saw the magician collect the parts of the boy in a basket, go back up the rope and return with the boy whole. When they developed their film, they saw to their astonishment the fakir and boy simply standing impassively by the rope, which was all the time coiled on the floor. The entire sequence had been imagined and conducted in silence. Puharich concludes that "the hallucination originated with the fakir . . . was telepathically inspired and extended to the several hundred people present". In 1934 the trick was performed twice in London, and on the second occasion the organizers concealed

FATE MAGAZINE

In December 1929 two crewmen died on board the *SS Watertown* and were buried at sea. The next day their likenesses were seen in the waves, always from the same position on deck. The vision recurred on the following two voyages and then disappeared.

the experience of two investigating psychologists, described in Andrija Puharich's *Beyond Telepathy* (1962), who saw the act with hundreds of other witnesses. In its full form a small boy goes up the rope, the magician follows with a knife, and both seem to vanish at the top. Screams are heard, followed by a grisly rain of dismembered parts. The magician comes down with a bloody knife, places the parts in a box, and soon the boy emerges whole and smiling. In some performances witnesses see

cameras. When developed, the film revealed the rope on the ground and the boy scuttling for the bushes. Those present were witnessing an event that did not take place in normal reality.

In an increasingly materialistic world, the growing list of apparition sites is a reminder that psychological and spiritual needs, unfulfilled by society, will find their expression often in new and surprising ways. For example, since November 1995, the Baptist Church at Copper Ridge,

Tennessee, has attracted great interest when some of its congregation reported seeing huge crosses of light in its windows. Rejecting any suggestion that they are created by street lighting or a product of the glass, Pastor Joe Bullard has encouraged investigation believing it to be a portent for a global revival of Christianity. Over several years, the phenomenon has grown. Crosses are also seen during daylight and seem to glow. Apparitions have been reported. Bullard reports how he and a number of others "were sitting on one side of the church when we saw a fully formed man wearing a turban appear on the opposite side of the church and walk slowly forward. Two other people with a cloudy appearance materialized and followed him. Every couple of steps the last person in line turned slightly towards us and waved in a friendly manner." When this curious procession reached the far wall it retraced its route again with the turbaned man in the lead. They marched thus, back and forward, three times before disappearing. Even the normally voluble Bullard was at a loss to say what this might signify. (Xan Phillips, "Do you see the light, brother?", *Fortean Times*, no.95, pp.24–26.)

The popular image of the Indian Rope Trick as performed by an English illusionist and assistant. In India itself, the illusion is created by fakirs who brilliantly manipulate the imaginations of their audience.

The best-known examples of mass visions of the Virgin Mary are those that took place at Lourdes, France, in 1858 and at Fátima, Portugal, in 1917. In the latter incident three peasant children experienced a series of apparitions which culminated in the famous incident of the "dancing Sun" observed by thousands. This event took place on 13 October but it had been predicted by the children at least two months earlier. On the appointed day a huge crowd of people gathered in the rain. The appearance of the Virgin Mary was only visible to the three children, but as the rain stopped many in the crowd saw the sun move and fall towards them.

The memoir of Father Ignatius Pereira, just nine years old at the time, recalls his school class being abandoned as his teacher led the rush to see what the tumult was outside. They found people in the public square weeping and shouting, pointing to the sun. "The solar prodigy was distinctly seen . . . It looked like a ball of snow turning on itself . . . Then suddenly it seemed to become detached from the sky and rolled left and right as if it were falling upon the earth. Absolutely terrified, I ran towards the crowd of people. All were weeping, expecting at any moment the end of the world." This and many other first-hand testimonies were collected by John Haffent for his *Meet the Witnesses* (1961).

The physics of an oscillating sun approaching the earth are not of this reality, so what *did* the expectant crowd see? Janet and Colin Bord, writers with a special interest in visionary phenomena, suggest that it might have been more than a simple delusion: "One person can hallucinate, two together *might* share a hallucination, but it is beyond all possibility that 70,000 people could share a hallucination." (*Modern Mysteries of the World*, 1989). Indeed, other witnesses reported a shower of what they believed to be white flower petals that disintegrated before they touched the ground just before the "dance of the sun"; still others felt its heat dry their clothes or saw prismatic auras and shadows around them.

Monsignor John Quareman, who was there, recalled the moment Lucia, the main visionary, reached the oak tree in which she saw the Virgin. "To my surprise, I saw clearly and distinctly a globe of light advancing from East to West, gliding slowly and majestically through the air." As the Bords put it, if we didn't know the context, the Monsignor might well have been describing a UFO. Another writer, D. Scott Rogo points out in his book *Miracles* (1982) that "Most writers on Fátima claim that the disc *was* the sun. But judging by the descriptions we have . . . the disc was at the wrong elevation and azimuth to have actually been the sun." He concludes: "[It] seems to have been an immense UFO-like silver disc."

An equally spectacular event took place in the small French village of Pontmain on the evening of 17 January 1871. Two young brothers became aware of a beautiful lady smiling at them in the sky, hovering about 25 feet above a neighbour's house. Their parents and a neighbour could see nothing; but twice more the boys described the same vision in the sky, unchanged for an hour or so. We take our details from a contemporary account by Abbé Richard, *What Happened at Pontmain*, reprinted in 1971. After supper, their excited cries soon attracted a crowd of neighbours, none of whom could see anything. The boys pointed out an equilateral triangle of three bright stars, one above the Lady's head, the others

The fourth stage of the Pontmain vision. Many people gathered but only five children actually witnessed the phenomenon.

by her elbows. The crowd saw these and nothing else and, curiously, these stars were never seen again. As more children arrived they were asked to describe what they saw but were not allowed to confer with the others. Three confirmed exactly the vision of the boys.

Then the vision began to change, and the children, now separated by the adults, spontaneously and together shouted out a joyful commentary. A white banner had unfurled at the Lady's feet and letters successively winked into existence. Hymns were sung as the children together called out the letters as they appeared. The first sentence went: "But pray, my children. God will answer your prayers in a short time." There were interruptions as the children exclaimed on the beauty of the apparition. The second line began: *Mon fils se laisse* . . . (My son lets himself . . .) to which a nun commented, "That doesn't make sense," and urged the children to look carefully." It should be *Mon fils se lasse* (My son is wearied)." Several times the children spelled out what they saw, with no mistake: "No, sister, there is an I". Then the sentence completed itself: *Mon fils se laisse toucher* (My son lets himself be moved to compassion). Finally a white vapour obscured the figure from the feet upwards, and slowly the blue oval and stars disappeared. The entire sequence had lasted from 5.30pm to 8.45pm, in the bitter cold of the evening.

Many of these apparitions seem to have been portentous. The very same evening as the Pontmain vision, the advancing Prussian army stopped at nearby Laval, and a few days later an armistice was signed ending the Franco-Prussian War. At Fátima, three secrets were revealed to one of the children, Lucia, by the Virgin Mary. The first was a message of peace (this was during World War I) and a vision of Hell. The second was more prophetic and controversial: "If you pay heed to my request," the vision declared, "Russia will be converted and there will be peace. If not, Russia will spread her errors through the world, causing wars and persecution against the Church."

The third secret, read by successive popes on their accession but supposedly too horrible to be revealed, was finally divulged to the world on May 13, 2000 following a Mass at Fátima in which Pope John Paul II beatified two of the original visionaries. Speaking at the Mass, Cardinal Sodano revealed that the children had spoken of a "bishop clothed in white" who "falls to the ground, apparently dead, under a burst of gunfire", and that this referred to the attempted assassination of the Pope which took place on May 13, 1981 – sixty-five years to the day after the original vision.

Although John Paul always attributed his survival to the direct intervention of the Virgin, and donated the assassin's bullet to the shrine, this is the first official statement that directly links the attempt on his life to the prophecy. It is unlikely to end the mass of speculation as to the prophecy's "true" meaning; especially since the Cardinal's statement insists that the prophetic text "must be interpreted in a symbolic way" and will only be released to the public "after the preparation of an appropriate commentary".

Social anxiety attacks

In times of great social stress it is understandable that large numbers of people are united by the strength of a shared emotion, as happened, for instance, during the London blitz, or in the wake of the tragic death of Diana, Princess of Wales. These cases and the sense of expectation felt by crowds at religious apparition sites (see SHARED VISIONS, p.106) are some of the more positive aspects of collective imagination.

However, it is the destructive aspect of collectively shared emotions that seem more common. Under the heading "Panic" in the indexes to 28 years of reportage in *Fortean Times*, evidence of mankind's capacity to over-react to the slightest (and strangest) provocation is endlessly recorded. The 1990s alone saw major social scares over body organ thieves; child-sacrificing Satanic cults; the preposterous blood-sucking beast of Hispanic America (called Chupacabras); sinister clowns or bogus social workers kidnapping children; and knife-wielding maniacs who hide under cars at shopping malls. The list of contemporary fears of this sort grows weekly – outstripping even cultish anxieties about the end of the world – and is chronicled by folklorists

In the mid-1800s, North America seethed with anti-Catholic propaganda. Popular lectures by Maria Monk and Edith O'Gorman convinced a credulous public that monasteries and convents were hotbeds of vice and corruption and that many captive nuns met horrible deaths under the pretext of exorcism or were walled-up with their unwanted babies. It was the forerunner of the scare in the early 1990s in the USA and Britain about babies bred for sacrifice by all-powerful Satanic covens. Exorcisms often provide a sanctioned opportunity for collective hysteria among the exorcists at the expense of the unfortunate victim. Illustration from O'Gorman's *Convent Life Unveiled* (1871).

such as Jan Harold Brunvand as well by as forteans.

The common thread seems to be a sense of vulnerability and helplessness before an overwhelming threat to personal and social stability. It is not surprising, therefore, that huge numbers of people today are prepared to believe that they are the "prey" of insidious conspiracies run by impersonal, complex and secretive government agencies.

Many of these panics involve either a fear about supernatural assault or, less specifically, the threat from forces beyond our control. At the end of the first millennium, a shift in the perception of evil meant that theologians felt increasingly under direct attack from the agents of Satan. The Devil was no longer content with mere famines and diseases, but began mounting personal assaults on the pious and the faithful. The proof was apparently self-evident; wherever the Church authorities looked they managed to find it. By the fourteenth century the accusation of devil-worship

– imagined or real – had proved so useful in the suppression of heresy, and as a means of social control, that it was extended to attack Jews, who were accused of sacrificing Christian children and stealing Eucharist wafers, and then to witches (see Norman Cohn's *Europe's Inner Demons*, 1976). Demonic possession became an explanation not just for obsessional and deviant characteristics but also for behaviour that was simply eccentric or unusual. Cases of "demonic assaults" abound in the literature, like the famous case of the Ursuline nuns of Loudon whose mass hysteria culminated with the execution of their priest, Urbain Grandier, in 1633.

The catastrophic notion of "Satanic child abuse" that obsessed some Fundamentalist groups and social workers in Britain in the 1980s, led to the break-up of many families. Convinced that Satanic "covens" were kidnapping or breeding unbaptized children for sacrifice in Cleveland, Rochdale, Nottingham, Orkney and Wales, well-meaning childcare workers conducted dawn raids to "rescue" children thought to be at risk. Unorthodox examinations for "tell-tale" marks and relentless questioning of children failed to secure any convictions in court (and made still harder the work of social workers investigating genuine cases of child abuse).

The parallels with the "questioning" of those accused of witchcraft in earlier times was not lost on Jean La Fontaine, commissioned to report on the issue to the Department of Health in 1994. In her unofficial account, *Speak of the Devil* (1998), she describes a modern version of the "witchfinder". In one case – which would be funny if the consequences were not so tragic – a sinister Latin-like chant taken as evidence of a Satanic ritual turned out to be based on a child's description of the "Doh, Re, Mi" song from *The Sound of Music*. A similar series of high-profile cases in the US led at first to extraordinary miscarriages of justice, as recorded by Mark Pendergrast in *Victims of Memory* (1997). Many of these were over-turned in court as judges condemned the use of hypnosis and related methods by psychotherapists to "recover" alleged suppressed memories.

Psycho-sexual anxiety is a particularly fertile area of investigation as Sigmund Freud was quick to realize. Freud's idea of a castration complex applies not just to the case studies of individuals. In *Sex and the Paranormal* (1999), Dr Paul Chambers examines the widespread social panics involving anxiety about penile loss or disfigurement. In the fear known throughout the Far East as "koro" – from the Malay word for turtle – the sufferer imagines his penis is withdrawing into his body; in females this applies to breasts and labia. Koro is not a trivial phenomenon; the outbreak in Singapore in 1967 resulted in the hospitalization of 446 men and 23 women in a single day. Medical studies of the phenomenon are full of tales of victims' bizarre attempts to prevent their genitals being seized by "fox spirits" or vanishing forever, including the application of special clamps. The novelist Anthony Burgess, in his autobiography *Little Wilson and Big God* (1987), describes the desperate behaviour of a terrified Chinese koro victim in Kuala Lumpur: "He stole a superfine jeweller's knife and rammed it in [his penis], screaming on the sunlit street."

Koro panics, observes Chambers, tend to be short-lived as they spread in precisely the same way as rumours. Their subjective nature is evident, as thoughtful doctors have successfully ended epidemics by treating victims with placebos. One panic was sparked by a boy frightened by an insect bite on his penis, while another, in Thailand, was blamed on duck eggs sold by immigrant Chinese farmers.

In the African variant, chronicled in *Fortean Times* (no.56, p.33), black magic is blamed. It seems to have begun in 1990, in Nigeria, with rumours that magicians seeking penises to sell as magical amulets could steal them with a simple touch. In the town of Enugu, a man getting off a bus suddenly screamed that his penis had been stolen. The passenger in front of him was grabbed on suspicion of being a magician and a riot ensued in which the bus driver was accidentally shot dead by police. Similar incidents occurred across West Africa. In August 1996, a mob in Cameroon hung three men for penis thefts and others were badly beaten. One eighteen-year-old said that, after shaking hands with a Nigerian friend of his, he "felt an electric-like current run through him, and a feeling that his manhood had retreated into his stomach."

In January 1997, the panics spread west along the Gold Coast to Ghana, where at least twelve people accused of being sorcerers died at the hands of mobs. In Abidjan, the capital of neighbouring Ivory Coast, a suspected penis-snatcher was burnt to death by a mob, triggering three days of rioting in which a further two people died. In an attempt to calm the situation the Ivory Coast government issued a statement denying the penis-snatching rumours. Other, minor, incidents were reported from Gabon, Cameroon and Togo until, in August 1997, over forty "suspects" were lynched during serious rioting in Senegal. Chambers points out that most of these locations lie along the same international highway and speculates that "the rumours were spread along it, possibly by truck-drivers".

In 1985 Enugu was once again the location of a strange panic when a rumour circulated that a female spirit, called "the mermaid", was due to visit schools in the town to avenge the killing of her daughter. When several children at a school near the Idaw River screamed that they saw the mermaid entering their classroom, the others fled in terror and nine were killed in a crush on the staircase (see *New York Post*, 1 November 1985).

In 1993, an extraordinary rumour spread rapidly through the south-western Chinese city of Chongqing. For reasons that were never explained, children had convinced each other that a huge American robot was out of control and heading their way. They believed it would destroy the city and devour any child dressed in red. Soon most of the city's children were refusing to go to school unless they were protected by garlic and crucifixes made from chopsticks (see *South China Morning Post*, 22 March 1993).

A very similar panic had occurred ten years earlier in Houston, Texas, where, in January 1983, a story flashed through several junior-high schools that an army of Smurfs – the blue cartoon characters – carrying guns and knives, had invaded several other schools, killing their headmasters. According to the rumour, anyone wearing blue clothing would also be killed. To add to the confusion the opposite rumour – that anyone wearing blue was safe – also circulated. Many children refused to go to school. The panic took a few days to wind down, helped by teachers claiming other cartoon characters were being drafted in to fight the Smurfs and by the appearance of the supposedly dead headmaster. It seems the story was sparked by a garbled version of an innocuous local TV report of the arrests of forty members of an adolescent gang called The Smurfs, for petty crimes (see *Newsweek*, 4 April 1983).

Children figure prominently in many of these social anxiety attacks. The famous Salem witchcraft persecutions of 1692 began with the careless talk of children, as did the awful pogrom at Mora in Sweden in 1669 which ended with 85 people burned alive accused of taking 300 children to a witches' sabbath. What interests us here is the role of the imagination – which children possess in unfettered abundance – in creating anomalous experiences. When communicated to other children who participate enthusiastically, a kind of collective "possession" takes place. This applies to adults too; in fact the capacity to "play" imaginatively, by the so-called "high fantasizers", seems to be a key ingredient in many accounts of strange phenomena. Some UFO investigators automatically assess the fantasizing ability of those who have claimed abduction by aliens. In many of the phenomena we discuss in this book the question of whether an event "really" happened takes second place to the fact that the witness *believes* that it did. And their tales, told with conviction, go on to convince others. This might not be scientific in approach or content, but these matters are a core part of human experience. Dreams and beliefs can change "reality" just as much as anything factual or physical can.

5

The Good Folk

5

The Good Folk

The little people

In the summer of 1998, an exhibition in the Manx Museum at Douglas, Isle of Man, recorded some of the last native speakers of the Celtic Manx language. One old man, a blacksmith who had never left his own parish, complained that, since the language had died out, people no longer saw fairies as commonly as they once did. He himself had not seen one for thirty years.

It is the same story everywhere. Records of old country life tell of regular encounters with a mysterious kind of people, generally smaller than ourselves and less solid. At one time they played an active part in daily existence and it was important to keep on good terms with them. In tribal societies and wherever the modern world has not intruded, the existence of fairies and spirits is accepted as an observed fact, and there are various traditional ways of relating to them. As the link between human and fairy folk has gradually weakened, the smaller race seems to have retreated into wilder regions.

Systematic persecution of fairies began in early Christian times and intensified during the Middle Ages. Zealous friars and exorcists or "limitours" were sent through every district to drive out "demons". Services were held in remote fairy glens, by woods, springs, streams and country dwellings.

"This maketh that there be no fairies" explained Geoffrey Chaucer in the fourteenth century. Previously, he said, "all this land was full of fairies". Their expulsion was not an unmixed blessing. Women could then walk about the country without fear of being molested by elves and incubi, but the new danger to their virtue was from the "limitour himself".

Dr Ingram, a famous preacher who died in 1879 at the age of 103, is said to have driven the last of the trows, the local fairies, out of the Shetland Islands, forcing them to migrate to the Faroes. John Nicholson, author of *Some Folktales and Legends of Shetland* (1920), was told this by an islander who had it direct from an old trow-woman, too feeble or obstinate to make the journey with the rest of her kind. Yet according to Mr W.E. Thorner of Luton, Bedfordshire, whose letter is printed in Marwick's *The Folklore of Orkney and Shetland* (1975), the trows of the northern isles are not quite extinct. Mr Thorner, who spent some time in the Orkneys during World War II, came across a party of them one stormy winter's day on the high cliffs of Hoy. There were about a dozen of them, "wild men" with sallow complexions and long dark hair, small in stature and with unkindly expressions on their faces. All of them were dancing.

A once popular theory about Little People was put forward by David MacRitchie in 1890. He suspected that the fairy Fin Folk of northern

This cache of delicately made 'fairy coffins' containing dressed wooden effigies was discovered in a cleft below Arthur's Seat, in Edinburgh, in 1836. Some had rotted away, from which it was thought that a series of burials had been made over many years.

Scotland, and fairies in general, were memories of actual Finns or Eskimos or some other small aboriginal race who had never become extinct but had retreated into ancient mounds and underground places in remote areas. This could be plausible in some cases, but it does not explain the majority of fairy sightings. A more likely suggestion was put forward by the Reverend Sabine Baring-Gould, the prolific nineteenth-century folklore writer. As a small boy he saw fairies running about and playing among the horses, as he sat in the sunshine on the side of his father's coach. He told his father who took him inside the coach and out of the sun, whereupon the vision faded. This made him believe that fairy-sightings were generally caused by sun or light. He admitted that this theory did not entirely explain why different people saw the same kinds of fairy forms, but his reasonable suggestion was that children see fairies in the forms that they have been accustomed to from stories and illustrations.

Relevant to Baring-Gould's theory are the many accounts of apparitions which begin with a sighting of strange lights. One example is the story told to W.Y. Evans-Wentz, a scholar of Celtic and Tibetan traditions, by T.C. Kermode, a member of the Isle of Man parliament. He and another young man were walking through the country one autumn night, when his friend pointed across a small river and exclaimed, "Oh look, there are the fairies. Did you ever see them?" Kermode looked and saw "a circle of supernatural light which I have now come to regard as the 'astral light' or the Light of Nature, as it is called by the mystics and in which spirits become visible". Into the circle of light he saw, arriving in twos and threes, "a great crowd of little beings . . . dressed in red. They moved back and forth amid the circle of light." When Kermode's friend shouted and waved his stick, the fairies vanished. The description of their movement as "in order like troops drilling" recalls the linear progression of phantoms through the Copper Ridge Baptist Church (see SHARED VISIONS, p.106) or of ghostly military formations (see SPECTRAL ARMIES, p.216).

Modern reports of luminous apparitions and mysterious little entities tend to support Baring-Gould's suggestion, that fairies are seen in forms that are conventional at the time. The convention these days is that they are alien beings from space – in other words space-age fairies. Janet Bord, in *Fairies: Real Encounters with Little People* (1997), and French ufologist Jacques Vallée, in *Passport to Magonia* (1969), both make a good case for UFO aliens as the modern equivalents of the fairies.

In all the numerous accounts over the last

fifty years of strange lights and creatures seen together, there is no real evidence of extraterrestrial origins. But the myth has become established, and nowadays every strange light is identified as a spacecraft and every strange entity as a space person! That is merely guesswork, and it conceals something that has become obvious to modern folklorists – that most of the elements in modern UFO lore are repetitions of traditional folkloric themes. The phenomenon of "UFO abductions" is a good example (see ENCOUNTERS WITH ALIENS, p.137).

This continuity between traditional folklore and modern UFO reports has been noticed by many writers. For example, in *Flying Saucer Occupants* (1967) by C. and J. Lorenzen there are some fifty reported encounters with "little men" in the 1950s and 1960s, always associated with a spherical or disc-shaped airship and all described in detail by named witnesses. To quote just one example, at noon on 20 August 1965 an engineer, Alberto Ugarte, his wife and another man were visiting Inca ruins near Cuzco, Peru, when they saw a shiny disc, only about five feet in diameter, land on an ancient stone terrace. Several little creatures – described as of strange shape and dazzling brightness – stepped out of the craft, but on seeing people climbed back in and departed.

Similarly, on 7 January 1970, two farmers near Imjärvi, Finland, were skiing through a glade at sunset, when they observed a strange reddish luminous cloud descend to hover quite close to them. The swirling mist seemed to shroud a metallic UFO that emitted a buzzing sound. An intense beam of light shone from its base down to the snow and within it they saw a small humanoid figure, about 90cm high, holding a box. The men described the "creature" as having small pointed ears and a weird hook-like nose, claw-like fingers and wearing a conical hat, green overalls and boots. It was "luminous like phosphorus but its face was very pale". A light shot from the box at the men, nearly blinding them; it was followed by trails of coloured sparks. Then the lights withdrew into the cloud-craft and it flew off. The men said they were not frightened, but laughing with awe and excitement. One of them collapsed when he went to move and found his leg paralysed; the other helped him back home. (Kim Hansen in Hilary Evans's 1987 anthology, *UFOs 1947–1987*.)

The significant detail in these cases, as in Kermode's fairy sighting in the Isle of Man, is that the little creatures developed out of the initial strange light. This accords with Baring-Gould's belief in light as a principal cause of fairy apparitions. The source and nature of that mystical light has never been identified.

An interesting department of fairylore concerns the "physical fragments of fairyland", referring to objects alleged to have been made by fairies and taken away from them. One of these is an exquisite glass vessel, the "Luck of Edenhall", taken from the fairies by a butler to the Musgrave family of Cumberland and now in the Victoria and Albert Museum, London. In the Royal Irish Academy, Dublin, is an ancient medical treatise which was

A 17th-century woodcut of fairies dancing. Other interesting ingredients include the face of the Green Man in the tree and the door to the Otherworld in the hill shaped like a classic UFO.

presented by fairies to a Connemara man whom they took away to their land of Hy Brasil and later restored to his people, having initiated him into all the secrets of medicine.

More mundane objects include the fairy coat, a description of which is given in Patrick Harpur's *Daimonic Reality* (1994). Found in 1868 in an Irish fairy ring by John Abraham ffolliott, "It was only six and a half inches long and only one and three quarter inches across the shoulder. Fully lined and with cloth-covered buttons, its high velvet-trimmed collar was greased and shiny from, presumably, long wear, while other parts were frayed

Peter Vangslev-Nielsen, the sexton of Agerup Church in Holbek, Denmark, shows the silver chalice that is kept there. It was said to have been part of a fabulous fairy hoard and to have been stolen from the fairies several hundred years ago.

and the pockets holed and scorched as if from a tiny pipe." Also in Harpur's book is a picture of a tiny, well-worn shoe, thought to have been discarded by a fairy. It was found by a farm labourer in southwest Ireland in 1835. It is just two and seven-eighths inches long and obviously worn through use. On a lecture tour of America, the author Dr Edith Somerville gave the shoe to Harvard University scientists, who examined it minutely. They confirmed it had tiny hand-stitches and well-crafted eyelets (but no laces), and was thought to be of mouse skin.

Photographs purporting to show fairies and such are few and questionable, but one case has been particularly influential. In the Christmas 1920 number of *Strand Magazine*, Sir Arthur Conan Doyle, who spent his royalties from the Sherlock Holmes stories on psychical research, announced an event "so sensational as to mark an epoch in human thought". Printed with the article were photographs of two young girls with elves and fairies. Their names, not disclosed at the time, were Elsie Wright of Cottingley, near Bingley, Yorkshire, and her cousin, Frances Griffiths. Behind their home was a glen where the girls liked to play, making friends with its tiny inhabitants. In 1917, when Elsie was sixteen and Frances ten, she borrowed her father's camera to photograph them.

Mr Griffiths, a Theosophist, showed them to Edward Gardner, a friend of Conan Doyle. Until recently, the photographs defied analysis and many authorities were impressed by the girls' sincerity. Conan Doyle in particular; in *The Coming of the Fairies* (1922) he declared that the photos may be proof of "the existence on the surface of this planet of a population which may be as numerous as the human race, which pursues its own strange life in its own strange way, and which is only separated from ourselves by some difference of vibration."

Perhaps the most complete summary of the case of the Cottingley Fairies is that by folklore professor Paul Smith. In his contribution to Peter Narváez's collection of new studies of fairylore, *The Good People* (1991), Smith describes the detailed forensic inquiry into the photos by Geoffrey Crawley, editor of *The British Journal of Photography*. In a series of ten articles (beginning in December 1982), Crawley concluded that the girls had used cut-out illustrations of fairies, retouching them to create fakes. To Crawley and several other modern interviewers, Elsie and Frances, admitted unequivocally that they had fabricated the images but, to their dying day, they insisted that they had actually seen fairies at the Cottingley glen, and that at first, for their own pleasure, they had tried to represent what they had actually seen.

Fairies, today, languish in a backwater of folklore, overshadowed by cute Disneyesque images and storybook illustrations. But the field still has its scholars and collectors. One of them, Janet Bord, recently told us: "Contrary to popular belief, fairies are not simply part of folklore. Many real-life sightings continue to be reported today. Researchers who collect accounts of fairies are sometimes surprised by reports from the most unexpected sources, often people who would never have expressed any belief in fairies – until they saw one for themselves."

For any modern or new reader, we recommend Janet Bord's well-referenced study, *Fairies* (1997), which includes such bizarre experiences as the Hull policeman who, in 1977, challenged three strange figures in a peculiar patch of mist on a playing field (they vanished); the sisters who, in 1940, looked out of their bedroom window in Cornwall to see a small white-bearded man in a pointed red hat driving a tiny car in circles on their lawn; and the children in Hertford who saw a tiny "biplane", with a wingspan of about a foot, "swoop over the garden fence [to] land briefly, almost hitting the dustbin and then took off again," its leather helmeted pilot waving to them as he flew off.

This otherworldly nature of encounters with little people seems to have a modern element in it, perhaps snatches of half-remembered TV or cartoon imagery (see also the attack of the Smurfs in SOCIAL ANXIETY ATTACKS, p.110). When a group of children playing in Nottingham's Wollaton Park, in 1979, reported seeing a cavalcade of thirty brightly-coloured little cars each with two gnome-like figures in (smaller than themselves) much was made of the Noddy-like descriptions they gave to their headmaster. The children were not frightened but unusually excited, saying the cars had chased them. Curiously, the cars had no steering wheels and "flew" over obstacles in their path.

Many of these experiences are reported by children under the age of ten, but these are not simple or trivial psychological events. They seem to flourish in the boundary between the conscious and subconscious mind where the nature of "reality" is to be malleable (see also ENCOUNTERS WITH ALIENS, p.137) and this seems an appropriate ground for a body of belief that is in transition. Reviewing these and other "high strangeness" narratives, in his book (*Borderlands*, 1997), historian Dr Mike Dash comments: "If the fairies that used to get around on foot or on horseback can now drive cars and fly aeroplanes, there is no reason why they could not pilot UFOs."

This illustration by Phiz, from Keighley's *Fairy Mythology* (1828), shows a similar theft of a chalice from the fairies.

One of the 'fairy photographs' taken by two young Yorkshire girls which so fascinated Sir Arthur Conan Doyle.

Mystical lights

Lights in the sky, under the sea and in caverns deep beneath the earth. Mysterious lights that flit across marshes, hover over ancient burial mounds and haunt the paths to cemeteries. Lights that enter houses and explode. Lights that seem to follow people. We hear of fairy lights, spook lights, aerial lights and others that cannot be categorized – playful or menacing, gaseous or animate, casual or purposeful.

The phenomenon has many names and identifications – UFOs, fireballs, spirits of the dead, fairies, will-o'-the-wisps, jack-o-lanterns, earth lights, sky dragons. Ball lightning is a comfortable name for floating balls of light, but no one quite knows what it means. As recently as 1943 W. J. Humphries in *Ways of the Weather* still upheld the traditional opinion that light balls were "a humbug" or optical illusions. Here are the conflicting views of two other "authorities": "Floating ball lightning is not dangerous to human beings, even when it appears in the middle of a group of persons; it appears to avoid them [as] it avoids good conductors." (Professor B.L. Goodlet, *Journal of the Institute of Electrical Engineers,* July 1937.) "It is very dangerous to touch a fireball. An inquisitive child once kicked one and thereby caused an explosion which killed eleven cattle and threw the child and a companion to the ground." (Frank Lane, *The Elements Rage*, 1945.)

Explanations for the will-o'-the-wisp vary from ignited marsh gas to spirits of the dead. Often it is said to display intelligence or purpose, sometimes malevolent in intent but sometimes revealing treasure.

A 'ghost light' photographed in Basle Zoological Gardens in 1907.

to support this belief. Several examples were collected from witnesses by the former US Consul in Wales, Wirt Sikes, author of *British Goblins* (1880). He heard about the pale, moving lights called "corpse candles"; their appearance on a path leading to a burial ground was taken as a warning that a funeral party would soon pass that way. On one occasion three corpse candles were seen by all the passengers on the coach from Llandeilo to Carmarthen as they crossed the river bridge by Golden Grove. A few days later three men were drowned at the spot when their coracle capsized.

The number of lights is supposed to foretell the number of coming deaths. John Aubrey's *Miscellanies* (1696) contains the story of a woman who saw five lights in the room occupied by five maids in the house where she worked. The room was then plastered, a fire was lit to dry it, and the fumes stifled the girls in their beds.

Baron von Reichenbach, famous for his earnest inquiries into the nature of the "magnetic" lights which some people see as auras, was curious about the lights, wraiths, spectres or whatever, often seen in graveyards. One of his colleagues, Miss Leopoldina Reichel, had the gift of seeing such things. They appeared to her as dancing lights, some as big as men, others small, "like dwarfish kobolds". She was able to move among them and whisk them about with her skirt. Reichenbach, who believed himself to be the discoverer of an essence he called "odic force", applied his theory to the evidence and produced this impressive-sounding explanation of graveyard luminescence. "It is a carbonate of ammonium, phosphuretted hydrogen and other products of putrefaction, known and unknown, which liberate odic light in the course of evaporation. When the putrefaction comes to an end, the lights are quenched the dead have atoned." (*Letters on Od and Magnetism*, 1926.)

The Reverend Sabine Baring-Gould in *A Book of Folklore* (1913) also invoked "phosphuretted hydrogen" as the explanation of graveyard lights.

Lane illustrates the "ball lightning" phenomenon with the following incident: "A young girl was seated at a table when she noticed a large ball of fire moving slowly across the floor of the room in her direction. As the fireball neared her it rose and commenced to spiral round her. It then darted towards a hole in the chimney and climbed up it. On reaching the open air it exploded just above the roof with a crash that shook the entire house."

Tradition associates the appearance of floating lights with death, and many incidents are recorded

On one occasion his brother's overcoat, thrown over a grave, became impregnated with the stuff, causing him to faint. Baring-Gould quotes several instances of lights which have appeared to give warning of death by travelling along a coffin route or entering the house of a doomed person; but though he is prepared to accept the reality of stationary lights above graves, he rejects the moving variety: "That these flames should travel down roads and seek houses where there is one dying is, of course, an exaggeration and untenable."

"as bright and stable as electric lights". One procession of such lights was seen to fly in formation from their usual haunt, a "fairy fort" named Crillaun near Castlebar in the west of Ireland, to another such earthwork on the opposite side of a lake. About the nature of the will-o'-the-wisp MacManus is undecided. Sometimes it seems to be inanimate and may be kicked or whisked about like Leopoldina's kobolds; yet there was a girl he knew, "very intelligent and well balanced", who was followed by a moving light, coming for her at running speed and changing direction to pursue

A fireball seen during a storm in Salagnac, France, in September 1845.

The moving lights which are called ball lightning when they occur indoors become wildfire or will-o'-the-wisps in the open air. They are variously explained as combusted methane (marsh gas), fairies or spirits, but there is no proof for any theory. According to the 1970 *Encyclopedia Britannica*, "no entirely satisfactory explanation has been put forward" for the phenomenon. It may be significant that as the fairies disappeared from their once familiar haunts, so did the will-o'-the-wisp. In 1855 a correspondent in *Notes and Queries* asked whether in fact such a thing existed outside poetic tradition and was answered by several people claiming direct experience and providing descriptions.

Dermot MacManus in *The Middle Kingdom* (1959) tells of personal encounters with "fairy lights", which he says are different from the will-o'-the-wisp because they are of many colours and

her home. "To this day she is convinced that it was directed by real intelligence."

A terrifying moving light chased and caught Terry Pell of Spalding, Lincolnshire, as he drove his vegetable lorry towards Warminster in Wiltshire in the early morning of 10 August 1965. Warminster at the time was undergoing one of its periodic plagues of weird aerial visitations, details of which are faithfully chronicled by local journalist and author, Arthur Shuttlewood, in his book *The Warminster Mystery* (1967). Forty-five minutes before Mr Pell had his adventure, at 3.45am, Mrs Rachel Atwill a few miles away, saw what many others in the district have reported seeing, a bright staring light in the sky. She was awakened by a loud droning noise, looked through the window of her bungalow and saw the light, dome-shaped on top, hovering over the range of hills opposite.

It stayed there for twenty-five minutes, humming and flickering, then vanished. Mrs Atwill suffered a headache and had to drink brandy. She recognized the shape in a photograph taken nineteen days later by Gordon Faulkner of Warminster and published in the *Warminster Journal* and the London *Daily Mirror*. When Mr Pell saw the light it was floating fifty yards in front of his lorry, having flashed into view from over the hills to his left. It was red and looked like a giant headlight or a human eye. It advanced on Mr Pell's lorry and fastened itself to the windscreen, vibrating. The lorry stopped. Its sleeping passengers, Mrs Pell and daughter Wendy, woke up to see the light ball soar aloft and away. They were frightened but unhurt.

This incident is far from unique. UFO literature abounds in modern events of the sort, and many older cases are to be found in collections of folklore. Here is a report from Brad Steiger's *Flying Saucers are Hostile* (1967), given without reference to its original source. Mr William Howell of Texas was driving home at 11.15pm in the summer of 1965. Like Mr Pell he had two sleeping passengers,

his brother's children, and he was also near a prominent local landmark, Foggy Hill. A light appeared overhead: "It seemed to head directly for my car. It gave off a bluish light that became so bright the entire car seemed bathed in a blue haze. If that thing would have been a meteor, it would have landed with a big crash. It didn't. It made a sharp turn to the southwest and shot off in a burst of speed."

When religious people see visions, they may identify them as saints or archangels, but their accounts usually begin with the appearance of a glowing light. Modern encounters with "extra-terrestrials" often begin the same way. Strange lights feature in many sections of this book, associated with many different kinds of phenomena. Some of them have an otherworldly quality, as if they are the lights of fairyland, the underground kingdom or some other world which we can never deeply explore. Reichenbach and other scientists have tried to find explanations, but nothing has ever been established, and it may be in the nature of things that nothing ever will be.

Phantom music and strange voices

In every treatise on hallucinations there are references to phantom music and disembodied voices, discussed in terms of mental and nervous aberrations. Psychiatrists are suspicious of this phenomenon, and a patient who admits to hearing voices is usually a candidate for the mad-house. The following example of "fallacious perception" by a patient is quoted by Edmund Parrish in *Hallucinations and Illusions* (1897): "Every tree which I approach, even in windless weather, seems to whisper and utter words and sentences . . . the carts and carriages rattle and sound in a mysterious way and creak out anecdotes . . . the swine grunt names and stories, and hens seem to scold and reproach me, and even the geese cackle quotations." In the sounds of nature, however produced, men have always heard the music and poetry of other worlds. To reduce the phenomenon to clinical terms is to damn at a swipe all that is intuitive and mystical in human nature.

Voices seem to manifest both internally and externally, though we are aware that this distinction may be an illusion. This question was raised by C.G. Jung in his *Alchemical Studies*. He tells of an African soldier who was spoken to by a tree. Modern psychology assumes that the voice was imagined or "projected" by the soldier. But between that and the traditional belief that the tree actually spoke, Jung suggests a third attitude that accepts the reality of a spiritual or daimonic existence, often mingling with our own. Patrick Harpur's *Daimonic Reality* (1994) demonstrates the advantages of this overview of irrational phenomena.

Among examples of voices heard internally are the famous cases of Martin Luther, St Ignatius Loyola, Benvenuto Cellini and Sigmund Freud. Socrates had a *daemon,* a voice that warned him of actions likely to offend the gods. Some voices torment the listener, and others urge on to action, as in the cases of St Joan (who heard the Archangel Michael and Saints Catherine and Margaret), St Francis of Assisi (who heard a voice from a crucifix

In 1765 the violin virtuoso and composer, Giuseppe Tartini, had a dream in which he gave the devil his violin who then played it 'on a level I had never before conceived was possible'. Tartini awoke and tried to transcribe what he had heard but the resulting 'Devil's Trill' Sonata, though better than anything he had written before, was apparently a pale reflection of the demonic original.

bidding him to "rebuild my church"), or George Fox (who founded the Quaker movement at a similar prompting). The phenomenon continues today and is interpreted by many UFO "contactees" as telepathic contact with beings from other worlds or dimensions.

Of the "externalized" voices, there can be no greater claims than those of the gods who thunder down laws, messages and warnings from above. Before this materialist age people were more sensitive to communications from nature; objects and animals could speak like men if the spirit moved them. The classical historian Herodotus was told by the priestesses of the Dodonian oracle of Zeus that the sacred grove containing the famous whispering oak was revealed by a talking bird that alighted in its branches. Wood from this tree was said to have been set into the keel of the *Argo* by Athena, giving the ship the vocal power to warn Jason of danger ahead. Disembodied voices are still associated with portents, especially warnings of the death of a friend or relative, and are so astonishingly common that even Camille Flammarion's great three-volume compilation, *Death and its*

Mystery (1922) could not exhaust the fund of anecdotes. Newly-bereaved widows – including Anna, the wife of Charles Fort – often tell of hearing their late husband's voice.

We are interested in the sounds and voices that often accompany "poltergeist" activity. They have a very strange quality; sometimes faint, sometimes so abnormally loud that they are more like shockwaves of great force. Consider the fantastic story of Calvados Castle in France, which suffered an astonishing range of phenomena from October 1867. They were still continuing when reports were published in the *Annales des sciences psychiques* in 1893. They told of furniture levitating and moving about, the vanishing of Lourdes medals and other holy charms used in a continuous exorcism, doors and windows opening by themselves, and the pulling-off of bedclothes. With these effects came a variety of sounds. They ranged from creaks, groans and footsteps to organ music being heard for hours after one of the occupants had ceased playing. The castle constantly shook under heavy blows "so strong that objects suspended on the wall rattled in their places. . . To acquire some idea of their violence, one must imagine a wall collapsing, or a horse, or cannon-balls thrown against a door." At times the whole building shook violently "from top to bottom", yet there was little damage, and the noises could only be heard inside the castle.

These effects are typical of poltergeist sounds, the characteristics of which are exaggeration and imitation. Alfred Monin's biography of the Curé of Ars, St John Vianney, says he was particularly persecuted by this kind of phenomenon. At times his courtyard would ring with the noise of a great army, camping, marching or charging. In the winter of 1824–25, the Curé could not sleep for the noise of a large flock of sheep passing over his head, and whenever he entered a lower room of his house, everyone could hear sounds, as though "a large, escaped horse" was prancing round him invisibly. The Curé was a noted ascetic, but a demon voice used to mock him and accuse him of indulging in luxury, crying, "Vianney, Vianney,

you truffle-eater, you! Are you still alive; haven't you died yet? I'll get you!" A similar vocal perse-cution is described by Evelyn Waugh in *The Ordeal of Gilbert Pinfold* (1957).

One of the strangest of the loquacious entities in our records took up temporary lodgings with the Dagg family of Clarendon, Quebec, in 1889. According to *Light*, December 1889, an investi-gator, Percy Woodcock, visited the family on 15 November, and was taken by the adopted daughter of the house, Dinah, to a shed where previously she had seen a strange man. Nervously she called out, "Are you there, Mister?" To Woodcock's astonishment, from the middle of the empty shed, about four feet away, came the clearly audible voice of an old man. It cursed them both in deep, gruff tones, using language that Woodcock would not record and which *Light* would hardly have printed. It said, "I am the devil. I'll have you in my clutches. I'll break your neck." Woodcock and Mr Dagg talked to the voice for several hours, during which

An engraving illustrating Robert Burns's poem *Tam O'Shanter*. As he passes by Kirk Alloway, the inebriated Tam witnesses 'Warlocks and witches in a dance' presided over by 'Auld Nick in shape o' beast'.

it admitted causing the mysterious fires (see Fiery Persecutions, p.150) and teleportation of household objects. It apologized for the inconvenience it had caused. During the conversation the foul and obscene language abated, and the voice promised to leave the following Sunday night.

When the news spread, people came from miles around. On the Sunday the voice was on good behaviour, though at times rather tactless. It answered questions and seemed to display an intimate knowledge of anyone who entered the house, often proclaiming aloud embarrassing details of their lives that they would rather have kept private. On being congratulated about his change of character the voice said: "I am not the person who used the filthy language. I am an angel from heaven sent to chase him away." The transformation was not yet complete, for the entity occasionally lost its temper in a volley of blasphemy, but by Sunday evening it was joining the crowds in singing hymns in such a "beautiful flute-like voice" that it was now implored to stay. The next day the Dagg children announced that it had finally left them. They described how a "beautiful man", resplendently dressed in shining clothes, had hugged them and bid them goodbye. They sang a final hymn together (the "angel" playing a small harp-like instrument) and as the children watched they saw a light, "red like a fire", blaze at his feet, rising to surround him as he ascended, singing sweetly, into Heaven. Fort adds a typically laconic footnote to his account of the story – "It sang a hymn and departed."

Some of these voice phenomena must have been quite impressive. A poltergeist case recorded by Dr Reid Clanny, *A Faithful Record . . . of Mary Jobson* (1841) features "exquisite music", heard by many witnesses independently, followed by a voice of "angelic sweetness" quoting from the scriptures. Another person who attracted disembodied voices was Clement Hofbauer, who later became a saint. In 1801 his sermon to a crowded church in Warsaw was frequently interrupted by the cries of a phantom baby. When he continued, voices broke out in the air all over the church, crying that it was on fire. Flames and smoke were seen everywhere, even from the street. Some minutes later, after panic subsided, these were found to be as ethereal as the voices. In the process of St Clement's canonization, the Church accepted the evidence of demonic intervention in his mission.

Phantom music is a favourite ingredient in ghost and fairy stories: here are two modern accounts. An empty office in Peter Street, Manchester, was haunted by thin piping tunes heard by many people in the building. A letter to the *Manchester Evening News* (24 October 1968) suggests it was the same phantom flautist heard in the same office block two years previously. A weird strumming from a piano gave over a hundred

FORTEAN PICTURE LIBRARY

The phantom drummer of Tedworth, Wiltshire, as represented in Joseph Glanvill's *Saducismus triumphatus* (1681). The Tedworth case, in which a noisy and violent haunting made life a misery for the Mompesson family, is probably the first major poltergeist case in British annals. The disturbances were blamed on the spirit of a drummer boy but, over the course of a year from January 1662, the drumming noise gave way to heavy blows which shook walls, moving furniture, foul smells, leading to physical assaults and levitations of Mompesson's children.

impromptu concerts in a house in Humber Avenue, Coventry, Warwickshire. According to Bill Duncan, the occupier, quoted in the London *News of the World* (13 January 1974): "It sounds as though someone is plucking the strings. . . It doesn't sound anything like modern music."

We have emphasized the strange, demonic side of phantom voices and music, but these phenomena have their positive aspects. Many people have been inspired to sainthood or great deeds by voices from the far blue yonder. And many favourite tunes in Celtic and other traditions of folk-music owe their origin to someone who heard the music played by fairies. At one time, it seems, every spot of supernatural reputation had its own particular music which could be heard there on the appropriate day. In W.Y. Evans-Wentz' classic, *The Fairy Faith in Celtic Countries* (1911), is a typical story of this kind, recorded in the Isle of Man.

"William Cain, of Glen Helen, was going home in the evening across the mountains near Brook's Park, when he heard music down below in the glen, and saw there a great glass house like a palace, all lit up. He stopped to listen, and when he had the new tune he went home to practise it on his fiddle; and recently he played the same fairy tune at Miss Sophia Morrison's Manx entertainment in Peel."

Finally, in another account from Wales, we have the remarkable adventure of David Williams of Penrhyndeudraeth in Gwynedd, as told by Elias Owen in his *Welsh Folk-lore* (1888). One evening, Williams, a servant, was walking home behind his mistress; he thought she was a few minutes ahead of him but, when he arrived at the door, he was amazed when he was told she had arrived three hours earlier. He told of seeing a brilliant meteoric light "followed by a ring or hoop of fire, and within this hoop stood a man and woman of small size, handsomely dressed . . . When the hoop reached the earth these two being jumped out of it and immediately proceeded to make a circle on the ground [in which] a large number of men and women instantly appeared and to the sweetest music that was ever heard commenced dancing round and round the circle."

Owen says the sight was so entrancing that Williams stopped a few minutes, or so he thought, to observe the legendary dance of the fairies. "The ground all around was lit up by a kind of subdued light," and he could see every movement with clarity. Owen continues: "By and by, the meteor . . . appeared again and then the fiery hoop came to view and when it reached the spot where the dancing was, the lady and the gentleman who had arrived in it jumped into the hoop and disappeared in the same manner in which they had reached the place." Immediately, the other Little People "vanished from sight" and Williams was left alone in the darkness to continue his journey.

If this is an honest account, we must accept that these events did not happen in everyday "reality" but in what some folklorists call the "mythical landscape" – more a state of mind than a geographical location. They reinforce our view that fairylore has much in common with ufology and the association takes place in our psyches as well as in our culture. Apart from the strange light, the luminous transport, repetitive movements and the celestial beings, this case embodies the motif of "missing time" that so strongly features in modern UFO encounter cases, preceding its famous exemplar (the Betty and Barney Hill incident) by nearly a century (see ENCOUNTERS WITH ALIENS, p.137).

Taken away and brought back

People are always vanishing. Some do it fair and square, once and for all, either of their own volition or somebody else's; others turn up again. Not surprisingly, those who return from mysterious absence feel the need to explain, but some of these explanations, far from enlightening, only make us wonder more about the people who did not return. Whatever explanation is on offer – "murdered by colleagues"; "went out for a pack of cigarettes and wandered off"; "abducted by fairies" or "extra-terrestrials" – the phenomenon is essentially the same: a person inexplicably vanishing and unaccountably returning. Any hypothetical explanation, as we keep pointing out, varies with fashion.

We have many records of people disappearing, suddenly, mysteriously and finally, but from the storyteller's point of view there is something wrong with all of them. They are too short, without proper endings. For example, the London *Daily Chronicle* (30 July 1889) said that on the thirteenth of that month Mr Macmillan of the famous publishing firm had climbed to the top of Mount Olympus. He was seen waving from the summit but, despite careful searches and rewards offered, no trace of him was ever afterwards found. That is all. Again, on 25 November 1809, Benjamin Bathurst went to enter his carriage outside a German inn. Then, says the Reverend Sabine Baring-Gould in *Historical Oddities* (1889), "he stepped round to the heads of the horses – and was never seen again".

As Dr Mike Dash explains, in *Fortean Times* (no.54, pp.40–44), Bathurst was a British intelligence agent on active service in Prussia during the Napoleonic Wars and his disappearance took place in a busy courtyard at night, so perhaps we should not make too much of it. Of course famous and notorious cases are often explained in time or by diligent research but many others have no satisfactory conclusions.

In December 1800 the boat from Lewis in the Outer Hebrides went to relieve the three keepers of the lonely Flannan Islands lighthouse. They were not there and no one knows what happened to them. Two RAF pilots, Day and Stewart, crash-landed in the Iraqi desert in 1924. Their footprints were clearly visible in the sand some distance from the aircraft, and then suddenly there were no more prints and no further news ever again of the two airmen.

Hoaxes and false cases clutter this field and obscure the material of value. For example, through poor scholarship, early ufologists have enthusiastically promoted a clutch of stories that seemed to suggest people could be abducted into another dimension through a vortex in full view of witnesses. These stories generally concern a young man – variously called David Lang, Oliver Lerch or Charles Ashmore – who is last seen crossing a field. Search parties find nothing. Sometimes there are a trail of footprints which end suddenly, or a faint voice calling for help is heard on the anniversary of their disappearance at the very spot the person vanished. We confess that we too were taken in by some of these stories but excellent work has gone into investigating many of them. No fewer than seven stories of this type have been found to be variants of some of the supernatural stories of Ambrose Bierce, an American writer whose own disappearance in war-torn Mexico in 1914 is still unsolved.

But genuinely mysterious disappearances do happen. Sometimes they lead to dreadful miscarriages of justice. The seventeenth-century legal writer Sir Edward Coke refers, in his *Institutes*, to a case in Warwickshire in which a little girl of eight or nine went missing. She was an orphan, looked after by her uncle, and due to inherit the family estate at the age of sixteen. The uncle was required to produce her, could not do so, and in panic dressed up another little girl and presented her as his niece. He was exposed, charged with the niece's murder, convicted and hanged. Years later the girl, having reached the age of sixteen, turned up and claimed her estate. She had run away, she said, and had been living with some kind people in the next county.

In earlier times, similar incidents probably gave rise to the kind of stories recorded by nineteenth-century folklorists, such as T. Crofton Croker. In his *Fairy Legends* (1825), Croker repeats a firsthand account he heard in the Vale of Neath, South Wales, of the disappearance of a certain Mr Rhys. One evening Rhys and another man, Llewellyn, were driving some horses to the farm where they worked. On the way Rhys fancied he heard music and told Llewellyn to go on ahead with the horses as he wanted to stay behind for a while and have a dance. By morning his friend still had not returned and when searches failed to discover him, Llewellyn was suspected of Rhys' murder. Fortunately a local farmer persuaded all parties, including Llewellyn and the narrator, to revisit the scene of the disappearance. There Llewellyn heard the

Illustration of Travis Walton's abduction by UFO in November 1975, from *Official UFO* (July 1976). Walton, of Snowflake, Arizona, said he was hit by a bolt of light and awoke on an alien craft, managing to escape a few days later. At first highly influential, his story is now widely believed to be a fantasy based on his interest in science-fiction and ufology.

music. His foot was on the edge of a fairy ring. "Put your foot on mine, David," said Llewellyn to Croker's informant. The man did so, and the others likewise. Then all heard the music and saw a crowd of little figures dancing in the ring with Rhys among them. Llewellyn dragged him out of the ring and it seemed to Rhys that he had only been dancing for five minutes or so. The experience left him so melancholy that he soon died.

A record of an abduction by fairies, reprinted in J.O. Halliwell's *Illustrations of the Fairy Mythology* (1845), from a pamphlet of 1678 in the British Museum, is the most interesting we know of. Its details are remarkable – not least because it illustrates how many of our phenomenal sections overlap – and it is attested to both by the man who was taken away and by the witnesses to his disappearance and return. Three weeks before the pamphlet was written, a Dr Moore with two companions was travelling in Wicklow, Ireland, and staying at an inn in Dromgreagh, near Baltinglass. He began to speak of fairies, saying that as a child in that country he had several times been taken off by them, on which occasions his mother would call in a local wise woman who was effective in retrieving him. As he spoke it seemed to him, as he said later, that a troop of men entered the room (see also SPECTRAL ARMIES, p.216) took hold of him and dragged him off.

All that his companions saw was that Dr Moore was being drawn out of the room by an unseen force (see also INVISIBLE ASSAILANTS, p.143). They tried to hold on to him, but he vanished and they raised the alarm. The innkeeper, who was apparently used to such happenings, sent for the old woman. She declared that Dr Moore was in a wood about a mile away with the fairies and that, if by her magic she could prevent him from eating or drinking during his absence, he would be restored unharmed; otherwise he would return in a consumptive state and would soon pine away. Early the next morning Dr Moore re-entered the inn, hungry and thirsty from a night spent in rapid travel between places of fairy feasts and revelry. Every time his abductors had offered him food, he said, it had been unaccountably struck out of his hand – presumably through the woman's magic – and at daybreak he had found himself alone within sight of the inn.

Local histories everywhere are full of such incidents, and the theme continues in the many similar reports of our own time. We can even find them shorn of any association with fairies or spirits, except that these are often replaced by appeals to a "fourth" dimension, or aliens. Consider the tale of a terrified elderly couple, in December 1873, who were discovered dazed and in their nightclothes at a Bristol railway station. As reported by

Dragged from the fairy ring. Illustration from Wirt Sikes's *British Goblins* (1880).

the *Times* (11 December 1873), Mr and Mrs Cumpston were asleep in a Bristol hotel when they were wakened by noises. Mr Cumpston stepped out of bed onto the floor, which seemed to open, he said. He felt he was falling into a black void and was saved only when his wife seized him and pulled him back. Panic-stricken, they climbed out of the room by a window and went in search of a reassuring policeman.

A phenomenon which was once very active, but seems scarcely to have been reported in recent years, is that of the changeling – the substitution, by the fairies, of a sickly alien child for a healthy human one. An old history of the Isle of Man, quoted in Halliwell's *Illustrations of the Fairy Mythology* (1845), provides the story of a Manx woman whose babies strangely disappeared shortly after their births. On the first two occasions, the disappearances were attended by various noises and disturbances in her house, which brought the neighbours running. The babies were each found some distance from the bed . . . dropped by the fairies, as they explained it. Soon after her third baby was born, the woman saw it being levitated out of the room by an invisible force. She cried out and her husband came in and pointed to the baby by her side; but it was a sallow, wrinkled child, not like her own, and it lay naked with the original baby's clothes tied in a bundle beside it. It lived on for a few years, never speaking, walking or defecating, and eating nothing but a few herbs.

Wirt Sikes, in *British Goblins* (1880), has an anecdote about Jennet Francis of Ebwy Fawr valley in Wales. One night she awoke to feel her infant son being pulled from her arms. Screaming out and praying, she succeeded in pulling him back. An interesting detail, in view of the spiritual powers which many cultures attribute to people who have been teleported (see also AVIAN ABDUCTIONS, p.333) is that the son grew up to become a famous preacher.

In earlier times, when the existence of an abducting or teleporting force was recognized in the terminology of the fairy faith, local witches or magicians were at hand with the appropriate spells to remedy the "sudden disappearance" effect. In the case of changelings, the folklore record is full of various procedures by which parents can regain their abducted baby. Other traditions hint at forgotten methods of recapturing older people whom the fairies had taken. Robert Kirk, minister of Aberfoyle in Scotland and the author of *The Secret Commonwealth of Elves, Fauns, and Fairies* (1691), is said to have died on the Fairy Hill near his home in 1692. One legend about him is that on the anniversary of his death (or, variously, the christening of his posthumous child) he appeared again with the fairy host and could have been liberated if the right spell had been enacted.

Fairies abducting a human baby. Illustration from Wirt Sikes's *British Goblins* (1880).

6

Invisibles and other Assailants

6

Invisibles and other Assailants

Encounters with aliens

Perhaps the single largest subject dominating the spectrum of strange phenomena today concerns extra-terrestrials, a lively topic which has seen a succession of bloody skirmishes between many different schools of interpretation. Are aliens really in control of Earth space and, as some claim, abducting humans with ease and impunity for their nefarious experiments?

It is only a matter of time before scientists will decide whether the origin of life on Earth was a unique event – an idea that Bible Fundamentalists share with some conservative scientists – or that life in the universe *must* be prolific. Through the 1990s, biologists discovered several different kinds of terrestrial nanobacteria (a nano is a billionth of a metre) capable of living in hostile or toxic environments without light, heat or oxygen. Their tiny size and toughness are perfectly suited to travel through space in meteoric or cometary debris. If nanobacteria are discovered on Mars, by the armada of probes that will be sent there in the first decade of the new millennium, the ubiquity of life will be confirmed.

This makes it more probable that other civilizations could have crossed space to visit Earth in our distant past, intervening in our biological and cultural development, as the ancient gods were

said to have done. This is the view of the "ancient astronaut" theorists, who interpret suggestive myths and anomalous archeological data as evidence of alien intervention. Modern ufology revolves around whether this intervention has continued to the present day and accounts for UFO sightings and abductions. This is the "extra-terrestrial hypothesis" (ETH) and is in direct opposition to the cultural and behavioural interpretations of UFO abduction phenomena which maintain they are the product of folkloric and psychological processes.

To unravel this important mystery we have to make a small detour to understand how sightings of "lights in the sky" could become so intimately associated with alien spaceships. The sighting which kick-started the "UFO era" was made by pilot Kenneth Arnold while flying a plane over the Cascade Mountains, Washington state, on 24 June 1947; he described the motion of several shining bat-winged craft as like "saucers skipping over water". Fascinated, first the US press then the rest of the world's media, adopted the term "flying saucers" and reports of mysterious lights in the sky became commonplace in daily papers.

These reports and the people who made them might have remained figures of fun if not for a significant development that occurred about a fortnight later. On 8 July 1947, an unspecified accident occurred at the Roswell Army airfield, in New Mexico (the precise details of which have

INTERNATIONAL UFO MUSEUM, ROSWELL

From time to time, this picture of a dead alien surfaces on the Internet or in news media as evidence of the recovery of alien bodies from the legendary UFO crash at Roswell, New Mexico. It is, in fact, a model made for the 1994 TV movie *Roswell* and was donated to the International UFO Museum in Roswell by producer Paul Davids.

always remained unclear). The USAF spokesman of the day made a lighthearted reference to a crashed flying saucer and produced debris. At the height of the Cold War, this was a clumsy attempt to distract media attention from several top secret projects. The base was home to the first nuclear bomber and high-altitude radar balloons and parachutes were being tested, the latter using crash-test dummies (which may account for the later rumours of alien bodies). When it was apparent that the ploy had backfired – it was headline news across the world – the military commanders again mishandled the story by denying the initial flying saucer story for one involving one of their balloons. The farce provided the stereotype for most cases of official denial of UFOs and the now-common accusation of "cover-up".

British sociologist and ufologist Hilary Evans, called the popular imagination in 1947 "prepared ground". Recognizing the influence of ancient myth and legends about inhabited other worlds, Evans and others sought specific origins for the key motifs of ufology and found them in the pulp science-fiction of the 1930s and 1940s. In the anthology *The UFO Mystery* (1998), he wrote: "It is no exaggeration to say that virtually every feature of the flying saucer myth – paralyzing rays, levitating beams, telepathic communication and alien abduction – was anticipated by the ingenious authors."

Between 1898 (when H.G Wells's *War of the Worlds* was published) and the mid-1940s, popular science-fiction had become increasingly interested in secret and exotic civilizations (both terrestrial and extra-terrestrial). By the time of Arnold's sighting, the idea of encounters with aliens was well-known to avid readers and it seemed a logical step to suppose the many reports of strange lights in the sky might be the craft of alien visitors. The very first edition of *Fate Magazine*, launched about six months later, featured Arnold's sighting on the cover. It mimicked the appearance of a science-fiction magazine but its monthly "factual" servings of fortean and paranormal mysteries, mixed with increasingly lurid tales of strange encounters and cover-ups by government agents, laid the foundations of modern ufology and the complex mythology of alien abductions.

By 1950, the UFO phenomenon was rampant and firmly entrenched in the popular imagination worldwide, through pulp magazines and the burgeoning genre of "B" feature films such as *The Flying Saucer* (1949) – thought to be the first representation of a UFO in a movie. This film and the Roswell incident inspired two hoaxers to convince a well-known journalist of the day, Frank Scully, to write *Behind the Flying Saucers* (1951), a book notorious for introducing the idea that the military had recovered dead aliens from a crashed UFO and puzzled out some of their technology.

Historically, the 1950s were the "golden age" of ufology; the overall tone was optimistic, with prophets, like George Adamski, Howard Menger and George King, among others, claiming contact with "space brothers" either telepathically or in person. The channeled messages warned of impending doom if mankind did not mend its ways but also offered salvation in the form of an airlift by flying saucers.

The encounters with aliens described in this period are thoroughly romantic. For example, South African Elizabeth Klarer claimed, in 1956, an interstellar affair with Akon of the planet Meton. "I found the true meaning of love in mating with a man from another planet," she wrote later. The honeymoon between aliens and earthlings was gradually soured by more frightening experiences, such as science-fiction author Whitley Streiber's claim to have been sodomized by aliens who burst into his bedroom in December 1985.

But the first big case of abduction and medical examination was that of Betty and Barney Hill in September 1961, driving on a lonely New Hampshire road late at night. Puzzled by a short journey that somehow took seven hours, unusual nightmares and strange, painful marks that had suddenly appeared on their bodies, the Hills eventually sought medical and psychiatric help. In 1963, they began sessions of hypnotism with Dr Benjamin Simon, to reconstruct their memories of that night

of "missing time". To their collective astonishment Betty and Barney told of being dragged from their car by little beings and subjected to a curious fertility examination. Betty had samples of skin and hair taken, a fingernail cut off and a needle inserted into her navel. Barney suffered the indignity of a device attached to his groin to remove sperm. Betty continues to believe in the reality of her experience, long after Barney's death in 1969. Dr Simon – cited in John G. Fuller's *Interrupted Journey* (1966) – later concluded that the episode was a fantasy, a type of *folie à deux*, based on Betty's unsettling dreams which she had discussed with Barney.

Other abductions, following a more or less similar formula, were reported all through the 1970s, their publicity establishing the now familiar description of large-headed, large-eyed, slit-mouthed beings, pallid and impassive (dubbed Grays). This was only one type in an increasingly surreal line-up that included reptilians, avians, insectoids, hairy dwarves, tall blond "Nordics", metal slabs and shapeless fleshy blobs (see Patrick Huyghe's *Field Guide to Extra-terrestrials*, 1997).

If the variety of aliens visiting Earth doesn't strike you as absurd then consider the "most unsettling development to date", as Huyghe calls the 1991 publication of the results of a poll by the Roper Organization on the extent of belief in alien abduction. The figures caused consternation and laughter in equal measure; extrapolating from their sampling figures, it was estimated that two percent of the American population had been abducted at some time in their lives – that is around five million per year, or 22 million per year if you extend it globally. Even Betty Hill was moved to comment, sarcastically: "With 4,000 people being abducted every night, I don't know how the planes would get through!"

This highlights one of the biggest problems facing those seeking to explain the abduction mystery – the dream-like character of so many narratives. A good example is the disturbing experience of Jean Hingley, of Rowley Regis in the Midlands, who was visited by fairy-like aliens on 4 January 1979. Investigating an orange glow in her garden, Mrs Hingley saw a hovering orange sphere. She felt its heat and noticed her dog frozen as if time stood still. Three child-sized winged beings shot indoors, past her, and began shaking the Christmas tree. They had "dead faces" and flew without using their wings. She was aware of them jumping on her sofa "like naughty children" and talked to them about Jesus, the Queen and the place of women in the home. From time to time, they would paralyze her by shooting a dazzling beam of light from their helmets.

Thinking they wanted something to drink, Mrs Hingley went to the kitchen and returned with glasses of water and some mince pies on a tray. Their motions were jerky and often concealed by the blinding ray but she thinks that they ate and drank her offerings. When she tried to show them how to smoke a cigarette they recoiled from the flame of the lighter. Deafening noises heralded the end of the visit and they glided back to their glowing sphere. Immediately upon their departure into the sky, Mrs Hingley felt pain in her arms and legs; feeling weak she crept slowly over to the sofa and lay there for a long time, numb and confused. She later had a nervous breakdown and reported trouble with her eyes and ears. Albert Budden, who investigated the case, at first suggested that Mrs Hingley experienced some kind of altered state of consciousness that had facilitated poltergeist-like and stigmata-like phenomena but later suggested that she had hallucinated due to "pollution" from power-lines and other sources of electromagnetic fields and radiation. (*Psychic Close Encounters*, 1995.)

Beyond the simple apocalyptic mission attributed to the ufonauts of the 1940s and 1950s, modern abductions are not without a mystical dimension of their own. Jean Hingley was a deeply religious woman who saw continuity, not difference, between her faith, the psychic experiences she had experienced since childhood and her alien encounter. Likewise, George King believed he was contacted in May 1954 by a telepathic "voice" from a 3500-year-old divine "Master" on Venus. The Aetherius Society, founded by King in 1956, mixes yoga, Theosophy and a science-fiction version of spiritualism involving trance channeling of alien entities.

Betty Andreasson Luca, whose experiences began in 1967, also believed her abductors were sent by God. Her experiences, recalled with the aid of hypnosis, began in childhood (1944) and were still happening in the 1990s. They include the sublime (a heavily symbolic vision of a giant phoenix) and the ridiculous (a vision of hundreds of headless "monkeys" with eyes on stalks crawling

A sketch of a huge mystery airship which appeared over Oakland, California, on 20 November 1896. A wave of similar sightings across the USA in 1896–97 led to panic and curiosity in equal measures and talk of a 'mysterious inventor'. The craft's speed and powerful lights were in advance of anything known at the time.

all over a building). Like Dante, Betty was granted a guided tour of the Otherworld, accompanied by a classic Gray called Quazgaa. (Raymond Fowler, *The Andreasson Affair, Phase Two*, 1982.)

Jacques Vallee's 1969 book *Passport to Magonia*, first presented the view that UFO abductions are simply continuations, in space-age imagery, of the

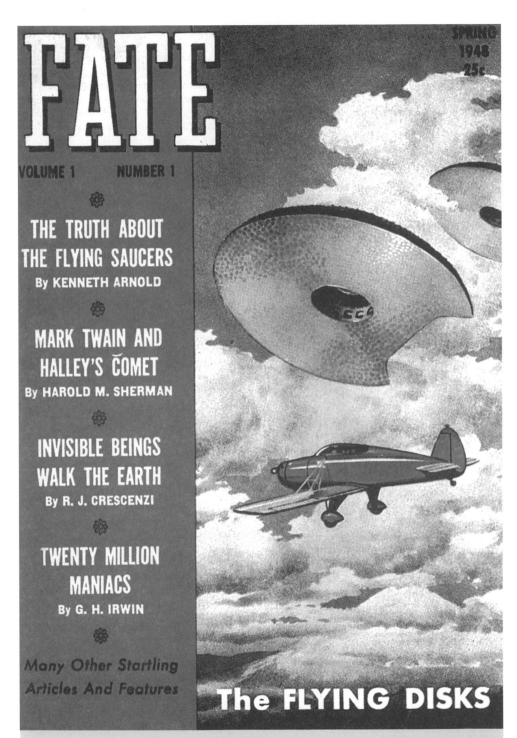

FATE

SPRING 1948 25¢

VOLUME 1   NUMBER 1

THE TRUTH ABOUT
THE FLYING SAUCERS
By KENNETH ARNOLD

MARK TWAIN AND
HALLEY'S COMET
By HAROLD M. SHERMAN

INVISIBLE BEINGS
WALK THE EARTH
By R. J. CRESCENZI

TWENTY MILLION
MANIACS
By G. H. IRWIN

*Many Other Startling
Articles And Features*

The FLYING DISKS

Pilot Kenneth Arnold sighted a formation of flying objects over the Cascade Mountains in June 1947. This cover illustration to *Fate Magazine* Spring 1948 was based on his description.

traditional kidnappings by fairies. Today, this theory is seen as rather simplistic and a new generation of writers, led by Patrick Harpur the author of *Daimonic Reality* (1994), have extended the idea by arguing that the fairy mythos and the alien mythos are not contiguous but both spring from the same core of subjective experience. Regardless of the different cultural imagery that colours such experiences, nearly all of them share the characteristics of shamanic visions. Folklorist Thomas E. Bullard, who analysed over thirty years of abduction cases, noted how many of them seemed to "hark back to primitive initiatory rituals and shamanic journeys, suggesting archetypal patterning behind human experience with otherworldly beings." Such experiences seem to mark out the experiencer from the rest of society, changing their lives in some profound way and giving them a sense of mission. We suspect that in an archaic society, Jean and Betty would have been honoured as shamans, people who have access to a realm of good and evil spirits.

The physical and mystical phenomena of shamanism, as described in Mircea Eliade's *Shamanism* (1964), include an initiating sickness, a descent or ascent to the Otherworld, negotiation with elemental spirits or gods and magical flight – all elements paralleled in close encounters. The initiatory trance of shamans, from Australia to the Arctic, includes variations of ritual dismemberment and resurrection – surely the prototype of the operations of the alien doctors. Eliade describes this dismemberment as an "initiatory death . . . an ecstatic experience that can be brought on by the suffering of a sickness". We think it is significant that many abductees were physically ill or under great stress mentally, emotionally or socially, at the onset of their visionary experience; the characteristic of many shamans is that they incorporate their "sickness" into their mythologizing, just as abductees do.

In our Western industrialized, computerized world there is little place for shamans and, denied a function, these individuals do not fare well. Some are resilient enough to find a niche for themselves – as teachers or alternative healers – but the rest, without a personal or social use for their visions become disturbed and even self-destructive. It is in that negative state of mind – depressed, alienated, helpless and purposeless – that the "contact" experience or vision takes on a terrible malevolence.

Against this "psychological" explanation of abductions stands the influential school of ufology led by Dr David Jacobs, a historian at Philadelphia's Temple University, John Mack, a professor of psychiatry at Harvard, and Budd Hopkins, a New York artist. In their various writings, these three urge us to believe in the literal reality of an ongoing alien invasion. Many confused people have come to them for help, only to be told that aliens have "prepared" selected humans for a long-term "career", using sophisticated mind-control techniques to cover their tracks (clearly with little success). The "chosen" ones are repeatedly abducted for their ova and sperm, and the women used as surrogate mothers for implanted alien-human hybrid foetuses which are removed before full-term.

Patrick Huyghe, writing in *The UFO Mystery* (1998), notes: "The ideal abduction case would involve two or more people who did not know each other but who gave corroborating details of the same abduction incident to independent investigators." Despite his familiarity with the key investigators and their material, Huyghe concludes that no such case has ever come to light.

Our conclusion is that "abduction" is a species of visionary or spontaneous shamanic experience rooted in the human psyche, and that the potential for it is widespread throughout the population. So-called "rationalists" will, no doubt, be shocked to realize that after several centuries of fighting the forces of supernaturalism and superstition, modern man is just as vulnerable as he ever was to attacks by invisible and malevolent entities: but as long as the experiences of alien abductees are taken literally and their visionary elements isolated and ignored, we suspect there will be little progress in understanding them.

Invisible assailants

In May 1876 there was panic in the streets of Nanking, China. Invisible demons were on the loose, snipping off people's pigtails. The citizens took to walking about with their hair clutched in their hands for safety. The terror spread to Shanghai and other towns, and then another panic developed. This time it was the "crushing mania", a fear of being crushed while sleeping. The rampage of these demons lasted for nearly three years. Other outbreaks have occurred since, and the phenomenon has a long history. According to De Groot's *Religious Systems of China* (1892), the first recorded outbreaks of the hair-snipping panic were under the Wei dynasty in 477 and 517 AD.

Newspaper reports of these panics in China raised many a smile at English breakfast tables, but these were wiped away when in December 1922 a similar scare broke out in London. Young ladies were being seized by a man who hacked off their hair and then disappeared "as if by magic", eluding the bands of would-be gallants who came rushing to the rescue. We have heard psychological explanations for this and respect them on their own terms, but they do not account for the physical fact that people have suddenly and mysteriously been deprived of their hair in a public street in broad daylight.

Thefts of hair seem to feature in attacks of all kinds, from poltergeists to UFOs. During the haunting of the Dagg family in Canada, as reported by the *Brockville Daily Times* (13 November 1899), one of the little girls "felt her long braid suddenly pulled; she cried out, and the family found it almost cut off, simply hanging by a few hairs. The same day the little boy said that something pulled his hair all over.

BLOWS INVISIBLE.

MR. Brograve, of Hamel, near Puckridge in Hertfordſhire, when he was a young man, riding in a lane in that county, had a blow given him on his cheek: (or head) he looked back and ſaw that no body was near behind him; anon he had ſuch another blow, I have forgot if a third. He turned back, and fell to the ſtudy of the law; and was afterwards a Judge. This account I had from Sir John Penruddocke of Compton-Chamberlain, (our neighbour) whoſe Lady was Judge Brograve's niece.

A 17th-century account of an unseen attacker from John Aubrey's *Miscellanies* (1696).

Immediately it was seen by his mother that chunks of his hair, also, had been cut off."

In *The Other Side* (1969) Bishop James Pike tells of the strange disturbances that followed his son's suicide. In one incident, a female assistant awoke one morning to find some of her hair singed off in a perfectly straight line. This was repeated again the next morning, and three weeks later one of the burned-off locks mysteriously appeared on a bedside table. An even stranger case can be found in the *Religio-Philosophical Journal* (4 October 1873). During a succession of poltergeist-type happenings at Menomonie, Wisconsin, a young girl was standing by her mother with no one else present when her hair was sheared off in chunks close to her scalp, vanishing as it was cut.

We now turn to a more shocking sort of violation, the symptom of which is the appearance of wounds, as if the victims had been stabbed or shot with invisible weapons. The *New York Times* (8 December 1931) printed a story by the captain of the German steamer *Brechsee*, which had put in at Horsens, Jutland, the day before. The captain had seen a man unaccountably wounded during a storm. Before his eyes a four-inch-long wound appeared on the man's head and he fell unconscious to the deck. On 16 April 1922 a man was brought to Charing Cross Hospital in London with a stab wound in his neck. All he could say was that he had strolled into a turning off Coventry Street, received a wound and fallen to the ground. A few hours later another man was brought to the hospital with same wound and the same story; and later that day a third man was unaccountably wounded in that same turning off Coventry Street. The story was reported in *The People* (23 April 1922).

Charles Mackay in *Extraordinary Popular Delusions and The Madness of Crowds* (1841) relates in detail the alarm in Paris in March 1623 at the rumoured powers and antics of the Rosicrucians, a clandestine, esoteric and mystical brotherhood. The Marais du Temple quarter soon acquired a bad name, for "no man thought himself secure of his goods, no maiden of her virginity, or wife of her chastity . . . and people were afraid to take houses in it, lest they should be turned out by the six invisibles of the Rose-Cross". Similarly, on 26 September 1923, the *Daily Mail* facetiously reported that Indian coolies in Lahore believed that a *mumiai* was abroad, an invisible thing that grabbed people in broad daylight. In 1890 the *Religio-Philosophical Journal* reported a scare from Japan, in which an "invisible" was blamed for slashes about an inch long that appeared on people's necks. This reminds us of the tale told in the second branch of the *Mabinogion* (a collection of medieval Welsh myths and folktales) in which Caswallawn, son of Beli, donned the Veil of Illusion to slay some rival chieftains, who could see nothing of the assassin, only the sword as it materialized seconds before cutting them down.

The coat of Kaspar Hauser. After mysteriously appearing in 1828, Hauser was fatally stabbed on 14 December 1833 by a 'black-cloaked man' of whom only the snowy footprints were found.

Frank Edwards in *Strangest Of All* (1962) details the case of Jimmy de Bruin, who worked at Farm Datoen, South Africa, and who seemed to be the centre of poltergeist disturbances in August 1960. During an investigation, Police Chief John Wessels and three constables heard twenty-year-old Jimmy

scream with pain. He was wearing shorts and they could see cuts appearing on his legs even as they watched. The next day, in the presence of two officers, a deep gash appeared on his chest, although nothing had penetrated his shirt. These cuts continued for several days. They were clean, as though made with a razor or scalpel – and all who saw them agreed that the young man could not have inflicted them on himself. Fort advanced the idea that if other things could be teleported, then perhaps wounds could be projected to appear on people. It is a common detail in cases of invisible assailants that the wounds appear on flesh beneath clothes which show no signs of penetration – a phenomenon that also occurs in cases of STIGMATA (see p.76).

The poltergeist connection was more clearly demonstrated in the celebrated Phelps case in Stratford, Connecticut, in 1850. The disturbances centred on Dr Phelps's twelve-year-old son, Harry. From the description of them in Father Herbert Thurston's *Ghosts and Poltergeists* (1953) it seems as if the boy was under constant attack. Stones were pitched at him, and a violent force would lift him off the ground to strike his head on the ceiling. Once he was thrown into a water-tank; and before the eyes of shocked visitors he was caught up and suspended in the branches of a tree while his clothes were methodically torn to ribbons by something invisible. In a pamphlet published by a Mr Durbin in 1800, *A Narrative of some Extraordinary Things that Happened to Mr Richard Giles's Children*, it is said that the damage done to the children by invisible assailants included teeth-marks on their flesh. This was also a feature in the case of Eleonore Zugun (see PROJECTED THOUGHT-FORMS, p.72). Witnesses in the Giles outbreak described the horrific sight of the little girl throttled by an invisible hand, seeing the sides of her throat pushed in, but without any obvious contraction of her neck muscles. Later the children were pushed and pulled, slapped and spat upon. On one occasion, five witnesses saw "their arms bitten about twenty times that evening . . . They could not do it themselves as we were looking at them the whole time. We examined the bites and found on them the impression of eighteen or twenty teeth, with saliva or spittle all over them, in the shape of a mouth . . . very wet [and] clammy like spittle, and it smelt rank".

We have many reports of "phantom snipers" whose "bullets" leave no other trace of themselves than a wound. In Chapter twelve of *Wild Talents* (1932), Fort mentions three murders in which the police could only suspect that the murderers had changed the clothes of the victims, for they had bullet wounds with no penetration of their clothes. The oldest similar account we can find is of a man pushing a cart near Berigen, Germany, on 2 October 1875. According to *Popular Science* (vol.15, p.566), he heard a whirring sound, inaudible to his two companions, and found that his right arm had been shot through as if by a musket ball.

Here is the most gruesome account we know of assault by "invisibles". In 1761 five women were returning from collecting sticks near Ventimiglia, in northern Italy. Suddenly one of them cried out and dropped dead. Her companions were shocked by what they saw. Her clothes and shoes were torn into fine shreds and scattered up to six feet around her. There were wounds on her head that exposed the skull; the muscles on her right side had given way exposing her intestines; her sacrum was broken and most internal organs were ruptured or livid; her abdominal region bore many deep and parallel incisions, and the flesh of one

Invisibly inflicted wounds on 13-year-old Romanian Eleonore Zugun in 1926.

hip and thigh was almost carried away, exposing the pubic bone and the broken head of the femur which had been forced from its socket. This horrific event was reported to the French Academy of Sciences by M. Morand, and the *Annual Register* for that year quotes him as noting that these grievous effects took place with no sign of penetration of the woman's clothes, nor was there any blood on the scene, nor any sign of her missing flesh. It was as though she had been the focal point for an instantaneous, silent and deadly explosion.

Mysterious mutilators

In 1973 panic and strange rumours spread across the American Midwest. Rustlers were using unmarked, cargo-type helicopters to spot vulnerable herds of cattle from the air and radioing information to hidden ground teams. There were hundreds of reports that these objects had been seen hovering over herds and rising from cow-pastures. A strange thing about them was that they were completely silent, as if without engines. Farmers were warned to bring their livestock in at night and some even began taking potshots at anything that flew over their property.

Stories of these phantom rustlers lasted into 1974 when they were overtaken by an even more extraordinary development: UFOs were reported to be landing and mutilating cattle. One of the first accounts was in the Florida *Miami Herald* (16 October 1973). Police at Dayton, Ohio, had received about eighty reports of flashing UFOs in the area, one of them from a woman who claimed "hysterically" that a UFO had landed, killing a couple of cows. By 1974, reports of strange lights and unidentifiable helicopters had become inextricably tied up with the ever-growing number of stories about mutilated cattle from Colorado, Utah, North Dakota, Minnesota, Mississippi, Pennsylvania, Iowa, Missouri, Arkansas, Illinois and Nebraska.

Many of these cases are detailed in *INFO Journal* (14) and by Ed Sanders in the magazine *Oui* (August 1976). The most striking feature of the outbreak was the nature of the mutilations. Ears, eyes, lips, udders and tails were carefully removed and internal organs were surgically extracted in a purposeful, even ritualistic manner. Some carcasses were found entirely drained of blood. In one case the intestines had been drawn out through a hole in the cow's side and piled neatly by its head (recalling a similar gesture by Jack the Ripper). A sinister aspect of these mutilations was the absence of footprints or bloody trails – an encouragement to the UFO and other conspiracy theorists. Evidently gangs of mad, airborne butchers or surgeons were abroad; many believed that a rich, well-organized occult fraternity was responsible. The press had a field day, revelling in gory descriptions and

The mysterious death of a horse called Snippy during the 1966–67 UFO flap. No explanation was ever found for Snippy's bizarre wounds, the missing brain and vital organs, and the skin stripped cleanly from head and neck.

stoking up the paranoia, even hinting at secret human sacrifices. Several investigators of the mystery claimed they were being threatened by "Satanists".

Tom Davies, writing in the *Minneapolis Tribune* (20 April 1975) attempted to scotch the occult and UFO theories. About 400 cases, he claimed, could be explained by a peculiar combination of blood disease (accounting supposedly for the complete absence of blood in most cases) and predators, which naturally go for the soft flesh first. But this does not cover all the observed facts. Witnesses and investigators have confirmed the surgical precision of these mutilations. The draining of blood is a feature still unexplained, and so is the lack of tracks or footprints around the carcasses, which have often been found on snowy or muddy ground. Besides, the authorities have never explained why, if disease was a factor, it was not more widespread, and attacks by predators cannot account for all the bizarre details of the mutilations.

This is a disgusting subject, but it is neither new nor localized. Outbreaks of mysterious animal mutilations and killings were known to the ancient Romans, who blamed them on "demons". For lack of anything more concrete, this type of explanation has remained popular, even in modern times. The demons could be in human form, but if so they are remarkably elusive. In all the many, world-wide epidemics of animal mutilations, human culprits have scarcely ever been detected. A rare prosecution took place in 1903 when, following a spate of sheep, cattle and horse rippings across Staffordshire, a young Anglican clergyman, George Edalji, whose father was a Hindu, was arrested and found guilty. The evidence was weak, the police were suspected of prejudice and, when Sir Arthur Conan Doyle intervened on his behalf, Edalji was exonerated. Conan Doyle believed that the atrocities were caused by demons. (Mr X, "The Edalji Case, Again", *Fortean Times* no.21, pp.8–9.)

Typical of our data is a series of obscene attacks on horses and cattle in western Sweden during 1991 and 1992. Police were looking for a gang of perverts and sadists, but none was ever found and the horrors gradually ceased. They began again in England. In 1992, particularly in the southern counties, horse-owners were shocked to find that their animals had been tortured and sexually violated overnight, slashed with sharp knives, with broomsticks shoved into them and barbed wire attached to their genitals. Once again, sadists and cultists were sought in vain. A detail that puzzled the owners was that their horses seemed not to have resisted or kicked out against interference with their hindquarters. A suggestion was that they had been drugged or anaesthetized. This passivity on the part of the victim has also been noticed in American cattle-mutilation cases, and some veterinarians believe that, before being assaulted, the creatures were made placid by the drug Ketaset.

As in many other strange subjects, Charles Fort was an early investigator. In chapters 13 and 14 of *Lo!* (1931) are his notes on the winter of 1904–05, during which time there occurred wave after wave of dreadful attacks on animals. At Hexham, Northumberland, something was killing sheep nearly every night, sometimes on both sides of the River Tyne on the same night. That winter there was more slaughter at Gravesend in Kent and Badminton in Gloucestershire, involving "terrible losses for poor people".

In May 1910 something began killing six or seven sheep a night, biting into their necks and sucking their blood, but leaving the bodies untouched. In 1874, sheep were killed in a vampiric manner around Cavan, Ireland; as many as thirty a night had their throats cut and blood sucked, but none of their flesh was eaten. Wolves were blamed (the last wolf in Ireland was killed in 1712), and finally a dog was shot. But the killings continued in the same region. In 1906 something killed over sixty sheep in two nights at Guildford and Windsor. At Llanelly in 1919 hutches were entered by "something" that broke the backs of rabbits. In 1925 a strange black animal "of enormous size" tore sheep apart, terrifying the Edale region of Derbyshire into fears of werewolves.

In 1995 a similar phenomenon initiated a panic that swept through many Hispanic American communities, it was feared that a strange beast, characterized as a "demonic, alien, kangaroo vampire", was killing small livestock and domestic animals by sucking their blood through small puncture marks – hence its name Chupacabras (or Goatsucker). The scare began among rural farmers in Puerto Rico in March and spread to Miami, largely as a result of excited reports on Hispanic radio and TV. Despite many frightened witnesses, widespread searches found nothing and when deaths of goats and other small animals were investigated in Miami, in March 1996, they were found by police and city veterinarians to be "classic canine puncture marks" and "contrary to popular belief, all the animals were full of blood."

Cryptozoological interpretation of El Chupacabras, Goatsucker, by John Sibbick based on eye-witness descriptions.

While sociologists and folklorists were classi-fying this as "a social panic driven by mis-identi-fication", dozens of Chupacabras incidents were reported from as far afield as Mexico and San Sal-vador and in several states of the US. These did not trail off until June 1996 (see *Fortean Times* no.89, pp.34–38). In Arizona, a family called police saying their home was under siege, but nothing was found. In Mexico a girl said she had been attacked by the creature but her "wounds" were shown to be love-bites. Attacks in Salvador were traced to starving bats forced to forage further than usual. The panic was so great in certain parts of

Mexico that important eco-systems came under threat as farmers lit fires to ward off or kill "vam-pires". In each outbreak, hundreds of animals were reported killed by an uncatchable monster that was said to have come from outer space, been created by witches, or even by the US military (see SOCIAL ANXIETY ATTACKS, p.110).

Sometimes there are features in these mutila-tions (e.g. backbreaking, the siphoning of blood, removal of specific organs) that bring to mind ele-ments of shamanistic or Mithraic sacrifice; but, as in the classic pattern of UFO paradox, the matter is devastatingly elusive. In their *Devil Worship in*

Britain (1964) Peter Haining and A. V. Sellwood confessed that they did not get far investigating the discovery of a pile of six heads of cows and horses in a wood near Luton, Bedfordshire. The eyes had been extracted, the jaws wrenched open and two jawbones removed. Nearby were two rings of trampled grass round a gnarled tree. There were no other tracks, no blood and no sign of the bodies. The heads were heavy enough to have needed two people to carry them down the two mile bridlepath to the spot, suggesting to the police a conspiracy. No farmer for miles around admitted to losing any animals, and the case remains unsolved.

The trampled rings recall similar patches reported from the sites of many of the Midwest mutilations and also the ground markings associated with UFOs. The *Sunday Mirror* (9 November 1975) tells of a black sheep, at Bray, Berkshire, found stripped of skin and meat from the neck down in a manner that suggested skill at flaying. There had been two other mutilations at Bray the week before. Phantom helicopters too are familiar objects in the UFO repertoire; and indeed their *modus operandi,* with silent night manoeuvrings and powerful spotlights, is reminiscent of the great airship flaps of the late nineteenth century (see PHANTOM SHIPS, p.221).

Other cases link animal mutilation to another of our sections, THE GREAT AMERICAN MONSTER (see p.298) with its foul-smelling mystery anthropoids. In *The Unidentified* (1975) Jerome Clark reports on his investigation into a series of bizarre animal killings around Rochdale, Indiana, during which about fifty people claimed to have seen a "gorilla-like" thing in the area. On 22 August 1972 two members of the Burdine family returned to their farm to discover about sixty chickens ripped apart but not eaten. After a close encounter with the "thing", they saw it again, by the lights of their car, framed in the door of the chicken coop. They shot at it as it lumbered off. Inside the coop all but thirty of two hundred chickens were "ripped open and drained of blood".

Now, as if to confound the UFO-link argument, we bring in the weirdest correlation of all. Fort had an inkling of what he called an "occult criminology" – that all these attacks on animals were part of one mysterious phenomenon, including "attacks, some of them mischievous, some ordinarily deadly, and some of the Jack the Ripper kind, upon human beings". Perhaps, like all great fictions, the terrifying destructive "monster from the Id", as in the 1956 film *Forbidden Planet,* is a mirroring of a repressed fact. In our INVISIBLE

As the co-ordinator of interstate investigation into the spate of mysteriously mutilated cattle in the 1970s, Gabe Valdez, a state police officer in New Mexico, attended many scenes like this one in Rio Arriba County.

ASSAILANTS section (see p.143) we review some cases where wounds appear mysteriously on human bodies. Nandor Fodor, echoing Fort, suggested that childish passions of anger, hate, jealousy and frustration could be "exteriorized" and vented on objects or people in the vicinity, causing the smashing, burning and spoiling pranks of poltergeists. For example, in FIERY PERSECUTIONS (see p.153) we tell the story of the girl in the kitchen at Binbrook Farm, who was severely burned on her back although quite unaware of the fire consuming her. In reporting the incident, the *Louth and North Lincolnshire News* (28 January 1905) mentioned incidentally the bizarre killing of 225 chickens on the property. Despite a constant watch on the hen-house, "whenever examined, four or five birds would be found dead". They were all killed in the same way: "the skin around the neck, from the head to the breast, had been pulled off, and the windpipe drawn from its place and snapped."

This sounds like a malevolent kind of poltergeist effect. And the more widely we examine this whole nasty business of mysterious mutilations, torture and killings, the more we are drawn towards the traditional acceptance of demonic powers or energies behind them. We should like to go further and be able to say whether such powers are inherent in nature or whether they are located in and projected by ourselves, but that is one of the many questions to which we have no firm answer.

Fiery persecutions

If researcher Larry Arnold is correct, there are many instances of SPONTANEOUS HUMAN COMBUSTION (see p.154) which are not fatal or stop just short of being fatal. Some of these look like attacks by poltergeists; others appear to be cases of people who attract fire (or runs of bad luck involving fire); while in others victims seem to be the object of persistent fiery assaults.

Spontaneous outbreaks of fire are a familiar feature of "poltergeist" disturbances. In the dramatic case of the Dagg household in 1889 (see INVISIBLE ASSAILANTS, p.143), the investigator, Woodcock, made a public statement citing no less than seventeen witnesses to the effect that "fires have broken out spontaneously throughout the house, as many as eight occurring in one day, six being in the house and two outside; that the window curtains were burned whilst on the windows, this happening in broad daylight, whilst the family and neighbours were in the house". The statement is quoted in full in Father Thurston's *Ghosts and Poltergeists* (1953).

The *New York World* (8 August 1887) says that as many as forty fires had been found in two hours in the Hoyt residence in Woodstock, New Brunswick, and that they had burnt themselves out or had been inexplicably confined to very small areas. They began on 6 August, and no origin could be found for them: "Now a curtain, high up and out of reach, would burst into flames, then a bed quilt in another room: a basket of clothes on a shed, a child's dress hanging on a hook." Fort mentions a case in which fires broke out in the presence of a girl adopted into the MacDonald household, of Antigonish, Nova Scotia, until in March 1922 their house finally burned to the ground.

This brings us to a significant aspect of many "poltergeist" cases and outbreaks of inexplicable fires. They generally seem to involve the agency of young girls, often lonely girls who had been adopted or working as maids in the afflicted households. In many cases, as we shall observe, these involuntary fire-agents are bullied by authorities into "confessing" their responsibility for mysterious fires, because this suits the authorities' convenience. In April 1908, Margaret Dewar, a retired schoolteacher of Whitley, Northumberland, was bullied by the coroner, the police and the gossip of neighbours into changing her story that on 22 March she had found her sister burned to death in a bed untouched by signs of fire. Her terror was taken to be the incoherence of intoxication, and when she told the story again under oath in court, it was again suggested that she was drunk. She persisted and the coroner adjourned the inquest until she came to her senses (see *Blyth News and Wansbeck Telegraph* for 23 and 24 March and 3 April, 1908).

The *New York Herald* (6 January 1895) tells of twenty fires the previous day in the home of Adam Colwell in Brooklyn. Policemen investigated and saw furniture burst into flames, one oficer even stated that he had seen wallpaper near Colwell's son, Willy, suddenly begin to burn. It was thought that the family's adopted girl, Rhoda, was responsible, but there was simply no way in which she could have started so many fires in full view of the firemen. A man came forward the next day to say that during the period Rhoda had been employed as a maid in his house in Flushing, New York, there had been fires, and that they ceased after he expelled her. The same paper on the next day records how the girl "sobbed her confession" when faced with the "facts" during a long interrogation. We wonder how many other confessions have been imposed on bewildered children by authorities in need of a tidy solution to an untidy mystery.

The agency behind mysterious outbreaks of fire is sometimes blatantly apparent. Fourteen-year-old Jennie Bramwell was an English girl adopted by Robert Dawson of Thorah, Canada. According to the St Louis *Globe-Democrat* (19 December 1891) the girl went into a trance after an illness. "Look at that!" she would exclaim, and the spot on the ceiling at which she pointed would start to blaze. As Mrs Dawson and the girl sat facing a wall, flames burst out of the wallpaper. In the week that followed there were many fires in the girl's vicinity, burning her dress, the furniture, and even a kitten's fur. The *New York Sun* (2 February 1932) reported many fires of undetectable origin in the house of C.H. Williamson, of Bladenboro, North Carolina. His daughter seemed to be the centre of the disturbance, and once, as she stood in the middle of a room with no fire near her, her dress suddenly ignited. And again, it was told of twelve-year-old Willie Brough, in the *San Francisco Bulletin* (October 1886) that he set things on fire "by his glance". His parents thought he was afflicted by the devil and threw him out. A local farmer took him in and sent him to school: "On the first day, there were five fires in the school: one in the centre of the ceiling, one in the teacher's desk, one in her wardrobe, and two on the wall. The boy discovered them all, and cried from fright. The trustees met and expelled him that night." We have on file corroborating stories of fireprone people. Consider, for example, the case of Barbara Booley, who was involved in seven different fires in Devon, Gloucestershire and Somerset within four years (see *News of the World*, 19 October 1975).

In 1713 the Abbé Girolamo Leoni de Ceneda was terrified by a flame which suddenly burst with a roar from the ground in a village near Venice. It hovered over the spot for a while and then vanished. There are several records of the same phenomenon elsewhere. Illustration from W. de Fonvielle, *Thunder and Lightning* (1894).

In December 1983 an astonishing spectacle occurred in Livorno, Italy – a Scottish girl was led through a crowd as they chanted "Strega!" (Witch!) The girl, twenty-year-old Carole Compton had been working as a nanny for the Cecchini family, was accused of arson and the attempted murder of her three-year-old charge. The previous year there had been several inexplicable fires in the house and one night, while the child slept, its cot burst into flames. The Cecchinis believed Carole was responsible for the fires, while the grandmother went even further and accused the girl of casting the evil eye on the child. There is some evidence that Carole was the focus of some poltergeist activity which – according to one theory – could have been triggered by a failed affair, her loneliness and her strained relations with other employees and with the Cecchini family. The maid of her previous employer spoke of madonnas falling off walls

and things spinning in Carole's presence and that her charge at the time used to cry out at Carole's touch. The crowd around the Livorno court were apparently from the more superstitious south (where the Cecchinis lived) and were whipped up by Ciara Lobina, a healer and clairvoyant whom reporters called "the Black Nun". Lobina was frequently ejected from the court, wailing and waving her large black crucifix, claiming the Devil had revealed to her in a dream that Carole and her mother were possessed. Carole was convicted, sentenced to two and a half years, but released immediately as she had already spent sixteen months in prison awaiting trial. She later published an account of her ordeal under the title *Superstition* (1990).

An interesting contrast of reaction to fire-proneness is the case of Benedetto Supino, a sixteen-year-old boy from Formia, near Rome, of whom mention was made during Carole's trial.

St Martin of Tours (d.400AD), celebrating Mass in Tours Cathedral, once saw a 'globe of fire' hover over his head. Despite the numbers present, only five others saw it. His successor, St Gregory, recorded other encounters, including one at St Martin's death and one during a parade of his relics.

Things would catch fire when he gazed at them, machinery would stop in his presence and someone claimed to have seen his hands glow on such occasions. But in the reportage – from November 1983 – there is none of the hysteria that coloured Carole's case, perhaps because his story lacked a superstitious grandmother and an eccentric lay-nun. After conducting some tests, Dr Giovanni Ballesio, Dean of Physical Medicine at Rome University, concluded that Benedetto was not an "electric boy". Even an archbishop stepped up to say the boy was "not malign" or "miraculous". (*Fortean Times*, no.42, p.21.)

Let us now look at a few cases of a more sinister nature, in which the outbreaks of fire actually seem to be directed at some poor individual. In *Poltergeist Over England* (1945) Harry Price tells of a case that happened near his home. On the night of 18 November 1943, Mrs Madge Knight's screams awoke the other occupants of her house. They found her in bed, bare but covered by the bedclothes; the skin had peeled off her back, but otherwise there was no smell or evidence of burning. A doctor identified the injury as a severe burn and administered morphine. According to the *West Sussex Gazette* (23 December 1943) Mrs Knight died from toxaemia on 2 December. At the inquest forensic experts testified that, despite a thorough examination, no evidence of fire or corrosive compounds or liquids could be found on her clothes or the bed linen. The jury gave an open verdict.

This recalls a more horrifying incident in Marylebone, London, more than a hundred years earlier. On 5 January 1820, and thereafter, fires broke out in the Wright household, where a ten-year-old girl, Elizabeth Barnes, was employed as a servant. Twice Mrs Wright found her clothes on fire while sitting in the kitchen with the girl. Once Mr Wright, hearing his wife's screams, found her in flames when the girl was not present. The Wrights' daughter moved in to guard her mother, who still caught fire by "some unknown means" and "was so dreadfully burned she was put to bed". Wright had accused Elizabeth of causing the fires, but Mrs Wright had defended the girl. They put Mrs Wright to bed, and upon leaving the room, Wright and his daughter were immediately brought back by her screams, and found her in bed surrounded by flames. The Wrights had Elizabeth arrested. The *Annual Register* (1830–31) ends its account of this remarkable case with the magistrate saying that he had no doubt the ungrateful girl was responsible in some way, but would adjourn the matter until Mrs Wright, who had always believed the girl innocent, was well enough to testify.

At Binbrook Farm, near Market Rasen, Lincolnshire, for nearly two months objects were thrown about rooms or moved on their own, and fires broke out in unexpected places. This time the girl in the case, whom the farmer had taken from the workhouse to be a servant, was in no condition to be dragged to the police station. The farmer himself told the *Louth and North Lincolnshire News* (28 January 1905) that he saw the girl sweeping the kitchen, at the opposite end of which there was a well-guarded small fire. "I suddenly came into the kitchen, and there she was, sweeping away, while the back of her dress was afire. She looked around as I shouted, and, seeing the flames, rushed through the door. She tripped, and I smothered the fire out with wet sacks. But she was terribly burned, and she is at the Louth Hospital, now, in terrible pain." The extent of her injuries meant that her back must have been on fire for some time, but the girl was certain that she was nowhere near the fireplace when she ignited.

During the same case something was killing the farmer's chickens in a horrible way (see MYSTERIOUS MUTILATORS, p.146). The girl's trance-like ignorance of the fire seems remarkably like the strange lulling in fatal cases of SPONTANEOUS HUMAN COMBUSTION (see p.154). Curiously, earlier that same month, something burned a woman, Elizabeth Clark, in the Trinity Almshouse, Hull, not many miles from Market Rasen. The *Hull Daily Mail* (6 January 1905) reported that on hearing groans from behind a partition in the dormitory at 6am the woman's fellow-inmates found her covered in burns. "Not a shred of her nightdress remained." The bed was undamaged and during the actual burning she had uttered no cry. Elizabeth Clark could give "no articulate account" of what happened and died shortly after.

Finally we mention the fiery persecution of Paul Hayes, a nineteen-year-old computer programmer in London. On the night of 25 May 1985, he was walking in Stepney Green when, suddenly and inexplicably, he was engulfed in flames. He thought he had been doused with petrol and set alight. "It was like being plunged into the heat of a furnace . . . from my shoulders to my wrists my arms felt like they were being prodded by red hot pokers . . . my chest felt like boiling water had been poured on it. I thought I could hear my brains bubbling." Screaming, he fell to the ground and curled up thinking he was dying but, as suddenly as it began it was over. "I opened my eyes. There was no flame, no smoke . . . then I began to shiver with shock." He stumbled to the nearby London Hospital and received treatment for burns on his hands, forearms, face, neck and ears. The report in *National Enquirer* (23 July 1985) says that police and medical investigators were left with a mystery. If the attack had not stopped, we might have had to tell Paul Hayes' story in the following section . . .

Spontaneous human combustion

The phenomenon of a living human body suddenly bursting into flames and rapidly becoming ashes has a long history; yet no one has discovered precisely how and why it takes place or the reasons behind its selection of victims. For a body to take fire in this way from no readily apparent outside source is the opposite phenomenon to the one we describe in the section FIRE-PROOF PEOPLE and FIRE STARTERS (see p.150).

A popular nineteenth-century theory was that spontaneous fire victims were drunkards who had somehow saturated their bodies with inflammable spirits. Another old explanation was that of divine retribution, which parallels the view of victims of lightning as sinners or blasphemers. There was, however, at least one dissenting voice in antiquity, that of Lucretius. "Why", he wondered, "do the gods not ensure that those who have perpetrated some abominable outrage are struck by lightning? Why, instead, is some man with a conscience free of sin . . . trapped and entangled without warning in the flame from heaven?"

It is a strange fire that consumes only living flesh – normally the most incombustible of materials due to the circulation of blood and the great percentage of water in its cells – leaving almost untouched the victim's clothes and other surroundings. Since the development of the theory of combustion (in the eighteenth century) the notion of such a fire has been scientifically regarded as preposterous. However, in defiance of the scientific view, cases still occur where people are suddenly attacked by fire as if from "nowhere".

One of the earliest scientific explanations of spontaneous human combustion sought to link it with those spheres of lambent light that floated over stagnant marshes. These will-o'-the-wisps, as they were known in folklore (see MYSTICAL LIGHTS, p.123), were known to be largely methane (CH_4) bubbling up from decaying vegetable matter; the real mystery was how it could ignite, something methane does not do on its own. Similarly, bacterial action in the guts of animals and humans produce methane and also hydrogen (H_2) and phosphane (PH_3, also known as "phosphoretted hydrogen"), all inflammable once they have been ignited by an external source.

In 1888 Dr J. Mackenzie of Aberdeen attended this case of an old soldier burnt to death in a hayloft. He was resting on a beam and surrounded by unscathed bales of hay. No fire had been seen, no cries heard, and, from the preserved features of the face, no pain felt.

Related to phosphane is diphosphane (P_2H_4), which really does spontaneously ignite on contact with oxygen; but chemists have long maintained that conditions in the human gut make the production of diphosphane unlikely. However, John Emsley, in *The Shocking History of Phosphorus* (2000), cites German research that has detected both phosphane and diphosphane in human faeces. The amounts are tiny – billionths of a gram – but according to Emsley, it is possible that on rare occasions sufficient diphosphane could build up and ignite on a chance encounter with some oxygen and set alight a pocket of methane and phosphane. This would satisfy John Heymer's observation that, in so many cases, the seat of the destruction has been the stomach region.

Emsley refers to a curious example from *Spontaneous Human Combustion* (1992) by Jenny Randles and Peter Hough. During World War II, an army patrol, crossing a field in Dorset, were "absolutely astonished" when a sheep burst into flames not far from them. They believed it was already dead but "in no way decomposed"; as it lay on its side "from its stomach issued blue flames". Why spontaneous combustion in animals (especially cows which produce huge volumes of methane) is not more frequently observed has yet to be worked out.

One of the best documented cases of spontaneous human combustion is that of Mrs Mary Reeser, of St Petersburg, Florida, who departed this life by fire on the night of 1 July 1951. The following morning, her landlady, on taking her a telegram, found the doorknob to Mrs Reeser's apartment too hot to touch. Two painters working nearby managed to open the door and were met by a blast of hot air. They could see no sign of the plump, sixty-seven-year-old lady. Her bed was empty, and though the room bore signs of a fire, there was only a little smoke and a feeble flame on the beam of a partition that divided the single room from a kitchenette. Firemen easily put out the flame and tore away the burnt partition. Behind it, instead of Mrs Reeser and her armchair, they found a blackened circle on the floor, a few coiled springs, a charred liver, a fragment of backbone, a skull shrunk to the size of a fist, and just on the edge of the scorched patch, a black satin slipper enclosing a left foot burnt off at the ankle.

The case was investigated in detail by firemen, arson experts, pathologists and insurance men. Appliances and wiring were checked but no cause for the fire could be found. Strangely, there was no sign of fire except in the vicinity of the chair, but there it had been unnaturally intense. A mirror on a wall had cracked with the heat, plastic switch-plates had melted, and in the bathroom more plastic items were damaged. At the inquest it was said that crematoria normally use a temperature of 2500° F, sustained for hours, to incinerate a body, and

Illustration, by Phiz, of the famous scene in Dicken's novel *Bleak House* when the smoking remains of Mr Krook are discovered. 'Here is a small burnt patch of flooring; here is the tinder from a little bundle of burnt paper, but not so light as usual, seeming to be steeped in something; and here is – is it the cinder of a small charred and broken log of wood sprinkled with white ashes, or is it coal? O Horror, he is here! and this from which we run away, striking out the light and overturning one another into the street, is all that represents him.'

even then they have to resort to grinders to pulverise the remains to the state in which Mrs Reeser's body was found. Assuming that a heat of this intensity was somehow generated, why, it was asked, was the wall not scorched behind the chair and why was a pile of newspapers less than a foot away not burnt? The FBI released a statement on 8 August, suggesting that Mrs Reeser had taken her usual sleeping pills and fallen asleep in the chair while smoking – their report is quoted in full in Vincent Gaddis's *Mysterious Fires and Lights* (1967). But experts testified that even if her clothes had caught alight they could only have burned her superficially, and that neither they nor the smouldering armchair stuffing could have generated and sustained anything like enough heat to ignite a human body.

By coincidence, one of America's foremost pathologists specializing in deaths by fire, Dr Wilton Krogman, was on holiday nearby and joined the investigations. He publicly expressed his bafflement at the event, regarding it as the most amazing thing he had ever seen. Never, in all his experience, had he seen a human skull shrunk by intense heat, normally the opposite effect occurs. In an interview with fortean researcher Larry E. Arnold – for his book *Ablaze!* (1995) – Dr

Krogman seemed to revise his opinion of a half a century earlier; it was a hoax, he seemed to suggest, a "set-up", largely because the facts were so anomalous and the critical evidence (Mrs Reeser's ashes) "vanished" en route to the FBI for examination. "I think the case was closed with undue haste," he told Arnold. "That's all I can say."

There are many references to spontaneous human combustion (or SHC) by eighteenth- and nineteenth-century writers, including de Quincey, Dickens, Melville and Zola. These were often based on famous cases like that of Countess Bandi of Casena, of whom only a head, three fingers and both legs were found in a heap of ashes, four feet from her bed, sometime before June 1731. (The earliest account of the Countess being in the *Gentleman's Magazine* of that date.) Many similar accounts can be found in the early textbooks on medical jurisprudence, as such fires have often given rise to suspicions of criminality. For example, the *Enzyklopädisches Wörterbuch* (Berlin, 1843) mentions the pile of ashes that were the remains of the wife of a Frenchman called Millet, of Rheims, in 1725. Millet was accused of an affair with his pretty servant girl and charged with murdering his wife and using fire to conceal the evidence. At the inquiry, however, it was acknowledged as a

A typical scene of 'spontaneous human combustion'. The fire, in Pennsylvania, in November 1964, seems to have been intense, rapid and localized, leaving only Helen Conway's legs.

"genuine" case of spontaneous combustion and Millet was acquited.

Dr E.S. Reynolds, addressing the Manchester Pathological Society on the topic of spontaneous combustion in 1891, resorted to the current theory that most victims are inebriates. Today it is often said that they fall asleep while smoking, ignoring the cases where the victim neither smoked nor drank. But even sceptics like Reynolds tell of cases that defy their own criteria; he writes of a woman's legs carbonized *inside* her unscathed stockings – see *British Medical Journal* (21 March 1891). In the London *Daily News* (17 December 1904), is an item on the case of Mrs Thomas Cochrane of Rosehall, Falkirk, who burned to death in her chair, surrounded by unburned pillows and cushions and without uttering a cry. Clearly there is a mystery about such cases, with hints of occultism that inhibit serious investigation by doctors and scientists.

The *Madras Mail* (13 May 1907), tells of two constables carrying a woman's body, still smoking, to the District Magistrate near Dinapore, India, after it had burst into flames. Her room was untouched by fire and the clothes she was wearing were unscorched on her burnt body. What sort of fire can consume a body and leave clothing and surroundings unnaturally intact? This astonishing feature is met with time after time. Maxwell Cade and Delphine Davis in their *Taming of the Thunderbolts* (1969) suggest some kind of subatomic transaction may be involved – an idea that could be given currency by the new field of energy research called Cold Fusion – but as far as we know, no one has taken a Geiger counter to a suspected SHC scene. In another example of this strange localization of the combustion, the *New York Sun* (24 January 1930) reported an inquest on Mrs Stanley Lake, at Kingston, New York, at which the coroner said: "Although her body was severely burned, her clothing was not even scorched." In our other sections on strange fires we notice this same selectivity at work.

Several scholars of SHC have identified another recurring aspect; the victims often seem to be in a kind of trance. In *Cosmos* (ser.3, vol.6, p.240) is an account by a Dr Bertholle to the Société Médico-Chirurgicale of his investigation of the case of a woman found burned to death in an almost unscorched room in Paris on 1 August 1869. He said that it was as if the body had been in an intense furnace, yet only the floor under the body had been scorched. He could not understand why the woman had made no outcry to be heard

by the other occupants of the house. Another case: the charred bodies of five men were found sitting in casual positions in a car in a back road near Pikeville, Kentucky. The account in the *Syracuse Herald-Journal* (21 November 1960), does not describe the condition of the car, but quotes the coroner as being baffled at the absence of any sign of a struggle to escape.

One of the strangest cases was summarized by Fort from an English paper, the *Dartford Chronicle* (7 April 1919). At 2.30am a well-known author, J. Temple Johnson, was found dead, scorched from the waist down. There was no trace of fire on his clothes nor in his room; but outside the door of that room, firemen found a blaze and could not understand how it started or why it should have been confined to that spot. Johnson was fully clothed and alone in the house. He still had money in his pockets, and there was no sign of the fire being used to mask a robbery. The inquest produced a verdict of death by heart failure brought on by inhaling smoke, and once again surprise was expressed that, if Johnson had been up and about when he discovered the fire, he had not escaped or called for help from his neighbours.

A number of TV documentaries have tried to explain SHC, often with very suspect demonstrations of the "candle effect" (in which body fat is the fuel and the victim's clothing the wick). In August 1998, BBC TV's science series *QED* conducted a careful and impressive demonstration; Dr John de Haan, a forensic specialist at the California Criminalistics Institute, wrapped a dead pig in a blanket and placed it in a replica living room. A small amount of petrol was poured on one shoulder and set alight. Five hours later, the "body" was still burning and would have continued had it not been doused.

Proponents of SHC have tended to think in terms of an intense, localized inferno, but de Haan showed that once started, a prolonged low-intensity blaze could convincingly reproduce many of the characteristics of SHC: the pig's extremities were intact and bones were friable, crumbling when poked. Effects in the room were localized: a plastic radio partly melted and a nearby wooden table was lightly scorched. However this still leaves many questions about reported SHC cases unanswered (despite the claim of the *QED* publicity). We note that an "accelerant" was used to get the fire going in the first place when, in many cases, there is no indication of a source of ignition at all or when there is clear evidence of the rapidity of the combustion.

Firemen clean up after the discovery of the remains of Mrs M.H. Reeser at St Petersburg, Florida, 2 July 1951.

only the vicinity of the body was charred; smooth surfaces (like the windows and lightbulb) were coated with yellow grease and the room was dripping with condensation of water originating in the body.

Heymer's research is detailed in his book *The Entrancing Flame* (1996), including other British cases that he learned of during his investigation. One concerned the death of a tramp (known as Bailey) on stairs in a deserted building in Lambeth, London, 13 September 1967. The fire crew was led by Jack Stacey who, in 1986, told Heymer of the most bizarre sight that he had ever witnessed in his entire career. "There was a four-inch slit in his abdomen from which was issuing, at force, a blue flame which was beginning to burn the stairs. We extinguished the flames by playing a hose into the abdominal cavity. Bailey was alive when he started burning and must have been in terrible pain. His teeth were sunk into the mahogany newel post of the staircase." The importance of this case cannot be over-emphasized as a highly experienced Fire Officer is emphatic that "the fire was coming from within the abdomen".

Larry E. Arnold researched the topic for 23 years, his painstaking historical research complemented by many hours talking to fire investigators. His book is crammed with new cases and sensible discussion of theories and the first-hand observations of police and fire officers. "Contrary to what was once believed," he says, "SHC is not always fatal and the existence of survivors poses a profound challenge to the debunker."

To Arnold the chief characteristic of "true" SHC cases is the indication that the fire originates within the body and burns outwards; with conventional fire deaths it is the other way around and this is why most authorities regard SHC as scientific heresy or mere superstition based on poor observation. John Heymer – a retired Scenes of Crime Officer for Gwent CID – agrees with Arnold. Heymer's experience with SHC began with his investigation of the charred remains of 73-year-old Henry Thomas in Ebbw Vale on 6 January 1980. What he saw was contrary to his experience of "normal" fire deaths: the extremities protruded from a heap of ashes; domestic objects nearby were singed or partly melted but

In *Fortean Times* (no.35, pp.6–9), archivist Peter Christie describes his search for original documentation of the oft-cited case of Grace Pett of Ipswich who combusted on 9 April 1744 and popularized by a devoted chapter in Sir David Brewster's *Letters on Natural Magic*. Grace was found by her daughter on a wooden floor "like a block of wood burning with a glowing fire without flames". Her abdomen had burned to ashes. Brewster dutifully mentions that Grace had been drinking and that clothes and a paper screen nearby were "untouched". Christie found an account of the inquest on Grace Pett which generally confirmed that, apart from her extremities, she had been "so farr reduced to ashes as to be put in ye coffin with a shovel". An additional source (given by Christie) reveals the previously unknown local opinion that Grace was suspected of being a witch. Apparently, a neighbour who farmed sheep consulted a conjuror over why some were dying and was advised to burn one (presumably in the belief that this would summon whoever bewitched them). Coincidentally, on the night the farmer burned a sheep, Grace also died; her unburned feet were said to correspond to the tied legs of the sheep.

7

The Haunted Planet

7

The Haunted Planet

The hollow earth

We have innumerable reports, evidences, legends, superstitions and fantasies, indicating that the earth is hollow and that there is a living world within it. There is no real proof of this, but the idea is ancient, and its persistence in all ages up to the present suggests that, on some level, there may be a hidden truth in it.

Plato in *Phaedo* repeats Socrates's account, given confidentially to close friends just before his execution, of how the world really is. It is a beautiful sphere perforated throughout by hollows and channels and with a great chasm running through it. Through these passages the rivers, winds and spirits of the earth pass in constant circulation. We do not live on the surface but in one of the upper hollows, where we do not see the full beauty, and there are entrances, both upwards and downwards, into the other levels. A similar picture was given by Athanasius Kircher (1602–80), the great Jesuit scholar. His earth was also riddled with caverns and deep tunnels, with an axial passage between openings at the north and south poles. In its crevices lived giants, demons and monsters.

Creatures of the inner earth, offspring of the earth goddess, are recognized in myths and folklore everywhere. Typically they are gigantic and misshapen, like the primitive Greek gods, the Titans.

Among them are dragons and other creatures that guard buried treasures; these are also guardians of the earth's wisdom and are encountered by initiates into the Mysteries. Lesser sprites, gnomes, elves, kobolds and such, live in caves and tunnels nearer the surface, and they are the kind most often seen and heard. This is the underworld of elemental spirits and souls of the dead. It is a dread world, a source of madness and nightmares, but it is also a source of benefits – of healing, oracles and inspiration. By all accounts there was once considerable traffic between the lower world and the upper. The old Irish histories tell of a battle between the invading Milesians and a magically skilled native race, the Tuatha De Danaan, for possession of the country. Finally it was split between them, the victorious Milesians taking the upper half and banishing the older race to the country below the surface. There they merged with the fairies, and in that guise have been familiar apparitions to every Irish generation.

A suppressed archeological secret is the existence of vast, inexplicable tunnel systems beneath the surface of a great part of the earth. All over Britain and Ireland are records, legends and relics of underground routes between the ancient and sacred places. Sabine Baring-Gould's *Cliff Castles and Cave Dwellings of Europe* (1911) has amazing records of the extensive cave and tunnel structures beneath France and other countries. Like the tunnels much used during the Vietnam war, those

GLOBE SHOWING SECTION OF THE EARTH'S INTERIOR

The earth is hollow. The poles so long sought are but phantoms. There are openings at the northern and southern extremities. In the interior are vast continents, oceans, mountains and rivers. Vegetable and animal life are evident in this new world, and it is probably peopled by races yet unknown to the dwellers upon the earth's exterior.

THE AUTHOR.

A page from William Reed's *Phantom of the Poles* (1906).

through". Other writers tell of a vast, "technologically impossible" network of mysterious tunnels in South America, running throughout the entire Andes range between ancient, forgotten stone cities.

In 1906 William Reed wrote *The Phantom of the Poles* in the hope of re-establishing the ancient theory of the hollow earth. "I claim", he began, "that the earth is not only hollow, but that all, or nearly all, of the explorers have spent much of their time past the turning-point, and have had a look into the interior of the earth." At each of the poles, so Reed sought to prove, there is a large, round-lipped hole, into which all polar explorers inadvertently sail. Many of these, including Peary, Franklin, Nansen and Hall, penetrated quite deeply into the world of the interior, and Reed found much evidence in their writings to support his theory. Accounts of the atmosphere growing warmer as the Poles are approached, of fertile Arctic territories abounding with animals, of floating timber and vegetation far from any known source; these he combined with noted instances of compass irregularities and displays of the Northern Lights (which he thought were reflections of light from within the earth) to prove the existence of the inner world. Later writers have lent their enthusiasm to his cause. Much has been made of the strange aerial expedition made by US Admiral Richard E. Byrd to the Antarctic in 1956, during which it was announced on the radio (3 January 1956) that the party had penetrated to a land 2300 miles *beyond* the South Pole. Before his previous flight, in 1947, the Admiral told reporters: "I'd like to see that land beyond the Pole. That area beyond the Pole is the Centre of the Great Unknown." Speculative writers on the hollow earth have misinterpreted this remark by claiming that Byrd was referring to the North Pole. In fact, as made plain by the journalist Walter

of Europe were resorted to as refuges by the local people in troubled times. They also contained shrines where the underworld deities were invoked. In Harold Bayley's *Archaic England* (1919) there are reports from early travellers of great tunnels stretching under much of Africa, including one beneath a river called Kaoma, "so lengthy that it took the caravan from sunrise to noon to pass

Sullivan, who accompanied Byrd in both his expeditions and described them in *Quest for a Continent* (1957), the Admiral's 1947 flights were in Antarctica.

The modern pioneer of hollow-earth theory was John Cleves Symmes (1779–1838) of New Jersey. His studious life was devoted to proving that the earth and all heavenly bodies were made up of concentric shells with entrances at top and bottom. The doughnut-holes in the earth were so large – 4000 miles across at the north pole and 6000 miles at the south – that ships sailed into and out of them without noticing. Symmes was an energetic promoter of his own theory and attracted a popular following. Politicians were also persuaded that his ideas should be investigated. In a circular to rally support he summarized the matter.

"TO ALL THE WORLD! I declare the earth is hollow, and habitable within; containing a number of solid concentrick spheres, one within the other, and that it is open at the poles 12 or 16 degrees; I pledge my life in support of this truth, and am ready to explore the hollow, if the world will support and aid me in the undertaking."

A full account of Symmes is in *Subterranean Worlds* (1989) by Walter Kafton-Minkel, a valuable compendium of hollow-earth lore. Also valuable – uniquely so in much of its subject-matter – is Joscelyn Godwin's *Arktos: the Polar Myth in Science, Symbolism, and Nazi Survival* (1992). Part of it describes the pole-centred, hollow-earth cosmologies that were popular in Nazi Germany and

A satellite picture of the North Pole claimed by UFOs-from-the-Earth's-interior advocates to show the hole there. In fact the dark area is the combined effect of the planet's tilt in the sun's light and a photo-mosaic technique compiled over 24 hours. This explanation does not convince the hollow-earthers.

have since been developed by fantasists of the far right. Evolutionary orthodoxy has it that humankind first arose in Africa and spread northwards. Against that is the Nordic myth, that humanity and culture were generated at the centre of the earth, in a land of paradise that lay (and perhaps still lies) behind the ice-barriers around the north pole. From there it is but a short step to supposing that the first people on the earth's surface came from inside it.

That step was taken by several of the writers mentioned in *Arktos*, and some of them have taken the further step of locating the last stronghold of "Nordic superiority" within the hollow at the south pole. A much repeated story is that Hitler and certain henchmen escaped from Berlin in 1945 and were conveyed, either by a Nazi flying-saucer craft or by the U-boat that surrendered in South America long after the war was over, to a subterranean base in Antarctica. The most active promoter of this myth is a Canadian citizen of German extraction, Ernst Zündel, whose books, including *UFOs: Last Secrets of the Third Reich* and *Secret Nazi Polar Expeditions* (1979), serve the principal purpose of sensationalizing his neo-Nazi opinions.

Ray Palmer, editor of the American magazine *Flying Saucers*, was a keen promoter of hollow earth theory, claiming that the interior is a more likely source of mysterious lights and UFOs than outer space. The idea also occurred to the pioneer ufologist, Brinsley Le Poer Trench. In *Secret of the Ages: UFOs from Inside the Earth* (1974) he suggested that many of our phenomena come from within the earth, and hinted at evidence that the intra-ter-

Subterranean kobolds excavating a fossil *Ichthyosaurus*. Engraving
from Pouchet's *The Universe* (1870).

restrials may already be plotting a military operation against our world of the surface.

There is much to enjoy in the hollow earth theory, but in this modern age of satellites etc. it is difficult to take entirely seriously. Yet we do not underestimate the power of military secrecy, and there is no doubt that much was suppressed in the official reports of Admiral Byrd's strange flights. More seriously, there is an established connection between faults and rifts in the earth's crust and apparitions of monsters, phantoms and mysterious lights. It is as if the underworld seeps out through the cracks. Loch Ness is on the geological crack across Scotland; and the Monster of Bolinas Swamp in California inhabits the fault line running north from San Francisco – the territory also of the hairy Bigfoot. Paul Devereux and others have pointed out the connection between UFO sightings and areas of geological faults. We find significance in this clustering of phantoms round clefts and caverns, traditional gates to the underworld. Perhaps they are indeed passing in and out. If we suppose, as many have before us, that there is life in a subterranean world which occasionally interpenetrates with our own, many of the strange phenomena in this book begin to seem more reasonable.

Phenomenal highways

We have written of phantoms and fireballs, of mystery animals, strange lights, Black Dogs and fairies, all of them participants in the intermediate state of reality we call phenomenal. In terms of the hard reality recognized by science their existence cannot be proved. It is evident only in its symptoms, and by analysing these symptoms we detect patterns. Haunted tracks for example; why are so many phenomena associated with certain spots and certain routes. Do the alternative realities of our records have an alternative highway system?

Reports of an elemental force that passes regularly on particular routes through the country, sometimes with destructive or ominous results, are universal. One version of it, widely known throughout Europe, is called the "Wild Hunt", the "Wild Troop" or the "Furious Army". It is rarely seen, and those who stand in its way are in danger of being killed or abducted to another world. Most terrifying is its noise, described as a

PAUL DEVEREUX/FORTEAN PICTURE LIBRARY

The alignments of churches, roads and other landscape features are known as leys. This ley runs for 3 miles NNW–SSE in the Cotswolds at Saintbury, Gloucestershire.

rushing roar in which can be heard the neighing and pounding hooves of horses, human cries and hunting horns. The appearance of this ghostly troop is generally upon a certain day – often around Christmas or the New Year – and it follows the same lines across country, not always straight but often between ancient monuments and landmarks.

In some cases its passage is marked by bent or broken trees, and houses built in its path are destroyed. A well-recorded example is the Wild Troop of Rodenstein in Germany. This dis-

after the authorities had lost interest, for Wirth was shown recently ruined houses as evidence of the passage of the Wild Troop.

Sabine Baring-Gould described the Nordic Wild Hunt in *Iceland: Its Scenes and Sagas* (1863), and again in his *Book of Folk-Lore*. On the lonely wastes of Dartmoor, the sound of galloping horses, baying hounds and voices in the air was supposed to signify the Wild Huntsman, urging on his hounds in their hunt for human souls. The hunt is said to follow the prehistoric Abbot's Way and

The Four Stones at Old Radnor, like many ancient stones, were said to be mobile, travelling to Hindwell Pool to drink. Several 'leys' and legendary tracks converge on them.

agreeable force steers a straight course between the castles of Rodenstein and Schnellert, blasting all in its path. Up to the middle of the eighteenth century the local authorities recorded the dates of this phenomenon. Catherine Crowe's *The Night Side of Nature* (1854) states that, in about 1850, a traveller named Wirth inspected the local court records and found its last reported occurrence was in June 1764. However, it apparently went on long

other ancient paths across the moor. The chronicler Gervase of Tilbury wrote that in the thirteenth century the Wild Hunt was frequently seen in the hills and forest lands of England. It was called the Harle-thing and its leader was King Herla, the German Erl-king. In Teutonic legends the leader of the Wild Hunt is the ancient pagan god Woden.

A rational explanation for this destructive and roaring force would be something meteorological like a whirlwind or electrical storm. But this does not explain its regular appearances on the same routes, and the strange stories that arise from it could hardly refer to a known, natural weather effect. Baring-Gould had another idea: that the mysterious noises from the sky are the cries of geese migrating southward by night at the approach of winter. This might explain the noise of the Wild Hunt, but not the damage and havoc it is said to cause.

Another kind of otherworldly force which is known to proceed along traditional paths between ancient sites is the fairy troop. W.Y. Evans-Wentz in *The Fairy Faith in Celtic Countries* (1911) writes about the haunted paths of Ireland and Brittany, which run in straight lines between the ancient hilltop forts inhabited by THE LITTLE PEOPLE (see p.117). On certain days of the year people avoid these paths for fear of interrupting a fairy procession and, for the same reason, it is considered unwise to build houses on them. An Irish seer told Evans-Wentz that fairy paths are seasonal channels of terrestrial "magnetic" energy. No explanation is given for the visible part of the phenomenon, the fairies themselves.

Some incidents connected with fairy paths are related by Dermot MacManus in his book of modern Irish fairy lore, *The Middle Kingdom* (1972). They warn against building houses on the traditional routes of fairy processions. Anyone who does so is likely to suffer regular disturbances, poltergeist effects, constant bad luck and, in extreme cases, the destruction of their property. In 1935, Michael O'Hagan inadvertently blocked a fairy path through building a westward extension to his house into an open field which lay in direct line between two ancient hillforts. O'Hagan's five children all fell ill and one almost died, to the bafflement of the local doctor. When a visit to a wise woman, versed in local mystical topography, revealed the problem, the new building was pulled down and the children straightaway recovered. MacManus gives other quite recent examples of Irish people being influenced in their choice of a building site by considerations of the fairies and their ways.

A similar elemental force, active at certain seasons and best avoided, is conventionalized in England in terms of BLACK DOGS (see p.286). Most books of local folklore refer to Black Dog tracks, which have the same mystical properties as our other examples. In one of the best collections of Black Dog legends, Patricia Dale-Green's *Dog* (1966) gives an

account of a phantom creature rushing at midnight through a Devonshire village, along a road from the church, and demolishing a corner of the schoolhouse. Or rather, it seems to demolish it because, though falling masonry is heard, no actual damage is discovered. We have another reference to the phantom dog's habit of destroying buildings in its path, near Lyme Regis, Dorset, where it is said to have knocked down the corner of an inn called the Black Dog. This makes us wonder whether the inn was called after an existing phantom or the phantom was attracted by the name.

In Scotland, according to A.A. MacGregor's *Ghost Book* (1955), the phantom Black Dog is called *cu sith* and travels in straight lines along customary routes. The sight of it is ominous and often followed by death. A modern case illustrating this connection between phantoms, their tracks and hidden dangers is given by Ruth Tongue and Katherine Briggs in *Somerset Folklore* (1964). A straight track on the north Somerset coast is referred to as Death Mile because it is haunted by a Black Dog that is fatal to whoever sees it. In 1960, a man to whom it appeared died within a year, as did a young girl who saw it – though her companion, who did not, was unaffected.

Another reference to the dangers of spirit paths appears in the magazine *Fate* (October 1972) which

Photograph from MacManus's *The Middle Kingdom* showing the cut-off corner of an Irish cottage which had been obstructing a 'fairy path'. With the corner's removal, the disturbances plaguing the cottage dwellers ceased.

quotes a first-hand account, originally published in Honolulu, by a native author, Napua Poire. One evening, as a little girl, she found herself alone on a spirit path in a forbidden part of the island. Standing rigid with terror, she heard the marching footsteps of an invisible procession drawing nearer and nearer. It was almost upon her when she felt a hand push her out of the way. Her parents later explained that she had been on a path reserved for the wandering spirits called the "night marchers", and it was the kindly shove of an ancestor spirit that had saved her from death.

A similar story is told by Sir Arthur Grimble in his book, *A Pattern of Islands* (1952). It also tells of spirit path in the Pacific, on one of the Gilbert Islands where Grimble was a colonial adminis- trator. The ghosts of the dead, he was told, took this path on their way to a spot on the north- ernmost tip of the island, from whence they pro- ceeded to the otherworld. Grimble investigated and, as he walked back to his village along the path, he met an old man who ignored him and did not even return his greeting. Back in the village when he described this person and asked who he was, he learnt that it was the spirit of a man who had died there that afternoon.

A modern writer who has made a special study of mystical pathways is Paul Devereux, one-time editor of *The Ley Hunter* magazine. In two of his books, *Symbolic Landscapes* (1992) and *Shamanism and the Mystery Lines* (1992), he summarizes the evidence of this phenomenon all over the world. In Germany they are called *Geistenvege* (spirit ways); in Holland *Doodwegen* or roads of the dead; while in England the name Dod or Dodman (dead man), attached to certain ancient paths, has a similar meaning. The formerly straight path, Dod Lane at Glastonbury, lies on the extended axis of the old Abbey and was evidently regarded as a way by which the spirits of the dead entered the sanctuary. Strange events of many different kinds are asso- ciated with these lines – phantom animals, moving lights, ghosts, wild hunts, fairy processions and the flights of witches. In some cases these mysterious,

haunted paths have an underground dimension, coinciding with actual or legendary tunnels. Dev- ereux's suggestion is that the networks of straight lines, discovered across landscapes in all continents, are relics of tribal shamanism, laid out in con- nection with magical and out-of-the-body flight.

Leys – or "leylines" as they are now generally called – were first recognized in the British Isles by Alfred Watkins, a local businessman of Hereford. He observed that prehistoric monu- ments, traditional landmarks and churches built on sites of ancient sanctity were often arranged in series of straight lines. Upon these lines or leys he found lesser, unrecorded relics of the past, such as mounds, markstones and stretches of local tracks, which in many cases ran between hilltop earth- works and "fairy forts". In his controversial classic, *The Old Straight Track* (1925), Watkins suggested that leys were forgotten traders' routes, but he was also aware of their mystical character, their asso- ciation with witches, phantoms and ancient reli- gious practices. Later researchers have established that prehistoric sites were indeed laid out in straight lines, probably in connection with a rit- ualized form of astronomy which was itself con- nected with necromancy and the spirits of the dead.

There is something ominous about these lines and the natural or supernatural forces that use them. The *feng-shui* masters who designed the sacred land- scape of old China were suspicious of unbroken lines of straight tracks and avenues, seeing them as pathways of a disruptive force called *sha*, which brought death or bad luck to anyone exposed to it. Similar misfortunes occur to people who see the Wild Hunt, obstruct fairy paths or interact with the forces that move along the mystical highway system. This is an area of experienced reality that modern science has hardly begun to recognize and investigate. That is not surprising, since everything known about the subject indicates that the phe- nomena behind it are spiritual forces, unbound by the laws of physics and therefore beyond the reach of the science that prevails today.

Invisible barriers

This section is about a phenomenon that is surprisingly common yet little studied – the occurrence of invisible barriers that unaccountably inhibit people, animals and even machines.

In the Old Testament story about Balaam and his ass, Balaam's instructions from God forbade him to take a certain way, which he immediately did. His ass shied away from the path but Balaam beat it back again. It repeated this behaviour and, finally, it lay down in the road and no amount of blows could persuade it to continue. The biblical explanation, put into the mouth of the ass, was that its refusal to move was caused by a vision of the Angel of the Lord standing in its path.

his house that he made a brass horse and buried it in the street. Thereafter no horse could be made to travel that way, even when whipped.

Similar legends can also be found in a modern context. UFO reports often feature car engines that stall in the presence of a UFO or when a UFO directs a beam of light at the car. Witnesses also speak of radios failing and watches stopping.

A ghostly variation on this theme appears in *Weekend* (21 October 1970); several witnesses spoke of a phantom army which had been seen in November 1960 on a road near Otterburn, Northumberland, the site of a fourteenth-century battle. One of the witnesses, Mrs Dorothy Strong, was in a taxi. She said: "Suddenly the engine died, the fare-meter went haywire and the taxi felt as if it was being forced against an invisible wall. The soldiers seemed to close in on us then fade into

A lubin bewitches a Norman ploughboy. Lubins, like the English boggarts and fairies, could stop animals and carts.

Frequently we read in accounts of fairy sightings that horses – with or without carriages – are unable to pass beyond a point in the road adjacent to where fairy music is heard or where fairies are seen at their revels. It is said that St Thomas Aquinas, who learned the art of making magical models from Albertus Magnus, was so disturbed in his studies by the clatter of horses outside

thin air." Several people said it had happened around that location before.

Some believe that the interference is caused by mysterious "rays" and energy fields, similar to those beloved by early science-fiction stories and movies. The subject of "secret rays" which could stop machines or cause "mysterious" accidents was enthusiastically discussed in the popular press of

1923–24 and Oliver Grindell-Matthews, the eccentric British genius, even claimed to have invented such a "projector" (*Daily Mail*, 5 April 1924). Another, long forgotten, manifestation was the incident in 1930 in which about forty cars stalled simultaneously on a road in Saxony. None of them were able to restart for about an hour (*New York Times*, 25 October 1930). Later on, the idea of "death rays" and machine-stopping rays was revived in the classic rumours of World War II.

Today, we know that powerful magnetic pulses can be directed in such a way as to stop machines, even car engines, at some distance and these have been developed as military and police devices. But still there is a kind of fascination in recognizing that the "tractor beams" of *Star Trek* have their counterparts, if not roots, in the older traditions of fairy and ghost lore.

A similar effect to an "invisible ray" is the inhibiting magical spell which can be lifted only by the person who placed it – a power attributed to George Pickingill said to be one of the last of the old "cunning men" of Essex who died in 1909. In Katherine Wiltshire's

George Pickingill (d.1909), the last witch of Canewdon, Essex, was said to be able to stop farm machinery with a glance, and was feared throughout the Rochford Hundred.

collection of tales from the living memory of her English county (*Ghosts and Legends of the Wiltshire Countryside*, 1973), a ninety-year-old shepherd tells of a carter who worked on the same farm as himself at Newton Tony. One day the man was driving a wagon-load of wood and encountered a woman, known locally as a witch, who asked if he would carry her small bundle on his cart. He refused and tried to drive on, but the horses were unable to pull the wagon beyond that point, and he had no choice but to unhitch them and lead them home. The farmer returned with him the next morning, and again the wagon would not budge; it remained stuck until they consented to carry the woman's small bundle of wood.

In the 1820s, General Andrew Jackson (a future President of the USA) heard stories about the "Bell witch" – an active poltergeist at the Tennessee farm of John Bell – and went out of his way to investigate the matter. Approaching the farm, his horses halted as the wheels of his coach suddenly "froze". Jackson examined them himself and could see no reason why the pushing and pulling could not budge them. The exasperated members of his party were startled by a metallic voice ringing out in the air: "All right, General, let the wagon move."

Charles Bailey Bell, a descendant, wrote a history of the four-year "infestation", *The Bell Witch of Tennessee* (1934), which included another pertinent story. A family friend, William Porter, was sleeping in the Bell home when the "unmistakable" voice of the entity informed him it would sleep with him to keep him warm. Porter, a man not given to fear lightly, said the chilly sensation of something snake-like was "simply awful". The covers were pulled from him, forming into a roll on the other side of the bed. Porter seized the roll and carried it, struggling, towards the fireplace with the intention of throwing the "witch" into the fire. With every step the bundle seemed to get heavier and "smelled awful", he wrote later. "I had not got halfway across the room before the baggage got so heavy and became so offensive that I was compelled to drop it on the floor and rush outside."

Other accounts of invisible barriers come from fairy-lore, in particular the tradition of the "stray sod", a patch of soil on which fairies have placed a spell. Anyone who steps on this enchanted ground has great difficulty on finding his way off it. Dermot MacManus devotes a chapter to it in his *The Middle Kingdom* (1973). In 1935, his aunt in Mayo hired a girl from a neighbouring village and sent her on an errand which meant passing Lis Ard, a beechwood-capped hill ringed by a famous fairy-fort. As she was homesick and had time to spare, she climbed up the hill into the enclosed wood to gaze at her village from its summit. Then she walked back down the slope towards a gap in the bank. "She had just got to the opening when she felt a queer kind of jerk, a muscular jerk inside her rather than from outside, and before she realized what had happened she found herself walking quickly in exactly the opposite direction towards the centre of the wood again." The same thing happened when she tried the gap a second time. She then made for the point at which she had entered, "but now she received her greatest shock, for she felt an invisible wall which she could not pass". She was trapped for hours behind this magic wall, which felt so solid that she could follow it round with her hands. Meanwhile her absence had been a matter of concern; evening passed into night, and four search parties set out. The girl later said that one party had passed within twenty yards

of her, but they could neither see her nor hear her frantic yells for help, although she could see and hear them well enough. Some time later she became aware that the barrier had gone and was able to set off home, frightened and exhausted.

There are many "haunted" locations, popularly believed to be the centre of strange forces or gateways to other worlds. Typical are those where gravity is said to be out of kilter, making cars or other objects roll backwards "up hill". Often they are not geo-magnetic anomalies at all but odd optical illusions created by the lack of familiar indicators of the horizontal or vertical. Of this type is the famous "mystery vortex" near Gold Hill in Oregon. Now developed as a tourist attraction, its claimed characteristics include plumb-bobs being "pulled" towards the centre where cigarette smoke forms strange eddies and the light is oddly dimmer. (A sceptical account is in Jim Brandon's *Weird America*, 1978.)

There are indeed places with geo-magnetic anomalies which can affect the navigation of ships and planes as well as that on dry land. Remember the "Bermuda Triangle" – which, as Janet and Colin Bord point out "is neither a triangle nor centred on Bermuda" – where some tragic losses have been attributed to strange interference with navigation and radio equipment. Although Lawrence Kusche, in *The Bermuda Triangle Mystery, Solved* (1975), makes a diligent attempt to attribute fifty-one disappearances to misreporting (some ships never did "vanish"), lies, mistakes and natural disasters (hurricanes, etc), there are occasions when things go wrong with instruments inexplicably, such as during sun spot activity. The Bords tell of a flight over the English Channel in 1978 that experienced a sudden and sustained change of 100° in the direction indicator and compass, twenty-five miles south of Bournemouth. On the return journey, the deviation over the same location was 20°. In both cases the new course would have taken them over Portland, Dorset. "Was something secret being tested at Portland Navy Base," the Bords ask, "some sort of weapon which might affect the magnetic field?"

We have heard of local legends of cars being forced to turn dangerously or being unable to turn as though ghostly hands had seized the steering wheel. A series of "attacks on automobiles" of this sort was noted by Fort in April–May 1927, in which cars were forced off roads into ditches, rivers and lakes. In one incident the driver described how he tried to keep the car to the right as it was being forced mysteriously to the left. Could something

A scene from the classic science-fiction film *The Day the Earth Stood Still* (1951) in which an alien creature succeeds in stopping all the machines on earth simultaneously.

similar have happened to Mrs Celina Legris in Sunbury, Ontario, who was found guilty of driving negligently and causing a death when her car hit another? According to the *Recorder and Times* (24 January 1969) her defence was that "some unseen force seemed to pick my car up and violently throw it into the wrong lane just before the head-on collision". Whatever the truth of her claim, the court did not believe her.

Again, an invisible force in a car park at Durham, England, frustrated Mrs Dilys Cant's repeated attempts to back her car into a vacant space. In the *Newcastle Journal* (8 December 1975), she said that it felt as if she were always coming up against a kerb, though no obstacle was visible. Her daughter was also prevented from entering the space by "an invisible force-field". Two other motorists tried to drive and then to push their cars into the space, but were unable to do so. Typically, by the time officials of the council investigated, the "haunted" bay had reverted to normality.

Our final account returns the subject once more to the realm of poltergeists, whatever they are. According to the *Daily Mail* (1 May 1907), an elderly woman in Paris complained to a magistrate that "something" compelled her to walk on her hands every time she went through the door of her apartment. The magistrate detained her, thinking she was mad, and sent an officer to investigate. He returned with the woman's son, who told the court: "I do not pretend to explain it. I only know that when my mother, my uncle and myself enter the flat, we are immediately impelled to walk on our hands." The uncle was sent for, and he too confirmed the story. Finally the magistrate summoned the concierge of the building, who said: "All you have heard is true. I thought my tenants had gone mad, but as soon as I entered the rooms occupied by them, I found myself on all fours, endeavouring to throw my feet in the air." The magistrate ordered the rooms to be disinfected!

Anomalous fossils

The geological record, as Charles Fort pointed out, is a prime example of circular reasoning in science; fossils being dated from their surrounding strata, and the strata from the fossils found in them. The matter is not helped by the bitter controversies of recent years over the anomalies and errors in such scientifically respected dating techniques as the carbon-14 and thermoluminescence tests. This lack of precision in archeological dating is emphasized by science-writer Richard Milton in his book *The Facts of Life: Shattering the Myth of Darwinism* (1992).

Yet despite the impossibility of any really positive proof, academic orthodoxy firmly upholds the cosmogonic myth that we have ascended to our present enlightened, civilized state through uninterrupted development from savage, superstitious beasts, our ancestors. This view is in opposition to the older and universal theory of human history as a decline from the primeval "Golden Age" and discounts the Platonic belief that civilizations rise and fall in cycles with intervening cataclysms.

What interests us here is the evidence of a human presence and technology on this earth long before the evolutionists would have us believe it was possible. Some of this evidence has been actively suppressed and deliberately ignored; some have quietly and mysteriously disappeared from museum stores and records; some are probably on display somewhere dismissively labelled as a "Ritual Object".

We are referring to, among other things, apparently human footprints in sandstone laid down in the Carboniferous period, between 225 and 280 million years ago. That is about 200 to 250 million years before our ape ancestors split from the mainstream of monkey evolution. The *American Journal of Science* (vol.3, p.139) details the discovery of a series of human footprints found in sandstone near Carson, Nevada, in 1882. Three years later tracks, easily identified as human, were found in sandstone near Berea, Kentucky, according to the *American Antiquarian* (vol.7, p.9). There are other discoveries, any one of which, if accepted, could collapse the geological order of the ages overnight, bringing with it the whole Darwinian edifice.

In recent years there has been an explosion of books that have exploited heretical ideas about evolution and anomalous fossils. Significantly, some of these are vehicles for the "Creationist" view that the world was created relatively recently – anywhere between 10,000–4000 years BC. As this does not leave much time for geological and evolutionary processes, creationists argue that the current scientific interpretations are simply wrong.

The main opposing strand of active anomaly research states that the earth is immeasurably more ancient than geologists or creationists will credit. In *Forbidden Archeology* (1993) Michael Cremo and Richard Thompson sifted through much of the evidence for anomalous and "out-of-date" fossils.

A photograph of a coin, dated 1397, found embedded in Carboniferous coal, from the *Strand Magazine* (1901).

Most academics regard such material with undisguised hostility, and in some instances the authors were actively hindered from gaining access to museum specimens and reports. This reaction was fuelled by the fact that, in casting about for a view of human origins that would accommodate artefacts apparently a million years old or older, Cremo and Thompson had to turn to the Hindu-Vedic cosmology. It was here that they found the suggestion that technological and other civilizations have risen and destroyed themselves or been destroyed many times over.

Yet another strand of interpretation holds that fossil footprints and artefacts derive from visits to this planet by aliens far in the formative past. The popular writings of Graham Hancock have developed the thesis that we were visited in this way in 10,500 BC, a magic date when, it is argued, most of the formative early civilizations appeared

to gain major advances in architecture, astronomy, agriculture and mathematics.

Many of these fossil tracks, while distinctly human in appearance, are giant in size. According to a US Department of the Interior booklet, *The Story of the Great White Sands*, a government trapper, in 1932, found a line of thirteen prints in the gypsum rock of White Sands, New Mexico. They were about twenty-two inches long by eight to ten inches wide. In 1896, the *American Anthropologist* described some fourteen-inch human prints found in West Virginia. Brad Steiger gives other examples in his *Mysteries of Time and Space* (1974), including what appears to be a fossil imprint of a shoe, showing a well-cut and double-stitched leather sole, found in 1927 at Fisher Canyon, Nevada. The rock was identified by a geologist as Triassic limestone (laid down 160 to 195 million years ago). This sort of data has been eagerly collected by "Bible scientists" and two groups, the Films for Christ Association and the *Bible Science Newsletter*, have attempted to retrieve a set of prints from the bed of the Paluxy River in Texas. They are in Palaeozoic strata and show the tracks of a human being and a three-toed dinosaur crossing each other, one of the human prints squashing the edge of a dinosaur print. Indeed the large size of some of the fossil tracks, and their shape, seem very similar to the prints associated with our modern mystery anthropoid monsters (see IN SEARCH OF APE-MEN, p.292).

While critics try to dismiss these anomalies as "artifacts of erosion and weathering", it is rather more difficult to explain away objects. The *Times* (24 December 1851) tells of a miner returning from California with a block of auriferous quartz which he accidentally dropped. It split open to reveal a straight-cut iron nail, firmly embedded near its centre. According to a note in the *Report of the British Association* (1845) Sir David Brewster once announced to a meeting the finding of a two-inch nail half-embedded in a lump of solid limestone from a Scottish quarry. A report of a gold thread found in a stone in Berwickshire appeared in the *Times* (22 June 1844). A lady cracking lumps of coal to fill her scuttle, says the *Morrisonville Times*, of Illinois, 11 June 1891, was surprised to find two halves of one lump linked by a small chain, the ends of which were still embedded solidly in the coal which bore a clear imprint of chain. The *Scientific American* (5 June 1852) contained a plea for help in solving a puzzle. Quarrymen blasting out fifteen feet of pudding-

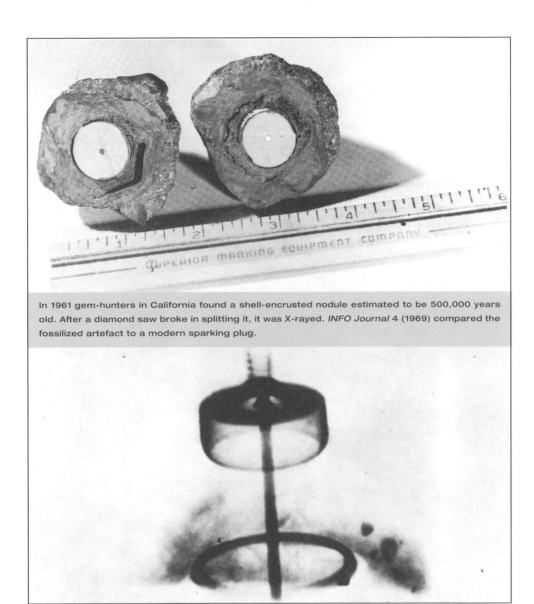

In 1961 gem-hunters in California found a shell-encrusted nodule estimated to be 500,000 years old. After a diamond saw broke in splitting it, it was X-rayed. *INFO Journal* 4 (1969) compared the fossilized artefact to a modern sparking plug.

stone on Meeting House Hill, Dorchester, Massachusetts, had found in the rubble the two halves of a metallic bell-shaped vessel. It is described as about four and a half inches high, made of some alloy and inlaid with silver in an intricate floral design. The quarrymen were in no doubt that it had come from deep within the rock. The best the editor of *Scientific American* could come up with was to suggest that it might have been made by "Tubal Cain, the first inhabitant of Dorchester". In his *Secret Treasure* (1931) A. Hyatt Verrill gives two incidents where coins have been found inside

masses of flint, one in Chute Forest near Stonehenge, and the other in a gravel pit at Westerham in Kent.

Between 1786 and 1788 coins, tools, stumps of columns and other worked stones were found in a quarry in Aix-en-Provence, France, fifty feet down and below eleven beds of compact limestone. An anonymous writer in the *American Journal of Science* (vol.1, p.144) quotes from the *Mineralogy of Count Bourbon* the details of this astonishing find. Among these artefacts from another age was a wooden board, one inch thick and about eight feet long, now turned into a "very fine and agreeably coloured agate". The Count noticed with astonishment that the utensils, board and stoneworkings followed the same pattern used by his men (even the board was worn in the same manner, being rounded and wavy at the edges). An ancient and a modern technology had duplicated each other on the same site; predictable, perhaps, and yet, as the Count remarks, one of them "preceded the formation of this stone".

There are several different theories to account for artefacts which have been found out of their proper time or place. Quite possibly there have been civilizations in the remote, unknown past,

much more evidence – even if we widened our acceptances to imagine the hypothetical civilization to be non-human (e.g. reptilian). Another idea arises out of Fort's speculations on falls and missiles from the upper regions, and on the mysterious force of teleportation, which transports objects through solid matter. Perhaps the same forces might transport occasional objects back in time to when the sedimentary strata were laid down.

We have another idea, equally preposterous and therefore no less worthy of consideration – the spontaneous generation of these anomalous buried objects *in situ*, within the womb of the earth. Consider our section TOAD IN THE HOLE

This trilobite crushed beneath a sandalled heel, was discovered by a fossil-hunter at Antelope Springs, Utah, who split open a slab to find the tableau fossilized in its interior. The trilobite was said to have been alive when it was squashed – which puts the incident some 300 million years before the advent of dinosaurs.

but to postulate technological civilizations hundreds of millions of years back in time on the basis of a single nail, thread or pot is as irrational as, say, Sir Richard Owen inventing the absurdly crosslegged *Labyrinthodon* to explain fossil tracks which had "thumbs" pointing outwards! We would need

(see p.342), in which we examine the phenomenon of living animals found inside rocks. Can one seriously imagine that these animals appeared on earth before their due time to become encased in mud and compressed into rock and to survive across millions of years against all biological reason? Is this any less incredible than spontaneous creation or teleportation? The medieval naturalists often debated whether there was a "shaping force" (*vis plastica*) that formed fossils in the earth. Some thought it a divine trick to test men's faith. But the basic nature of fossils has been well known since the Greek philosophers, so that Michael Valentini's belief that stones copulated and bore young in the earth was to his eighteenth-century colleagues deplorable backsliding. Nevertheless the *vis plastica* theory has had strong adherents including Kepler, Avicenna and Aristotle, and though regularly refuted it persists in dreams and popular traditions, as in the dream-theme of finding coins or other "lucky" objects in unexpected, hidden places.

In the book that he wrote with physicist Wolfgang Pauli, *Synchronicity* (1955), Carl Jung suggested that Kepler's notion of an earth-soul, an *anima telluris*, was the forerunner of his own theory of synchronicity. The forces which harmonize the myriad independent yet interrelated systems of life and matter on the living planet are essentially the same as those which order the contents of the mind. The mind and the earth are wombs in which things are brought into being. Among the dreams, which Jung uses to illustrate how these two great spheres of existence interpenetrate, is one in which the dreamer finds human heads in low relief on slabs lodged in Triassic rock. In another dream, an earth-coloured gnome leads the dreamer into a deep cave where he finds columns of hard "lignite", shaped into life-like human busts. They extend far back into the living rock "and must therefore have come into existence without the aid of man". If some synchronistic process can so unite mind and matter as to impress visible images onto a film or body (see PROJECTED THOUGHT-FORMS, p.72), perhaps there is an analogous force which projects forms into the earth.

Arkeology

We would not like to say that anything is impossible, but few things seem to us less likely than that Noah's Ark should still be where the Flood left it on Mount Ararat. We were taught at school that the Old Testament story was a myth or allegory, and at the time we believed it. After all, the legend of a great flood that destroyed all but one family is a universal one – from Mexico to Mesopotamia – and Ararat is not the only mountain reputed to be the Ark's last resting place. Mount Nisir in Mesopotamia is named in the early Babylonian account, and Al Cudi (also known as Mount Judi) two hundred miles to the south of Ararat is mentioned in the Koran and favoured by the Syrians and other Muslims. There could of course have been many floods and many arks.

In 1829 Dr Johann Jacob Parrot, professor of natural history at the University of Dorpat, was the first European to climb Mount Ararat. Though not looking for the Ark, he was shown alleged relics of it in a monastery that was destroyed by seismic activity just eleven years later. Parrot has his place in the history of arkeology for breaking an ancient taboo that prevented the local inhabitants taking foreigners up the mountain.

In 1876, Viscount Bryce discovered on a rocky ledge some 13,000 feet up the slopes of Ararat a piece of shaped wood about four feet long, possibly gopher wood. Supposing it might be a spar from the Ark, Bryce cut off a small piece as a souvenir.

Archdeacon Nouri, a dignitary of the Chaldaean Church, conducted three searches for the Ark between 1887 and 1892. On 25 April, 1892, he approached the summit of Ararat and there it was! The *English Mechanic* (14 October 1892) described his feelings, as with five or six companions he contemplated from various angles the great wooden vessel. He wrote: "I was almost overcome. The sight of the ark, thus verifying the truth of the Scriptures, in which I had before had no doubt, but which, for the sake of those who do not believe, I was glad, filled me with gratitude". The Turkish government refused him permission to ship the Ark to the World's Fair in Chicago (if he found it). Nouri was later incarcerated in a mental institution.

Noah's ark perched on Mount Ararat as imagined by Hieronymous Bosch (c.1485).

Sightings of the Ark had been made centuries before the claims of Bryce and Nouri. As early as 275 BC, a Babylonian historian called Berosus, whose record was preserved by later Greek writers, stated that an ark was still to be seen in the Kurdish mountains of Armenia, and "the people scrape off the bitumen, and carry it away, and make use of it". The Jewish historian Josephus also refers to pilgrimages to Ararat around 50 BC.

In the cathedral of the monastery at Echmi-adzin, near the foot of Ararat, is a small fragment of wood, the relic of an earlier archeological expedition by a monk of the time of St Gregory the Enlightener (credited with bringing Christianity to Armenia in the fourth century). He is said to have made several attempts to climb the mountain but each time, after ascending a little way, he fell

into a deep sleep and found himself teleported back to the monastery. Finally he was told in a vision that the summit of Ararat, where the Ark lay, was forbidden territory, but that as a reward for his persistence he would be given a piece of its timbers. The piece, duly received, became the monastery's greatest treasure. At the time of the monk's expedition the survival of the Ark was a well-established tradition. These could have been the relics shown to Parrot in 1829.

Since the invention of the airplane the number of Ark sightings and explorations of Greater Ararat have increased. In 1916, a Russian pilot, V. Roskovitsky, reported a large vessel lying on the upper slopes of Ararat. Tzar Nicholas II dispatched an expedition, and the object was found and identified as the Ark. Unfortunately the report was

A photograph of Mount Ararat, showing the 'outline of the Ark', was printed in the *Daily Telegraph*, 13 September 1965. The shape was later thought to be a natural occurrence, possibly a fossilized mud flow.

lost during the Russian Revolution the following year. These things tend to happen in arkeology. An article in the US magazine *Christian Herald* (August 1975), tells of an Armenian immigrant and a lost newspaper cutting. The Armenian, who died in America in 1920, told people that in 1856, when he was a young man living near Ararat, "three foreign atheists" had hired him and his father to guide them up the mountain on an anti-arkeological expedition to disprove the Ark's existence. To their fury they found it. They tried in vain to destroy it but it was too large, so they made their guides join them in an oath to say no more of the matter. The lost newspaper item (which several people claim to have seen but no one has yet produced) reported the death-bed confession of a British scientist confirming the Armenian's story.

Another unlucky piece of evidence was the six large, clear photographs taken in the summer of 1953 from a helicopter less than a hundred feet above Mount Ararat by an American oil worker, George Jefferson Greene. They showed the apparent outline of the Ark half buried in rocks and ice on the edge of a cliff. Greene tried without success to raise an expedition and, since his death in 1962, the photographs have vanished.

For the last half century the Ararat region (where Armenia joins Turkey, Iran and Azerbaijan) has been under strict military control, and both expeditions and overflights have been extremely difficult. Nevertheless, the period between the end of World War II and 1974 was the great age of arkeology. In the summer of 1949 two parties set off to find the Ark. One led by Dr A.J. Smith, a retired missionary of North Carolina, who raised funds by convincing investors that he had had a divine revelation of its location (*Le Monde*, 24 September 1949). Smith failed in the shadow of a rival Turkish expedition, whose colourful account appeared in *France-Soir* (31 August 1949). "We have seen Noah's Ark", they cabled, "but not on Mount Ararat." The find had been made on Mount Judi, in southern Armenia which is believed by the Kurds and others to be the true resting place of the Ark. It was described as an impressive craft − 500 feet long, 80 feet wide and 50 feet high − together with some bones of marine animals and, not far away, Noah's burial place. The explorers, two Turkish journalists, also mentioned the local legend that the Ark sometimes appears like a ghost ship beneath a covering of mud. It is not clear from the account whether it was the actual Ark that was spotted or its phantom apparition.

Many arkeological expeditions have used the Kurdish border town of Dogubayazit, beneath Ararat, as a base. Farhettin Kolan, proprietor of the hotel in the town, acted as a mountain guide for the great Riquer expedition of 1952, the successful Navarra attempt of 1955 and the seven unsuccessful ones by John Libi up to 1969. Libi, a San Franciscan who claimed to have seen the exact site of the Ark in a dream, retired frustrated at the age of seventy-three after an adventurous archeological career which included the experience of being chased by a stone-throwing bear − a phenomenon unique in our records. Another familiar face on the Ararat scene was Eryl Cummings, "the grand old man of arkeology", who made thirty-one ascents, beginning in 1961.

The most successful arkeologist of his time was Fernand Navarra, whose record was published in French in 1956 and in English in 1974 under the title, *Noah's Ark: I Touched It!* From beneath a glacier and a frozen lake high on Ararat, Navarra excavated a number of planks and a hewn L-shaped beam. In 1969 he guided a party mounted by an American organization, Search, which discovered more such timbers and brought back samples. Experts using the radio-carbon method of dating declared them to be some 1400 years old, though other experts at laboratories in Bordeaux and Madrid thought this result was due to the samples becoming contaminated with extraneous carbon-14 and produced the more biblical date of about 3000 BC.

Such breakthroughs have now become regular events in arkeology, each new discovery upstaging the last. Mr George Vandeman, a director of the Archaeological Research Foundation of New York, was reported, in *Antiquity* (1965), as stating that worked wood recovered by an Anglo-American expedition to Ararat was part of a large boat and hundreds more tons of the same timber still lay buried under the ice. Apparently, it was so hard that electric saws had been broken trying to cut it. Mr Vandeman estimated the size of the boat to be about two-thirds that of the *Queen Mary*, similar to the size of Noah's Ark as given in the Bible. In the summer of 1974, just before the Turks closed the area, there were no less than eight Ark-hunting expeditions in the field.

Then we have the excellent satellite photographs. One of which prompted Senator Frank Moss of the US Senate Space Committee, to comment: "It's about the right size and shape for the Ark." However it is is not on Ararat but near Tendurik, fifteen miles to the south and closer to

Mount Judi and the Iranian border. David Fassold, one of the last Americans granted an excavation permit for the vicinity of Ararat, made nine trips to the Tendurik site between 1960 and 1994, and in the end was forced to accept that it was a petrified mud-flow.

In the last decade, we have seen the application of satellite imaging and digital enhancement techniques to photography of the Ahora Gorge, one of the locations favoured by California filmmaker Robin Simmons. Simmons, who grew up in the company of Ark-hunters, joined several expeditions and has spoken with many people who claim to have seen the Ark. One of his informants was Ed Davis, who was taken by a guide on a secret route up the mountain, in July 1943, stopping on the way to see relics preserved in a cave by locals. After several days more climbing, the guide pointed into a crevasse, partly obscured by mist. "Then I saw it," says Davis. "A huge rectangular, man-made structure, partly covered by ice and rock, lying on its side. At least one hundred feet were clearly visible. I could even see inside it, into the end where its broken off timbers stuck out." His guides told Davis that the Ark had broken into three or four pieces, and that in it were forty-eight rooms and animal cages both large and small. They planned to climb down to it the next day but had to cancel because of bad weather.

Inspired by such stories, Simmons attempted his own search in the mid-1990s. One of his guides, climbing alone, radioed back excitedly that he had photographed an object about a quarter of a mile away, "a dark area in the ice, like a barn". Simmons had the film enhanced using specialized satellite imaging software and studied by an aerial reconnaissance expert. Months later, on another visit, flying close to the Ahora Gorge, Simmons believed he saw dark shapes resembling Ed Davis's description of the Ark broken into several parts on the sheer glacier.

Over many years of collecting accounts and stories about the Ark on Ararat, Simmons is convinced that not all has been revealed and that the "truth" is considerably stranger than imagined. Much of his research contains elements that would not be out of place in a typical crashed UFO scenario, complete with recovered bodies and suggestions of high-level conspiracy. For example, he was told by a "protected" source that an espionage team, returning across Ararat in secret in 1974, fell into a structure they took to be an ancient Byzantine shrine. When it was realized what this might be, a classified report went "all the way to the White House".

This strange twist to the story has seemingly been corroborated by other accounts. A pilot, flying secret missions that took him over Ararat many times in the first half of 1960 said that he regularly saw, and photographed, a huge rectangular object protruding from the ice at an altitude of around fifteen thousand feet. Stranger still is the tale of David Duckworth, a young volunteer worker at the Smithsonian Institution in Washington DC who stumbled upon a secret shipment of artefacts from Turkey including a sarcophagus containing a body. There the curtain of silence falls as Duckworth was apparently ordered to keep quiet by two FBI agents.

Why the secrecy and conspiracy? Simmons' theory is that the US military, in a case of classic Cold War paranoia, believes that public confirmation of the Ark's existence would incite Islamic Fundamentalism on a global scale. He was told by an Islamic scholar at the University of Erzurum that "the Ark is a bomb in the world", referring to a belief that its reappearance would herald the return of Mohammed to purge the Earth of heretics and unbelievers.

Judging by its post-diluvian history, Noah's Ark has an existence like that of the Loch Ness Monster or the Abominable Snowman – phenomenal rather than physical. As is usual with such things, there are legends, sightings and ambiguous relics and photographs, all of which fall short of scientific proof. Yet people continue to dream of Noah's Ark and some go in search of it, and it responds with dream-like evidence of itself, which never quite achieves hard reality.

Crop circles

From the early years of the post-World War II UFO phenomenon, there were occasional reports of alleged landing sites – areas of crushed vegetation, sometimes in association with unidentified lights or objects. The most famous of these sites, called "saucer nests", were in Australia, and ufologists saw a continuation of these when, in about 1980, an apparently similar phenomenon began to be noticed by farmers in southern England. Circles were appearing in their fields of wheat and barley. These were not disorderly messes, as might be caused by something landing but regular, neatly swirled circles of laid-down crops, still growing and virtually undamaged.

A masterpiece of the 1997 season appeared on 8 August in a wheatfield near Alton Barnes, Wiltshire – a well-known centre of crop circle activity. Measuring 234 feet across, its 'fractal snowflake' outline was fringed with 192 small circles, 150 outside and 42 within. The central area of wheat was untrodden, raising the problem of how this geometric design could have been constructed. In this and a neighbouring formation, the crop had been laid down in a way that suggested wave action rather than physical labour.

The ufologists were not alone in their investigations. Among the first in the field were a pair of Hampshire technologists, Pat Delgado and Colin Andrews, forming the nub of a circle-spotting group which included veteran ufologist Don Tuersley and a local pilot "Busty" Taylor. Also in this group, though following his own line of research, was Dr Terence Meaden, a Wiltshire meteorologist. Together and separately they visited and recorded hundreds of crop circles during the following summers.

Sometimes, instead of simple circles, they would discover square formations or rings and other features. Delgado and Andrews were conscious of a spooky effect and saw the circles as the workings of an "unknown intelligence". But Meaden stuck with science. "Stationary whirlwinds" was his first explanation and this was elaborated into a theory of "electrically-active plasma vortices", unrecognized by modern science. These vortices, thought Meaden, had been known in the past; the ancient British had venerated them and temples, such as Stonehenge, were built on the sites of prehistoric crop circles.

By the end of the 1980s, crop circles had become a full-blown mystery, sensationalized by newspapers and television and provoking all kinds of ingenious theories. Supporters of whirlwinds argued with extra-terrestrialists, and cases were made for fungi, fertilizer, rutting deer, hedgehogs, hippies, helicopters and hoaxers.

Geometric spirals featured in many crop formations during the 1990s. A particularly subtle design from 1999 was this 300-foot wide example in a wheatfield not far from Avebury in Wiltshire.

Decoders joined in, identifying the crop markings as symbols in ancient scripts – Sumerian, Phoenician, Tifinag and the Hopi Indian language were among those claimed – producing messages of hope or doom. In 1990, the Koestler Foundation, promoters of paranormal research, offered £5000 for a definitive solution to the circle mystery and the *Sunday Mirror* made its own headlines by adding a further £10,000 to the prize.

1990 was a golden year for the crop circles. There had been a spate of books on the subject, one of which – the beautifully illustrated *Circular Evidence* by Pat Delgado and Colin Andrews – became a best-seller. Mystery-seekers from all over Britain and abroad headed for Wiltshire, the acknowledged centre of the phenomenon. Among the visitors was a well-equipped team of Japanese scientists, invited by Meaden to record the circle-making effect in action and to discover the nature of the energy behind it. Expectations were high and the circles phenomenon lived up to them.

The season began with a series of new crop formations, quite different from any in previous years. Researchers called them pictograms. They were elaborate compositions, up to 150 yards long, featuring not just circles but rings, rectangles and strange shapes that looked like protruding claws. The sensation of the year came on 12 July, when a huge pictogram appeared overnight in a field at Alton Barnes, near Pewsey, a place now famous for circles and a rallying-point for their investigators. Many other formations followed, not only in Wiltshire and neighbouring counties but in the north of England, East Anglia, Kent, Sussex, Cornwall and elsewhere. Circles were also recorded appearing in America and Canada, on the Continent, in eastern Europe, Japan and Australia. It was an epidemic and a very exciting one.

Yet, behind the euphoria, some of the older researchers felt twinges of unease. Near the end of the 1990 season, there was a nasty incident in which prominent circle experts were publicly humiliated by an unknown team of hoaxers. "Operation Blackbird", sponsored by British and Japanese television, assisted by the Army and staffed by leading researchers including Andrews and Delgado, was mounted on a Wiltshire hillside with surveillance equipment, hoping to record the

One of the most beautiful crop patterns of its time, this 'spider's web' of 1994 was significantly placed just outside the great circular earthwork of Avebury in Wiltshire, the main prehistoric temple of southern England. From the beginning of the phenomenon there has been a marked connection between crop circles and ancient sacred sites.

formation of a crop circle. Six circles duly appeared in a field below and BBC listeners were told to stand by for sensational news. But when the researchers entered the circles they were dismayed to find objects in the centre of each circle, deliberately left there to prove trickery. George Wingfield, describing the event in the *Cerealogist*, the independent journal and forum for crop circle studies, edited at the time by John Michell, claimed that the hoax was a disinformation exercise by a government agency aimed at discrediting the circles phenomenon. The incident was particularly disturbing because the experts and authors of crop circle books had always insisted that the circles could not possibly be man-made.

The least popular explanation for crop circles was that they had been hoaxes. According to the experts, the plants in circles were not trampled but laid down organically by some unknown natural force. Sometimes the stalks were woven together in a skilful way that seemed beyond human art. Delgado, Meaden and most of the leading researchers had taken up dowsing and the movements of their rods told them that powerful energy fields were active within the circles. These were thought responsible for the strange experiences of circle visitors, including luminous visions and incidents of healing. Yet as the circle forms grew more elaborate, it became ever more obvious that they were not just chance products of natural forces but intelligently designed. Solly Zuckerman, former British government adviser on science, argued that, since we are the only known intelligent beings, the circles must be human artefacts. The

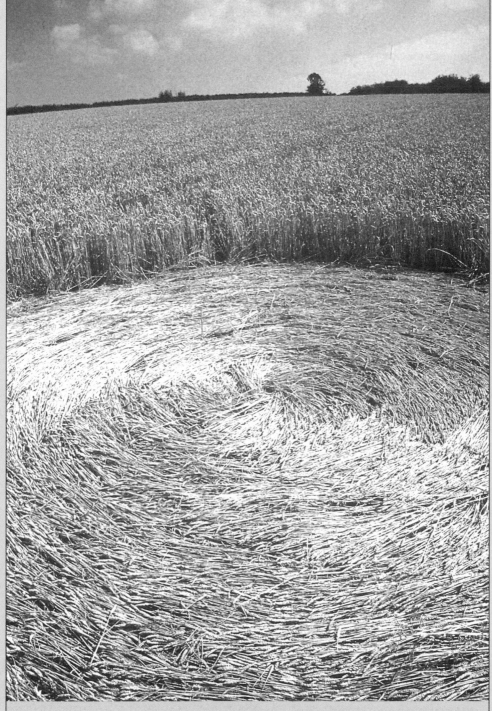

Crop circles cause little damage to farmer's fields. Laid down in regular, sometimes elaborately woven patterns, the plants continue to grow and ripen.

phenomenon, he added, is still a mystery. Who is making the circles, how are they doing it and what is their motive?

The crop circles of 1991 were hailed as even better than those of the previous year. Among them was a huge, faultless "Mandlebrot Set", a fractal design discovered in a Cambridgeshire wheatfield. Other wonderful designs followed and, at the *Cerealogist*'s end-of-season "Cornference" in Glastonbury, speaker after speaker talked excitedly about millennarian revelations to come. The magazine had already published an article by a sceptic, Peter Williams, claiming that the circles were all man-made but this was widely ignored.

This woodcut of a 'mowing devil' is from a broadsheet, published in 1678, describing a remarkable event that took place in Herefordshire that summer. A farmer employed a labourer to cut his field of oats but they quarrelled over payment. The farmer declared that he would rather the devil himself mow the field than pay what the man asked. That night a fiery light was seen in the field and the following morning revealed the crop cut, with supernatural exactness, into "round circles". When rediscovered in 1989, the story was claimed as an early record of the crop circle phenomenon. But in this case the crop was cut rather than laid down.

It came as a bombshell then, when, in September, *Today* newspaper published a sensational account of how two men in their sixties, Doug Bower and Dave Chorley, had fooled the world by making circles themselves. Delgado, Meaden and Taylor were among those who had been caught out by identifying "Doug 'n' Dave" circles as the genuine article. Crop circle followers who had invested high hopes in the phenomenon were disillusioned and many of them abandoned the subject.

Next year, prompted by the biologist and author Rupert Sheldrake and organized by the *Cerealogist*, a circle-making contest, with a prize of £3000 for the winner, was held in a Buckinghamshire wheatfield. Eleven teams entered, some with many hands and much equipment, but the third prize was won by a young American, Jim Schnabel, working alone. The result was to prove how much easier it was to reproduce the subtle features of crop circles than the experts had proclaimed.

For many people the phenomenon was over. It was all a hoax. Schnabel's book, *Round in Circles*, made it plain that he and others had created some of the acclaimed circle designs. The press lost interest in the subject and only the die-hard enthusiasts continued to make the annual pilgrimage to Wiltshire. Yet, against all reasonable expectations, the phenomenon did not die. Every year up to the present (1999) a great many further designs, as beautiful and mysterious as before, have appeared in the usual fields and districts. Like the masterpieces of earlier years, these are still of unknown origin. Even the known circle-makers, who like to take credit for their work, are baffled by these superior designs. They attribute them to a hypothetical "A team". Despite heavy surveillance, no team of circle-makers has ever been caught in the act.

If crop circles have a meaning, it is probably indicated by the effect they have on people. Many researchers say that their minds and lives have been changed by the phenomenon. New friends have been made, new interests developed and the mystery in the cornfields has drawn attention to other mysteries, in archeology for example. Crop circles are often to be found near ancient sites, appearing alongside the old temples of Stonehenge and Avebury and other Wessex monuments. There is much speculation on the geometry of their designs, some of which are hard to construct, even on paper. To create them on a large scale, illegally, flawlessly, in the short hours of summer darkness, often in full sight of main roads, is an impressive feat, unequalled by any of the self-proclaimed hoaxing teams.

Far from dwindling away, the mystery has actually deepened. Like most of the phenomena recorded in this book, it has been explained often and in many different ways, but never finally. Veteran researchers recall the early days when circles on remote farms were unvisited, unpubli- cized, sometimes peppered with little swirls of "grapeshot" and with features that convinced them that no ordinary people could possibly have made them.

Is there really an "A team", persistent, dedi- cated, practising their art secretly in farmers' fields year after year? Are they trying to tell us some- thing? Or is the answer something else entirely?

Discs of ice

Ice-discs are circular plates of ice many metres across, circumscribed by a narrow, usually ice-free, ring or "ditch" in which the disc slowly revolves. Like crop circles, they have an immediate and striking visual appeal, but the phenomenon is rel- atively unfamiliar, even to scientists, and remained largely uninvestigated until the 1980s. There are no references to the phenomenon in any standard texts on meteorology, geology or hydrology.

The geometric perfection and size of the ice- discs, like that of their cereal cousins (see CROP CIRCLES, p.184), has been taken by the credulous as a sign of alien intervention. Most attempts at scientific explanation, as with crop circles, have involved discussion of vortices – only this time in the form of whirlpools rather than whirlwinds.

Many have wondered, if this was indeed a natural phenomenon, why they had never heard of ice-discs before. Thus were sown the seeds of doubt that flowered into suggestions of hoaxing. But the question of motive was even more charged than it was with crop circles: why would anyone go to the trouble of making something so difficult in places so remote that it was unlikely ever to be seen?

As in so many cases of strange phenomena, ufologists were among the first to draw public attention to this mysterious and entrancing occur- rence. In January 1987 Clas Svahn, head of UFO- Sweden and editor of its journal *UFO-Aktuellt*, published an account of his visit to two rivers in northern Sweden earlier that month. The first ice- disc that he found (50m in diameter) was located a few kilometres south of the town of lvsbyn, at a bend in the Piteälven ("the River of Pite"). The entire formation of the ice-disc had been observed by a local man in mid-December 1986. "At first, all that could be seen was a large central area of ice surrounded by many smaller chunks, all moving in a circle", wrote Svahn. By 22 December, this rotating system of ice planets was frozen together, and in early January (when Svahn visited) the huge circle was complete. The ice was 50cm thick, deep enough to support the adven- turous ufologist who completed a revolution in eight minutes. "It was great fun!" said Svahn.

According to Svahn, the rate at which the Piteälven ice-disc revolved slowed from about two minutes in its early stages to about ten minutes weeks later. This was presumably due either to variations in the flow beneath it or, more likely, to the slush freezing in its ditch – or possibly both. A few weeks later, Svahn was called to Kalixälven where he saw a similar but smaller ice-disc. It was unable to revolve because its ditch had frozen, fastening the disc to the rest of the ice sheet. Clas also told us that in January 1992, a pair of discs, both frozen in situ, had been found on Hotagssjön, a lake near Östersund.

Inquiring at Sweden's Meteorological and Hydrological Institute (SMHI), Svahn was referred to Mrs Birgitta Raab, who took more than a passing interest in the phenomenon. She told him: "I know of three or four rivers in Sweden and Norway in which rotating discs of ice have formed, but as far as I know this phenomenon doesn't yet have a name." Mrs Raab said that a particularly massive disc formed every spring in the River Ljusnan in central Sweden. (It has been known to measure an astonishing 200m in diameter.) In her opinion the critical factor is the

This early record of a slowly revolving disc of ice appeared in the *Scientific American*, February 1895. The 25-ft diameter disc was seen on the Mianus River, near Bedford, New York.

way a river current flows through a bend or narrow part to form a suitable back eddy. It was possible, she said, that the shape of the shoreline in some lakes could also influence the currents to form ice-discs.

In fact an earlier ice-disc formation, was reported in the *Illustrated London News* (15 February 1930), under the heading "Jack Frost Describes a Circle": it was located "in the Valley of the River Don, within a few miles of Toronto, Ontario, at a sharp turn in the stream where there is a slow-turning whirlpool, or eddy." The anonymous account went on to describe how when "this part of the river froze over, a sheet of ice in the shape of a perfect circle was formed in the centre of the whirlpool. This disc floated on a round patch of water, which was surrounded by ice on all sides, and turned slowly around with the water beneath it."

The UFO connection surfaced in October 1991 when the *UFO Journal* of the Mutual UFO Network (MUFON) carried an account of a cir-

cular formation of ice on the River Mzha in the Ukraine. It had been sent to editor Dennis Stacy by MUFON's Russian correspondent Vladimir Rubtsov. The circle was found on 7 January 1990 by Mr A.E. Vorontsov, a resident of Merefa (about 30km south of Kharkov), who had cycled to the river to check his baited fishing lines. Vorontsov claims he saw a huge, top-shaped object resting on the ice or hovering just above it. After ten minutes the luminous object, "as glorious as a sunset", sped eastward leaving the large disc of ice to sink into the water and rise again.

By chance, the story came to the attention of Dr Pyotr I. Kutnyuk of the Kharkov regional UFO group the very next day, and he promptly went to the location to see for himself. Kutnyuk noted that the ice layer was thin – it could not support a man, never mind a UFO seventy-five metres across. When Rubtsov himself visited the site five days later, on 13 January, the ice had thickened enough to support a man, and both researchers believed this ruled out a hoax. Rubtsov was intrigued by the metre-wide ring, which comprised a number of "concentric ridges, as if it had been made by a giant milling machine cutter." The rings were still visible at the end of January, but it was a relatively warm winter and thereafter the ice soon melted.

Whatever Mr Vorontsov saw may have had nothing (or everything) to do with the ice rings, and the comparison has been made with the rare description of glowing masses in association with formation of crop circles. Nevertheless, it is clear that the Mzha River ice rings are related to ice-discs, and probably represent a variation in the process of formation.

An early theory about the ring of ridges is that they might be frozen ripples. This was proposed by another MUFON investigator, Paul Rosenfield, in connection with a set of clearly defined concentric rings, 6m (20ft) in diameter, in the ice over a stretch of the Charles River that runs through the Mount Feake Cemetery in Waltham, Massachusetts. He had spotted the formation while jogging on 15 January 1991 and submitted his report to the MUFON *UFO Journal* (April 1992). Rosenfield, who was fascinated by reports of crop circles, made the visual connection immediately

and ran home for his camera. As he judged, the ice was not safe and there were no footprints or tracks near the circle, it did not appear likely that anyone could have faked it.

Paul Rosenfield tried unsuccessfully to get a few scientists to look at his photos; then he met Dr Jerome Carr, who had an interest in geophysics, geology and limnology. Dr Carr's considered opinion was that the circle effect had been created by the near-perpendicular strike of a meteorite through the ice and the resulting wave patterns overlapped to produce refrozen rings of broken ice. Just how the pattern of breaking and re-freezing would create perfectly circular rings is not explained. Rosenfield also managed to test the theory; in March 1991, a police diving team were salvaging a small sunken boat not far from the ring site, and he managed to convince them to search the river bottom for any unusual rocks. There was no sign of anything seemingly meteoric.

As knowledge of ice-discs became more widespread, British sceptic Peter Williams launched an explanation of his own. Ice-discs, he asserted, were made by hoaxers using an ice saw (an adapted chain saw used in ice manufacture since the 1920s). Williams envisaged one man standing at the centre

A perfect disc of ice revolving clockwise on the River Don near Toronto, Ontario, in January 1930. Around the slow-turning whirlpool, areas of thin, slushy ice can be seen, especially on the outer edges of the ditch in which the plate of ice is revolving.

holding a rope that acts as the radius. Thus guided, his partner would carve the inner edge of the "ditch", then the outer, and then both smash up the ring to set the disc free (*The Crop Watcher*, September 1993). This theory would be fine, were it not for the fact that some of our accounts involve ice too thin for any anchorman and chainsaw artist. Moreover, the Piteälven disc was observed throughout its formation, and the Ukrainian ring at different stages in its growth.

The phenomenon was thrust on the scientific community in February 1993 when a strange constellation of concentric ice-rings began to form on the surface of the Charles River where it flows through the Massachusetts Institute of Technology (MIT) campus at Cambridge, Massachusetts.

graduate, confirmed the theory of two colleagues through first-hand observation. Crossing over the Harvard Bridge each day he observed the circles forming over several weeks. "First, a smooth sheet of ice formed over most of the river. Then large holes were formed by ice shearing and moving around." The driving force behind the ice formations were eddies from the piers of the Harvard Bridge itself. "Areas of open water froze over again . . . in circular patterns, even though they had irregular shapes when they were created. I saw that the ice *grew* into the holes, from the outside edge in. Evidently this made the holes more circular," said Ricks. (*MIT Tech Talk*, 24 February 1993). We find it amazing and amusing that this high-powered think tank was completely unaware of

Conrad Serfass surveys the ice disc that formed in Cranberry Creek, behind his home in Tannersville, Pennsylvania, in January 1993. The 8.5m-diameter disc, a good simulacrum of the Moon, was discovered by his wife while walking the dog.

Under the supervision of Professor John Marshall, of MIT's Earth, Atmospheric and Planetary Science Department, various supposed causes (such as effluent from submerged pipes, the down-draughts of helicopters, wind action, activity by aliens, bubblings of natural gas from decomposing matter, and underwater springs) were systematically eliminated. The mystery was finally solved when David Ricks, an Ocean Engineering

the more perfect concentric ice rings observed by Paul Rosenfield further up the same Charles River just two years earlier (see overleaf).

Over the past few years a consensus has begun to emerge about how ice-discs are formed. A slow-moving river current creates a slow-turning eddy in which a rotating disc of ice can grind out its edges, and those of the ditch, to perfection. According to Paul Fuller, writing in the *Crop*

Watcher (November 1991), "this is further proof that nature can and does produce precisely-defined geometrical traces without the need for alien intervention."

Could the phenomenon be related to, or explain, the rash of holes found in ice-covered lakes in Sweden in March 1968 (*Fortean Times*, no.24, p.41) and in Finland in 1983–84 (*Fortean Times*, no.45, p.47). In the Swedish case locals believed a large object had crashed into the lake at Upprämen, in southern Dalarna, through ice 35 inches thick. The curiously triangular hole, measuring 60 feet by 90 feet, was surrounded by a wall of large ice boulders several yards high. Military divers claimed to have found nothing below it but local people remained convinced that perhaps it was a bomb dropped by mistake or a crashed spy satellite. Two similar ice-holes were found in April 1968, some 93 miles further north in the river Dalälven at Hedfjorden and again searching divers found nothing. Upprämen lake was searched again by divers in the summer of 1998; thirty years after

the first incident it still worried the locals. There was some evidence that the huge wall of ice round the hole had been thrown up by an impact or explosion. (*UFO-Aktuellt*, issues 3 and 5, 1998).

Sweden seems to be a favourite target for celestial marksmen, because the phenomenon occurred again in mid-August 1999, this time in the lake at Backsjön in the province of Värmland, where people staying in summer cottages said they saw a mysterious flying object with fins falling into the lake. For a whole month, Swedish military forces searched in and around the lake for the UFO, but no trace of the object was found.

We believe that it is perfectly possible all these related phenomena have been in the open all the time, unnoticed because (like many topics in this book) they were quite familiar to country people and regarded as too commonplace by them to warrant any comment. There again, it may be – as is the case of many other things that were "there all the time"– that the evidence for them in historical records has, simply, never been noticed.

8

Signs and Portents

8

Signs and Portents

Honest codfish

On 23 June 1626, a Mr Mead of Christ's College, Cambridge, was walking through the city's market when exclamations from a rustic group around a fish stall attracted his attention. On the stall lay a battered book, its sail-cloth binding slimy with fish gut. The fishwife had just pulled it out from the inside of a plump codfish. In a letter to Sir M. Stuteville, Mead wrote excitedly: "I saw all with mine own eyes – the fish, the maw, the piece of sail-cloth, the book – and observed all I have written; only I did not see the opening of the fish, which not many did, being on the fish-woman's stall in the market, who first cut off its head, to which the maw hanging, and seeming much stuffed with somewhat, it was searched, and all found as aforesaid. He that had had his nose as near as I yester morning would have been persuaded there was no imposture here without witness. The fish came from Lynne."

In the name of scholarship Mead took possession of the fishy volume. It turned out to be a theological work by John Frith, written while the author was in prison at Oxford. We do not wish to be provocative, and merely for the sake of inclusiveness we record the fact that the place of his confinement had been a fish storage cellar where the smell was so overpowering that several of Frith's fellow prisoners had died of it. His book, thus miraculously restored to circulation, was reprinted by the Cambridge authorities under the title *Vox piscis* and illustrated with a woodcut showing the book, the fish stall and the knife which had cut open the fish.

This anecdote perfectly illustrates a principal theme of our book, the way in which certain apparently most unlikely events repeat themselves among all people and in all ages of which we have record. Some of these stories of lost treasures revealed by a fish we find rather incredible. Our title comes from an undated newsclipping (from the *Times*, sometime before 1900) in which a Scottish fisherman who lost his keys overboard in Loch Broom had them delivered back to him personally, six weeks later and a hundred miles away, while fishing off the island of Rassay, vomited up by a large cod. The report commented: "It is a remarkable circumstance that this fish, in its migratory course, should arrive at the same spot where the sloop was . . . and with its last breath discharging an act of honesty that would have honoured a higher grade or species of animal." By another such act of honesty, Ricky Shipman of Sunset Beach, California, had his driving licence returned to him after eleven years by a mackerel. (Associated Press, 10 Sept 1983).

Much less believable is the tale given in William of Malmesbury's *Gesta pontificum*, repeating a slightly different version in the *Chronicle of*

Evesham Abbey. The eighth-century founder of the Abbey, St Egwin, an early Bishop of Winchester, had become involved in some scandal and decided on a voyage to Rome to clear his name. Dramatically, before setting off, he locked fetters to his feet and threw the key into the River Avon. As he sailed to Rome, a fish leapt out of the sea and onto the ship's deck; it was opened and there was the key. The *Chronicle* says that the fish was actually caught in the River Tiber. At all events, the Pope took the matter to signify the complete innocence of St Egwin and he returned to England vindicated.

Among the earliest episodes in Japanese sacred history is the Shinto myth of two brothers – corresponding to Cain and Abel – who divided the

had the fish hook to return it. A mullet which had swallowed the hook obligingly threw it up again, and the brother took it back home.

In medieval versions of this story the object most commonly swallowed and returned by a fish was a ring. St Mungo, bishop and patron saint of Glasgow, who lived in the sixth century, was once applied to by a lady who had dropped her husband's ring into the River Clyde and was suspected of having given it to a lover. St Mungo, after prayer and meditation, asked for the first fish caught that morning in the Clyde to be brought to him. In its mouth was the ring. Another saintly bishop, Gerbold of Bayeux, threw his ring into the sea and retired into a hermitage after the people had driven him out of his palace. Later a man caught a fish. The Bishop's ring was in its belly. The hint was taken; Gerbold was sent for and reinstalled in his palace at Bayeux, which he continued for many years to sanctify, first with his living presence and thereafter with his holy bones.

All these stories, we know, bear a mystical interpretation. In Celtic mythology the salmon is the bearer of wisdom, and the oracular fishes, consulted by the Druids at Irish holy wells, were within recent years still spoken of by the country people. Accounts of being swallowed by a fish, or descending into a cavern or dark hermetic vessel, are allegories of the psychological process in which the soul in its quest for maturity sinks into the perilous depths of the mental underworld to emerge

Illustration from the lost book found within a codfish in Cambridge market – showing the market stall, knife, fish and book.

country between them, the elder living by the shore and becoming a fisherman, the younger taking to the mountains as a hunter. On a whim they decided to change roles, but neither was any good at the other's trade, and things would simply have reverted to normal had not the younger brother lost the elder's precious fish hook. Thousands of substitutes were offered, but nothing would do but the original, so the younger brother set out in quest of it to the palace of the fish king. After many adventures, including marriage to the king's daughter, he persuaded the king to summon all the fish of the ocean and to ask whichever one

tempered and purified. Christ's descent into Hell and Jonah's adventure in the whale's belly are among the many illustrations of symbolic death as a means to initiation.

In *Psychology and Alchemy* (1964) Carl Jung describes an episode from a patient's dream containing all the essential elements in our fish and ring story: "Then the dreamer is wandering about in a dark cave, where a battle is going on between good and evil. But there is also a prince who knows everything. He gives the dreamer a ring set with a diamond . . ." In Jung's interpretation, the cave is the unconscious mind, scene of deep mental

COLIN AND JANET BORD

Pictish inscribed stone from early Christian Scotland, bearing symbols of the worm bait, fish and mirror ring, reminiscent of the archetypal theme reviewed in this section.

conflict and the prince is the philosopher's stone, instrument of reconciliation. In accepting the ring the dreamer is pledging himself to the sacred quest.

Jung's purpose was to show the enduring, archetypal nature of certain themes and images, expressed in universal mythology, poetry and magical symbolism, and also recurring spontaneously in people's dreams, and to construct from them a model of human psychological reality. Ours is to take the matter a stage further by spotting these same archetypes as they emerge from the world of dreams into the world of actual experience. We do not know whether Herodotus was correct in stating that Polycrates (fl. 536 BC), tyrant of Samos, sacrificed his emerald and gold seal on the advice of a holy man by throwing it into the sea and later received it back from the belly of a fish; nor do we know just what truth there is behind the legend that the name of Pickering in Yorkshire comes from a ring lost by an old British king and restored by a pike. But we do know that when Mrs S. Judges of Chatham, Kent, lost an opal ring, she dreamed that night of finding it in the muck of her chicken run. Two days later, one of her birds was killed for dinner and, there in its crop, was her ring. (*Sun*, 6 February 1975).

Charles Fort regarded such tales as too conventional, simply because they were pretty common and he admitted neglecting to collect them in favour of stories "of the unconventional repeating". Nevertheless, such tales of the chance discoveries of long lost or forgotten objects are often to be found in odd newspaper reports and appear in *Fortean Times* from time to time. Our favourite story of this type comes from the *Half-penny Journal* (11 November 1861). An unnamed young man, a servant to an unnamed lady in an unspecified English town was charged, on a date not given, with delivering a ring to a jeweller. Stopping on a bridge over a stream, he took the

AN HONEST CODFISH.—A sloop, belonging to Rothesay, was recently lying in Lochbroom, the skipper of which, when fishing over the side, lost the keys of his lockers, &c., from his pocket into 10 fathoms of water. Attached to the bunch was a small piece of parchment, on which his name and that of the vessel were written. He, of course, gave up all hopes of ever seeing the keys again, and gazed on their rapid descent into the watery depository with deep regret. Six weeks afterwards the skipper cast anchor off the island of Rassay, about 100 miles from Lochbroom, and again resumed his piscatory employment. Among the results of his labours was a large codfish, which was speedily unhooked and thrown upon the deck; and, to the utter amazement of the skipper, the poor cod, when in the last agonies of death, vomited up his bunch of keys. The parchment, being partly preserved, proved his property beyond a doubt. At the same time, as if conscience-stricken, it disgorged a penknife belonging to a brother skipper, on which his initials were engraved. It is a remarkable circumstance that this fish, in its migratory course, should arrive at the same spot where the sloop was, sacrificing its life, and with its last breath discharging an act of honesty that would have honoured a higher grade or species of animals.—*Greenock Advertiser*.

An account of a particularly honest codfish as recounted in the *Greenock Advertiser*.

ring out to look at it and was horrified when it slipped from his grasp and fell into the water. He searched for it all day and until darkness fell, then feeling that he could not satisfactorily account to his mistress for returning so late without the ring he knew he would be accused of gambling it away. He never went back. Instead, he went to the Colonies where he eventually amassed a fortune of his own. But still the incident with the ring tugged his conscience and he returned to his hometown with the idea of clearing himself with his old employers. On alighting from the stage-coach, he fell in with a man following the old path through the fields and explained to him his purpose as they came up to the bridge that changed his life long ago. "There," he said, "it was just here that I dropped the ring and there is the very bit of old tree into a hole of which it fell . . . just there." As he spoke, he thrust his umbrella into the cavity and drawing it up, to the astonishment of both, there was the very ring jammed on the ferrule of the umbrella.

Coincidences

"When it comes to coincidences," wrote Charles Fort, "dark cynicisms arise. What if some of them were not coincidences?" In Fort's mind was his idea of Continuity: that there is an underlying Oneness in which all things merge with all other things. Apparently separate phenomena, as he saw it, were like a chain of islands, outcrops from the same invisibly submerged bedrock.

One of Fort's speculations was that things happen in their own natural time, as if in accordance with some script, pattern or ideal by which we are all controlled, like iron filings in a magnetic field. The rattling of kettle lids blabbed the secret of steam power for centuries, until finally "came steam engine time", as he put it. There are several cases of unconnected people simultaneously filing similar patents on their inventions, as happened in the case of bakelite. Fort would have been pleased to know that, at the same time he was writing about Continuity, Paul Kammerer was developing his own theory about "meaningful coincidences" which he called Seriality.

For phenomenalists, single events cannot be isolated from the continuum that embraces all reality and ensures that anything that happens, on any level, anywhere, influences and is influenced by everything else. Nineteenth-century science attempted to study objects and events as detached entities, whereas physicists now accept that the very act of observation affects the thing observed, and that perception is a powerful act of creativity.

One illustration of this is the phenomenon of coincidences, where two or more events echo each other so neatly and unexpectedly that they seem to indicate a meaning or pattern. Yet in most ordinary cases no particular meaning is apparent.

There is an endless supply of such anecdotes. Typical of its kind is one told to us by an American friend. As a little girl she was taken by her father to a soda bar. A man walked in through the door and the father recognized him as an old friend he had served with in the War and had not seen since. He rose to greet him, but then saw that he had made a mistake and it was not the man he thought. A few minutes later another man came in, and this time it really was the father's old comrade. A similar, common experience is thinking about someone, the phone ringing, and knowing before you have answered it that the caller is the person you were thinking about.

A bizarre coincidence that befell his friend, the poet Emile Deschamps, is recounted by Camille Flammarion in *The Unknown* (1902). While at a school in Orleans Deschamps shared a table with a certain M. de Fortgibu, who on a trip to England had acquired a taste for plum-puddings, then unknown in France. He insisted that Deschamps try one. Ten years later Deschamps passed a restaurant, and saw a plum-pudding being prepared inside. His early taste, long forgotten, urged him to enter and ask for a slice; but the pudding was reserved for another, and Deschamps was obliged to beg the favour from this stranger. It turned out to be M. de Fortgibu, and both were astonished at meeting again for the second time

SOUTH SHROPSHIRE JOURNAL

When Mrs Margaret Bell, a well-known beekeeper of Ludlow, Shropshire, died in June 1994, this swarm settled on the corner of Bell Lane for an hour during her funeral. According to country lore, bees should always be told of a death so they can pay their respects.

M. de Fortgibu!" said Deschamps. "My hair stood up on my head. A fourth time I should feel capable of anything . . . or nothing!"

In his book, *Synchronicity* (1955), Carl Jung proposes an unknown process which cuts across space-time to order events in the same manner as the archetypes order the pre-conscious contents of the psyche, so that events in both physical and psychological reality take on parallel meanings. Flammarion's interest was para-psychological, developing from his interest in phantoms as portents of a death. He pointed out that even if such visions are merely hallucinations, there is the problem of their synchronization with unknown events far away. Had Flammarion not turned away from his brief excursions into coincidences, he would have anticipated the work of Paul Kammerer, the ill-fated biologist, who published his work on the "Law of Series" in 1919. For twenty years he kept a detailed notebook on coincidences, meticulously analysed into categories, and was confirmed in his belief that "Seriality is ubiquitous and continuous in life, nature and cosmos".

Buried in Kammerer's work is the old alchemical notion of affinity, of like attracting like. Kammerer also noticed a periodicity of events, a theme picked up and amplified into a new area of study by Edward R. Dewey in his *Cycles: The Mysterious Forces that Trigger Events* (1971). A baby fell fourteen stories in Detroit and landed on Joseph Figlock passing below. A year later Joseph Figlock was hit by another falling baby (*Weekend*, 19 May 1976). He and both babies survived. A similar coincidence, which occurred in Bermuda and was reported in the *Liverpool Echo* (21 July 1975) ended in tragedy. Two brothers were killed by the same taxi and driver, carrying the same passenger. They were riding the same

over the same dish. Many years passed again and Deschamps was invited to a dinner party which featured an English plum-pudding. At dinner he delighted his hosts with the tale of his extraordinary encounter with Fortgibu. They all joked about the possibility of the old man turning up, which he duly did having been invited to dinner at another apartment in the same building and having lost his way. "Three times in my life have I eaten plum-pudding, and three times have I seen moped in the same street – but each accident happened exactly one year apart.

Fort said that he was not so much interested in things as in the relations between things, and saw all phenomena as a vastly complex continuity whose peaks occasionally project into the field of our notice: "Not a bottle of catsup can fall from a tenement-house fire-escape in Harlem, without . . . affecting the price of pajamas in Jersey City; the temperature of somebody's mother-in-law in Greenland; or the demand in China for rhinoceros horns."

Not only are coincidences a common factor in everyday life, but according to Ira Progoff, in *Jung, Synchronicity and Human Destiny* (1973), they can to some extent be induced, by keeping a daily record of coincidences, as Kammerer did. That effect was also observed by Alan Vaughan in his book, *Incredible Coincidence* (1979): "The more I focused on synchronicity", he wrote, "the more it began happening". John Keel in his UFO classic, *Operation Trojan Horse* (1970), found the same thing, that as soon as he began investigating the subject of UFOs the phenomenon "zeroed in" on him and he was "plagued by impossible coincidences". Many writers tell of helpful coincidences, the type that Koestler attributed to "library angels", whereby some much-needed book or reference turns up in an apparently miraculous way. In his introduction to *The Occult* (1971) Colin Wilson wrote: "On one occasion, when I was searching for a piece of information, a book actually fell off the shelf and fell open at the right page." Flammarion recalls, in *The Unknown*, that when he was writing a chapter on the force of the wind for his *L'Atmosphere,* a gust of wind carried his papers off "in a miniature whirlwind beyond hope of recovery".

Notice of the capture of 'a loyal fish' appeared in the *Daily News*, 19 October 1926. The synchronicity of its distinctive markings – in the form of the Union Jack – at a time of an intense debate in South Africa about the design of their new flag, did not go unnoticed. W. Thompson of Durban, who claimed that an Indian caught the fish locally, sent this photograph to several Natal papers.

A few days later he received the proof of that chapter from his publisher, complete with the missing pages. The whirlwind had carried them down a street and deposited them at the feet of a man who worked in the publisher's office. He gathered them up under the impression that he must have dropped them.

In the "library angel" type of coincidence we see evidence of intense desire spontaneously attracting its object – or, in religious terms, acting as an answer to prayer. Solzhenitsyn gives a wonderful example in his *The Gulag Archipelago* (1976). When he was in the state prison in Leningrad, a new prisoner – a famous physicist – was brought in. This man was obsessed with a certain technical problem which required mathematical tables. He seemed to have no chance of obtaining the book of tables, because the only books in the prison library were works of Party propaganda. A library worker came round each week, distributing the books to each prisoner at random. The physicist prayed for a miracle, and received one. Among the library books allotted to him was the very book of tables he had been praying for. Quickly he began memorizing the relevant tables, and managed it just in time, before a prison warder noticed the book and confiscated it.

The most commonly recognized form of coincidences – apart from the "talk-of-the-devil" effect that so fascinated Flammarion – involves words and numbers. Fort quotes a classic example ("a savage pun mixed with murder") from the *New York Herald* (26 November 1911). Three men had been hanged in London for the murder of Sir Edmundbury Godfrey at Greenberry Hill: the names of the murderers were Green, Berry and Hill. There is a punning sense of humour abroad in the world, childish at times, ominous at others.

Vic Burnside was attending a meditation course at the Manjushri Institute, Conishead Priory, at Ulverston, in Cumbria, in 1986, and appears in the second of two personal photos without a head. In his pocket at the time was the book *On Having No Head* by D.E. Harding.

The *Scunthorpe Evening Telegraph* (26 April 1975) tells of golfer Jim Tollan, who teed off toward the fourteenth hole at the local golf club. His ball soared up and struck a mallard duck flying overhead, bringing it down on the green in front of the Mallard Inn. A striking example of the portentous coincidence occurred with the *Daily Telegraph* crosswords that preceded the Normandy landing on 6 June 1944, and included many of the top-secret codenames for the operations: Omaha, Utah, Mulberry, Neptune and the blanket code for D-day itself, Overlord. The innocent compiler of the crosswords, a schoolmaster, found himself under interrogation by Military Intelligence.

There is a category of coincidences in which nature appears to follow art, and fact fiction. As

FORTEAN PICTURE LIBRARY

phenomenalists, we see little point in arguing out chicken-and-egg-type paradoxes, accepting that in Continuity there is a little of everything in everything else, so that it is difficult to tell where "hard" and "soft" realities merge except in an arbitrary and local way. This is a realm of intermediary reality that is virtually unexplored. For example: Noel McCabe of Derby was listening to a record, "Cry of the Wild Goose" by Frankie Lane, when a Canadian goose crashed through his bedroom window (*Sun*, 19 November 1974). The Melkis family of Dunstable, Bedfordshire, were watching a TV film when, just as the doomed *Titanic* was about to collide with the iceberg, their house shook under an impact of a large block of ice that had "chosen" that moment to fall from the sky and smash through their roof (*Daily Mail*, 8 July 1975). In a *Sunday Times* article Arthur Koestler notes that the *Titanic* incident itself was preceded fourteen years earlier by Morgan Robertson's 1898 novel, *Futility*, in which a giant ship, the *Titan*, collides with an iceberg on her maiden voyage in about the same place in the Atlantic. Koestler also pub-

lishes a letter from a man who was at the helm of a ship in 1939, at the exact position of the *Titanic* disaster, when he stopped the ship on a premonition. And just in time, for a giant iceberg loomed up, striking and damaging the vessel, this time with no loss of life. The ship's name was *Titanian*.

Finally we have noted a form of coincidence that would have amused Fort, where an expert scientist witnesses something strange in his own field, as though it were a show put on for him alone. *Science* (22 April 1949) reports that Dr A.D. Bajkov, an ichthyologist, was bombarded with fish from the sky "shortly after breakfast" in Biloxi, Mississippi. Dr W.M. Krogman, a pathologist who specialized in fire-deaths, happened to be on holiday nearby on the night Mrs Reeser spontaneously combusted (see SPONTANEOUS HUMAN COMBUSTION, p.154) And on 2 April 1973, a meteorologist out strolling in Manchester was nearly brained by a falling block of ice that shattered at his feet. According to the *Meteorological Magazine* (September 1975) it was one of the best documented falls of ice on record.

Accidents to iconoclasts

Some archeologists proceed to a cheerful old age. Yet, on the evidence of history, their profession would seem a dangerous one. That so many old stones and buried treasures have survived the centuries intact is certainly due to the popular belief that no good will come to him who disturbs them. Records of the misfortunes of grave-robbers, vandals and iconoclasts are universal; and their ill luck is often inherited by later owners of relics sacrilegiously obtained.

It was widely reported in the press (15 September 1997) that a British tourist, who stole a lump of stone from the base of the Great Pyramid five years earlier, returned it to the Cairo Museum with a letter saying that "it had brought him bad luck ever since". The Museum authorities were not surprised; several such items had been returned by people who felt cursed after

stealing them. A good reason for caution is the largely bogus story of an Egyptian coffin lid – or fragment of a coffin lid. It was told to Arthur Weigall, author of *Tutankhamen* (1923) by its onetime owner, Mr Douglas Murray who purchased the coffin some time in the 1860s: "no sooner had he done so than he lost his arm, owing to the explosion of his gun. The ship in which the coffin was sent home was wrecked, and so was the cab in which it was driven from the docks; the house in which it was deposited was burnt down; and the photographer who made a picture of it shot himself. A lady who had some connection with it suffered great family losses, and was wrecked at sea shortly afterwards . . . The list of accidents and misfortunes charged to the spirit which is connected with this coffin is now of enormous length."

The presence of an Egyptian mummy on board is sometimes blamed for the loss of the *Titanic*. It was said to have been shipped to New York on the supposedly unsinkable liner. Its coffin, no. 22542 in the British Museum, is associated with the curse, and Museum authorities caution people who propose to photograph it.

There is an extensive record of accidents to those who vandalize tombs and ancient monuments. Some quite recent examples are given in the last chapter of *The Secret Country* (1976) by Colin and Janet Bord. Many others have been recorded in S. Menefee's articles in *Folklore* (1975 and 1976) and in L.V. Grinsell's *Folklore of Prehistoric Monuments* (1976).

People who disturb megalithic sites, even to the extent of measuring them or counting their stones, are liable to be themselves disturbed by meteorological or other portents. On 12 August 1740, John Wood, architect of Bath, proposed to take a plan of Stanton Drew stone circles in Somerset, whose stones are said to be wedding guests petrified by the devil. As he later recalled, in *A Description of Bath*, his researches were resisted: "No one, say the country people about Stanton Drew, was ever able to reckon the number of these metamorphosised [*sic*] stones or to take a draft of them, though several have attempted to do so, and proceeded until they were either struck dead upon the spot, or with such illness as soon carried them off." Nevertheless Wood persisted, "and as a great storm accidentally arose just after, and blew down part of a great tree near the body of the work, the people were then thoroughly satisfied that I had disturbed the guardian spirits of the metamorphosised stones, and from thence great pains were taken to convince me of the impiety of what I was about." Wood repeated his "impiety" by taking a plan of Stonehenge with the same results – a violent storm which drove him to shelter in a nearby hut.

Some years later, Dr William Borlase excavated a "giant's grave" in the Scilly Isles. That night a hurricane destroyed the islanders' crops of corn and potatoes – a direct consequence, so they claimed, of the Doctor's archeology. The incident is described in Halliwell's *Rambles in Western Cornwall* (1861).

It is well known that no one in Ireland will, or would, take timber from a rath, which is a sacred enclosure or fairy grove. The railway companies in their early days found many such impediments on their chosen lines, and the same inconvenience is still occasionally suffered by road-making contractors. At the other end of the world the Japanese refrain from cutting trees on Mount Miwa or at any other rural sanctuary. The innumerable instances of disasters visited on people who destroy sacred timber begin with that of the Empress Saimei, who, in 661 AD, felled a sacred grove to build a palace. The building was immediately destroyed by the

A report in the *Times* of 15 December 1967, tells of the discovery, the previous night, of the body of Evalyn McLean of Dallas, Texas, with no obvious cause of death. Evalyn inherited the infamous Hope Diamond from her grandmother (also Evalyn) but was never allowed to touch it. The elder McLean acquired the diamond in 1907 after which she lost a son in a car accident, a daughter to suicide and a husband to mental illness. The diamond is named after its first known owner, Henry Thomas Hope, an English banker, who bought it in 1830 and whose family suffered a catalogue of disasters. Before Hope, the diamond was owned by two ill-fated kings of France; and between Hope and the elder McLean its string of owners committed suicide, were dethroned or assassinated. Others had tragic accidents, like Simon Montharides, whose carriage was dragged over a cliff by a shying horse killing him, his wife and their child. The legend of the diamond is the stereotype of the cursed gem, said to have been stolen from the forehead of an ancient Hindu idol.

Tutankhamen's death mask is said to have a blemish corresponding to the mark of Lord Carnarvon's fatal mosquito bite.

elements, together with its Grand Treasurer and many members of the court. A young Samurai, seeing good timber lying waste, took the logs to build his own palace – with the same results.

To the delight of local wiseacres at the time – and of wiseacres generally ever since – the Puritan who, in the time of Cromwell, chopped down one of the two stems of the sacred Glastonbury thorn (the tree which sprang from St Joseph of Arimath-aea's staff and blossoms every Christmas morning) received a splinter in his eye which prevented him from continuing work on the second stem.

Dr Robert Plot, the old historian of Oxford-shire, records with relish the misfortunes of Cromwell's commissioners who took up quarters in the King's apartments at Woodstock Palace on 13 October 1649 and warmed themselves by burning the locally revered King's Oak. They seem thus to have invoked some of the most unpleasant classes of phenomena described in these sections. A black dog rushed through the rooms upsetting chairs, phantom foot-steps were heard, papers were torn and scattered and ink spilt. The logs of the King's Oak were mysteriously hurled around. On 20 October the commissioners were attacked in their beds, and from then on were continually buffeted by "invisible assailants". Other poltergeist effects followed. Windows were broken by volleys of stones and – some-thing we have never heard of before in this connection – horses' bones. For all this Dr Plot blamed "immaterial beings". The last straw was when the commissioners, having planned to set aside some of the estate for them-selves, and drawn up an agreement to that effect and hidden it in a pot beneath the roots of an orange tree, found the earth in the pot burning with a blue, sulphurous flame; at which point they fled.

Of all such curses, coincidences, strokes of ill luck or whatever they may be, the most famous is the "Curse of the Pharaohs", which started its career of entertaining the public and infuriating the Egyptologists on 6 April 1923 with the death of Lord Carnarvon shortly after his expedition had forced open the funerary chamber in the tomb of Tutankhamen. Arthur Weigall, who was present at the opening, describes the frivolous atmosphere of that occasion. On Carnarvon boasting that he would give a concert down in the tomb, Weigall was inspired to remark, "If he goes down in that

PROFESSOR Walter Emery, the British Egyptologist has died in Cairo from a stroke suffered after discovering a statue of the ancient Egyptian god of death.

Prof. Emery, who was 67, was digging in his final quest-seeking the tomb of the ancient god Imhotep (god of medi-cine) — at Sakkara, near the Pyramids, when he collapsed.

The Middle East News Agency said the Professor dis-covered a statue of the Egyp-tian god of death (Osiris) and was handling it when he col-lapsed with cerebral throm-bosis.

Prof. Emery followed in a distinguished line of British Egyptologists, including the discoverers of Tutankhamen's tomb, in Upper Egypt, in 1922.

A curse was supposed to rest with anyone desecrating the Tutankhamen tomb, and about 20 people connected with the tomb were said to have met sudden or mysteriou sdeaths.

An example, from the *Birm-ingham Evening Mail*, 12 March 1971, of the apparent link between tomb-defilement and sudden death.

spirit, I give him six weeks to live." That was on 16 February. Carnarvon's death, attributed to a mosquito bite, was soon followed by that of Mr A.C. Mace, one of the leading excavators; and then, to the delighted applause of the press ("ninth victim . . . tenth . . . twentieth victim", etc.), the other members of the Tutankhamen party began to die off, several in mysterious or tragic circum-stances. Weigall (unknown fever) was claimed as the twenty-first victim, following Carnarvon's half-brother (suicide during temporary insanity), and old Lady Carnarvon (insect bite again), until by 1930 only one of the original tomb invaders was left alive – their director, Howard Carter.

The belief that the Curse of the Pharaohs accounted for Lord Carnarvon is naturally unpopular with archeologists, yet it is a fact that before he opened Tutankhamen's tomb Carnarvon received clear warning that if he did so he would soon die. The warning came in a letter from Count Hamon, the famous mystic, better known as Cheiro. With the letter, written on 30 November 1922, was a message Cheiro had received by auto-matic writing. It read:

LORD CARNARVON NOT TO ENTER TOMB. DISOBEY AT PERIL. IF IGNORED WOULD SUFFER SICKNESS; NOT RECOVER; DEATH WOULD CLAIM HIM IN EGYPT.

This message worried Carnarvon and he sought advice from another noted seer of the time, Velma. She inspected his palm and saw the probability of his early death in circumstances connected with the occult. A few weeks later he visited her again and she declared that his hand looked even more ominous than before. Lord Carnarvon considered with-drawing from the Egyptian enterprise, but things had gone too far, and he bravely decided to "challenge the psychic powers of the ages" – his own phrase. His death and those of his colleagues is now attributed by Egyptologists to infectious microbes, possibly left in the tomb to deter grave robbers.

With his usual significant inconsequentiality, Charles Fort's only comment on the Carnarvon affair was to draw attention to reports from British newspapers of the time: "Upon Lord Carnarvon's estate near Newbury, Hampshire, a naked man was running wild, often seen, but never caught. He was first seen upon March 17th. Upon March 17th Lord Carnarvon fell ill, and he died upon April 5th. About April 5th, the wild man of Newbury ceased to be reported."

Another of the "wild people", this time an atavistic Orcadian, was the portent of tragedy in the household of an Orkney farmer, whose son-in-law guaranteed the truth of every detail in his account published in *Old Lore Miscellany of Orkney, Shetland, Caithness and Sutherland* (July 1911). The farmer was in the process of excavating a large old mound on his land when he was approached by a wild man, its spiritual guardian, old and grey-whiskered, "dressed in an old, grey, tattered suit of clothes, patched in every conceivable manner, with an old bonnet in his hand, and old shoes of horse or cowhide tied on with strips of skin on his feet". This apparition warned the farmer that, should he persist in his attack on the mound, he would lose six cattle and there would be six funerals from his house. The six cattle actually died as predicted, and six deaths followed in the farmer's household. The writer of the account · was present at the fourth death, when he was told the story.

Family retainers, weird and ominous

Viscount Gormanston is a very charming and handsome man, but even his best friends admit that he looks a little like a fox. Foxes run in his family. There is one running on the Gormanston crest, and another, erect, supports the coat of arms. It is also a matter of repeated record that when the Viscount Gormanston of the day is on his death bed, foxes gather round the castle to honour the passing of one whom they evidently regard as of their own kind.

In the *New Ireland Review* for April 1908 is an account of events at Gormanston Castle on the night of 8 October the previous year, when Jenico, the fourteenth Viscount, was dying in Dublin. At 8pm the gardener and coachman saw about a dozen foxes lurking about the castle and its chapel. They were barking and "crying". Two days later, at three in the morning, Jenico's son, Richard Preston, was in the chapel watching over his father's body. Outside he heard stealthy footsteps, whimperings and scratchings. He opened a side door and saw a large fox sitting just outside. There was another one behind it, and others could be heard in the bushes. Preston then went to the end door of the chapel, opened it, and there were two more foxes, one so close he could have touched it. For two hours the foxes continued to haunt the chapel and then suddenly departed.

Earlier records of the Gormanston foxes are summarized in *True Irish Ghost Stories*: "When Jenico, the twelfth Viscount, was dying in 1860, foxes were seen about the house and moving towards the house for some days previously. Just before his death three foxes were playing about and making a noise close to the house . . . The Hon. Mrs Farrell states as regards the same that the foxes came in pairs into the demesne, and sat under the Viscount's bedroom window, and barked and howled all night. Next morning they were found crouching about in the grass in front and around the house. They walked through the poultry and never touched them. After the funeral they disappeared." At the death of Edward, the thirteenth Viscount, in 1876, the foxes were once again in attendance: "He had been rather better one day, but the foxes appeared, barking under the window, and he died that night contrary to expectation."

There is something about these Gormanston foxes which makes them seem more like were-foxes than natural ones. In some of the cases in our collection of family death omens, the warning

Viscount Gormanston and his family crest.

SANS TACHE

were last seen in 1913. Many other pedigree Irishmen are warned of their deaths by the moanings or apparitions of that dread female spectre, the Banshee.

In England we hear of knocks. According to Dr Plot's seventeenth-century *Natural History of Oxfordshire*, a death in the family of Wood at Brize Norton was always preceded by "knockings on doors, tables, or shelves". The Cumberfords of Cumberford Hall were similarly affected by rappings, while the Burdets foretold the end of one of their number by a drumming sound issuing for several weeks from their chimneys. From other sources we are informed that the Roman Catholic Middletons of Yorkshire see a ghostly Benedictine nun before dying, and that the Breretons are similarly advised by a mysterious tree trunk floating in the lake before their mansion. In Scotland, the head of the Campbell clan is warned of his death by a sailing ship that appears in the loch in front of his castle (for further details see PHANTOM SHIPS, p.221).

Returning to living creatures, real or spectral, as family death omens: a white owl performs this service to the Westropp family in Ireland, its last recorded appearance being in 1909; the Arundels of Wardour were also warned by owls, two remarkably large ones which perched ominously on the battlements of their castle; and the Cliftons of Nottinghamshire had as their death omen a rare sturgeon swimming up the Trent past Clifton Hall.

In the ancestral park of the Ferrers family of Chartley near Lichfield dwelt – and maybe still dwells – an ancient herd of white cattle. To the Ferrers the birth of a black calf into this herd was fatal. The *Staffordshire Chronicle* of July 1835 gives details: "The decease of the seventh Earl Ferrers and of his Countess, and of his son, Viscount Tamworth, and of his daughter, Mrs William Jolliffe, as well as the deaths of the son and heir of the eighth Earl and of his daughter, Lady Francis Shirley, were each preceded by the ominous birth of the fatal-hued calf. In the spring of 1835 a black calf appeared at Chartley, and before long the beautiful countess, second wife of the eighth Earl, lay on her death-bed."

The see of Salisbury is not an hereditary post, but its incumbent inherits a death omen. When a Bishop of Salisbury is dying, white birds of an

is given by something other than a natural living creature. There is a merging here between animals and wraiths. At the death of a Scanlon of Bally-knockane, County Limerick, strange lights appear to illuminate their residence and have always so appeared ever since the time of a seventeenth-century Scanlon who was King of Ossory. They

Iohn Oxenham Gentleman Aged: 22: Died with
his Aparition aboue witnesse Robert Woodley and
Humphrey King

Rebecka Oxenham Aged: 8: Died with the
same Aparition witnesse Elis: Auerie widdow and
Mary Stephens

Tomasin the wife of Iames Oxenham the younger
Gentleman Aged: 22: Died w y like Aparition—
witnesse Elizabeth Frost & Ioane Tooker

Tomasin a Child in cradle Died with the like
Aparition witnesse Elis: Auerie & Mary Stephens

Frontispiece from J. Oxenham's *A True Relation of an Apparition* showing various appearances of the white bird of the Oxenham family.

unusual kind are seen on Salisbury Plain. Kathleen Wiltshire describes them: "They are large birds like albatrosses, with dazzling white wings which do not move as they fly." The first recorded incident was in 1414. The Bishop of Salisbury died abroad, attending the Council of Constance. A great flock of strange white birds descended on the roof of the hall where he lay in state and stayed all night making harsh noises. It was called "a great sign of the birds".

Miss Moberly, the Bishop's daughter, saw the white birds fly up out of the Palace gardens as her father lay dying in 1885. Again, on 15 August 1911, Miss Edith Olivier, returning from a village choir outing near Salisbury, saw two curious white birds, flying but not moving their wings. She knew nothing of the bird/bishop connection at that time, but on reaching home she was told that Bishop Wordsworth had suddenly died. Her report of the white birds was then recognized as the conventional omen.

Quite the best and longest-documented history of a family haunted at times of death by a particular creature relates to the white bird of the Oxenhams. The origin of this family's connection with their white bird is lost in antiquity. An old country ballad in Devonshire tells of Sir James Oxenham preparing for the wedding of his daughter, Margaret. In the background is a jilted lover. Sir James gives a banquet. A white bird appears and Sir James shudders at the omen which, even in those legendary times, was long known in the family. Next day Margaret and her bridegroom stand at the altar. The jilted lover steps forward, stabs her and then himself. As she dies the white bird flies through the church.

The first historical record of the white bird was just before the death of Grace Oxenham in 1618. Twenty-three years later her son, James, published a tract about the circumstances of certain recent deaths in his family. His son, John, aged twenty-two, had suddenly died two days after a bird with a white breast had appeared in his room and hovered over the bed. Five days later, on 7 September 1635, James Oxenham's wife, Thomasine, fell ill, saw the white bird and died. The same thing happened soon afterwards to her little sister, Rebecca, aged eight, and on 15 September Thomasine's infant daughter also died, the ominous bird having previously been seen in her bedroom also. James Howell in *Familiar Letters* (1646) claims that he saw in a London stonemason's yard a marble slab about to be sent into Devonshire, with an inscription that "John Oxenham, Mary his sister, James his son, and Elizabeth his mother, had each the appearance of such a bird fluttering about their beds as they were dying."

Up to 1873 the white bird was still faithful and active. On 15 December of that year Mr G.N. Oxenham died in Kensington. According to a statement by his nephew, The Revd Henry, reproduced in F.G. Lee's *Glimpses of the Supernatural* (1885), flutterings were heard in the dying man's chamber. And, a week before his death, there was an odd incident when his daughter and a friend, who knew nothing of the family tradition, heard a commotion, opened the window and saw a strange bird, like a pigeon but larger and white, perched on a bush just outside. Some workmen were trying to drive it away by throwing their hats at it. In Dr Mogridge's *Descriptive Sketch of Sidmouth* is an account of the death of old Mr Oxenham of Sidmouth in the second decade of the nineteenth century. Just before he died, the gardener and his wife, who both looked after him, saw a white bird fly in at the door, pass over Mr Oxenham's bed and disappear into one of the drawers of his writing desk.

We had intended to compare this sort of thing with various anthropological phenomena such as totemism and tribal affinities with animals, hoping to provide some reasonable background for our collection of family death omens. But there are certain aspects of this family/animal connection which defy comparisons and hint at the existence of some guiding – or occasionally interfering – principle behind life on earth. This supposed principle, whatever its other qualities, is certainly not without a sense of humour. There is an old Border family called Herries, whose crest is a hedgehog because, say the heralds, it is a pun on their name, *herisson* meaning hedgehog in French. Somehow this joke has penetrated to the hedgehogs themselves, for whenever a Herries is dying the little creatures turn up in droves to haunt his dwelling.

The Fowlers are an ancient family, and ever since the time of the Crusades their crest has been an owl. The following story was told to Mr William Fowler of Cumberland by his father and is repeated in Kathleen Wiltshire's *Ghosts and Legends of the Wiltshire Countryside* (1973). It is a story which supports our notion that there is a sense of humour in nature, and that the guiding or interfering principle referred to above enjoys the sort of joke that superior people might find rather infantile. "The Reverend W.W. Fowler, a canon of Lincoln, retired to a rectory in Wiltshire to write a book on ornithology. On the day he died, all the owls in the neighbourhood seemed to have gathered around his house, perching on the roof, gateposts, pinnacles, or any convenient place. There they remained till he was dead, when they all disappeared. On the day of the funeral, however, when the coffin was being carried under the lychgate to the church, a large white barn owl swooped down, almost touching the coffin before disappearing into the large yew trees in the churchyard."

Cities and islands in the sky

If we were to have the apparently not uncommon experience of seeing a city in the sky, a city embellished with the most noble architectural effects, white marble towers, domes, etc; if we were lucky enough to see such a thing, we might be sufficiently curious to seek an explanation. From the list of explanations authoritatively offered over the centuries we could select one of the following causes for our vision: that it was (i) a holy city like the New Jerusalem, as seen by St John "coming down from heaven, prepared as a bride adorned for her husband" (Revelation 21:2); (ii) a reflection, due to some undetermined atmospheric function, of an actual city elsewhere (but we wonder why cities should project themselves so much more frequently than the landscapes in between them); (iii) a city of the blessed dead such as is occasionally seen, particularly off the coasts of Celtic realms; (iv) a peculiar effect of cloud and mist; (v) an actual flying city like Laputa in Swift's *Gulliver's Travels*; (vi) a delusion of drink or religious excitement.

An image in the sky "giving the impression of distant land with wonderful white buildings" was seen from the island of Sanday in the Orkneys in 1840; it was seen again in 1857 when it lasted for about three hours. E.W. Marwick, who quotes these records in *The Folklore of Orkney and Shetland* (1975) adds that the phenomenon is not uncommon in the North. Local people explain it as being the crystal and pearl city of the mysterious Fin Folk, occasionally revealed to mortal eyes; or it may be the intermittently manifest isle of Hether Blether, whose quasi-location is west of the actual sacred island of Eynhallow. Marwick explains it as a mirage but does not suggest what it is a mirage of.

Roderick O'Flaherty, writing in 1684, describes a phantom island that often appears off the west coast of Ireland. He gives several possible explanations; that it is the island of Hy Brasil, known to cartographers but to nobody else; that it is the terrestrial paradise kept hidden by special ordinance of God; that it is a fabrication of evil spirits or merely an illusion of the clouds. Which of these speculations is to be preferred, says O'Flaherty wisely, "is more than our judgments can sound out".

The New Jerusalem descending from heaven, as revealed by an angel to St John the Divine. Illustration by Gustave Doré (1866).

The photograph of the 'mirage of Bristol' from Miner Bruce's *Alaska* (1900). Identified as an actual view of the real Bristol, its similarity to the mirage may have confused its Alaskan claimants.

W.G. Wood-Martin in 1902 records several appearances of Hy Brasil. It was seen off Sligo in 1885, and after a previous sighting a correspondent wrote: "I myself, upward of half a century ago, saw a wonderful mirage resembling that recently described as having been visible off our Tireragh coast (county of Sligo); and had I been looking on the Bay for the first time, nothing could have persuaded me but that I was gazing at a veritable city – a large handsome one too, trees, houses, spires, castellated buildings, etc." Wood-Martin explains that such cities are reflections of real cities somewhere else, and he offers as analogy the claims of sailors in Dublin Bay that they can sometimes see Mount Snowdon "looming" a hundred miles away. But looking out to sea from the west coast of Ireland the nearest known city in that direction that could loom would be New York, whose distinctive architecture is never a reported feature of the west Irish city vision.

On 18 July 1820 Captain Scoresby of the *Baffin* pointed his telescope at the unexplored shore of West Greenland and spied "an extensive ancient city abounding with the ruins of castles, obelisks, churches and monuments, with other large and conspicuous buildings". He drew some of these features. Sir David Brewster put the drawings together into a panorama, which is reproduced in his book, *Natural Magic*. But in his engraving the architectural features are reverting to natural rock forms and have not the "distinctness of reality" as Captain Scoresby said they had.

One of the attractions of Alaska is that its local sky is peculiarly receptive of images of the city of Bristol in England. Fort in *New Lands* (1923) lists several reports of the appearance of Bristol over Alaska and quotes the tradition that this city is there visible every year between 21 June and 10 July. It, or something like it, is said to have been regularly seen by the Alaskan Indians before white settlement. In 1887 the famous pioneer Willoughby saw and photographed this aerial city, or so it was claimed, but his print looks so like the city of Bristol that many people have supposed it to be a photograph of material Bristol rather than its Alaskan phantom. Yet there is ample evidence that some remarkable city or other is at times apparent in the Alaskan skies. In the *New York Times*, 31 October 1889, Mr L.B. French reported seeing quite plainly in the sky near Mount Fairweather, Alaska, "houses, well defined streets and trees. Here and there rose tall spires over huge buildings, which appeared to be ancient mosques or cathedrals . . . It did not look like a modern city – more like an ancient European city". Fort quotes another correspondent from the Yukon who in June 1897 had seen a great city in the sky. Members of his party speculated on whether it most resembled Toronto, Montreal or Peking, but concluded that it was more like "some ancient city in the past".

The archaic and splendid features. often attributed to aerial cities, even when viewed in non-religious contexts, link them, phenomenally speaking, with the ideal cities of mystical vision,

The flying city of Laputa appeared to Gulliver, in Swift's *Gulliver's Travels*, in a form which has since become popular with UFO and science-fiction illustrators.

such as St John's vision of Jerusalem. An example of this type, cited in Flammarion's *L'Atmosphere*, is the "vast and beautiful city, adorned with monuments, domes and steeples" seen by the traveller

Grellois between Ghelma and Bône in North Africa. He knew of no earthly city resembling it. However, the tendency of most modern viewers is to seek a local origin for their vision. Thus in the case quoted by Fort from the *New York Sun*, 6 March 1890, of a large unknown city seen at 4pm, over Ashland, Ohio: although some declared it to be the New Jerusalem, the majority were divided between Mansfield, thirty miles, and Sandusky, sixty miles away, as its original. The incident produced a typical Forteanism: "May have been a revelation of heaven, and for all I know heaven may resemble Sandusky, and those of us who have no desire to go to Sandusky may ponder that point."

To emphasize the recurrence of the "city" phenomenon we select from Fort's collection in *New Lands* the apparition of Edinburgh, so-called, seen over Liverpool, 27 September 1846; the snow-covered, icicle-hung, inhabited village which appeared over Pomerania on 10 October 1881, and was said to resemble a settlement on the island of Bornholm a hundred miles away; and the series of phantom cities, islands and other scenes which were reported from Sweden between 1881 and 1888. From the classic phantom-city land of Ireland: an aristocratic town of mansions set in shrubberies behind white palings seen over Youghal, Cork, in June 1801, and two other visions of a walled town viewed earlier from the same city in 1796 and 1797; at Ballyconneely on the west coast a phantom city of assorted houses in different styles of architecture was on view for three hours on 2 August 1908.

Those whose favoured explanation for phantom cities is that what is seen are actual cities, detached, mobile and airborne, can respond to the obvious objection that any such bodies would be reported by astronomers or radar stations by pointing out that they are indeed so reported. The UFO literature is full of examples of sighted or radar-detected objects, often of apparently vast size, all of unknown nature. Many earlier observations of such things are to be found in Fort's collections.

The phenomenon of a recurrent landscape, most often a city or island, appearing annually or seasonally in a particular area of sky, is one which we do not think has been fully covered by any explanation yet devised. We suggest that the tradition of an enchanted land or island of the dead, described so frequently in Celtic folklore and the mythologies of many other races, is partly derived from actual visions of such a landscape. Its regular appearance at certain times may have given the old Druid priests the opportunity of predicting a vision of paradise, or of crediting themselves with its invocation. Legend attributes to them the habit of creating such grandiose phantasmagoria. A survival of ancient practice may lurk in the incident quoted in Davies Gilbert's *Parochial History of Cornwall* (1838): "The editor remembers a female relation of a former vicar of St Erth who, instructed by a dream, prepared decoctions of various herbs, and, repairing to the Land's End, poured them into the sea, with certain incantations, expecting to see the Lionesse country [legendary lost lands] rise immediately out of the water, having all its inhabitants alive, notwithstanding their long submersion." Unfortunately no such country appeared.

Spectral armies

Phantom soldiers in battle array marching over the land or in the sky – this is a spectacle which cries out for an explanation. In times when traditional mythology was an active force, it was well known throughout northern Europe that the gods and heroes of Valhalla were occasionally to be seen fighting in the sky, and no Breton peasant would have been surprised at the vision of King Arthur and his retinue passing overhead on their way to battle or the chase.

The recurrent phenomenon of phantom armies could everywhere be explained in terms of local myths. As these lost their power, other explanations were developed. The apparition of an army in the sky was interpreted as the portent of a battle to come or the spectre of an ancient one, or a mirage reflecting real soldiers somewhere on earth, or a function of second sight, or a meteorological freak, a psychological projection, or extra-terrestrials on manoeuvres. We think there may be something in each of these explanations, but rather than judge between them we follow our usual policy of emphasizing the phenomenon itself rather than its possible causes.

The phenomenal reality of spectral armies is well established. St Augustine records a case in *The City of God*. During the Roman civil wars a noisy battle between "evil spirits" was seen and heard taking place on a plain in Campania, so realistically that the saint tells of footprints of men and horses afterwards observed on the ground. This event shortly preceded an actual battle which took place on the same site. Note the explanation, typical of the time, in terms of spirits and portents.

A curious legend arose in 1537, when the Turkish army of Suleyman the Magnificent threatened the city of Otranto. Burmann's eighteenth-century *Thesaurus of the History of Italy* cites contemporary records which claim Otranto was saved by the apparition of the city's "800 martyrs" which appeared on the city walls in the company

the Turks and were executed "for their short-sightedness."

When fairies are believed in, they of course provide the explanation of "phantom soldiers". W.G. Wood-Martin in *The Elder Faiths of Ireland* records an instance in 1797 of an army of "fairies" marching across the bog between Maryborough and Stradbally. They were observed at the unghostly hour of midday. In 1836 another phantom army was seen on the hills at Ballyfriar, and there is a case like St Augustine's, of a fairy battle which left physical traces on the ground. In 1800 two little armies were reported to be fighting from the ditches on each side of a road in Kilkenny, and afterwards bushes were found crushed, trees broken, and there was blood on the grass.

The fairy cavalcade is regarded by folklorists

The Wild Hunt or fairy cavalcade, two names for a phenomenon which has repeated itself over the centuries.

of "innumerable" angels. According to the annals of an early Christian bishop of Otranto, the 800 were killed during a previous Ottoman seige, led by Mehmed II in 1480. Their bodies were left unburied for thirteen months but "showed no sign of corruption, nor were they once violated by birds or beasts" (E.C. Brewer, *Dictionary of Miracles*, 1884). This phantom army once again rescued the city from an Ottoman onslaught in 1644. Brewer refers to a story that Christian galley slaves, pressed into service on a Turkish ship, claimed not to see the spectres striking fear into

as synonymous with the Wild Hunt or Furious Host, the passage of an unusually destructive force through the countryside. Such was the hold of this phenomenon on the imagination of early Europeans that a whirlwind could be perceived as a mob of spirits, fairies, hounds and tormented souls led by a horned being (whose identity ranged from the Teutonic Woden to the more elemental Herne the Hunter). This animistic force was often said to travel in straight lines (see PHENOMENAL HIGHWAYS, p.167). As widely as it was feared, it was believed that any who glimpsed the Wild Hunt were withered or struck mad. Woden/Odin, his wife Frigg and other Teutonic deities were shape-changers and rode or flew on animals, brooms or hurdles to a gathering which J.B. Russell has argued, in *Witchcraft in the Middle Ages* (1972), was the forerunner of the medieval witches' sabbat and just as bad luck to witness.

Apparitions of unearthly battles were recorded quite frequently during the sixteenth century and were linked by several historians with the outbreaks of millenarian fervour at that time, such as the Anabaptists' rising at Münster in 1525. Ronald Holmes in *Witchcraft in British History* (1974) cites other instances from seventeenth-century Scotland which he relates to the religious revivals of the Covenanters. According to a contemporary record, on Clydeside in the summer of 1686 there were "showers of bonnets, hats, guns and swords, which

covered the trees and the ground; companies of men in arms marching in order upon the water-side. . ."

Similar rains and phantom armies seen in Scotland towards the end of the eighteenth century coincided with John Wesley's warnings about the diabolical reality of such things. Holmes blames them, not implausibly, on mass hysteria, but this psychological explanation does not account for the many cases of phantom armies seen during times of no particular religious excitement and by people not subject to it.

The year 1642 was a good one for phantom battles and for pamphlets on them. One such, printed in London, and now in the British Library, tells all in its title: *A Signe from Heaven, or a Fearful and Terrible Noise heard in the Ayre at Aldborow* [Aldeburgh] *in the County of Suffolke, on Thursday, the*

Good Newes to Christendome (1620) contains an account of how thousands witnessed a radiant female above Mohammed's tomb, putting a Muslim army to flight. The vision lasted 21 days.

On 29 September 1914 the London *Evening News* published a short story by Arthur Machen called *The Bowmen*. It was inspired by newspaper reports the previous month of the harrowing retreat from Mons, in Belgium, in which the British army, despite overwhelming German forces, managed to retire in good order and hold the line. Machen's story was about the intercession of St George with a spectral army on behalf of the British. It became very popular and was much reprinted, appearing the following year as a little book, to which Machen attached an Introduction, claiming that his story had been responsible for the crop of reports and rumours that angels had indeed appeared over the field of battle. This claim was hotly contested. Harold Begbie immediately wrote a book, *On the Side of the Angels: an Answer to 'The Bowmen'*, in which he abused Machen for his 'amazing effrontery' in pretending that it was his story which was being imitated by the 'angel' reports. Begbie quoted many accounts from individual soldiers of the visions they and their comrades had seen at Mons, accounts which were given to witnesses before Machen wrote his story. Machen, he said, had naively supposed himself to be the inspirer of the legend, whereas he had merely 'picked up' unconsciously something that was in the air at the time. Begbie's informants claimed to have seen a wide range of visions, including knights, bowmen, saints, glowing angels, mysterious clouds (hiding them from the enemy) and phantom armies. A Lieutenant-Colonel wrote to Machen that on the night of 27 August 1914, during the retreat, he and all his brigade had seen ghostly squadrons of cavalry, not in the sky but riding alongside their line of march.

4th day of August, at 5 of the clocke in the afternoone – wherein was heard the beating of Drums, the discharging of Muskets and great Ordnance for the space of an houre or more. The title goes on to claim as witnesses "many men of good worth" who will undertake to testify to leading Members of the House of Commons and to exhibit a stone of great weight which fell from the sky during the uproar.

The title of another contemporary pamphlet describes *A great Wonder in Heaven, shewing the late Apparitions and Prodigious Noyse of War and Battels seene on Edge-Hill, neere Keinton, in Northamptonshire, 1642.* On four successive Saturday and Sunday nights, visitors to the Civil War battlefield of Edgehill (near Kineton, Warwickshire) were treated to a repeat performance of the recent hostilities. Gentlemen of credit were dispatched by the King at Oxford to investigate. They personally witnessed the phenomenon and swore statements to that effect.

A modern sighting of a phantom army, which was given some publicity at the time, was reported by another gentleman of credit, well known to us as such, who swears it is a true account. In November 1956, our friend Peter Zinovieff and his half-brother, Patrick Skipwith, were camping in the Cuillin Mountains of Skye. At about three o'clock one morning Peter heard strange noises, opened the tent flap and saw "dozens of kilted Highlanders charging across the stony ground". He woke Patrick who also saw them. Both were very frightened. The next evening, after a day's walking and rock bashing (Peter was then a geology student at Oxford), they pitched the tent further up the mountains and sat up with coffee to see if the spectres would return. Nothing happened and they fell asleep. At 4am they were awakened by the same noise and again with terror saw the Highlanders, but "retreating, stumbling across the boulders, looking half dead". At first light they ran down to the Sligachan Hotel, and later that day they told their story to a local man, Mr Ian Campbell. He said they were not the first to see the same thing and explained the Highland soldiers as phantoms "either from the thirteenth century or the '45 Rebellion".

The age of enlightenment brought the theory of mirages, or rather the word "mirage", to account for spectral armies. Sir David Brewster applied this reasonable explanation to a wide range of unreasonable phenomena – in itself an irrational proceeding – in his *Natural Magic* (1832). One of the best attested "phantom army" sightings was on 23 June 1744, on the mountain of Souterfell in the Cumberland Lake District. At about seven in the evening Daniel Stricket, servant to John Wren of Wilton Hall, saw many troops of soldiers riding up and over the mountain. Mr Wren was summoned and also saw them, and so did "every person at every cottage within the distance of a mile, the number of persons who saw them amounting to about twenty-six". Brewster explains that they must have been reflections of real troopers on the other side of the mountain. But there were no soldiers then in the district, nor was there a road on the far side of the mountain; so Brewster explains further, incredibly: "But if there was then no road along which they could be marching, it is highly probable that they were troops exercising among the hills in secret, previous to the breaking out of the rebellion in 1745". Charles Fort, referring to this case, remarks on the amazing prescience of these troops, and he adds typically: "There has never been an explanation that did not itself have to be explained."

Fort, in *New Lands* (1923), goes on to assail the explainers with volleys of phantom soldiers, giving references mostly from contemporary reports. In 1785, at Ujest, Silesia, soldiers were seen marching through the sky at the same time as the military funeral of General von Cosel was being held. Later, long after the funeral was over, the phantoms were seen again. On 3 May 1848, at Vienne, in Dauphiné, an army in the sky was seen by twenty witnesses; on 30 December 1850, phantom soldiers in the sky near the Banmouth; on 22 January 1854, phantom soldiers over Buderich; on 8 October 1812, the same at Ripley, Yorkshire; from September to October 1881, white-robed figures in the sky over Virginia, platoons of "angels" in white robes and helmets marching above Delaware, and similar reports from Maryland, all summarized in *Scientific American* that year. For several hours a day on three consecutive days from about 1 August 1888, infantry divisions led by a chief with a flaming sword marched across the sky near Varasdin, Croatia. The event was recorded in Flammarion's *L'Astronomie* with the comment that investigation had failed to discover any corresponding terrestrial soldiers in the region; nor, had such soldiers been found, would their presence explain this repeated, localized apparition.

We have many more reports from all ages of the spectral army phenomenon, but no space here even to mention them. Catherine Crowe in *The Night Side of Nature* (1848) gives some excellent cases of this remarkably persistent phenomenon, including a full report of the 1881 Ripley incident referred to above and details of the sighting near Lanark, Scotland, in 1686, when only one man in a crowd failed to see the phantom regiments apparent to everyone else. Suddenly, with terror, he too saw them, and Mrs Crowe suggests that he may have temporarily received the second sight from a seer standing by him. This excellent writer rejects the mirage theory on the grounds that there is often no possible original image to be reflected, particularly in the cases when the phantom soldiers' uniforms are of another age. In speaking in terms of spirits, spirit-seers and impressions of ancient events occasionally reforming themselves as apparitions she voices a tradition that is ancient indeed.

Phantom ships

In the early morning of 11 July 1881, the future King George V as a young naval officer sighted the famous spectral ship, *The Flying Dutchman*, in the South Atlantic. It did not particularly surprise him; similar apparitions have been reported by seafarers from the earliest times. Sightings also include ships that appear to be navigating through the clouds. In the *Flying Saucer Review*, May–June 1971, there is a report from 1743 of a farmer near Holyhead in Anglesea, who saw a packet-boat sailing through the clouds 1500 feet overhead. Its keel was clearly visible, proving that it was no mirage of a ship at sea, and the farmer estimated its displacement as about ninety tons.

There is a reference in ancient Irish annals to "fantastical ships" seen in 1161, sailing against the wind into Galway harbour. W.G. Wood-Martin, quoting this in *The Elder Faiths of Ireland*, also gives another instance of the sighting of an aerial navy by hundreds of people on a hill at Croaghpatrick, Mayo "on a serene evening in the autumn of 1798". It was, explains Wood-Martin, "produced by the reflection of the fleet of Admiral Warren which was then in pursuit of a French squadron off the west coast of Ireland." He goes on to suggest that the Galway ships of 1161 must have been a reflection of Norse war-galleys.

Long before any known airship there was a belief that airships existed. Agobard, Archbishop of Lyons in the ninth century, was confronted with a crowd of local people escorting four prisoners

A sighting of *The Flying Dutchman*.

who, they said, had been caught landing from an airship. They requested the Archbishop's leave to stone them. Agobard refused, not believing the airship story, and later reported (we quote him from G.G. Coulton's *Medieval Panorama*) that the locals were so unreasonable as to "believe and assert that there is a certain region called Magonia, whence ships come in the clouds: the which bear away the fruits of the earth . . . to that same country".

The histories of Cornwall and Brittany contain many references to ships which are seen to sail across land, particularly on certain anniversaries, at times preceding storms or at the death of a notable person. The Land's End district of Cornwall was once famous for such apparitions, of which several are recorded in W. Bottrell's *Traditions and Hearthside Stories of West Cornwall*. The actual paths over which these ships navigate are sometimes noted; and we suspect that certain old roads were originally laid to follow the traditional route of a phantom ship (see PHENOMENAL HIGHWAYS, p.167). In about 1835 Robert Hunt, author of *Popular Romances of the West of England,* spoke to a man who had seen the wondrous ship of Porthcurno, also described by Bottrell, which "would drive into Porthcurno against wind and tide; oft-times she came in the dark of evening and, without stopping at the Cove, took her course over the old caunce towards Chapel-Curno; thence she sailed away, her keel just skimming the ground, or many yards above it, as she passed over hill and dale till she arrived at Chygwidden". The ship would then vanish at a rock, beneath which a hoard of coins was discovered.

On the arms of the Duke of Argyll, Chief of the Clan Campbell, is a vessel described heraldically as "a lymphad or ancient galley, sails furled, flags and pennants flying gules, and oars in action sable". At the death of a senior Campbell this ship appears on Loch Fyne by Inveraray, Scotland. Lord Halifax in his *Ghost Book* says he was told by the Duke that just after the death of his father, Lord Archibald Campbell, in 1913 the galley had appeared with its usual crew of three men and had followed its regular course over the

The crescent moon as the boat of souls, as on this 1st century BC chalcedony gem, demonstrates the antiquity of the idea of celestial craft bearing emissaries from other worlds.

Loch to a certain spot on the shore, whence it proceeded overland to the sanctuary of St Columba. A curious detail is that on this occasion it was seen not only by local people but also by a visiting Englishman who called out, "Look at that funny airship!"

A similar apparition was seen June 1959 over New Guinea. The incident, first reported in the Sydney *Sun* and later much discussed in UFO literature, is an interesting one because of the number and sobriety of the witnesses (Father Gill and the entire staff and inmates of the Anglican mission in Papua) and because it is another instance of a well-documented modern event for which there is much precedent in early records and folklore. The ship which hovered over the Mission was circular with a superstructure "like the bridge of a boat". Its crew of four leant over the rails, and when Father Gill and his flock waved to them, they waved back.

"The Great Airship Flap of 1897" is the name now given to the most remarkable phenomenon that ever defied explanation. The events of this saga are so bizarre as to seem incredible, yet if we are to give credence to any historical records of the very recent past, we can scarcely withhold it from the mass of contemporary statements which suggest that, throughout the nineteenth century (particularly during its last decade) the skies of North America were infested by a large miscellany of "impossible" airships.

In Charles Fort's *New Lands* (1923) is the first compilation of some of the many scattered reports of mysterious lights and airships in 1896 and 1897; and Fort was the first to make the revolutionary suggestion that the phenomenon might well be attributed to visitors from another world. Recently a great many more newspaper reports of the time have been unearthed by UFO researchers and quoted in such books as John Keel's *UFOs: Operation Trojan Horse* (1970) and Clark and Coleman's *The Unidentified* (1975). April 1897 was the peak of the "flap". There were airship reports from all over America, the majority from the Midwest and Texas. A cigar-shaped, winged object, with a canopy or superstructure and brightly lit with coloured lights, passed over Iowa, Michigan, Washington and many other states . Thousands of people saw it over Chicago. There were absurd but respectably attested reports of landings, messages received and occupants encountered, varying from dwarfish Orientals to tall, bearded white men;

The ship of Porthcurno engraving by Joseph Blight from Bottrell's *Traditions and Hearthside Stories of Cornwall.*

and there were hoaxes and strange rumours of secret airship inventors. There were at the time no known dirigible airships flying in America, yet on 19 April 1897 the *Dallas Morning News* reported the crash of an airship at Aurora, Texas, together with the remarkable statement that the dead pilot was "not an inhabitant of this world", and that "Mr J. T. Weems, the US Signal Service officer at this place and an authority on astronomy, gives it as his opinion that he was a native of the planet Mars". A recent proposal to reopen the grave and examine the "Martian" was defeated by residents' objections.

Of all the newspaper reports of 1897 airship activities, the most amazing is the following from the *Houston Daily Post,* 28 April: "Merkal, Texas, April 26. Some parties returning from church last night noticed a heavy object dragging along with a rope attached. They followed it until in crossing the railroad it caught on a rail. On looking up they saw what they supposed was the airship. It was not near enough to get an idea of the dimensions. A

light could be seen protruding from several windows; one bright light in front like the headlight of a locomotive. After some ten minutes a man was seen descending the rope; he came near enough to be plainly seen. He wore a light blue sailor suit, was small in size. He stopped when he discovered parties at the anchor and cut the ropes below him and sailed off in a north-east direction. The anchor is now on exhibition at the blacksmith shop of Elliott and Miller and is attracting the attention of hundreds of people."

Loren E. Gross, another patient scholar of the "airship flaps", suggested in his *Charles Fort, the Fortean Society and UFOs* (1976) that we should try to see the Aurora and Merkal cases against the popular imaginings of the time. This was the period, Gross points out, when Percival Lowell's telescopic surveys of Mars from his giant new telescope on a mountain near Flagstaff, Arizona, were receiving much attention in the press, and creating a boom in amateur astronomy. Another factor must have been the serialization that spring of H.G.

Wells's *War of the Worlds* in *Cosmopolitan* magazine. Not surprisingly there was much talk of "men from Mars". On 7 March 1897, the *Salt Lake Tribune*, Utah, published an article referring to beliefs in "cloud ships" under the title "A Sea above the Clouds – Extraordinary Superstition once prevalent in England".

Thus at least twelve days before the anchor-incident at Merkal we find that a newspaper in another state had told the story of a much earlier anchored "cloud-ship". This occurred in Bristol at the beginning of the thirteenth century and is recorded in the *Otia Imperialia* of Gervase of Tilbury. People coming out of a church after Mass heard a cry in the air and saw a "cloud-ship" overhead with its anchor and cable caught on a tombstone. A sky-sailor descended the cable to free it, but was detained by the people and drowned in the gross atmosphere of earth. The crew of the airship then cut the cable and made off. This story has yet another precedent. In *Fate* magazine, March 1958, is printed a translation from another thirteenth-century manuscript, the Norse-Irish *Speculum regale*, describing how in about 956 AD a sky-ship's anchor caught on the porch of St Kinarus' church in the borough of Cloera. Again one of the sailors descended the rope, but this time the bishop deterred the people from seizing him, and he sailed off unharmed with the rest of the crew, leaving the anchor as a souvenir of their visit.

In the early 1950s, George Adamski, a hotdog vendor at the Mount Palomar Observatory and founder of the Royal Order of Tibet, claimed regular meetings with beings from other planets who had come to save the Earth from nuclear destruction. As proof he offered an unparalleled variety of photographs of their craft, from small 'scoutships' to gigantic cigar-shaped 'motherships' like the one shown here.

Odd clouds

For previous ages clouds were a perfect symbol of the phenomenal universe, for in clouds could be seen all kinds of illusory forms. As Shakespeare noted, in *Antony and Cleopatra*,

"Sometimes we see a cloud that's dragonish;
A vapour sometime like a bear or lion,
A towering citadel, a pendant rock,
A forked mountain or blue promontory
With trees upon't, that nod unto the world
And mock our eyes with air . . ."

The *Prajna Paramita* (a Buddhist hymn of the first century AD) insists that the forms we take for everyday reality are transient and the true nature of reality is more like the ceaseless shape-changing of clouds and dream-images – a view consistently supported by all forms of mystical experience.

We begin our look at the phenomenon of odd clouds with an incident from the log of the barque *Lady of the Lake* found in the *Journal of the Royal Meteorological Society* (vol.1, p.157). On 22 March 1870, the captain and crew saw a "remarkable cloud" that remained stationary against the wind until it was lost in the evening darkness. They

DAVID SHURVILLE

This elephant-shaped cloud over a temple in Chiang Mai, Thailand, photographed in 1994, seems like an acknowledgement of the Buddhist reverence for elephants. The Buddha's mother dreamed of a white elephant immediately before his birth, and this particular temple features carvings of elephants.

Solitary lenticular clouds – sometimes referred to as 'pile of plates' clouds – have a distinctive shape and are sometimes mistaken for UFOs.

described it as a stable, circular form with an internal semicircle divided radially into four, from which extended a long "tail" which curved back towards the "body". This massive, fluffy tadpole of a cloud challenged everything they knew about the behaviour and constitution of clouds, but – being practical sailors – they were content merely to note the details and avoid speculation.

Many of the strange apparitions classified as UFOs are described as cloud-like, reminding us of the "cloud ships" reported by French country people at the time of Agobard, Archbishop of Lyons in the ninth century (see PHANTOM SHIPS, p.221). Photographs of UFOs commonly show objects which look half solid and half nebulous, like ghosts appearing or vanishing. A typical sighting which merges UFOs with meteorological effects was reported in the *Flying Saucer Review* (vol.9, no.4). In November 1958, Dr and Mrs M. Moore were in their car near the border between North and South Dakota. The sky was cloudless except for a "silvery, cigar-shaped object, like a giant windsock", which accelerated out of view leaving behind it a trail of strange purple clouds.

Another link between UFOs and clouds is indicated in *New Report on Flying Saucers* by Lloyd Mallan, a reporter for *True* magazine. He interviewed Allen Noonan, who believed that he was in touch with "Galactic Command" who maintained UFO bases within the earth (see THE

HOLLOW EARTH, p.163). Noonan told Mallan that two UFOs might appear in the cloudless sky outside their hotel window, so he loaded his camera with infra-red film and waited. Ten minutes later, "two saucer-shaped clouds had formed in trail between some buildings across the way". Mallan felt sure they were conventional lenticular clouds, but was astonished that they should have appeared when and where Noonan had predicted.

In the 1980s, farmers in southern France and Spain hired all sorts of rainmakers during months of prolonged drought. What few successes they had were inadequate and it was widely thought that rival marketing conglomerates were using every means (high-tech planes having superseded rogue magicians) to "steal" their rain clouds. We can only observe that cloud-summoning and cloud-busting have always been among the powers claimed by shamans and magicians of most cultures. Their traditions were continued by the "magnetizers" of the nineteenth century and by the followers of Wilhelm Reich's theory of "Orgone" energy – both of whom made weather control part of their general occult technology.

Cloud, mist and vapour are basic elements in mystery. In *Human Animals* (1969), Frank Hamel tells of fogs that aided the transformation of witches into animals and birds or that concealed them with cloaks of invisibility. The world over, supernatural beings and sages are said to use clouds as vehicles or messengers; for example, the seduction of the nymph Io by Jupiter in the form of a cloud (as recounted in Ovid's *Metamorphosis*). Indeed, one of the continuities in our data is that metamorphoses are often indicated or accompanied by mists or clouds. Most phantoms have this quality; thus, a Black Dog legend from Dorset (see BLACK DOGS, p.286) quoted by Patricia Dale-Green, says the beast will grow larger if watched, eventually swelling into a large cloud and vanishing. Several forms of the "transition-cloud" exist in the spiritualist cosmology, such as the soul likened to a vapour rising from the body at the moment of death, and the clouds of ectoplasm from which materialize faces, hands, and so on. Ghosts too often have a mist-like structure, and interestingly there are many accounts of ghostly human forms with parts of their anatomy hidden or replaced by a local cloudy mass.

Many religious apparitions begin or end with a small, curious cloud (see SHARED VISIONS, p.106). On 16 October 1984, Mrs Rosa Quattrini, known as Mama Rosa, was talking to a neighbour in an orchard at San Damiano in Italy, when both noticed a peculiar cloud forming in the air among the branches of a damson tree. It floated over to a pear tree where it seemed to solidify into a female form, resplendent with beams of light, a crown on her head and a flower in each hand. This was the first of many appearances of the Virgin Mary to Mama Rosa, and only she ever saw the radiant lady on these occasions. In contrast, the entire congregation of a church in Warsaw, in 1801, saw the shining Virgin Mary appear from a cloud.

In PHANTOM MUSIC AND STRANGE VOICES (see p.126) we tell of the day when "demons" interrupted the services of St Clement Hofbauer. Later the same day, as Zsolt Aradi tells it in his *Book of Miracles* (1957), as St Clement prayed before the altar of St Joseph, "hundreds of people saw a cloud forming above the altar, then enveloping the figure of the saint, who disappeared from their sight. In his place [they] saw a celestial vision. A woman of great beauty, with radiant features, appeared and smiled at the worshippers, who only a few hours ago had been frightened by the prodigies of the devil."

People who see apparitions in clouds are inclined, like Mama Rosa, to feel they are being communicated with and accept them as messengers. Medieval chronicles abound with this kind of celestial vision during strange meteorological events, and people continue to this day to see figures among the clouds. The phenomenon is not restricted to Christian cultures, as Robert Bartholomew, an American anthropologist and author of several studies of collective delusions and related phenomena, points out. In Algiers, in June 1990, for example, as the leader of the newly elected Islamic Salvation Front Party addressed an ecstatic crowd, they saw, in the direction of Mecca, a cloud take the shape of the Arabic script for Allah (*Daily Telegraph,* 16 June 1990).

The story goes that a USAF man in Korea took a picture of American and Communist planes in combat and was surprised, on developing it, to see the huge image of Christ dominating the sky below them. Editions of the Ashland, Kentucky, *Independent*, which carried the picture in the late 1960s, rapidly sold out. Many of the claims made about it are contradictory. Christ is not made up of clouds, no one connected with the photo is named or can be traced, and the barely discernible planes (above Christ and to the right) are identical bombers in tandem rather than different fighters in combat. Despite these doubts, the widespread belief in the authenticity of the image places it in the same meaningful tradition as the 'Bowmen of Mons'.

In December 1990, a tourist from Northern Ireland visited New York and took this photograph of the Statue of Liberty. The satanic features gazing down at the statue were only noticed later.

their religious background," he wrote in *UFOs and Alien Contact* (1998).

A curious case from the nineteenth century was recorded in a rare Canadian pamphlet, *Wonderful Phenomena* by Eli Curtis, from statements collected by Addison A. Sawin. On 3 October 1843, Charles Cooper, labouring in a field near Warwick, Ontario, heard a low rumbling in the sky and looked up to see a strange, solitary cloud beneath which hung, or hovered, three "perfectly white" figures, calling to him with "loud and mournful noises". He thought they were angels, and Sawin, a spiritualist, naturally saw in it "the glorious hope of the resurrection". What is more interesting to us is the selective nature of the phenomenon; just as Mama Rosa could see the Virgin where others could only see mist, other witnesses at Warwick – some nearly six miles away and some in an adjacent field – all agreed on the "remarkable cloud", though not all of them saw the "angels" or heard the sounds.

Sometimes we hear of clouds appearing in answer to an unspoken need. Harold T. Wilkins, in his *Strange Mysteries of Time and Space* (1958), quotes a British naval officer's story about the Allied invasion of North Africa. He said the sea was dead calm and the entire fleet was completely exposed, an easy target for German bombers. Before long, as though in response to their nakedness, an "immense black cloud" formed, staying directly over the armada for ten consecutive days. The officer said: "I was not alone in thinking that Providence set the cloud there." A similar story is told of clouds that "miraculously" veiled the retreat of the British army at Mons, August 1914 (see SPECTRAL ARMIES, p.219).

Tales of encounters with UFOs and their "occupants" sometimes involve terrifying vapours that paralyze, blind and suffocate. We have many data on clouds behaving malevolently: some bursting into flames, some which are luminous or magnetic, some which "bounce" along, and others which hiss or broadcast a series of loud explosions.

We have noticed in our sections on things which fall from the skies, that some of these falls originate in odd clouds. In *Strange World* (1964), Frank Edwards relates the story of Ed Mootz tending his Cincinnati, Ohio, garden on 22 July 1955, when it rained a blood-like, oily liquid. Mootz saw this grisly rain falling from a small, solitary red, pink and green cloud that appeared to be rolling along about a thousand feet overhead. Drops that fell on his skin began to sting him. He

A similar display of mystical picture-making clouds attracted the attention of an awed crowd at an Islamic school in the Malaysian state of Selangor. During the evening of 29 July 1992, twenty-six distinct images were seen, including a foetus in a womb, two corpses and women exposing their sexual parts. The event was interpreted by devout Muslims as depicting the ascension of the Prophet Mohammed. Bartholomew, who interviewed witnesses for a report on the incident for the government's Islamic Centre, said more images were seen the following day. "Drawings of the images were made by the students yet they appear to have misperceived clouds in the night sky reflective of went inside to wash, and when he returned the cloud was gone. Strangely, it was not reported elsewhere. The next day the trees and grass were dead; everywhere the red rain had fallen was now brown, shrivelled and dying. According to Edwards the incident was never explained, despite investigations. Similarly, we recall that in the case of the shower of "blood and muscle" on the tobacco-field at Lebanon, Tennessee (mentioned in RAINS OF SEEDS AND ORGANIC MATTER, p.47), a red cloud was noticed flying directly over the field.

Clearly then, there are clouds which are only "were-clouds". There is no way, in our conventional knowledge of clouds, to account for the hissing "ball of fog" that swooped down on a car in Minnesota. According to the *Eagle Bend News* (25 May 1961), the car was left unbearably hot and pitted with tiny holes. Nor can we explain the report by a postman in Thailand, quoted in the *San Francisco Chronicle* (23 April 1962), that he saw a red and green fog crumble into little pieces which he thoughtfully collected.

9

Images

9

Images

Simulacra: faces and figures in nature

In the fifth century AD the Armenians rose in revolt against their Persian rulers. Led by the saintly Vartan, their small army met the enemy at Averayr near Chermoog, where they were defeated with great loss of life. Among the victims was St Vartan, thereafter regarded as a martyr. After the battle a group of Armenians gathered in a nearby valley to mourn their loss and to pray that St Vartan would be restored to them. Suddenly it was noticed that a rock in the valley had taken on his appearance, complete with white beard and mitre. This greatly uplifted the spirit of the Armenians and inspired them in their fight for independence.

This story of a significant image, turning up in the right place at the right time, would fit just as well into our COINCIDENCES section (see p.201). So would the whole subject of simulacra – things that look like other things. Everyone occasionally sees shapes or pictures in clouds, trees, rock formations, flickering fire, running water and any mottled surface – even in the static of TV screens. The coincidence arises when a natural shape seems to relate to its locality.

This profile in rocks near Chermoog, Armenia, is revered as that of local hero and martyr St Vartan. The appearance of his gigantic portrait in the cliffside is accepted by the Armenian church as a miracle.

A cross-section of Mexican agate which reveals the mountainous landscape where it was found.

they are spots where nature seems to manifest the prototypes of Creation. The Forest of Fontainebleau outside Paris is an area of curious rocky outcrops, many of which are shaped like animals, some familiar some yet unknown. Among them are three different examples of nature's attempts at sculpting an elephant. In the north of England, above Pateley Bridge in Yorkshire, a fifty-acre ridge of millstone grit, called Brimham Rocks, has been carved by wind ino a menagerie of strange beasts which include camels, bears, turtles, apes and other forms suggestive of a past or future creation. A famous area for natural likenesses is the Arizona desert, where tall, eroded, red rocks combine with sunlight and shadow to produce a wonderland of fantasy creatures. Among them one can sometimes discern the features and religious symbols of the local Indians.

A common form of simulacra-coincidence is the natural rock-form which, seen from a certain angle, reproduces the typical features of the people or animals that live around it. These spontaneous images are often prominent in local folklore, and in times of pagan religion they were symbols of the gods and other characters of mythology. They give hints about the spiritual qualities and the natural products and uses of the country around them. In China *feng-shui* masters interpreted the symbolic shapes in hills and rocks as expressions of the general character of the people living within sight of them. If a local crag were shaped like a person at a desk, it might indicate that the people nearby were likely to be clerks or scholars. When, in modern times, a scientific expedition to a remote Chinese village sought to discover why so many twins were being born in that district. The locals pointed out the twin peaks of the mountain above them.

Certain spots on earth are seen by mystics as "generation centres"or *points d'amour*, because

The correspondence of shapes in the landscape with the looks and artefacts of the indigenous people is one of the fascinating aspects of simu-lacra studies. This correspondence was revealed most dramatically to the French artist, writer and visionary, Antonin Artaud. In 1936 he travelled through Mexico to the mountainous land of the peyote-eating Tarahumara Indians, intending to sample their drugs and to experience their states of mind. As he crossed the Sierra he became aware that, among the chance shapes and images that his eye picked out in the rocky landscape, certain figures kept recurring. Religious emblems and universal, esoteric symbols repeated themselves in the rock formations. "I shall not argue if someone says that all these forms are natural", he wrote. "It is their repetition that is not natural." In "The Mountain of Signs" (from an Artaud collection, *The Peyote Dance*) he declared that "the land of the

Tarahumara is full of signs, forms and natural effigies which in no way seem the result of chance". He eventually realized that the shapes he saw over and again in the rocks were reproduced in the sacred ritual symbols of the local people. And then, "the whole landscape revealed itself as the creation of a single thought, which had given shape to the rocks and to all indigenous life, plants, animals and men". From this perception, of a landscape and all its inhabitants, animal, vegetable and mineral, under the dominance of one formative spirit, Artaud came to see the former existence of a sacred science, the science of paradise on earth.

Artaud is far from being the only writer to have expressed that idea. In 1952 a Peruvian traveller, Daniel Ruzo, discovered gigantic artworks, as he called them, of a vanished civilization on the remote desert plateau of Marcahuasi, west of the Andes. There were huge carvings of people and creatures, rocks that looked like Inca heads and others figuring animals unknown or long extinct. Many of the most impressive forms were only made visible at the summer solstice by the play of light and shadow. Ruzo persuaded himself that these were the works of supreme, prehistoric artists, who had shaped mountains all over the world to represent gods and philosophical ideals. Peter Kolosimo supported this idea in his book *Timeless Earth* (1973): "The number of rock carvings to be seen in every continent suggests the handiwork of migrant artists with titanic powers and titanic chisels".

C.T. BALLARD

A striking example of a tree seeming to take on the appearance of a female torso.

Ancient sculptors may perhaps have worked on rock faces to make them more like one thing or another, but nature alone, aided by the imaginative human eye, is the supreme artist. And, like human artists, nature's favourite theme is the face. The staring eye-nose-mouth pattern occurs in the markings of many creatures, on the backs of crabs, on the hood of the cobra and widely among all kinds of insects. These and other examples of "mimicry" in nature are a constant puzzle to biologists. The evolutionist, Sir Julian Huxley, produced a quaint explanation for the fierce Samurai face on the shell of the edible Japanese crab, suggesting that superstitious fishermen who noticed something like a face on a crab threw it back. Crabs with the best faces therefore survived to produce offspring with even better ones. A response to this is that the English Cassivelaunus crab also bears a face on its shell, though with European features. This cannot have been developed by fishermen throwing the best ones back, since the crab was never eaten.

Obvious faces can be seen on the folded wings of moths, and these are sometimes accentuated when an insect displays the "eye spots" on its underwings. The probable effect of these and other face-patterns in nature is to scare off enemies. This implies that it has a universal meaning as an image of fear and dread – a bogeyman image. A staring face is naturally frightening. That seems to be true, not only on the human scale but also among smaller creatures. On the chrysalis of a small North American butterfly, *Feniseca tarquinius*, is a startlingly clear image of a face, but the chrysalis is only a quarter of an inch long. Strangely enough, the face is said to have the look of an American Indian. This is clearly not a case of the chrysalis mimicking an Indian, because of the discrepancy in scale. The same is true of the South American lantern bug. Markings on its head reproduce the features on an alligator, complete in every detail, with apparent teeth, eyes and nostrils. Yet this cannot fool its enemies into thinking that it is a real alligator, because its head is no more than three inches long.

Instead of mimicry we think of simulacra. Nature and our own imaginations are always conspiring to create illusions, and these are often repetitious. Artaud found repetitions in the simulacra shapes of the Mexican rocks, and this led him on to dream of a universal language of symbols, the Creator's pattern book. It is a dream that has always inspired artists, one of whom, Leonardo da Vinci, saw "the most exquisite landscapes" in the texture of a mildewed wall, and advised his students to let such random configurations feed their imaginations. The eighteenth-

Chrysalis of the Indian butterfly *Spalgis epius*. H.E. Hinton, an expert on natural camouflage, has explained the anthropoid face pattern as being a result of natural selection in mimicry of local monkeys. Illustration from the *Journal of the Bombay Natural History Society*.

century English water-colourist, Alexander Cozens, even went so far as to make random blots the starting point for his landscape paintings, while the Surrealist, Max Ernst, used rubbings onto paper from wood and stone as the basis for much of his imagery.

Unreasonable footprints

On the morning of 9 February 1855 the inhabitants of the South Devon towns of Topsham, Lympstone, Exmouth, Teignmouth and Dawlish awoke to find themselves in the centre of what the *Times* a week later called an "Extraordinary Occurrence". The report took the form of a letter, from which the following extract summarizes what happened:

"It appears that on Thursday night last there was a very heavy fall of snow in the neighbourhood of Exeter and the south of Devon. On the following morning the inhabitants of the above towns were surprised at discovering the tracks of some strange and mysterious animal, endowed with the power of ubiquity, as the footprints were to be seen in all kinds of inaccessible places – on the tops of houses and narrow walls, in gardens and courtyards enclosed by high walls and palings, as well as in open fields. There was hardly a garden in Lympstone where the footprints were not observed. The track appeared more like that of a biped than a quadruped, and the steps were generally eight inches in advance of each other. The impressions of the feet closely resembled that of a donkey's shoe."

A lively correspondence on the mystery developed in the *Times* and spread to the *Illustrated London News,* in the course of which further interesting details came to light. The "devil's footprints" had been found to stretch for a distance of over a hundred miles. At one point they had jumped over the two-mile wide estuary of the River Exe, continuing on one side opposite where they had left off on the other. Nothing had impeded their progress or broken their even spacing of eight inches. They were found on each side of a haystack, which was untouched, and on each side of a fourteen-foot wall. A curious feature of the prints was that they were placed one in front of the other rather than as in a normal animal trail.

Happily for those of us who enjoy explanations, the event happened during the high season of scientific rationalism, and a fine crop was raised in answer to the mystery. They included otters, leaping rats, a rope trailing from a balloon, and the devil (this one was particularly popular locally). Professor Richard Owen, who could always be relied on for an opinion regarding anything unexplained, weighed in authoritatively with his verdict – badgers. Even definitive study – by Dr Mike Dash in *Fortean Studies* no.1 (1994) – of 50 original sources failed to settle the matter. It is an abiding English mystery.

The thirteenth-century Japanese history, the *Kokon Chomonshu,* records how "In the year 929 the Imperial palace was found one morning full of demon's tracks as big as an ox's and coloured red and blue." Two incidents can be found in the *Chronicon anglicanum* composed by Abbot Ralph of Coggeshall in the early thirteenth century. In the first case, monstrous, pointed, hoof-like tracks appeared on the ground the day after a fierce electrical storm on 29 July 1205; and in the second, which took place at York in the reign of Richard I, "there appeared in certain grassy flat ground human footprints of extraordinary length; and

A comic-book illustration of the 1855 'Devil's hoofprints'.

Ancient national heroes have a penchant, it seems, for leaving their mark on the local landscape. Here a footprint in a stone at Corwen, Denbighshire, is attributed to the medieval Welsh hero Owain Glyndŵr.

everywhere the footprints were impressed the grass remained as if scorched by fire."

A correspondent in Heidelberg, on hearing of the Devon prints, wrote to the *Illustrated London News* (14 March 1855) that similar tracks could be seen every year in sand and snow on a hill on the Polish border; and in his account in *Oddities* (1965) of the Devon incident, R.T. Gould mentions the entry for May 1846 in Captain Sir James Ross's record of his Antarctic explorations, describing how on the sub-Antarctic island of Kerguelen a party found hoof-like prints in the snow, stretching for some distance, although there was no animal on the island to account for them.

In Dr E.L. Dingwall's *Tomorrow* (1957) there is an account of a man named Wilson who visited a secluded beach on the west coat of Devon in October 1950. He was the first person to walk on the cliff-enclosed beach after the tide had left the sand quite smooth, and was therefore surprised to see a series of hoof-like prints which began under a perpendicular cliff and led in a straight line to the sea. They were not cloven, but evenly spaced at six feet apart, and deeper than his own – a giant, heavy stride, unlike the mincing "devil's footprints" left in Devon snows nearly a century previously. Wilson also noticed that each print was not impressed, but appeared to be "cut out of the sand". Dingwall adds that similar tracks were

reported on New Jersey beaches in 1908 – "marks like the hooves of a pony in thick snow". Here again, he noticed, "we have the story of how tracks led up to wire fences and continued on the other side". They were attributed to the "Jersey Devil", a mystery animal of the region, that had been known from the previous century and was still generating sightings as late as 1930. Twin-lobed, crescent-shaped tracks, similar to but smaller and more irregularly spaced than the Devon tracks of 1855, were reported from Belgium in 1945.

Once in a while we discover a note of a single anomalous footprint, or rather a single footprint located anomalously such as that seen by Austin Hatton, a columnist for the *Sunday Telegraph*. He was trudging along the old pilgrim way from the Isle of Ely to the shrine at Little Walsingham when he came upon a 30-yard stretch of hardened sand. "In the centre, perfectly formed and dried hard was the imprint of a small, bare foot. Nowhere else could I find any other mark. Not a single explanatory indentation. The stretch was too wide for anybody, especially with such small feet, to have jumped across it . . . in a gigantic leap." Hatton, who declares his disbelief in fairies, said, "For once I feel the supernatural has set a trap for me." (*Sunday Telegraph*, 28 April 1974).

One of the most interesting theories about the tracks comes from the personal experience of the explorer, James Alan Rennie. During a venture into northern Canada in 1924, he and his mate, a French-Canadian dog-skinner, were crossing a frozen lake when they came across a set of large, bear-like, two-toed tracks, spaced equally in a single line. Their unnaturalness "reduced my companion to gibbering terror"; the poor man asserted that they were made by Windigo, the Canadian version of Bigfoot. Later Rennie returned across the same lake, and in bright sunshine caught sight of something that chilled him to the bone. He was half a mile from the shore, and saw the tracks "appearing miraculously before my eyes . . . in line-astern" with no animal, no sign of any life at all, to account for them, just "those tracks springing into being as they came inexorably towards me. I stood stock still, filled with reasonless panic. The tracks were being made within 50 yards of me – 20 – 10 – then smack! I shouted aloud as a large blob of water hit me in the face. I swung round brushing the water from my eyes and saw the tracks continuing across the lake" (*Romantic Strathspey*, 1956).

Fort pointed out that many of the reported sightings of strange creatures and monsters took place after earthquakes or volcanic eruptions (and, we might add, remembering Abbot Ralph, after electrical storms). The *Philosophical Transactions* (vol.50, p.500) reports that after the quake of 15 July 1757 marks resembling hoof-prints were found on a patch of sand 100 yards square at Penzance, Cornwall; these were not crescent-like but "little cones surmounted

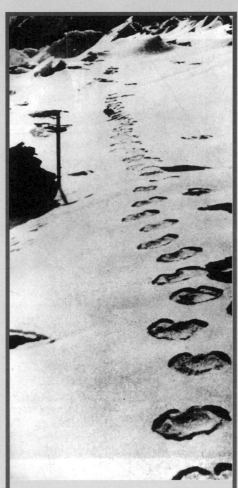

This trail – unusual both in size and shape – was found on the Menlung Glacier by the 1951 British Mount Everest Expedition. It was thought to have been made by a large bipedal creature, possibly a Yeti.

by basins of equal diameter". A correspondent in the *New Zealand Herald* (13 October 1886) writes of visiting the area desolated by an eruption of the volcano Rotomahana, and finding in the mud and ashes the footprints of a horse-like animal. He also refers to a story among the Maoris of a stag-like creature, unfamiliar to them, having been seen in the new wilderness. On 20 November 1970 the *Daily Mirror* reported that seven giant footprints, 4 feet long, 6 inches deep and 4 yards apart, had been found in a crater 10,000 feet up the volcano Etna in Sicily. They were being examined by scientists, but typically that was the last ever heard of them.

We have records from the Scottish Highlands of strange tracks and of strange animals; yet, the two are rarely matched. The *Times* (14 March 1840) reported that, for the second winter running, foal-like tracks "of considerable size", were discovered ranging for twelve miles in the glens of Orchy, Lyon and Lochay, south of the fairy-haunted Rannoch Moor. One of the legendary creatures of this district is especially interesting, the *Fachan*, with "one hand out of its chest, one leg out of its haunch, and one eye out of its head", hopping out in forays from its home in Glen Etive, a few miles northwest of Rannoch Moor. There is a similar beast in Brazil, known as *Pe de garrafa* or Bottle-foot, because it leaves a single line of deeply impressed prints suggestive of the bottom of a bottle. In Bernard Heuvelmans' *On the Track of Unknown Animals* (1995) there is a hunter's description of this creature, given in 1954, which confirms its humanoid appearance and single leg. Heuvelmans mentions that medieval geographies were frequently illuminated with delightful drawings of Sciapods (one-legged humanoids) each sleeping in the shade of an oversized foot. One of the few accounts that link a mythic image to physical evidence is in a medieval record, the *Chronicon de Melrose*. In August 1065, during a storm at York, an enormous image of the Devil riding a black horse charged through the sky to the sea: "The tracks of this horse were seen, of enormous size, imprinted on a mountain at the city of Scandeburch [Scarborough]. Here, on top of several ditches, men found, stamped in the earth, prints made by the monster, where he had violently stamped with his feet."

Yet another piece of the puzzle comes from the giants' stamping grounds in Scotland. Otta F. Swire tells, in *The Highlands and Their Legends* (1963), how she and her husband were motoring from Cluanie to Glengarry, near the southern end of Loch Ness, across a virgin blanket of snow when they saw on a small frozen lochan, not footprints but "marks as of cartwheels, clear and unmistakable in the new-fallen snow. Curious, we stopped and got out to see where they led. No sign or track of any living thing was to be seen . . . and there was no trace of footmark, wheel mark or sledge mark in the snow on the loch shore, either where the wheel marks began on the snow-covered ice or where they ended, or indeed anywhere else."

Despite enquiries they learned nothing more until some months later when an informant mentioned the "Devil's Coach": "He drives over the moors in the winter and his wheel marks are often seen on lonely frozen lochs, but never a sign on land, nor a sign of the horses that draw his coach."

Like many of our other categories, both the tracks and their interpretations have changed over the years; UFOs and laser beams have recently been suggested as the cause of the Devon 1855 prints. Any unilateral approach to the mystery brings out frustrating paradoxes. Mrs Swire put it thus: "I have been told that there are no hoof marks because the Devil's horses are spirits whereas his coach, used to carry mortals, must have earthly substance; but if this is so, why do the wheels leave tracks only on ice? And whom does he carry off? And why?" We remain equally perplexed.

Spontaneous images

"After the death of Dean Vaughan, of Llandaff, there suddenly appeared on a wall of the Llandaff cathedral, a large blotch of dampness, or minute fungi, formed into a life-like outline of the Dean's face." (*Notes and Queries*, 8 February 1902). Folklore is fabulously rich in such tales of images – from tile scorch-mark left by the devil on the north door of Blythburgh church, Suffolk (see BLACK DOGS, p.286) to the grave in Pekin, Illinois, of a man hanged for the murder of his sister, over which nothing will grow; the resulting bare patch is said to be an excellent likeness in outline of the woman's face (*Gentry Journal*, 30 April 1897).

Reports of spontaneous images seem to come in waves. On 12 March 1872 crosses appeared on windows in Baden-Baden, Germany. Authorities ordered them washed off, but they proved resistant, even to acids. Two days later at Rastadt more crosses appeared, followed shortly by death's heads. The same happened at Boulley, after which the appearances became epidemic. Religious and political symbols – crosses, eagles, skulls and others – were seen on window-panes across the countryside. The authorities were alarmed because feelings were still high after the recent Franco-Prussian war. In one house a squad of Prussian soldiers smashed windows, because people saw in them groups of French Zouaves and their banners. According to the *Religio-Philosophical Journal* (29 March 1873) the Zouaves could still be seen defiantly waving their flags in the fragments of shattered glass.

From that date up to 1890, Fort noted, reports of images in window glass were regularly featured in the American press. It could not be said that the American public was merely elaborating on the European events, because sporadic outbreaks had been reported in America since at least 1870;

and besides, events of this kind were recorded long before the advent of photography.

Another series of images began with "a faithful and unmistakable likeness of the late Dean Liddell, who died in 1808", appearing on a wall of Christ Church, Oxford, in mid-1923. Three years later, *TP's and Cassell's Weekly* (11 September 1926) reported that it was still there. "One does not need to call into play any imaginative faculty to reconstruct the head. It is set perfectly straight upon the wall as it might have been drawn by the hand of a master artist. Yet it is not etched: neither is it sketched nor sculptured, but it is there plain for all eyes to see."

Marie-Julie Jahenny, of the Breton village of La Fraudais, bore, in addition to her other spontaneous marks of distinction, a flower, a cross and the Latin words "O Crux Ave" (Hail, O Cross). Dr Imbert-Gourbeyre followed her case for over twenty years, throughout which the marks remained visible. In his *La Stigmatisation* (1894) he explains in terms of tiny beads of clotted blood forcing their way through the epidermis to lie just below the surface. But the interesting question, how the blood became organized into coherent images, is avoided completely.

All knowledge is founded on experience and first-hand testimony, yet the modern world-view

Dean Liddell of Oxford, shortly before his death in 1898, and the 'ghost portrait' that appeared above his wife's tablet in Christ Church Cathedral in 1923.

Later in that same year of 1926 reports of images came from Bristol and from Uphill, Somerset; and in the old Abbey at Bath an image of a soldier with a pack was clearly seen in a discoloured patch on one of the pillars close to a Monument to the Somerset Regiment. Local theosophists, reported the *Bath Weekly Chronicle*, identified it as a "thought image" created by pious visitors.

In the INVISIBLE ASSAILANTS section (see p.145) we mention the strange case of Eleonore Zugun, on whose arm, in front of witnesses, the word "Dracu" spontaneously appeared (*Evening Standard*, 1 October 1926). There is an even more striking case, of a young French girl whose responses to questions took the form of words and pictures that appeared on her body (*Daily Express*, 11 November 1913). Similarly, the modern stigmatic,

is so deep-rooted in most of us that we would rather doubt our sanity than question scientific authority. What then are we to make of the experience reported by a pilgrim who visited the Italian stigmatic, Palma Matarelli, in April 1872. A white cloth had been given to the stigmatic to wipe off the blood that trickled from punctures in her forehead. "This wiping left upon the linen not simple bloodstains, but emblems clearly outlined, representing inflamed hearts, nails and swords. This is truly a marvel and I saw it with my own eyes."

Spontaneous marks and images sometimes seem curiously related to their time or social context. In the first half of December 1680, the citizens of Rome were excited by a "strange and wonderful comet" that became visible near the ecliptic against the constellations of Libra and Virgo. At 8am on

On Good Friday 1993, Cyril Legge, a devout Catholic, took some glasses out of the dishwasher and noticed one was still dirty. Holding it up to the light, he saw 'the clear image of a saint-like figure'. A few days later, Cyril – manager of the Margaret Roper House for the mentally ill in Birkdale, Merseyside – discovered a second glass which bore the distinct head of a lion. Dr Ronan McGrath of Liverpool University, who examined both glasses, said the images appeared to be in layers with some areas more opaque than others. Cyril believes the lion represents his recent visit to Kenya and thinks it was a divine message to raise money to help the mentally ill in that country.

11 December, Rome buzzed with extra news: "A prodigious egge was laid by a young pullet, with a perfect comet in it, and as many stars, and in the same form as the enclosed figure shows." This account in the *Loyal Protestant and True Domestic Intelligencer* (2 April 1681) says quite clearly that the image was not on the shell, but "within the egge, most clearly exprest". The coincidence of a cometary visitation, the public expectation, and the miraculous egg sounds so fantastic that even the *Loyal Protestant* in that credulous age invited readers to believe it or not.

Our last item is singular by any standards: the day it rained Virgins. The *English Mechanic* (12 June 1908) reprinted from French sources the eyewitness account by the Abbé Gueniot of the church at Remiremont. On 26 May 1907 a severe storm swept over the Vosges area of France. Large hailstones fell profusely. The Abbé was reading in his presbytery (the object of his attention, oddly enough, was a treatise on glacial formation) when a neighbour urgently called him to see the "miracle". There was a message in the hailstones. The Abbé went to inspect, and, by his own account, found very distinctly marked on the hailstones, the bust of a woman with a robe turned up at the bottom like a priest's cope: "I should perhaps describe it still more exactly by saying that it was like the Virgin of the Hermits. The outlines of the image were slightly hollow, as though they had been formed with a punch, but were very boldly drawn."

Gueniot noticed that the hailstones were almost regular spheres, with what looked like a seam, as if they were moulded. "The imprint on the two I examined was so regular that it can hardly be due to chance." The logical hypothesis of human manufacture was also rejected, because of the vast quantity of image-bearing hailstones over the whole area of the fall, and the many observations of them falling. The Bishop of Sainte-Dié convened an inquiry, at which scientists heard 107 other witnesses, who vouched for the event although opinions on its cause varied.

This fall had other peculiar characteristics: it was confined to a strip of land three-quarters of a mile wide and several miles

A trick of the light produced this image of a Madonna-like-figure in the trees by a church at Metz in France (left of picture).

long; although many of the hailstones fell with sufficient force to do considerable damage to crops and greenhouses, many others were seen to fall without much force at all, seeming "to have fallen from a height of but a few yards". Since there was no evidence of imposture, this accords very well with the strange falls and flights recorded in Chapter 2. The Abbé Gueniot had his own very satisfactory explanation for the descent of hailstones bearing the image of the Virgin of the Hermits. A week earlier it had been the day of the Virgin's feast, but no feast had been held: "The town council of Remiremont, for profound reasons which I need not discuss, forbade the magnificent procession which was in preparation; but on the following Sunday at the same hour, the artillery of heaven caused a vertical procession which no one could forbid."

Veronica and the shroud

According to legend, St Veronica was a pious woman who accompanied Christ as he he carried his cross to the place of crucifixion. Moved by his suffering, she wiped his face with a cloth which thereafter carried on it the imprint of his face. The cloth was taken to Rome (where it allegedly healed the sick Emperor Tiberius) and eventually came **into the hands of Pope Clement I. It now resides in the basilica of St Peter's but there are no known photographs of it and it is never publicly displayed.**

Whatever the truth behind the image's origin, the name Veronica appears to derive from the Latin word *vera* meaning true, and the Greek word *icon* meaning image. Significantly the story of St Veronica did not become widely known until the sixth century, and the name was almost certainly attributed to the saint at that time. It seems to have

An engraving, by Albrecht Dürer, of the Sudarium displayed by two angels. It seems likely that Dürer used his own features to represent the face of Christ.

been coined by St Gregory of Tours (d.594 AD) and was also applied to the cloth itself which, like the relics of the True Cross, existed in multiple versions. Representations (usually paintings) of the saint carrying her Veronica (or "vernicle" in English) became quite common from the Middle Ages onwards. Ironically – given the apparent durability of the image – St Veronica is the patron saint of laundresses.

A Byzantine tradition of the "Holy Face" also emerged in the sixth century. In this version King Abgarus of Edessa requested an image of Christ from his archivist Hanaan who was unable to supply it. Instead an image "not made with hands" miraculously appeared on a cloth and cured the king of his leprosy. A variant of the tale suggests that this same cloth was the Shroud of Christ which had been smuggled to Edessa following the fall of Jerusalem in 70 AD and was only rediscovered when Edessa was rebuilt following a disastrous flood in 525. The Byzantines called the cloth the Mandylion and it became the prototype for all subsequent icons of Christ. The Mandylion remained in Edessa until 944 when it was transferred to Constantinople and received by the Emperor amidst great celebration.

But the most famous example of this type of relic is, undoubtedly, the Turin Shroud, a bolt of ancient linen, imprinted on both sides with fulllength images of the front and back of a bearded man. Supposedly the winding sheet of Christ, it now belongs to the papal authorities and is housed in Turin Cathedral. Unlike the Veronica image, it has undergone a great deal of investigation and has spawned a wide range of imaginative theories and explanations.

The pre-Renaissance history of the Shroud is rather hazy. There are a few records of a "shroud of Jesus" being seen in Jerusalem in 570 AD and on the Scottish isle of Iona in 670 AD, but it is difficult to say whether these were the same object as the Shroud of Turin. A more likely possibility is that the Mandylion and the Shroud are one and the same, and that its presence in the West is due to the involvement of the Knights Templar – an order founded to protect pilgrims in the Holy Land. In 1204 Constantinople was sacked by Crusaders; the following year the Byzantine leader, Theodore of Epirus, complained to Pope Innocent III about the looting of "the relics of the saints, and most sacred of all, the linen in which our Lord Jesus Christ was wrapped after his death and before the resurrection." The objection that the Mandylion only revealed the face of Christ, have

been countered by the suggestion that, when presented to the faithful, the cloth was folded into a rectangle which only showed the face.

The first record of the Shroud in the west occurs in 1353 when it is revealed by one Geoffrey de Charny at Lirey in France. Geoffrey was almost certainly related to the Templar Knight bearing the same name who was executed in 1314 at the height of Philip of Burgundy's purge of the order. The Templar connection provides the probable missing link between the Mandylion's disappearance from Constantinople and the Shroud's first appearance at Lirey. The Shroud was later sold to the Duke of Savoy and housed at Chambery before being moved to Turin in 1578.

Modern interest in the Shroud really began in 1898 when Secundo Pia was given permission to photograph it for the first time. While there are only faintly visible marks on the cloth, the photograph when viewed as a negative revealed the remarkable image which is so familiar today. Further photographs, taken by Giuseppe Enrie in 1931, simply increased worldwide interest in the Shroud.

Serious scientific analysis began with the setting up of the Shroud of Turin Research Project (STURP), and in 1978 forty scientists examined the cloth in detail for a period of five days. Their findings, published in 1981, showed conclusively the presence of human blood. Further attempts to date the Shroud began in 1988, when three independent laboratories were permitted to take small samples of the cloth. The resulting dates, arrived at using the carbon-14 technique, fell between 1260 and 1390, although believers in the Shroud's authenticity – Sindologists (from Sindone, the Italian for shroud) – refused to accept this, arguing that severe fire damage in 1532, and the contamination after centuries of handling rendered the dating process invalid.

In support of their claims that the Turin Shroud is the genuine article, Sindologists have put forward the following "evidence": that the figure's wounds are consistent with that of a scourged and crucified man, that the dimensions of the cloth conform to Middle Eastern measurements (e.g. Syrian cubits), that some mineral fragments within the Shroud correspond to rocks found in caves around Jerusalem. Some Sindologists, seeking an explanation for the imprinting of the figure, have suggested that the moment of Christ's resurrection may have resulted in a burst of radiation (rather like our LIGHTNING PICTURES, see p.247) and that this burned an image into the cloth.

GLENN MEYER

On the left the Turin Shroud, on the right Nicholas Allen's reconstruction of a shroud-like image using a camera obsura and medieval chemistry.

Those who oppose the believers fall in two main camps (though both accept a late medieval dating). The first group favours the idea that the image was painted onto the cloth; if so, the artist would have had to work in negative, a technique quite unknown five centuries before the modern discovery of photography. (The proposal of Leonardo da Vinci as a likely candidate is wishful thinking since he was born almost a hundred years after the first mention of the Shroud at Lirey.) While no one seems to doubt that similar images were painted and passed off as genuine relics, the scientific evidence for it is negligible and all attempts to replicate the Shroud by this method have failed to match the impressive quality of the original. In its favour is the fact that the figure does not correspond accurately to the norms of human anatomy but does correspond to the traditional, post-classical, iconography of a long-haired, bearded man.

The second group (probably inspired by Pia's famous negative) believes that the image was made by a primitive form of photography, using a camera obscura to project onto sensitized cloth. The experiments of Nicholas Allen, using only materials available in the fourteenth century, have produced some convincing images which include some, but not all, of the visual distortions characteristic of the actual Shroud. These experiments, as well as those made by Lynne Picknett and Clive Prince, and Christopher Knight and Robert Lomas, are detailed in Allens' book *The Turin Shroud and the Crystal Lens* (1998).

A new bout of excitement was generated in 1999 when pollen extracted from between Shroud fibres in 1978, was analysed by Avinoam Danin of the Hebrew University in Jerusalem. Among the plants identified was a species of thistle endemic to the Jerusalem area which set seed during the period corresponding to Easter. Unfortunately questions have subsequently been raised about the reliability of Max Frei, the criminologist who lifted the original samples of pollen from the Shroud in 1978 – the same man who pronounced the "Hitler Diaries" as genuine. Frei may well have studied genuine ancient pollen for comparison and accidently contaminated the Shroud samples. We will never know because he died in 1983.

In an exquisite way, these example show how science, far from settling an issue, only raises yet more questions about it. The central enigma of the Shroud – by what process was the image of a man formed – continues to elude analysis. Further scientific tests are scheduled for the year 2000 when the Shroud will once more be put on public display. Perhaps in this important anniversary of the birth of Christ the threads of this mystery will finally be unravelled.

Lightning pictures

Can a flash of lightning transfer an image of the local scenery onto bodies and objects? This question was debated in all seriousness by nineteenth-century scientists and the subject was given a name, Keranography. Yet the issue is still undecided. Cade and Davis in their *Taming of the Thunderbolts* (1969) say that in some cases lightning victims "do get peculiar markings on their bodies which give rise to incredible stories of 'lightning photographs'." On the other hand, Frank W. Lane in *The Elements Rage* (1945) says: "I am informed, however, that it is established today that lightning has no photographic properties."

On 17 June 1896 two labourers were sheltering from a storm in a hut in the south of France when a bolt struck very close to them, knocking them to the ground. A letter to the *Petit Marseille* the next day said: "The lightning cut open the boots of one man and tore off his trousers; but over and above this, like a tattooer making use of photography, it reproduced admirably on the arti-san's body a representation of a pine tree, a poplar and the handle of his watch." In his book *Thunder and Lightning* (1905) Camille Flammarion speculated whether the cabin could have acted like a pinhole camera with the flash determining the exposure, but this does not explain the selection of only certain images from the surrounding scene, nor the imprinting of images through the man's clothes.

In 1861 Mr C. Tomlinson read a paper on Keranography to the British Association in Manchester, later summarized in the *English Encyclopedia* article "Lightning Figures". He mentioned a little girl who stood before a window during a storm in 1853, and on whose body was found "the complete image of a maple tree", illuminated outside the window by a brilliant flash. In September 1825 a sailor sitting below the mast of the brigantine *Buon-Servo*, moored in the bay of Armiro, was killed by lightning; a line was seared down his back from neck to hips, and near his groin was etched the perfect image of the horseshoe nailed to the mast above him. Most dramatic of all: a boy climbed a tree to steal from a bird's nest; the tree was struck by lightning and the boy hurled to the

Flammarion, in L'Atmosphere, tells of people fixed in a rigid death tableau by lightning, sometimes with an image of the local scene engraved on their skin.

ground; and on his breast was seen "the image of the tree, with the bird and nest on one branch, appearing very plainly". This story and twenty-three others can also be found in *Chambers's Journal* (6 July 1892); other collections were compiled by Flammarion, Andrew Steinmetz, and Henry F. Kretzer.

Steinmetz, in his enthusiasm for a scientific-sounding theory, ignores the conflicting and significant details in his own evidence, and sees the explanation for stories of tree-images on the bodies of lightning victims in the well-known dendritic patterns of electrical discharges. Undoubtedly the root or branch patterns of radiating burns left by lightning has given rise to many of these stories; but there are many other incidents involving quite different images. One consistent detail that cannot readily be explained away is the realistic quality of the images in many lightning photographs. Steinmetz himself mentions "a perfectly engraved image of a cow" on the body of a woman who was tending it when it was struck by lightning (*Sunshine and Showers*, 1867).

In 1895 Henry F. Kretzer privately published a collection of reports on the antics of lightning, gleaned from American newspapers (*H.F. Kretzer's Lightning Record*). It contained such outrageous gems as the bolt of lightning that stripped silver-plating off swords hanging on a wall, while perfectly electroplating a cat sleeping on a sofa below. Also included is a tale of two men killed by lightning as they sheltered beneath a tree in Highland Park, Pennsylvania, on 19 July 1892. On removing the clothing from one of them (named Cassell), the undertaker witnessed an astonishing sight: "Across Cassell's breast was a picture true to nature. The browned oak-leaf of autumn was there. Twined among the foliage were a number of ferns. These too, with the exception that they were brown, were as natural as their model. So plain were the leaves and ferns that even the minutest vein was discernible." In about four hours the scene faded into a purple blotch.

We wonder if the phenomenon might not be more significant than any merely mechanistic explanation might suggest. In assembling data for this book we are constantly struck by the concurrences between phenomena and their imagery, so that the graphic similarity between lightning and the trees they strike begins to hint at more symbolic connections. This theme is developed further in our sections on SPONTANEOUS IMAGES (see p.240) and COINCIDENCES (see p.201).

If we look beyond the inadequate nineteenth-century attempts to rationalize this phenomenon of lightning photography, we find it well recognized in every age. When Vesuvius erupted in 1660 the attendant lightning flashes were blamed for the appearances of crosses on garments throughout the kingdom of Naples. Isaac Casaubon, in 1611, mentioned, in all earnestness, the images of crosses that appeared on the bodies of a congregation in Wells cathedral during a summer storm in 1596. Lightning "fell" into the church, and although no one was hurt, the terrific violence of the thunder threw many to the floor: "The wonderful part was this, which afterwards was taken notice of by many, that the marks of a cross were found to be imprinted on the bodies of those then at divine service." The Revd G.S. Tyack describes this incident in his *Lore and Legend of the English Church* (1899), quoting Casaubon: "The Bishop [of Wells] himself found the mark upon him, and others were signed 'on the shoulder, the breast, the back, and other parts'." Flammarion adds that the bishop's wife was among those who received the cross stigma. Another incident when crosses appeared on clothes was mentioned even earlier, by Joseph Grünpech in *Speculum naturalis coelestis* (1508).

The spectacular case of lightning striking the high altar in the church of Saint-Sauveur at Ligny, France, on 18 July 1689, is included by most of the encyclopaedists mentioned earlier. Father Lamy, a priest from a neighbouring town, investigated as soon as he had word of the strange effects, and published his report in 1696 in a little booklet that is a model of observation. The curtains surrounding the altar were blown off their rings, but without breaking the rings or detaching them from the curtain-rail or ripping the cloth. Various altar cloths were burnt in places, and the main cloth was torn in a huge X-shaped rent. As witnessed by the fifty people present, a statue of Christ was levitated and hovered in the air while its stand was shattered. But the incident that aroused the greatest astonishment and terror was the appearance of strange lettering across the main altar cloth. Deciphered when calm was restored, it proved to be the words of a printed text which lay face down on the cloth, but reversed and magnified. Yet this interpretation merely added to the horror when it was found that all the holy words and phrases were missing in this unholy transcription. However, Father Lamy was a match for this, seeing immediately that the omitted words were those printed in red ink on the card and that

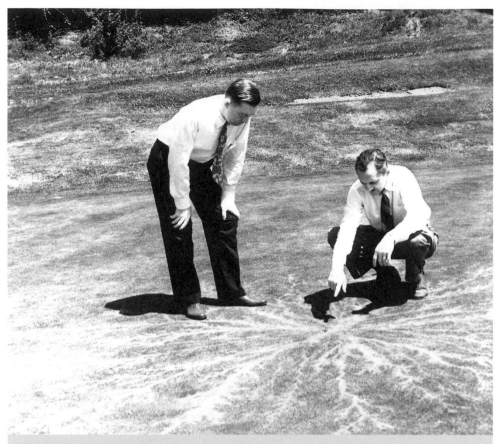

The branching pattern left by lightning explains some 'lightning photographs' but not all.

the lightning had transmitted only the main part of the text printed in black ink. This case was re-examined by Flammarion in *Thunder and Lightning* (1905) and found to be a factual report.

Andres Poey, director of the Physico-Meteorological Observatory at Havana, Cuba, published in 1861 his own collection of lightning stories. This book is very rare, and we have seen only references to and quotes from it in our authorities. One of Poey's examples occurred at San Vicente, Cuba, on 24 July 1852 when the image of a palm-leaf hut and its surroundings were found etched on some dried leaves. At Sibacoa on the same island in August 1823 lightning imprinted the image of a bent nail on the trunk of a tree. Poey adds that this was an exact but reversed copy of a nail embedded in one of the tree's upper branches.

We end with an aspect of our subject that, as far as we know, has never been researched – the imprinting of images *beneath* the skin. In 1812, at Combe Hay, Somerset, six sheep were struck dead by lightning in fields near a wood of oak and nut trees. As reported by James Shaw, in the *Journal of the Meteorological Society* (March 1857), when the sheep were skinned "a facsimile of part of the adjacent landscape" was found on the inside of the skins.

Images that weep and bleed

The old histories abound in references to idols and images that weep, sweat and bleed, events that were taken as significant portents. It is recorded, for example, that on the eve of Alexander the Great's main expedition of conquest, a cypress-wood statue of Orpheus, in Libethra, sweated profusely for several days. The soothsayer, Aristander, was not disconcerted; he delivered a favourable interpretation saying it was emblematic of the labour that future historians and poets would be put to in celebrating the monarch's exploits. Similarly, before the Sack of Rome in 1527, a statue of Christ was said to have wept so copiously that the fathers in the monastery where it was kept were continually employed in wiping its face. The same lachrymose tendency was attributed to a marble statue of St Lucy which wept during the siege of Syracuse in Sicily in 1719. Livy records that a statue of Apollo once wept for three days and nights; and Ovid tells of the dryad's oak at Eresicthon which gushed crimson, blood-like liquid when it was sacrilegiously cut down.

All these old stories of bleedings and weepings by various sacred objects may sound too fantastic to be taken seriously, and yet the same phenomenon continues up to the present day. In November 1996 a twelfth-century face of Jesus, painted on a marble pillar above his traditional birthplace in Bethlehem's Church of the Nativity, began winking and weeping blood-coloured tears. The first to notice this was a Muslim woman cleaner at the church, who saw it as "the will of God". Pilgrims and sightseers converged upon the church, and the weepings continued for many weeks. At times they were so profuse that cotton wool swabs were used to dry the icon. The moisture imbued them with "the most fantastic fragrance". One witness observed that the tears from the image's eye stopped at its cheek alongside the nose.

The event was proclaimed a miracle by the local head of the Greek Orthodox Church, Father Anastasios. "Jesus is crying because the world is not going well", he declared. The weeping had in fact begun about a month after a gun battle between Israeli troops and Palestinian police which left seventy-five people dead. But Catholics and Armenians, who share the Nativity church with the Greeks, were warned by their leaders to be cautious. A Franciscan, Father Michele, denounced the "miracle" as a fraudulent stunt to boost tourism. "How can it be that they saw Jesus crying at the exact spot there they sell candles?" he shouted cynically to a gathering of journalists. This, of course, is the same line that Protestants use against Catholic miracles! Our own piety is towards the phenomenon itself rather than for the religions whose images seem to attract it. Some cases occur outside any formal religious context. Years ago, a young listener called in to a radio discussion programme we were taking part in to tell how on the night of Jimmy Hendrix's

In 1911, this picture of Christ in a church at Mirebeau, France, began bleeding from the visible wounds of the stigmata. Tests at London's Lister Institute showed the blood to be a rare human type.

death, he looked up at a poster of the musician and saw drops of water running down the face from the eyes.

One reason why the Church authorities tend to be suspicious of weeping statues and the like is that they recognize in them remnants of "pagan

The 'Weeping Madonna' of Syracuse, Sicily, 1953, whose flowing tears were found to be similar to human tears.

superstition" – implying that they occurred before Christian times. Yet they undoubtedly serve, at least temporarily, as an aid to religious faith. In 1998 a woman waiting for a bus in Salt Lake City, Utah, noticed on a tree above her, on the stump of a lopped branch, a small "face of Jesus". A platform and ladder were erected, enabling people

to see it close up. When the face began exuding liquid, the "tears" were piously collected in cups and a shrine grew up at the base of the tree. The largely Mormon city administration did not at first approve and tried to suppress the cult, but they changed their tune when its effects became plain.

It was a poor district, inhabited by Catholic Hispanics, with a higher than average crime level. But the discovery of the Jesus tree caused a religious revival and lessening of crime. When John Michell visited it in August 1998, the shrine was strewn with flowers and well attended, the liquid was still flowing from the face and, when tasted, it could well have been identified as tears.

The *Sunday People* (11 January 1976) contained an article on a 300-year-old wooden image of Christ, in the Brazilian village of Porto das Caixas, and the miraculous healings attributed to the blood which periodically streamed from its painted wounds. Authoritative tests were said to have confirmed that the blood was real, though of an indeterminate species. More interesting to us is the fact that, despite careful watches and examinations since the first appearance of bleeding in 1968, the source of the flows remained undetected. In 1972, a bleeding limestone crucifix, belonging to the Pizzi family of Syracuse, Sicily, attracted so many pilgrims that the Church had to warn the public that this was not a recognized miracle – yet! Drops of blood formed on the statuette's breast, on the traditional site of Christ's lance-wound. According to Dr S. Rodante, president of the island's Catholic Doctors' Association, quoted in *Fate* (December 1972) the blood coagulated instantly, whereas samples taken from the Pizzi family (presumably on the assumption that they might be perpetuating a hoax with their own blood) reacted in the normal manner.

Bleeding and weeping images often occur in association with other strange happenings. For example, on 21 August 1920 all the religious statues and pictures belonging to James Walsh, a devout sixteen-year-old, began to bleed. He was lodging in the house of Thomas Dwan in Templemore, County Tipperary, Ireland. Statues in the house of Dwan's sister, Mrs Maher, were also found oozing blood after a visit by the boy. During the periods of bleeding, the furniture and other objects in Dwan's house moved on their own, in the best poltergeist tradition. In the months that followed many thousands of people saw these wonders. At first Dwan and Mrs Maher let small parties into their houses, but soon the great numbers became prohibitive, and they took to placing the statues in their windows as the columns of pilgrims trooped by, day and night. Many depositions were drawn up testifying to the miracle; and the *Tipperary Star* rarely appeared without some new account of the wonder of Templemore. There was another manifestation here of interest too. In the earthen floor of James Walsh's room a cup-shaped hollow kept filling up with water. Thousands of pilgrims took away quantities, but no matter how often it was drained, the hollow was always full. There were no signs of any hidden spring (the water never overflowed), but just enough water to replenish the hollow was

appearing as mysteriously as the blood on the statues.

Sometimes these mysterious appearances of liquids take a bizarre form. The *Worcester Telegram,* of Illinois (10 May 1970) reported that a "watery blood" was oozing from the neck, hands and feet of the body of St Maximina, in St Adrian's Church, Chicago. St Maximina's 1700-year-old bones, preserved in a glass coffin, are encased in a wax body portraying a beautiful lady, but the bones of the hands and feet are exposed to view. This seems analogous to the so-called "blood miracles" associated with many saints, whose blood has been found long after their deaths to be fresh and still capable of flowing, and whose bodies remain uncorrupted.

Father Herbert Thurston devotes several chapters to these aspects of hagiography in his *Physical Phenomena of Mysticism* (1952). A typical case is the blood prodigy associated with St Nicholas of Tolentino. In 1345, forty years after the saint's death, a lay brother cut the arms off the saint's still uncorrupt body, intending to carry them to Germany. Like the axing of Ovid's oak, this sacrilegious act was betrayed by a torrent of blood. The saint's arms were recovered and enshrined at Tolentino in reliquaries, and are said to repeat their

A plaster statue of Christ, now in St Luke's Church, Eddystone, Pennsylvania, started to bleed in November 1975. According to the *National Enquirer*, 20 January 1976, the blood is human, though of great age.

The weeping statue of the Virgin Mary displayed by the devoutly Catholic Rosa Mystica group in Maasmechelen, Belgium.

bleeding whenever some disaster threatens. Thurston had some doubts about the tale of the severing, but added that "there can be no reasonable doubt that from the two arms a curious exudation of a red fluid, described as 'blood', did take place from time to time in the sixteenth and seventeenth centuries. In 1699 this discharge seems to have continued pretty constantly for four months". That stringent critic and authority on miracles, Pope Benedict XIV, accepted the authenticity of this miracle.

In contrast, the Church has frowned on the way in which the miracle of the liquefaction of the blood of St Januarius has been popularly taken as a sign of luck for the city of Naples. Each year, phials holding dried particles of the saint's blood, kept in the Santa Chiara basilica, are supposed to turn liquid and froth for a while during services on the first Saturday in May, and on 19 September. On the occasions when the miracle fails, the Neapolitans fatalistically await a calamity. In 1976, the two most violent earthquakes ever to have shaken Italy both took place within a few days of the St Januarius festival. One happened in May on the sixth day after the failure of the miracle; the other happened in September during the week before a successful liquefaction. So you can interpret the portent as you please. The earliest recorded liquefaction was in 1329, since when there have been many attempts to explain the event away. Sir David Brewster, in *Natural Magic* (1831) speculates about compounds that would melt at low temperatures, so the "blood" would froth from the heat of the hand holding its phial. Other investigators have found the phenomenon to be genuine.

Most apologists and critics of miracles tend to argue specific events in isolation; Fort and Thurston, on the other hand, suggested that the enigma may only be understood when the phenomenon is studied as a whole rather than from a purely religious or sceptical point of view. Fort,

of course, was thinking of the teleportation of liquids, and we could extend this to include the well-documented, perpetually damp "bloodstains" that occur in "haunted" houses (see MYSTERIOUS FLOWS AND OOZINGS, p.51).

According to contemporary newspapers, Mrs Theresa Taylor of Walker, Newcastle-upon-Tyne was praying before her plaster-cast Madonna on 10 October 1955 when she saw the statue's left eye open and a bead of moisture form there. Later, neighbours were said to have seen a stream of tears. Another English case on our files involved a sixteen-inch crucifix, owned by Alfred Bolton of Walthamstow, London, which was observed to shed tears on at least thirty occasions between May and July 1966. A forensic scientist quoted in the *News of the World* (24 July 1966) said he was quite baffled after a thorough examination of the statuette.

In March 1960 Mrs Pagora Catsounis was praying before a portrait of the Virgin in her Island Park, New York home. She thought she saw Mary's eyes open and tears flow. Her husband saw them too, and called the priest of St Paul's Greek Orthodox church in nearby Hempstead. When he arrived, he saw for himself tears forming under the glass and running to the bottom of the frame *where they vanished*. In relating this story, the writer in *Grit* (26 July 1970) refers to other instances of weeping pictures. In 1953 several icons of the Madonna wept blood in Italy: in Syracuse the flow lasted eight days, and in Mezzolombardo blood appeared on a newspaper photograph of an icon!

Statues that come to life

At Limpias, in northern Spain, in March 1919, hundreds of people – many of them "scientifically educated persons" – swore statements that they had seen "certain pictures of saints perform miracles, step out of their panels, carry out actions, etc." The psychologist E.R. Jaensch, who briefly discusses the case in his *Eidetic Imagery* (1930),

attempts to explain this and other visions in terms of eidetic images: complex retinal images that persist in the visual memory and appear superimposed on normal visual images.

William A. Christian's more detailed study, *Moving Crucifixes in Modern Spain* (1992), takes a different tack, providing rare insight into the social and political contexts of such extraordinary beliefs. Most of his research deals specifically with the events in Limpias where local records show that, for nearly two weeks, a life-size crucifix in a church was seen by many people to be expressing agony – rolling its eyes, grimacing and sweating. Christian also demonstrates clearly that these experiences were, to a great extent, "enabled" at the time by the nine-day preaching "mission" of two Capuchin friars, who might well have known of the similar phenomenon at Gandia, in southeast Spain, the previous year (1918).

Although less well-known than other "miraculous" events in the history of modern Catholic

A painting by Gêrome showing the moment when Aphrodite brings the statue of Galatea to life.

phenomena, Limpias is on a par with the great post-World War I visions (such as those at Lourdes, Pontmain, Knock and Fátima) and undoubtedly influenced the popular culture of belief in such possibilities. Limpias was quickly followed by two other mass-witnessings of Christ's agony on the Cross in Spanish towns – at Piedramillera (1920)

and Melilla (1922) – setting the scene, as it were, for the more recent flaps of wobbling Madonnas in Ireland and bleeding Madonnas in Italy.

The idea that statues and paintings can take on a life of their own has its earliest expression in ancient cosmogonies in which the Creator breathes life into images he has made of human and other creatures. In classical mythology, the legendary King of Cyprus, Pygmalion, falls in love and eventually marries a statue that comes to life. In the eleventh-century Welsh epic *The Mabinogion,* the magician Math creates a wife for the hero, Lleu Skilful-Hand, entirely out of flowers. Shakespeare plays with the idea in the magical ending of *A Winter's Tale* when a statue of the dead queen, Hermione, turns out to be the living, breathing woman.

The sorcerer-poet Virgilius of Naples gained a great reputation for animating statues; among the wonders attributed to him, by Gervase of Tilbury and other medieval chroniclers, was the fabrication of a brass fly that chased other flies away from that city. He also made a bronze archer, who guarded a perpetual fire in the city's baths. The same art was known to medieval magicians. Gerbert (Pope Sylvester II), Robert Grosseteste, Albertus Magnus and Roger Bacon are all credited with the manufacture of talking bronze heads that would give advice and answer any questions put to them. Albertus Magnus is also said to have made a metal man which grew to be so loqacious that his student, Thomas Aquinas, finally smashed it to pieces.

The archetypal quality of the primal act of creation is evident in its persistence into the present. An example of this continuity is the ancient Jewish legend of the creation of a magic automaton, the golem. This creature was a man shaped from "virgin clay" and brought to life by the insertion into its mouth of a Cabalistic formula, written on parchment, containing the mystical names of God. Sometimes the formula was written on the monster's forehead.

In the legend of the golem, the creature, like Frankenstein's monster, runs amok and destroys its creator – a pattern that is repeated in similar stories of artificial men from other cultures. The Taoist classic *Lieh Tzu* (c. 300 AD) records an ancient story of an artificial man sent by an artisan to the court of King Mu of Chou. Able to dance and sing on command, the automaton enraged Mou when it began to wink at and beckon the royal concubines. Fearing for his life, the inventor Yen Shih, demonstrated to the king that it was not alive by showing him its components made of "leather, wood, glue and lacquer".

Steve Moore, writing in *Fortean Studies* (no.1, 1994), points to some evidence that the story of Yen Shih's lascivious android may well have originally come from India in an early Buddhist work. Moore provides a valuable assessment of the

legends concerning the automata-making skills of China's great military strategist of the third century, Chu-ko Liang, who is credited with creating a herd of "wooden oxen and flying horses" to transport the supplies of his army.

In an article in *Flying Saucer Review* (April 1976), Aimé Michel refers to the many records of lifelike automata in antiquity and suggests that they are evidence of an advanced ancient technology, possibly of extra-terrestrial origin. Certainly, the earlier the period the more is claimed for its artificers' skills, magical or otherwise. According to the *Asclepius* of Hermes Trismegistus, a book of Egyptian magic, certain statues in the Egyptian temples were so designed and placed that at certain seasons they would become animated by cosmic forces. At the end of the nineteenth century the scientist Sir Norman Lockyer began to investigate

NIALL O'MARA

For three days in September 1995, Hindus all over the world believed that statues of Shiva's elephant-headed son Ganesh were drinking milk offered to them on spoons. The story seems to have started in Northern India on 21st September and, as crowds flocked to their nearest temples with milk and spoons, the rumour spread to Hindu communities in other countries via email. Within days, the phenomenon was reported from Southeast Asia, the Middle East, Europe, Britain, Canada and the USA. While most sceptics dismissed the milk-drinking as due to 'capillary action' or absorption by hollow statues, we noted that the same phenomenon was reported of metal statues and glass-covered paintings. Before the frenzy itself diminished, we even heard of a statue of the Virgin Mary in Malaysia doing the same.

this ancient Egyptian science and discovered that the temples were orientated so that the statue in the sacred heart of the temple would be struck once a year by the rays of the rising or setting sun or of one of the other heavenly bodies.

Of course pious frauds were frequently perpetrated, such as the tricks used in ancient temples to encourage belief among the credulous. The Greek satirist, Lucian, in 155 AD, described the awe of worshippers at a temple at Hierapolis as a statue of Apollo seemed to levitate. In fact, to Lucian's amusement, it was actually being lifted by the priests.

These ancient stories of "living statues" can be interpreted as early examples of mechanical toys but we feel that their significance is far greater than that. The old texts are vague about what, in modern terminology, we would call the power source of such automata. What was clearly more important was the way in which the attention of the listener, reader or believer was directed towards the idea that the normally inert could be animated and then controlled by a touch or spoken command. The life-force of such an automaton was closely connected to that of its creator, and it followed that those things created by divine magic were the most miraculous of all.

Catholicism has been a particularly rich source of amazing stories of magical icons and statuary. St Francis of Assisi was advised by the crucifix in the church at San Damiano which spoke to him and charged him with his mission. In 1609 and 1610 there were two appearances in a church at Chiavari, Italy, of a tableau of the Madonna and Child, composed of lifelike moving statues. According to varied sources, when the Araucanians stormed the Chilean town of Concepción in 1600, an image of the Madonna left the church to pelt the invading Indians from a tree with stones and clods of earth. In 1906 teachers and pupils at a Jesuit college at Quito, Ecuador, saw a statue of the Madonna open her eyes and change her expression; and several people in the Italian town of Assisi saw a statue of Our Lady of Assisi move and smile in 1948. D.H. Rawcliffe mentions other Italian examples of self-moving images in his *The Psychology of the Occult* (1952): pictures that moved at Campocavello in 1893; a statue that moved its arm and hand at Soriano, in Calabria, in 1870; paintings seen to move their eyes and shed tears on a number of occasions at Rimini between 1850 and 1905. Cobham Brewer's *Dictionary of Miracles* (1884) also has a cluster of legends of

crucifixes that bleed, move and speak (see IMAGES THAT WEEP AND BLEED, p.251).

The phenomenon is still reported today. On the evening of 22 July 1985, two women passing the Virgin Mary grotto at Ballinspittle in County Cork, Ireland, believed they saw the statue rock to and fro. According to Lionel Beer's chronicle, *The Moving Statue of Ballinspittle* (1986), within a fortnight thousands of people were gathering each night; many witnessed the rocking motion,

A painting by Edward Burne-Jones showing St John Gulberto (d.1073) being embraced, during his Knightly vigil, by a life-sized wooden figure of Christ.

including some who were initially sceptical. By October similar sights were reported from over forty other shrines across Ireland, the most extreme being three children at Mount Melleray, County Waterford, who claimed the Virgin came down

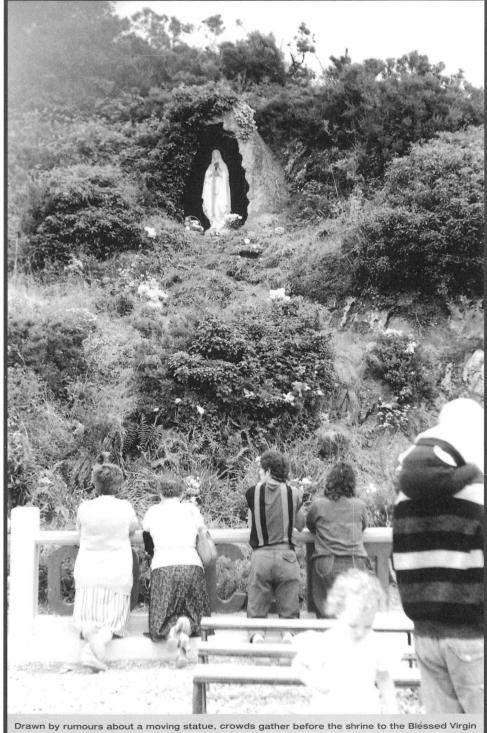

Drawn by rumours about a moving statue, crowds gather before the shrine to the Bléssed Virgin Mary at Ballinspittle, Co. Cork, in Ireland, in August 1985.

from her pedestal to tell them "God is very angry with the world." In most of the cases, the Church authorities were non-committal saying there was probably a reasonable explanation for such mass reaction.

The association between visions and animated images is continued in the story of Catherine Laboure who experienced a protracted series of visions of the Virgin Mary in 1830. Near midnight on 6 June 1830, in the Paris seminary of the Sisters of Charity, Catherine was woken up by a voice. A cherub surrounded by light conducted her to the chapel to meet the Virgin in person; the interview lasted two hours. As it began, Catherine heard a rustle of silk and looked up to see a radiantly beautiful lady "seating herself in a chair on the altar steps at the Gospel side, just like St Anne, only it was not the face of St Anne". The apparition had reproduced the pose and other details of a portrait of St Anne hanging elsewhere in the sanctuary. Catherine thought the vision was of St Anne, and had to be admonished twice by her inquisitors before she could accept she was in the presence of the Virgin.

It may be that Catherine *did* see a vision of the portrait of St Anne at first, but that the experience soon took off on its own inexorable course. Her second vision occurred on 27 November when she saw a bright three-dimensional tableau of the Virgin standing on the sphere of the Earth, crowned with stars and surrounded by a glorious light (the classic iconography of the Virgin of the Immaculate Conception as formulated by painters in seventeenth-century Spain). The Virgin then moved slightly, striking a distinctive pose. The whole scene became framed in an oval border on which some words appeared. Slowly the tableau began to revolve around its long vertical axis, and Catherine could see, on the back of the oval, the symbols of the Sacred Hearts of Jesus and Mary.

Catherine was ordered by the vision to arrange for the minting of a medallion that reproduced what she had just seen; the "Miraculous Medal" became so popular that many millions were distributed. Bernadette Soubirous was wearing this "medal" on 11 February 1858 when she first experienced the apparition of the Virgin Mary in the grotto at Lourdes. The story becomes even more interesting when we note that, according to Bernadette's own testimony, during her sixteenth vision (on 25 March) the Virgin struck a pose as she hovered above the rose bush. Bernadette recognized the pose as that portrayed on her medallion. This was the occasion on which the vision announced: "I am the Immaculate Conception." Both Catherine and Bernadette were later canonized and details of their visions, together with those of six others, can be found in *A Woman Clothed with the Sun* (1961), edited by John L. Delaney.

It is interesting to note the similarities in the accounts we have from people who have seen pictures or statues come alive. Frequently mentioned are the eerie brightness and unnatural quality of the light at the time of the vision and the inclination of the apparently animated figures to strike formal, conventional poses, as in a tableau or illustrated book. These descriptions remind us of holographically-generated images which are convincingly three-dimensional and contain a limited degree of movement. This was clearly demonstrated at Pontmain and when Catherine Laboure saw the *back* of her vision as it rotated.

Another important example is the strange mass vision at Knock (Cnoc), County Mayo. In this small Irish village, on 21 August 1879, many people saw a group of "shining statues" by the church wall where, in reality, there was no room for such a tableau. It took the form of a lamb standing on an altar surrounded by the Virgin, St Joseph and a bishop. As witnesses watched for an hour, the Virgin turned her arms and eyes to heaven in prayer, St Joseph turned to look at her, and the bishop read from a Bible. They were about two feet in the air and "full round as if they had a body and life". Kevin McClure includes many eyewitness accounts of this and other visions in his 1983 analysis *The Evidence for Visions of the Virgin Mary*. One witness reports being able to read the print in the bishop's Bible while another, prostrating herself at the Virgin's feet, clasped only empty space and "wondered why I could not feel with my hands that which I had plainly and distinctly seen?

Photographs of the gods

Almost as soon as photography was invented, the new medium was used to record (and often to fake) spiritualistic phenomena. In psychic photography one often comes across claims that peculiar patches of light – not always in human shape – have appeared anomalously and represent sentient beings (the souls of the dead, fairies, angels, aliens and the like). Another category, the classic "ghost photograph", reveals images, some faint and some solid, of definite human form, purportedly of people who were not present when the photo was taken. Yet another type is the "thoughtograph", in which someone wittingly or unwittingly causes an image to appear on unexposed film, an interference attributed to some undefined psychic ability like psychokinesis.

Our subject here goes beyond these categories and involves alleged photos of entities that either existed long before the invention of photography or who could more properly be called "mythical".

Probably the most famous of all "god" photos is the one known as "Christ in the Snow", which shows Jesus in the "Sacred Heart" pose – right hand raised in benediction, left hand clutching his robe as though about to expose his chest. The earliest extant account of this photo dates it to 15 July 1920, when Mildred Swanson, a housewife of Seattle, Washington, was posing her daughter Karin against a bank of flowers. Of its own accord, the shutter clicked and fearing she had ruined a frame, Mrs Swanson advanced the film to take the required photos of Karin. When the film came back from the drugstore, in Rochester, NY, the frame contained the image reproduced on the left.

Some years later, a *Fortean Times* reader, Julian North, of Victoria, BC, Canada, included the photo in his regular column in the *Victorian* (8 September 1976). By this time, the story, as received by North, had changed: it was said to have been taken in 1937 (not 1920) and placed Mrs Swanson in Winnipeg. Apparently the manager of the drugstore that developed the picture asked for, and was given, permission to sell reprints of "the picture that took itself". Hundreds were sold at a nickel each.

In subsequent years these details changed many times, but the captions usually agree that Christ is depicted against a bank of snow. This explanation might well have been invented in order better to explain the quality of the photo with its contrasted black and white areas. In fact when several versions of this image are compared one can see that the real cause of this high contrast is successive copying with its attendant loss of detail. Each time the photo is reproduced it generates a new batch of impossible claims.

The clearer image shows an early version of 'Jesus among the flowers', located by Julian North in 1976 and said to have been taken by a Mrs Mildred Swanson of Winnipeg, Manitoba, in 1937. An earlier account says Mrs Swanson took it in Seattle in 1920. Since then many versions of the photo have been circulated – many of them 'filled-in' by recopying from earlier copies – and with wildly different details. In our own researches, we were astonished at how many owners of prints believed the photo was taken by a relative under extraordinary circumstances.

In Britain, the image was first printed in the spiritualist newspaper *Psychic News* on 10 October 1936. Its editor, Maurice Barbanell, made it a personal quest to locate the original negative and it was reprinted many times in successive years. He eventually discovered that a copy had been sent to Sir Arthur Conan Doyle in 1926 by a woman who had obtained it in Vancouver. This copy was displayed in the Conan Doyle Museum, part of Doyle's psychic bookshop in Victoria Street, London, for at least ten years. Barbanell was told by one correspondent that it had been taken in 1917, "unexpectedly secured in the trenches in France" by a cleric. This is the earliest date we have seen claimed.

To celebrate their 5000th issue, on 13 Nov 1977, the *Sunday People* reproduced the image with the caption "the most famous picture we have ever printed". For them it was, "A snow scene in the Alps, taken from an aircraft, (in which) the face of Christ is etched in the melting snow." When the picture was first printed by them on 10 Oct 1958, it had generated 30,000 requests for copies and several new claims about its origin. Most intriguing was the assertion that the photograph was taken by a Chinese man troubled by the anti-Christian feeling in China at the time. One day, while walking through snow-covered mountains, he heard a voice telling him to take a photograph. Fortunately he had his camera with him, and snapped a hillside of melting snow and black earth: on seeing the "face" in the developed photo he became a Christian.

Another version of the photograph's origin was given in a UFO magazine, *Saucer News* of Spring 1968. It was sent to them, they said, by an unidentified "third party" and was taken "in the Swiss Alps by a vacationer attempting to photograph a UFO." We most recently saw copies of the image on the Internet (March 1998) being sold "for healing purposes". The vendor claimed his father took the photo during World War II. He was not the first with this idea as advertisements for a poster of it regularly appeared in the *National Enquirer* in 1980.

In *Psychic News* (8 March 1978) Barbanell confessed his dismay on investigating yet another claim of ownership of the original photo, only to be shown one more derivative copy. After forty years of searching, he told us, he was no nearer to pinning it down. However, the diversity of claims have not daunted the faithful; one pointed out that "the duplication of the pictures is further proof of the existence of Christ."

Tracking the provenance of other similar photographs has proved no less difficult. We first saw the famous "Christ in the Clouds" in the 1968–69 issue of *Saucer News*. The most common version of its origin is that it was taken by a US Airforce flyer during a combat patrol over Korea. Printed in the *Daily Independent* of Ashland, Kentucky (it had been sent in by a local man claiming to be a brother of a neighbour of the airman), its 14,000 first edition sold out, as did the second. But none of the people mentioned in its transmission are positively identified.

When it comes to other religions, two significant photos are known to Bob Rickard which purport to represent Kuan Yin (the Goddess of Mercy in Chinese Buddhism) in the clouds. Nothing much is known about the first image (opposite), except that it was allegedly photographed in 1975 through an airplane window. Copies of it are widespread among the Chinese communities of Malaysia. Despite the loss of the middle tones, it is possible to see the feet of the goddess resting on a curving black shape which, on reflection, takes on the shape of the head and neck of a dragon (also facing to the left). It could be a photograph of a sculpted devotional tableau in a temple or garden.

The other image of Kuan Yin looks more like a painted or drawn image than a photo. The accompanying undated inscription, translated for us by Susan Lung, is the account of the "photographer". "One day as I was strolling along in the open, I noticed an extraordinary cloud with a funny shape. It seemed to be approaching closer to me. It took on the shape of a respectable lady, but the image was vague. So I took out my camera and took a snap of it. To my surprise it turned out to be an image of our goddess. It hit the headlines at the time; the press and astrologers were all extremely interested. Because of this our humble chemist shop thought it would be nice to make copies from the original so that every household could put one up in their home. The kindness and blessings of our goddess is unlimited. Signed: A certain chemist, Shin-Tsi."

Steve Moore, editor of the *Oracle*, a journal devoted to studies of the I Ching, has found an even earlier Chinese example. In 1923 great excitement was generated in the city of Hochow, in Kansu province, by a photograph circulating that was said to be a portrait of one of the Eight Immortals, Lu Tungpin. The original notice, in the *North China Daily News* (10 March 1923), has a familiar ring to it. A native of the city, a Mr Têng, who worked for the government in Lanchow, received instructions from an unspecified source that "at a particular time on a designated day, he should observe the heavens and his efforts would be rewarded by seeing the god in the clouds, this to be followed by the use of his camera." The resulting photograph is said to show the Immortal "respectfully making prostrations at the Mountain gate in the Monastery of Mani at Uchuen, Lanchow."

According to Florence Ayscough, who includes this notice in her travel diary in the *Journal of the Royal Asiatic Society*, North China Branch (1923), there are several other, local and much older, traditions which link Lü Tungpin with "miraculous portraits". Mr Têng, who is described as a well-respected scholar and "an ardent disciple of China's ancient cults", would have known of these uncanny paintings and even if his photograph is a pious fraud in the manner of the Cottingley fairy photos (see THE LITTLE PEOPLE, p.120) it is interesting to note how an old tradition is given new currency with the aid of modern technology.

Alleged to be a photograph of the Buddhist goddess Kuan Yin, this print was widely circulated in Chinese communities throughout Southeast Asia with the unsupported claim that it had been taken through the window of an airplane in 1975.

to a retreat. As they were talking, Sai Baba, drew the outline of a human figure in the sand, and then drew out of the sand a small silver statue of Vishnu. Smoothing out the sand he continued the discourse until he began drawing once again. Then, ". . . he felt with his fingertips into the top of the mound and scraped a little sand away; less than an inch down was a photograph. He pulled it out . . . and held it up for us to see," wrote Murphet. "It was a glossy black-and-white print, about ten inches by eight. He passed it around for some of us to look at closely and later I examined it at leisure back at our quarters. It was a photograph of the Hindu gods and avatars, standing in two rows, to form a forward-pointing arrowhead, with Lord Krishna in the foreground at the tip. The heads of Satya Sai Baba and Shirdi Baba (his previous incarnation) could be seen as small inserts on the body of Krishna. This print, I felt was not produced in any earthly studio." The photo was given to a Mr T.A. Ramanatha Reddy and we greatly regret that Murphet did not include the photo as an illustration in his book. Perhaps a reader amongst Sai Baba's followers could trace it for us?

Satya Sai Baba (claimed as India's greatest living saint) is credited with the miraculous ability to produce photographic portraits of himself out of thin air. Howard Murphet in his book, *Sai Baba: Man of Miracles* (1971), tells of how he, his wife and a few other devotees accompanied Sai Baba

Today, the production of alleged photographs of extra-terrestrials, spirits, elementals and other entities is a burgeoning industry. Their origins are just as vague as those we have reviewed and not one of them is remotely convincing to anyone but a devout believer. As advances in the digital manipulation of images produces ever-more convincing pictures of objects and places that have never existed, so the notion of photography as a form of factual evidence is continuously undermined. Investigators of unexplained phenomena will no longer accept a photograph, on its own merits, as proof of anything — yet, paradoxically, photos of Jesus and his Mother have never been more widely circulated among the faithful.

10

Monsters

10

Monsters

Sea serpents and monsters of the deep

Sea serpents, together with lake monsters, are the most confusing of all the "borderline" creatures discussed in this section of our book. As with many of our topics there are some genuine, sincere sightings, some undoubted hoaxes and, in between, a multitude of cases where the evidence could be interpreted either way or in some other way altogether. This confusion goes back to the earliest writings on the subject, and particularly to those of Olaus Magnus, a Swedish ecclesiastic who left his native land at the time of the Reformation and went to Rome, where, in 1555, he wrote his famous *Historia de gentibus septentrionalibus*, a compendium of Scandinavian traditions, antiquities and folklore. He was a lover of curiosities, and it is hard to know what to believe among his marvellous tales. His book was illustrated with woodcuts, the most famous of which depict the soe orm, or sea serpent, and the kraken, a monstrous kind of octopus much reported by northern seamen. Although tales of marine monsters go back a long way – the Book of Isaiah (27: 1) mentions "the dragon that is in the sea" – Olaus Magnus was the first modern scholar to collect reports and make a serious study of these creatures.

Conrad Gesner, for his *Historia animalium* (1560), redrew most of Olaus's sea monster illustrations, making them even more fanciful, and helping to form the traditional, undulating sea-serpent image which persists to this day. One of the types he described was a huge, sinuous water creature which he called the Great Wall snake. In the text of his book Gesner rather craftily passed the buck, saying: "Such monsters were put on plates by Olaus, how well and right is his responsibility to bear".

Another cleric, Eric Pontoppidan, Bishop of Bergen, joined the debate nearly two centuries later with his *Natural History of Norway* (1753). He relied heavily on seamen's yarns, but included some authentic sounding details, such as whales in their death throes vomiting up tentacles twenty feet long, presumably bitten off some submarine giant in a recent battle.

The first scientist to take such stories seriously was a young French naturalist, Pierre Denys de Montfort, who devoted a major part of his unfinished *Natural History of Molluscs* – published as part of Buffon's voluminous *Histoire Naturelle* (1749–67) – to evidence of the giant octopus and kraken. He became a familiar figure to the whalers and deep-sea fishermen in the French Atlantic ports, from whom he collected accounts of sea monsters. For this he was scorned and reviled by his contemporary savants. One of his reports was of a ship nearly swamped by a giant octopus which pulled a sailor from the rigging with one of its tentacles. The other sailors managed to hack off a tentacle

Olaus Magnus's 16th century *Carta marina*, showing some of the mysteries and perils of northern waters, including types of destructive sea monsters, the Maelstrom (lower right) and a strange UFO-like vessel (upper left).

de Montfort ridiculed, he was ruined by the French Revolution and died in about 1820 in a Paris gutter.

If de Montfort had lived on to 1861 he would have found himself vindicated, because in that year the French corvette *Alecton* had a battle lasting many hours with a giant, brick-red squid. This was the event that inspired Jules Verne to include a similar battle in *Twenty Thousand Leagues under the Sea* (1870). While the seamen were trying to haul the monster aboard, its tail was severed, and after a few days it stank so badly that it had to be tossed back into the depths the fate of much valuable cryptozoological evidence. In the next two decades a number of huge carcasses were washed up on the east coast of America and Canada, some with amazing tentacles of up to 42 feet long. By the 1880s the existence of giant cephalopods was sufficiently established for at least one naturalist, Henry Lee, author of *Sea Monsters Unmasked* (1884), to go overboard in the other direction, explaining all sea-serpent sightings in terms of giant squids.

Among today's cryptozoologists interested in the giant cephalopods is the Connecticut biologist, Gary S. Mangiacopra, who has published a series of articles since the middle 1970s in *Of Sea and Shore* (USA) and other journals. He spent three years rescuing from obscurity the records of a giant octopus stranded at St Augustine, Florida, in 1806. Tissue samples from the carcass, which had an estimated tentacle length of over a hundred feet and a weight of eighteen to twenty tons, had been sent to Professor Addison E. Verrill the world's leading authority on cephalopods. On the evidence he announced his belief in the giant octopus, and promptly named it after himself, *Octopus giganteus Verrill*. Later, probably under academic pressure, he retracted, calling it a whale. In 1962 the tissue samples, preserved in the Smithsonian Institution, were re-examined and positively identified as octopus flesh. The samples were then "lost" – another common way of disposing of embarrassing evidence.

from the monster. It measured twenty-three feet. Even bigger creatures were told of. In a church at Saint-Malô, de Montfort found a painting of another ship attacked by a giant octopus. It had been placed there by the grateful sailors who had survived the adventure. He reproduced in his book a hand-coloured engraving of the picture as part of his proof of the existence of such monsters. The Paris savants remained sceptical, and when de Montfort challenged them to go to Saint-Malô to see the painting for themselves, not one of them accepted. Some time later the church was destroyed and the painting with it. Not only was

Pierre Denys de Montfort's reconstruction of a painting in the church of St Thomas (later demolished) at Saint-Malô, Normandy, showing a 'colossal octopus'. Although certainly exaggerated by the artist, it was based on accounts of an actual battle with a giant octopus.

An illustration derived from an eyewitness account of the 20-minute encounter between the British frigate *Daedalus*, and a sea serpent over 60 feet long, which took place off the Cape of Good Hope on 6 August 1848.

About the time de Montfort was becoming obsessed with the giant octopus, the scene of sea serpent sightings switched from Norway, and crossed the Atlantic to Maine and Massachusetts. In 1817 there was a long series of sightings near the port of Gloucester, Mass. Lonson Nash, of the Linnaean Society of New England, was dispatched from Boston with instructions to collect as much sworn testimony as possible. He ended up being a witness himself. He used new techniques, familiar to modern researchers, in what may have been the first on-the-spot investigation in cryptozoology. He separated witnesses to avoid collusion, and used a standard questionnaire drawn up by the Society. The results established the existence of at least one kind of giant sea snake. That same year the eccentric naturalist, Constantin Samuel Rafinesque-Schmalz, became sufficiently interested in the events at Gloucester to name the creature *megophias* (great snake).

In England these reports tended to be dismissed as "Yankee humbug". The credibility of American naturalists among their European colleagues had been damaged by the alacrity with which a number of them discovered and named "new species". It became almost a mania. Matters were helped when

it became known that Rafinesque-Schmalz had included some non-existent species in his study *Ichthyologia ohiensis* (1820) as the result of a hoax by his friend, the bird painter J.J. Audubon who had described them to him as a joke.

There were many other hoaxes and misiden-tifications, the most notorious being Koch's sea-serpent skeleton. Dr Albert C. Koch had "reconstructed" this 114-foot monster from bones dug up in Alabama, and had named it *Hydragos sil-limanii* after Benjamin Silliman, a professor of chemistry and geology at Yale who had declared himself in favour of the sea serpent's existence. After mounting it in an undulating pose, familiar from Olaus's legacy, he toured around with it, lec-turing. He was exposed in 1845 when Jeffries Wyman, a pioneer archeologist and a professor of zoology and anatomy, identified the bones as those of a Zeuglodon, an archaic type of cetacean which was normally no more than forty-five feet long. Koch had kept on adding the bones of more than one creature until he obtained an impressive length. Silliman was furious, but Koch, undaunted, was soon on the road again, with his money-making heap of bones renamed *Hydrarchos harlani* after someone more appreciative.

Koch was far from being a mere charlatan. He had done valuable excavations and was the source of many fine skeletons in museums, including that of a "matchless" mastodon now in the British Museum. His diggings had shown that people had lived in North America before the Indians came over from Asia, and that they had been contemporary with the mammoth and giant sloth. He found flint arrowheads associated with remains of these animals, but the implications of his finds were for many years disregarded, and his claims were ridiculed. As for Wyman, he went on to write, in 1847, the first scientific description of the gorilla, previously considered as mythical as the sea serpent.

Philip Henry Gosse, the popular Victorian writer, caused a stir by devoting the last chapter in volume I of his best-selling work, *The Romance of Natural History* (1860) to krakens and sea serpents, which were then being reported from all parts of the world. The excitement caused in scientific circles by these sightings is hard to imagine today. In 1848 Edward Newman, editor of the respected *Zoologist* magazine, took the brave step of opening its pages to sea serpent reports and discussions, and even contributed supporting statements himself.

Later that same year occurred the sighting which became the most celebrated of its time in Britain, involving the captain and officers of *HMS Daedalus,* off the Cape of Good Hope in the South Atlantic. On reaching England, Captain Peter M'Quhae sent details of the sighting to the Admiralty and to the *Times,* and personally supervised the now famous engravings of the sea serpent, published in the *Illustrated London News.* In one of the longest letters ever printed in the *Times,* Professor Sir Richard Owen, who had been knighted for his work in palaeontology, wrote a detailed criticism of the *Daedalus* report, insisting that the witnesses had seen a giant seal, or something. He added with all the force of his position that there is no such thing as a sea serpent, and therefore no sea serpent could have been seen.

Owen was the great authoritarian scientist of his time. In her entertaining account of the old naturalists, *The Heyday of Natural History* (1980), Lynn Barber describes Owen as "always willing to stand up as an expert witness, whether or not he had any experience in the relevant field". For almost any new species or scientific

work to be acceptable, it first had to be accepted by Owen. In cases where he did not know the answer to a problem of natural history, his own opinion was enough to settle the matter. But if Owen hoped that M'Quhae would be intimidated by his authority, he was wrong. The Captain bravely stood his ground and a strong body of public opinion supported him.

In December 1964, a Frenchman, Robert Le Serrec, with family and friends on his yacht, visited Hook Island, off the Queensland coast of Australia, and saw this huge tadpole-like shape resting on the sandy bottom in clear shallow water. His photograph of the 80-foot-long creature has met only scepticism from marine zoologists.

Twenty-nine years and many more sightings later, the sea-serpent again ran into trouble with Owen. In May 1877 Captain H.L. Pearson, in command of the royal yacht *Osborne*, described to the Admiralty a close sighting of an unknown sea creature off Sicily. The report was, of course, sent on to Owen, whose criticism of it boiled down to his opinion that the testimony was worthless because the observers were not zoologists. That objection could no longer be raised after 1905, when two naturalists obtained a clear view of a sea serpent from the yacht *Valhalla* off the coast of Brazil.

The first book by a professional zoologist to be devoted to the subject was *The Great Sea Serpent* (1892) by the Dutchman, Antoon C. Oudemans. For many years Oudemans had collected material, and in this first major bibliography of sea serpent references he listed 330 titles. His revolutionary conclusion, based on a morphological study of sighting similarities, was that the creature was a long-necked pinniped or seal. As expected, the scientific community was generally abusive, but the book marks the beginning of serious crypto-zoological interest in the sea serpent.

The publication in 1968 of Bernard Heuvelmans' *In the Wake of Sea-serpents* (inspired by Oudeman's pioneering work) was another landmark. He collected together no less than 587 sea-monster reports, and analysed each case, historically, statistically and morphologically. After eliminating probable hoaxes, misidentifications and vagaries, he was left with 358 serious, well-witnessed sightings. From these he categorized nine distinct sea-serpent types: the long-necked, the merhorse, the many-humped, the many-finned, the super-otter, the super-eel, the marine saurian, the "father of all turtles" and the "yellow-belly".

Heuvelmans acknowledged that there are dimensions to the problem of water-monsters that lay outside his own scientific field. For one thing, there is the tendency of witnesses to describe sightings so as to "fit an existing archetype". He also remarked, enigmatically, that "even the most common animal . . . is partly 'imagined'. And, reciprocally, all 'mythical' animals are partly real". This insight has been developed by the modern school of folklore, which draws its material not just from pre-industrial "folk" but from contemporary reports and rumours of paranormal phenomena. No sea serpent has ever been caught and exhibited, but in human imagination these creatures are more real than many other, more tangible species.

In 1998, a group studying animal behaviour at Oxford University developed a statistical method that allows them to estimate the diversity of the populations of rare creatures based on small samples. The group's spokesman, Charles Paxton, writing in the *Journal of the Marine Biological Association* (November 1998) declared that based on the discovery-rate of new species since 1748 (when the tenth edition of Linnaeus's *Systema Naturae* appeared) there were about forty-seven more unique salt-water species yet to be discovered, including a new whale and a few "totally weird sharks". The weight of evidence leaves us in no doubt that the sea-serpent exists. But somehow we do not expect ever to see one in a museum.

Nessie and other lake monsters

In 1933 newspapers all over the world found a diversion from the Great Depression in the beguiling form of the Loch Ness Monster. There is nothing new about reports of monstrous forms in lakes and inland waters. They feature almost universally in ancient myths and legends, and have been described by writers from before the time of Olaus Magnus in the sixteenth century. In the same year as media interest in Loch Ness began, there was a series of reports from the region of Vancouver Island about an aquatic monster called Caddy, or *Cadborosaurus*, from an appearance it made at Cadboro. The local Chinook Indians had known it for centuries by the charming name of *Hiachuckaluck*.

It was Nessie, however, who caught, the world's imagination. As more and more people came forward with claims to have seen the Monster of Loch Ness, the phenomenon assumed unusual dimensions. Nessie posed for photographs and, if witnesses could be believed, she had been seen in numbers, and even on the shore. It was one of those times of repeated sightings in an atmosphere of general excitement which the ufologists call "flaps".

The diversity of the sightings at Loch Ness, and the opportunity of studying a new animal mystery at first hand, excited Commander Rupert T. Gould. He had joined the British Navy in 1906, at the age of sixteen, and became interested in nautical mysteries. In 1930 he published *The Case for the Sea-serpent*. He was one of the first to realize that no one kind of animal could account for the variety of reported forms, so he offered three candidates: a long-necked seal, a giant turtle and, his favourite, a plesiosaur-like creature (favoured long before by Newman, Gosse and others).

When the Loch Ness story surfaced in 1933, Gould realized immediately the possibilities for first-hand investigation. He was forty-three years old and somewhat bulky, but he bought a motorbike and trekked to Scotland to interview witnesses. After the investigation Gould startled the world with a new theory, announced in his book, *The Loch Ness Monster* (1934). While most of the world happily contemplated the idea of a secret population of plesiosaurs stranded in the loch for millennia, Gould believed a sea serpent had recently become trapped in the loch, possibly by travelling upriver from Loch Linnhe, a sea loch,

This most famous of Loch Ness monster photographs was taken in 1934 by a London surgeon, R. Kenneth Wilson. Of his four shots, only this one and another even more vague have survived.

or through hidden tunnels or chasms below Loch Ness. But the big surprise was Gould's identification of the newcomer as "a vastly enlarged, long-necked marine form of the common newt".

The advantages of having a large, mysterious animal in a lake accessible to anyone who wishes to make the journey are obvious. In Britain, as in North America, a new breed of investigator appeared, the kind who would go out into the field and collect first-hand facts on their local lake monster.

kept private, was scandalized, and Dr Tucker's career was not exactly furthered.

The first unquestionably honest photographs of the Loch Ness Monster were taken in 1960 when an engineer, Tim Dinsdale, filmed a sequence of Nessie in the distance swimming away from the camera. Despite the small image, very grainy in enlargement, the film was authenticated by a military air-reconnaissance unit using techniques of analyzing photos for intelligence. The zigzag wake differed significantly from that

Tim Dinsdale, veteran of nearly fifty expeditions to Loch Ness, saw the monster on three occasions. His 1960 film of it has been exhaustively analysed by RAF scientists, and is now accepted as a genuine piece of evidence.

In 1934 Sir Edward Mountain footed the bill for a private expedition to Loch Ness, in which a thirty-day watch was kept on its murky waters by twenty men with cameras. The few resulting photographs, showing wakes, were disappointingly inconclusive. A similar expedition in 1960 was organized by students at Oxford and Cambridge. They were inspired by lectures given by Dr Denys Tucker, an ichthyologist at the British Museum of Natural History, who believed the monster to be a "lost plesiosaur". The Museum, which tolerates eccentricities in its staff as long as they are

of a boat and indicated a large body beneath the surface. The film was reanalysed in California in 1972, using computerized image-enhancing methods developed for the space probes. This disclosed new information: a second lump can be seen breaking the surface behind the first. So it appears, though sceptics disputed this interpretation. Dinsdale's belief in the plesiosaur solution, and the story of his regular expeditions to the loch can be read in his books, *Loch Ness Monster* (1961) and the revised *The Leviathans* (1976).

From among the many people who contacted him after learning about his photographs Dinsdale formed the Loch Ness Investigation Bureau (LNIB) in 1962. They continued to mount surveillance teams by the Loch under the leadership of Adrian Shire, while acting as a forum for research and discussion. The LNIB also keep a watchful eye on several other lochs with reputations for monsters. Later expeditions, well financed and technologically elaborate, included those of Robert Rines from the Academy of Applied Sciences in Chicago. His team achieved unprecedented success in 1972, photographing a "flipper", and in 1975 what appeared to be the head, neck and body of a large unknown creature.

In 1975 Anthony "Doc" Shiels, playwright, magician and well-known Irish-Cornish eccentric, brought to the attention of *Fortean Times* a series of sea-serpent sightings in the Helford estuary and Falmouth Bay area of Cornwall. One or

The photograph, taken in the depths of Loch Ness in 1975, which prompted some biologists to dignify the Monster with a Latin name but left others unconvinced.

more creatures were seen and photographed on many occasions, including once by Shiels and by David Clarke, editor of *Cornish Life*. Shiels first visited Loch Ness in 1958, and in 1977 he managed to take two full-colour shots of Nessie during a visit to Castle Urquhart – the clearest yet of a head and neck, recalling the famous photographs by the London surgeon, R.K. Wilson, taken in 1934, but with more detail. As with so many pieces of valuable cryptozoological evidence, bad luck dogged the photographs. One original was lost, and a glass copy of it was accidentally smashed, leaving only a poor copy print the value of which was lost amidst accusations of hoaxing. This sort of thing seems to occur regularly. Investigators into paranormal subjects frequently tell of jammed or forgotten cameras, malfunctioning equipment and vanishing evidence.

The subject is also made confusing by fakes and hoaxes. The best known picture of Nessie is the first of them all, the "Surgeon's photograph" taken by R.K. Wilson. Its image of a long-necked, dinosaur-like creature set the style for subsequent pictures, and it has long been accepted as a foundation stone of cryptozoological theory. In 1999 a book by David Martin and Alastair Boyd, *Nessie: the Surgeon's Photograph Exposed*, denounced it as a trick, showing how it was created from a model. Their evidence is carefully compiled and so convincing that it throws doubt on the whole record of Nessie photography. Other frauds have been detected or confessed to, and even in cases where the sincerity of photographers is not questioned, the images are too poorly defined to satisfy the doubters.

The first historical analysis of the Loch Ness Monster was Constance Whyte's *More Than a*

Legend (1957), tracing sightings back to the famous incident in Adamnan's *Life of St Columba*. She was the first to mention Nessie's cousins in other Scottish lochs. But treatment of the subject in a book by a professional zoologist had to wait until 1961 and the publication of Dr Maurice Burton's *The Elusive Monster*. Burton was willing to entertain ideas about plesiosaurs, giant eels, turtles and otters on the high seas, but explained the phenomenon in the Loch as misidentifications of gas-bubbles, wind-formed waves, diving birds and floating vegetable mats. However, Burton was not entirely negative. He accepted a residue of reports indicating the presence of "a large unknown animal", and deduced that it was probably "a long-necked otter-like animal".

There is now a Visitor Centre and Monster exhibition on the north shore of Loch Ness, and the literature on the subject keeps growing. Peter Costello's *In Search of Lake Monsters* (1974) summed up reports of lake-monster sightings all over the world, and in Roy Mackal's *The Monsters of Loch Ness* (1976) is a catalogue of Nessie's appearances

and photographs. Mackal's conclusion was that the Loch holds a population of giant amphibians, a species halfway between a giant newt and an eel. A later round-up of the subject is Paul Harrison's *Encyclopedia of the Loch Ness Monster* (1999). His cautious conclusion is that there really is something mysterious in the Loch.

In May 1981 there was great excitement about a photograph of a creature in Lake Champlain, on the border of Vermont and New York state, taken by Sandra Mansi in July 1977. It had come to light partly through the researches of Joseph Zarzynski, a New York schoolteacher who has made the identification of "Champ", the Champlain monster, a main ambition. According to Zarzynski sightings of Champ go back to the pioneer days when, in 1609, explorer Samuel de Champlain made its acquaintance, and found that it was already well known to the local Indians. Zarzynski joined forces with Professor Mackal to have the photograph scientifically studied. It is said to be the clearest yet of a monster in action and appears to show a type of Zeuglodon. Another monster

From the grounds of Castle Urquhart on the morning of 21 May 1977, Doc Shiels spotted Nessie surfacing, and managed to take two snapshots of the monster as it turned and sank out of sight.

hunter, X (his legal name) of Kingston, in Canada, has compiled a computerized catalogue of Canadian lake and coastal sightings; at the last count there were 204 items on his list. In the introduction (*INFO Journal*, March 1981) to his continuing survey, X observes that prior to the suffocating influence of nineteenth-century science, the existence of such creatures in Canadian waters was widely known and accepted.

These writers and researchers are all more or less followers of Bernard Heuvelmans, the "father of crypto-zoology", whose 1958 classic, *On the Trail of Unknown Animals,* was followed in 1968 by *In the Wake of the Sea-serpents.* Heuvelmans' thesis is that there are large creatures in many parts of the world, known to the local inhabitants but still unrecorded by science.

are never caught or adequately recorded on camera is that they do not physically exist.

In many cases the lakes are simply too small to hold the monsters attributed to them, or are too many and various to form a stable, or indeed feasible, ecology. Meurger devotes an appendix to the Champlain monster as an example of the influence of myth in both ancient and modern literature. Champlain was describing a new kind of fish – a gar-pike – and the illustration was exagerrated by European naturalists until it looked, on early maps, like a grotesque crocodile located in Canadian waters. The phenomenon Zarzynski is recording therefore has little to do with Samuel de Champlain and everything to do with modern cultural explanations.

GAMMA LIASON

This enigmatic photograph was taken at Lake Champlain, on the border between New York and Vermont states, by Sandra Mansi on 5 July 1977. Many believe it shows the head and neck of 'Champ', the legendary inhabitant of the lake, reports of which go back several centuries. Analysis to date reveals no evidence of trickery and the identity of the 'creature' is still unknown.

still unrecorded by science. This idea was formidably challenged in 1988 by Michel Meurger's *Lake Monster Traditions.* Meurger surveyed the entire field of lake monster legends, in Canada, Scandinavia and other regions, demonstrating that their fantastical details indicate that they are not records of flesh and blood animals but items of folklore. The reason that lake monsters

Meurger also accuses the cryptozoologists of literalizing myth and of distorting evidence by suppressing the fantastic details of monster legends so as to make them seem more reasonable. Nor does he have time for the supernatural or for those who believe that lake monsters are creatures of magic and enchantment. Human imagination naturally locates monsters in lakes and wildernesses, and everything strange or unexplained that people experience tends to be interpreted in the context of the local folk-tales. Meurger does not dismiss the lake monster but puts it into that intermediary state of reality that we call phenomenal, and locates its lakes and whirlpool haunts firmly in the landscape of myth. His arguments are subtle and compelling, but the hard-line cryptozoologists are still convinced of the physical nature of their prey and that one day there will be a lake monster in the scientific record. We cannot take sides here, because the evidence in this book seems to show that just about anything imaginable can at least appear to happen.

Globsters

If there are still unknown monsters, lurking in the depths of the oceans, there should be evidence of them in monstrous carcasses washed up on seashores. There are many reports of such things. Typically they are large, grisly, shapeless lumps of hair-covered flesh on a beach. Ivan Sanderson, the pioneer cryptozoologist, with his genius for inventing names, called them Globsters.

The first globster that came to Sanderson's attention was found at Temma, on Tasmania's west coast, in August 1960, apparently thrown up from the deep by a recent great storm. The huge, fleshy mass was roughly circular, fairly flat with a large central mound, marked with what may have been gill-slits. It measured eighteen feet by twenty feet and was covered with short soft hair, which one of its discoverers, a cattleman named Ben Fenton, compared to sheep's wool. From time to time Fenton and his two friends, Jack Boote and Ray Anthony, revisited the remote beach. The carcass was constantly shifted by the tide, which sometimes buried it and sometimes left it exposed. It took a year and a half for reliable information about the monster to reach Hobart and the ears of Bruce Mollinson, then working for the Commonwealth Scientific and Industrial Research Organization (CSIRO). He asked one of the Museum's trustees, G.C. Cramp, to finance an expedition of local naturalists to make an initial study of the enigma. Their report, with statements from Fenton, Boote and Anthony, prompted Mollinson himself to make two arduous trips to the site to see the astonishing new animal and to take flesh samples. Writing his own account in *Argosy* (June 1962), Mollinson refuted the explanations of faraway experts: "It wasn't fish, fowl or fruit. It wasn't whale, seal, sea elephant or squid. Sunfish, some had guessed, but this creature did not have fins. Devil ray? A devil ray has a mouth and teeth." He might have added that rays do not have hairs. The interest of the press was aroused when Mollinson came out with his opinion, that it was a large unknown animal, raylike in form, probably from the deep subterranean caverns off Tasmania.

Identifying the carcass became a game for journalists and experts all over the world. Suggestions ranged from a thawed out "prehistoric monster", perhaps a mammoth from Antarctic ice, to the body of a "space being". This latter idea naturally appealed to Sanderson, who had previously put forward the theory that UFOs themselves might be living creatures. CSIRO was slow to act, but after much delay and argument an official expedition set out to investigate the mystery carcass. Their report did more to obscure the incident than to clarify it. A few days after the expedition returned, a senior Australian government minister made a public statement, recorded in the Hobart *Mercury* (19 May 1962), in which he seemed to describe a quite different carcass, much smaller than the one originally reported. CSIRO claimed that what they inspected was a lump of decomposing whale meat, but Mollinson and others doubted whether the creature reported on by CSIRO was the same as that which the local naturalists had described, so different were the two accounts. The CSIRO team, which had omitted to take along any of the original discoverers, could have stumbled across a rotting whale and mistaken it for the body in question. Mollinson wrote: "I am not at all sure that Boote's monster and the one that became the center of attention are the same." Boote himself said: "The thing I saw was not a whale, or any part

Views of the carcass, found at St Augustine, Florida, in November 1896, with Dr DeWitt Webb, who conducted the first scientific examination of the remains and declared them to be of a giant octopus.

of a whale." So the incident ended in uncertainty.

"When we come upon assurances that a mystery has been solved," said Fort, "we go on investigating." That is what Sanderson did, and he published his conclusions in *Fate* (August 1962). He could add nothing essentially new, but he was profoundly suspicious of the official "wipe", preferring to believe that the first reports were an honest record of "an unknown, hairy, boneless invertebrate".

Fort in his time had kept an eye out for such records, "trying to come upon something about a hairy monster; furred, anything except scaled or with a hide like a whale's." The other unusual characteristic which intrigued him was the occasional mention of an elephant-like trunk. This is not characteristic of sea animals on this planet. "It may be," he wrote, "that there have been several finds of remains of a long-snouted animal that is unknown to the paleontologists, because, though it has occasionally appeared here, it has never been indigenous to this earth."

Fort was able to find only two suggestive items.

On 28 November 1930, the *New York Sun* reported that on Glacier Island, in Alaska, the carcass of a 24-foot-long monster, with a snout over 3 feet long, had been found preserved in ice; the creature was said to be covered in hair. The *New Zealand Times* (19 March 1883), reported that among the remains of a 40-foot-long unknown monster found on the Queensland coast was "what must have been an enormous snout, eight feet long, in which the respiratory passages are yet traceable." Such stories are tantalizing, but without precise details they are useless to science or cryptozoology. For this reason the long-snouted hairy one is not among Heuvelmans' sea-serpent types.

Included by Heuvelmans in his book, *In the Wake of the Sea-serpents* (1968) is the remarkable story of the Globster of Margate, a seaside town in Natal, South Africa. On 1 November 1922 a local farmer, Hugh Balance, noticed a disturbance off the coast. Looking through glasses, he thought he saw "two whales fighting with some sea monster" which looked like a huge polar bear. According to a statement he made to a local newspaper, cited in the *Daily Mail* (27 December 1924), Ballance said: "This creature I observed to rear out of the water fully 20 feet and to strike repeatedly with what I took to be its tail at the two whales, but with seemingly no effect." The battle continued for several hours, watched by growing crowds on the beach. Eventually the whales moved away leaving the strange giant floating without a sign of life. That night the carcass drifted ashore on a beach near the aptly named Tragedy Hill. It was colossal and it spread out upon beaching, as do all large sea creatures without their natural element to support their bulk. It was 47 feet long, 10 feet wide and 5 feet high. It had a 10-feet-long tail, matched at the other end by a curious trunk-like appendage. "Where the head should have been," said Ballance, "the creature had a sort of trunk 14 inches in diameter and about five feet long, the end being like the snout of a pig."

But the most astonishing feature of the monster, which could be seen clearly from the beach during the previous day's battle, was its impressive fur or hair, "eight inches long and snow white, exactly like a polar bear's." There was no sign of any wound or blood-stains. For ten days it lay there on the beach, attracting sightseers and flies, until the stench became intolerable. A team of 32 oxen failed to move it far and abandoned it near the water's edge, from where the night tide washed it back into unknown depths. This story,

Globsters for which photographic evidence have failed to settle any of the arguments (see the St Augustine carcass in SEA SERPENTS AND MONSTERS OF THE DEEP, p.267). The mythical dimension of the Margate monster is an interesting issue; undoubtedly some carcass was washed ashore and many people had an opinion about it. Penny Miller's *Myths and Legends of Southern Africa* (1979) interprets it in the context of the folk belief of the Zulu tribes. To the natives it was a vivid confirmation of what they had always known – that every pool, waterfall, river and coastal inlet had its own weird forms of life: mermaids, watersprites, *tokoloshe* spirits and "strange sea beings who danced upon the moonlit sands at night and left their footprints for all to see." Ballance said that the day after the carcass vanished, he met some natives "who told me that while fishing they had seen the monster out at sea, going up the coast, and this is the last we have seen of it."

As a curious sequel, we remember that a very similar creature, though less than half the size, was washed up at Machrihanish, in the Mull of Kintyre,

An artist's impression of the Hobart 'monster'.

of an aquatic polar bear 47 feet long, reminds us of a passage in Darwin's *Origin of Species*. On hearing about a bear in North America, swimming in the sea with its mouth open, and he wrote: "I can see no difficulty in a race of bears being rendered, by natural selection, more and more aquatic in their structure and habits, with larger and larger mouths, till a creature was produced as monstrous as a whale." It is a pity he never saw the evidence for his theory in the bear-whale on Margate beach.

This is an incredible story and one which could have been settled if only someone had had the foresight to take photographs. And yet there are

in 1944. According to the *Daily Mail* (5 October 1944) it was 20 feet long, had the bulk of an elephant and was headless. The *Mail's* headline proclaimed it was a polar bear, mainly because of its "long white fur", but no naturalist could be found who would endorse polar bears of that size, with or without a head. A careful reading of Ballance's description of the Margate monster raises the idea that its, "appendage" might not be a trunk but a headless neck which brings the overall form of the Margate carcass in line with the popular idea of what a sea serpent should look like – except for the white fur.

In his review of monster-carcass beachings, mentioned above, Heuvelmans notes that in almost every well-documented case it has been possible to identify the corpse as that of an "oarfish, basking shark or some well or little known cetacean" which has disintegrated into a bizarre heap of flesh but is still recognizable to a competent zoologist. (For ten days no competent zoologist went near Margate beach, so we will never know what *that* carcass was.) Hair or fur of any kind is unusual in large sea creatures and is unknown on the scale we have described here. Heuvelmans explains: "The appearance of stiff hair is soon produced by decomposition both in sharks and whales, once the skin comes off and the very fibrous connecting tissue begins to dry out." This almost certainly accounts for the "mane" of the Stronsa Beast, and other shredded "hairy" remains discovered several times in the Orkneys in the 1940s. But somehow we doubt if decomposition could account for the impressive white coats and hairy skins described in some of the cases.

Records of two earlier globsters turned up in a marine explorers' journal, *The Log* (April 1968), in an article by Michael Harvey. In 1948 a man wrote to the Sydney *Sun* about a carcass which he and some friends had found on Dunk Island, Australia. "It was like a huge jellyfish, with several slits and no eyes, and had a tough skin covered with fur. It was huge and must have weighed tons." Whatever it was, it was no jellyfish, the biggest of which are no more than half that size and have no "hide". A government scientist tried to tell the witnesses it was a malformed whale embryo. The Dunk Island folk were naturally eager to rid themselves of the stinking remains, but found them impossible to burn, so they resorted to axes and dynamite, dumping the bits far out to sea. It took ten days. The second incident occurred in 1958, when a globster turned up in the nets of two fishermen sailing from Melbourne to Hobart. The apparently lifeless carcass was likened to a huge bowler hat, 6 feet high with a tail on it. Its thick smooth skin was hairless and, like our other globsters, it showed no signs of fins, flippers, a mouth, eyes or other sense organs. The fishermen took photographs before they tossed it back, but in Hobart there was no marine scientist who could identify it.

The strange carcass, suggestive of a plesiosaur, found on 25 April 1977 by the Japanese fishing vessel *Zuiyo Maru* in waters east of New Zealand.

The man-eating tree

This terrible picture shows a person in the toils of a Ya-te-veo ("I can see you") a carnivorous plant said to grow in parts of Central and South America, with cousins in Africa and on the shores of the Indian Ocean. It comes from J.W. Buel's *Land and Sea* (1887) and illustrates a description given to the author by "a gentleman of my acquaintance,

who, for a long time, resided in Central America". This is his account:

who, for a long time, resided in Central America". This is his account:

"Travelers have told us of a plant, which they assert grows in Central Africa and also in South America, that is not contented with the myriad of larger insects which it catches and consumes, but its voracity extends to making even humans its prey. This marvelous vegetable *Minotaur* is represented as having a short, thick trunk, from the top of which radiate giant spines, narrow and flexible, but of extraordinary tenaciousness, the edges of which are armed with barbs, or dagger-like teeth. Instead of growing upright, or at an inclined angle from the trunk, these spines lay their outer ends upon the ground, and so gracefully are they distributed that the trunk resembles an easy couch with green drapery around it. The unfortunate traveler, ignorant of the monstrous creation which lies in his way, and curious to examine the strange plant, or to rest himself upon its inviting stalk approaches without a suspicion of his certain doom. The moment his feet are set within the circle of the horrid spines, they rise up, like gigantic serpents, and entwine themselves about him until he is drawn upon the stump, when they speedily drive their daggers into his body and thus complete the massacre. The body is crushed until every drop of blood is squeezed out of it and becomes absorbed by the gore-loving plant, when the dry carcass is thrown out and the horrid trap set again."

The Ya-te-veo tree as described to J.W. Buel by an informant from Central America. Reports of this obnoxious vegetable are rare, perhaps because few who encounter it live to describe it.

A type of vine in the swamps of Nicaragua, which devours small animals and will even try to capture men, was described in the *Illustrated London News* (27 August 1892). The report, in Dr Andrew Wilson's "Science Jottings", is reproduced opposite. In a later column Dr Wilson reported further, on a carnivorous tree discovered on the edge of the Sierra Madre in Mexico. It had slimy, serpentine branches which it wrapped round its prey. It seemed to live mostly on birds, for the ground beneath it was covered with little bones and feathers, and it accepted gifts of live chickens, ingesting their blood through suckers on its tentacle-like branches. But it did not refuse larger game, for when Dr Wilson's informant touched it, one of the branches grabbed his hand, and it was only with painful loss of skin that he was able to break free.

In 1924 a former Governor of Michigan, Chase Salmon Osborn, published a book called *Madagascar, Land of the Man-eating Tree*. He dealt with the tree in Chapter 1, the rest of the book

SCIENCE JOTTINGS.

BY DR. ANDREW WILSON.

I have lately met with the description of a very singular plant, given originally, I believe, in a provincial newspaper. As one is always interested in the strange and weird as represented in nature, I give the account for what it is worth. It may be nothing more than a piece of fiction, of course (I have learned caution from more than one instance of a joke being stated in the gravest of terms) ; but if, on the contrary, the incident described was a real one, I shall expect to hear something more about this wonderful plant. Perhaps some of my readers may be able to inform me whether or not the matter is a " plant," vulgarly speaking, in another sense.

It appears that a naturalist, a Mr. Dunstan by name, was botanising in one of the swamps surrounding the Nicaragua Lake. The account goes on to relate that " while hunting for specimens he heard his dog cry out, as if in agony, from a distance. Running to the spot whence the animal's cries came, Mr. Dunstan found him enveloped in a perfect network of what seemed to be a fine, rope-like tissue of roots and fibres. The plant or vine seemed composed entirely of bare, interlacing stems, resembling more than anything else the branches of a weeping willow denuded of its foliage, but of a dark, nearly black hue, and covered with a thick, viscid gum that exuded from the pores. Drawing his knife, Mr. Dunstan attempted to cut the poor beast free, but it was with the very greatest difficulty that he managed to sever the fleshy muscular fibres (*sic*) of the plant. When the dog was extricated from the coils of the plant, Mr. Dunstan saw to his horror that its body was bloodstained, while the skin appeared to be actually sucked or puckered in spots, and the animal staggered as if from exhaustion. In cutting the vine the twigs curled like living, sinuous fingers about Mr. Dunstan's hand, and it required no slight force to free the member from their clinging grasp, which left the flesh red and blistered. The tree, it seems, is well known to the natives, who relate many stories of its death-dealing powers. Its appetite is voracious and insatiable, and in five minutes it will suck the nourishment from a large lump of meat, rejecting the carcass (*sic*) as a spider does that of a used-up fly." This is a very circumstantial account of the incident, but in such tales it is, of course, absurd " to leave such a matter to a doubt." If correct, it is very clear we have yet to add a very notable example to the list of plants which demand an animal dietary as a condition of their existence ; and our sundews, Venus flytraps, and pitcher plants will then have to " pale their ineffectual fires " before the big devourer of the Nicaragua swamps.

The man-eating tree of Nicaragua: a description published in 1892 in the *Illustrated London News*.

being a general account of the topography, history and folklore of this huge East African island. The best evidence he found of the tree's existence was a letter, written in 1878 by Carle Liche, a German traveller, to a Polish friend, Dr Fredlowski. The letter was published over the next few years in a number of journals and newspapers, but nothing more was ever heard of Liche, nor of his companion, one Hendrick. Osborn printed the letter in full, in all its flowery, gory detail. The following is a summary.

Liche and Hendrick had made friends with a reclusive tribe of cave-dwelling pygmies called the Mkodos, and were invited by them to attend a sacrifice. They went deep into a forest and stopped at a clearing by a bend of a stream, where grew the dreaded tree. Its trunk was about 8 feet tall, brown, iron-hard and shaped like a pineapple. From its top grew eight leaves, each of up to 12 feet in length, which drooped limply to the ground. Their exposed inner sides were covered with spikes like the hooks of a teasel. A bowl-like growth on the apex of the tree held some sticky, intoxicating liquid, and from below the bowl a number of green, hairy tendrils, about 7 or 8 feet long, stuck out stiffly in all directions. Also from the top grew six tall, thin palpi, whitish or transparent looking, which waved about in the air in a sinister way, like serpents.

The victim about to be sacrificed to the tree was a young woman. With shrieks and chantings the Mkodos forced her to climb its trunk and stand on top of it. They then urged her to drink of the treacly liquid in the bowl. No sooner had she done so than the sinuous, waving palpi began to coil themselves round her limbs and body. The tendrils quickly jerked upwards to hold her in a firmer grip, and then the great leaves gradually rose up, closing over the body of the wretched girl and pressing tightly together so that her blood, mingled with the sweet, intoxicating fluid from the tree, flowed down the trunk.

On seeing the liquid, the Mkodos rushed up to the tree and began drinking the grisly flow, gathering it in cups, leaves and bare hands or lapping it with their tongues from the trunk. They became at once frantically intoxicated and began a "grotesque and indescribably hideous orgy" – at which point Liche and Hendrick made excuses and left. In the days that followed they kept the tree under regular observation. For ten days after its meal the leaves remained upright, after which its various members returned to their previous positions. At the foot of the tree was a new, white skull.

Despite its weakness as evidence and its lack of information on where exactly in Madagascar the tree was supposed to grow, Governor Osborn was impressed by this report. He travelled the thousand-mile length of the island and went across it many times, and everywhere he went he heard stories about the terrible man-eating tree. But he never managed to see it. All the tribes knew about it, and some of the local missionaries found reason to believe in it too, but no one would show him a specimen. He returned to America empty-handed, but not disillusioned about the possible existence of Madagascar's man-eating tree. Of the pygmy Mkodos there has since been neither trace nor record.

In defence of his notion Osborn pointed out that Madagascar has been known from ancient times as the Land of the Man-eating Tree. Much of the island was then still unexplored, and the only improbability about the man-eater was its size, which, as Osborn observed, "is not always a safe measuring standard of values". He described a similar plant, but on a smaller scale, which he had seen in London.

"At the London Horticultural Hall in England there is a plant that eats large insects and mice. Its principal prey are the latter. The mouse is attracted to it by a pungent odor that emanates from the blossom which encloses a perfect hole just big enough for the mouse to crawl into. After the mouse is in the trap bristle-like antennae infold it. Its struggles appear to render the Gorgonish things more active. Soon the mouse is dead. Then digestive fluids much like those of animal stomachs exude and the mouse is macerated, liquefied and appropriated. This extraordinary carnivorous plant is a native of tropical India. It has not been classified as belonging to any known botanical species."

The closest any currently existing carnivorous plants get to fitting the above descriptions are those belonging to the, increasingly rare, genus *Nepenthes*. These are large and vine-like, and grow in Malaysia, northern Australia and Madagascar. It is not unusual for them to capture frogs, and, less commonly, they consume birds and rodents – although these are almost certainly sick animals unable to put up much of a struggle. If there are such things as man-eating plants, the natives of the places where they grow might have good reasons for not revealing them to outsiders; and botanists who came across specimens, and examined them too closely, might find themselves in no position to report on them. Whether or not this plant will ever become available for scientific study, we feel that its legend will continue to flourish. We knew

Another view of the man-eating plant of Central America, illustrating a short story, 'The Purple Terror', published in 1899.

in childhood the terror of dark woods, from which claw-like branches seem to reach out to grab the passer-by, and we have often seen this illustrated – notably by Arthur Rackham. It is that image of universal imagination which ensures the survival of the man-eating tree.

Black dogs

A large, dark, mysterious beast roams the English countryside. Every year there are hundreds of sightings; some of them are reported to the police or in local newspapers, but many go unrecorded and remain private experiences. The creature is often described as a great, black dog with weird features such as glowing eyes. It is not just a modern apparition but is mentioned in every volume of local folklore, and it has always been such a common part of people's experience that

Similar to this was the experience of a Devon farmer. We quote from the fine collection of black dog myths, legends and modern sightings in Patricia Dale-Green's book *Dog* (1966). This farmer was on Dartmoor (no date or other details are given) when he heard the footsteps of an animal coming up behind him. It was a large black dog. He made to stroke it but his hand touched nothing. The creature ran off while "a stream of sulphurous vapour issued from its throat". The farmer chased it to a crossroads, where it seemed to explode in a blinding flash, throwing him to the ground.

A black dog, eyes glowing, invades the study of Cardinal Crescentius.

in each part of the country it has its own familiar name: Black Shuck in Norfolk, the Pooka in Ireland, the Gurt Dog in Somerset, and so on. Whatever it is called, the phenomenon is everywhere much the same, a fearful creature haunting certain spots and old tracks, the sight of which can make a man faint with horror. "'Twas awful. It had four legs, and it was black, and had great fiery eyes as big as saucers." This description is of a black dog seen in 1907 by a Somerset man near Budleigh Hill. But this was no ordinary beast, for "it ran on until it came to where the water crosses under the road, and they things, of course, can never abide running water, so it just couldn't get across, and it went up in the air like a flash of fire".

There are strange features of this black dog apparition which link it with several of our other types of phenomena. Its habit of vanishing in an explosive flash, for instance; in this detail it resembles the fire-balls, will-o'-the-wisps and corpse candles in our MYSTICAL LIGHTS (see p.123) section and the phenomena of PHENOMENAL HIGHWAYS (see p.167). Like them, it is connected to churchyards, crossroads, watercourses and stretches of old roads. It is also commonly taken as an omen of death. In the Somerset volume of *County Folklore* is a reference to a black dog haunting a road from St Audries to Perry Farm, which was said in 1960 to have appeared recently to two people just before their deaths. The luminosity of many black dogs and their evil appearance have caused them to be identified as the devil or his agents. "In some places it is said that, when spots where Black Shuck has been seen are examined, they are found to be scorched and smelling strongly of brimstone", writes Dale-Green. The same effect is mentioned by a correspondent in *Notes and Queries* (18 May 1850) on the subject of East Anglian black dogs. One witness, "on bringing his neighbours to see the place where he saw it, found a large spot as if gunpowder had been exploded there". In another incident, at Hatfield Peverell, Essex, a waggoner went to hit a large black dog that was blocking his path in a country lane, with the result that he caught fire and was burnt to ashes along with his horse and waggon. Another case is recorded of a farmer near Aylesbury, Buckinghamshire, who struck out at the two eyes of a black dog glowing in the dark. The dog and its bright orbs vanished instantly; the farmer was left speechless and paralyzed, never to recover.

We would like to be rational and identify the black dog with one of those familiar though still unexplained atmospheric phenomena such as ball lightning. The difficulty is that all the black dog witnesses are unanimous that it is definitely in the form of an animal. Nor is the creature always said to be a dangerous force. The Pooka of Ireland is often represented in a favourable light as a companion or guide to country people on dark, lonely roads. Another reference to a friendly protective aspect of the black dog is in the book of Somerset folklore. In the 1930s women in the isolated valleys of the Quantock hills allowed their infants to roam the hillsides in the secure knowledge that the Gurt Dog up there would keep them from harm. It is a general rule that the more simply and unhysterically people accept their local phantom the more amicable it becomes.

In the Suffolk volume of the Folk-Lore Society's county series the local black dog is described in the words of an old writer: "Old Shock is a mischievous goblin in the shape of a great dog, or of a calf, haunting highways and footpaths in the dark. Those who are so foolhardy as to encounter him, are sure to be at least thrown down and severely bruised, and it is well if they do not get their ankles sprained or broken; of which instances are recorded and believed."

The most terrible outbreak of black dog in Suffolk, involving worse than broken ankles, took place on 4 August 1577 on a Sunday. An account of what happened was published in a pamphlet by some of the witnesses. Between 9 and 10am, while the people of Bungay, Suffolk, were in church, there was suddenly a most unusual thunderstorm of extreme violence. The sky darkened, the church quaked, and the parish clerk who was cleaning out the gutters on the roof was struck to the ground by lightning, though not seriously hurt. In the church a fearful prodigy appeared – a black dog. Illuminated by lightning flashes it was clearly seen by the whole congregation, and the contemporary record is insistent that it was in the form of a dog. It ran down the church aisle and through the congregation. It passed between two people on their knees praying, and both were instantly struck dead. Another man whom it touched was shrivelled up like a drawn purse but stayed alive. The machinery of the church clock was left twisted and broken, and there were found marks like the scratches of claws on the stones and the metal-bound door of the church. On the same day, at Blythburgh about seven miles from Bungay, a black dog also ran down the church, smiting the congregation and killing two men and a lad as well as "blasting" others.

Like many other black dogs this Suffolk fiend sounds as if it was something meteorological, but something which defies rational explanation as being an effect of natural forces in the atmosphere while at the same time having the form of a recognizable animal. Such a creature of paradox must belong to the realm of magic and witchcraft. Not that this should put it beyond further inquiry. Magicians are no less bound than anyone else by the laws of nature; they merely understand them better. No witch can invoke what is not there in nature to be invoked in the

THE BLACK DOG

Sir, –The legend of the black dog occurs in many localities, and our corner of North Staffordshire is no exception.

A particular stretch of road has been well known to be haunted by a big black dog. Many years ago, my grandfather came home in a state of shock, after encountering the phantom one night. My aunt, not an imaginative woman, told me she once felt something sniff at her hand, when she was walking home one evening, but on turning round, saw nothing to account for the sensation.

A modern black dog story from Country Life.

The Suffolk black dog. The marks on Blythburgh church's north door are still visible.

first place. If phantom shapes can be conjured up by magic there must be a phantom potential in nature for the magic to act upon; and if there is this potential it may on occasions manifest itself spontaneously. The dreadful black dog of Bungay was evidently a spontaneous manifestation, but there are many cases of black dogs reputed to be witches' familiars or sorcerers disguised as were-animals. Katherine Wiltshire, who in her book of Wiltshire legends cites over forty instances of black dogs in that county alone, says she has heard that Norfolk witches can still produce these saucer-eyed creatures by the power of concentrated thought.

A witchcraft trial involving a magical black dog was reported in the *Sunday Express* (23 November 1975). Five men of a tinker family, a father and four sons, were accused of attempted manslaughter, for trying to burn an alleged witch near Varasdin, Croatia. They claimed that the old woman had attacked them in the form of a large black dog with blazing eyes, knocking one of the brothers from his bicycle. Neighbours disturbed them as they were lighting the bonfire beneath the stake to which they had tied her.

A survey of all our black dog material suggests that these apparitions belong to a side of nature which was better recognized in the past than it is today. There is a pattern in the peculiar association of black dogs with water, bridges, underground streams, buried treasure, old churchyards and certain lengths of road, which is shared by some of our other phenomena and hints at one mysterious principle behind them all. If anyone should see a large black dog with bright eyes and a sinister appearance, our best advice from the experience of others is to stand well clear and not to touch it.

Werewolves

Wer is the Old English word for "man" and werewolves are people who turn into wolves and then back into men again. We are not doctors, but we believe this sort of thing is physiologically impossible. If we were lawyers, however, we should have no option but to believe in werewolves because of the vast amount of legal precedent for convicting and executing the creatures. Evidence against people accused of transforming themselves into savage animals and committing crimes while in that shape has often been given by unanimous witnesses of good repute, firmly convinced from personal experience of the accused's ability to assume animal form. On the one hand werewolves are impossible; on the other they actually occur. Here again is a phenomenon which can not be reconciled with any rational system of explanation.

The most direct evidence of werewolves is from people who have actually seen the transformation taking place. One of these was said to be Pierre Mamor, a fifteenth-century Rector of the University of Poitiers in France, whose writing on the subject is quoted in The Revd Montague Summers' book, *The Werewolf* (1933). The learned Mamor contributes a disgusting story of a peasant's wife in Lorraine who saw her husband at table vomit up a child's arm and hand which he had devoured while in the form of a wolf.

This event is explained by Mamor as a "demoniacal illusion", because his theory is that werewolves are actual wolves possessed by the spirits of men, whose bodies meanwhile are safely hidden away, all this being the work of evil demons. This theory does not account for such cases as the one recorded in Olaus Magnus's *Historia de gentibus septentrionalibus* (1555) as having happened some years earlier. A nobleman's wife was heard by her slave to deny the possibility of men becoming wolves. The slave disagreed and proved her wrong by there and then making the transformation. He was at once set upon by dogs but managed to shake them off and flee away in wolf's shape after they had torn out one of his eyes. The next day the slave appeared, human but one-eyed.

The werewolf lives on in science fiction and horror comics. A still from the 1935 film, *The Werewolf of London*.

A more recent account is quoted in C. Dane's *The Occult in the Orient*. In 1960 Mr Harold M. Young, a former official in the Burmese administration and at the time proprietor of the zoo at Chiang Mai, Thailand, was hunting in the Lahu mountains near the Burm–Thai frontier when he encountered one of the locally dreaded "taws", a jungle werewolf. Entering a village he was told there was a taw nearby. A shriek was heard, and Mr Young ran over to a hut where in the bright moonlight he saw the taw chewing the neck of a dying woman. He raised his gun and shot the beast in the flank, but it escaped into the jungle, leaving a trail of blood. In the morning Young and others followed the trail which led out into the jungle and then back to the village to a hut, in which they discovered a man with a bullet wound in his side.

This modern account repeats in detail the classical werewolf story which recurs in all times and places with remarkable consistency. We do not know what happened to Mr Young's taw, and we pass on the story at second-hand, but we have direct evidence of the careers and fates of many European werewolves from the most satisfactory sources, the contemporary reports of their trials. In December 1521 two French peasants, Burgot and Verdun, were accused at Poligny of a long series of cannibalistic murders committed by them while in the shape of wolves. Both men confessed. Burgot said that he had long been in the service of the devil and had extended his activities to shape-shifting with the encouragement of Verdun, who was a practising werewolf and a member of a witches' coven. Verdun was the more agile of the two and could change his shape with his clothes on, while Burgot had to strip naked and be rubbed with werewolf ointment which they obtained from their diabolist superiors. This special ointment for effecting transformations is often referred to in these cases. Montague Summers suggests it was composed of such bewitching drugs as belladonna, aconite, hemlock or henbane. Whatever it was, its influence on Burgot and Verdun was bestial. They attacked and devoured many locals until Verdun was wounded by an armed traveller, who followed the bloody wolf-spoor to a hovel where Verdun was having his wound bandaged by his wife. Both men were executed together with another local werewolf, and it is said that portraits of all three were to be seen in the church at Poligny.

Throughout the sixteenth century werewolves were rampant in Europe. So many of those caught and burnt in France during that period were also practising witches, and claimed to have learnt the art of transformation from others of their coven, that we suspect some traditional magic ritual was involved, inherited from ancient times and still active in remote districts of Europe almost to the present. Many of the classical authors on the subject of werewolves refer to this traditional knowledge. In eleventh-century Ireland it was the practice of the inhabitants of Ossory always to have two of their people in the shape of wolves, each pair serving seven years. Giraldus Cambrensis, who gives this information in his *Topographica Hibernica*, tells of an Irish priest who spoke with one of these Ossory werewolves in 1182. He was on a journey between Ulster and Meath, passing the night in the woods, when he was approached by a large wolf who explained his circumstances and asked the priest to come and bless his dying wife. The priest was unwilling to extend religious privileges to a she-wolf, but the wolf reassured him by pulling back his wife's wolfskin and revealing an old woman beneath it.

Fort on werewolves: "I think that the idea of werewolves is most silly, degraded, and superstitious: therefore I incline toward it respectfully." From the *Cornhill Magazine* (October 1918) Fort quotes the experience in northern Nigeria of a Captain Shott. Hyenas had been raiding a native village. Hunters who followed their tracks were surprised to find that at a certain point the animal prints gave way to human ones. One night Captain Shott's party wounded a particularly large beast, shooting off its jaw. The trail of blood was followed to another village where next day a man died of a terrible wound. His jaw had been torn off.

Reports of werewolves from all times and continents are innumerable, and so are were-tigers, foxes, hares, bears, cats and weasels, enough to fill an alternative menagerie. The phenomenon as experienced is as well established as anything could be. What everyone wants to know, of course, is whether the transformation from man to animal takes place in actual fact, in defiance of the doctors, or whether it is an illusion affecting the senses of both the person transformed and the people who see him. It may make little difference to a man having his throat torn out by something which looks and behaves like a wolf whether the creature is actually a wolf or merely seems like one, but this question has been disputed by the learned from very early times. Paracelsus thought the change was actual and physical, taking the magical view that the power of human will and imagination could be concentrated to affect external reality through the medium of the spiritual substance of the universe. Other authorities disagreed, explaining the phenomenon as an effect of drugs or the magical enchantment they call "glamour". They in turn were contradicted by Sponde in 1583, who reasoned that "if a herb and the power of evil can have such control over the higher part of man, his reason and his immortal soul, why can not man's body be subject to similar disturbances?"

An old explanation, put forward as early as the second century AD by the Roman medical writer Marcellus Sidetes, sees the phenomenon in terms of the affliction known as lycanthropy, whose victims become convinced that they are savage wolves and behave accordingly. Though whether lycanthropy is, as Marcellus thought, a "species of melancholy", to be treated with cold baths and a diet of curds and whey, or whether it is a form of diabolic possession, as Summers and many others have believed, is a question which may never finally be resolved. In any case the lycanthropy theory accounts for only one half of the werewolf phe-

A number of medical conditions – such as the genetic defect causing porphyria and hypertrichosis, excessive hair growth – almost certainly contributed to the popular conceptions about werewolves. In modern times, some famous 'hairy people' were brought from Burma, Laos and Mexico to be exhibited in circus freak shows. Theodore Petrof, for example – whose successful career as 'JoJo the Dog-faced Boy' spanned several decades – was said to have been found at the age of eight living wild in a forest in Kostroma, Russia.

nomenon, the delusion of the werewolf himself, and says nothing about the delusions of the witnesses who see him in his wolf's form. The same objection of incompleteness can be brought against other popular explanations in terms of self-hypnosis and the ritual wearing of animal skins. The Viking "berserkers" wore bear skins while transforming themselves into savage killers by invoking the spirits of beasts, and members of the secret leopard-men societies, still active in east Africa, practise the same sort of rites. A certain Mr K., whose story is quoted, though without reference to its original source, in *Fate and Fortune* magazine, no. 6, was present early last century at a ritual in Orissa, India, where a local youth was transformed before his very eyes into a were-tiger. It is impossible to understand the effectiveness of these ritual transformations through any of the part-explanations already mentioned, such as lycanthropy, hypnosis or illusions created by the wearing of make-up and animal skins. Not that we reject any of these; we accept them all, in combination with other causes, as contributing towards the production of a magical effect which, whatever the degree of physical reality one may choose to attribute to the transformation, has a terrible reality indeed to the man who seems to change into a savage beast and to all who come within the sphere of his activities.

While working in northern Spain in the 1980s, soil engineer Jack Romano gained a unique insight into the werewolf beliefs of the inhabitants of the mountainous region of Galicia. Still remembered throughout Spain is the case of the self-confessed werewolf Manuel Blanco Romasanto, who was tried in 1852 for a series of murders of young or lonely women he had tricked into going with him into the mountains. Unlike the notorious trials of medieval witches, the Spanish courts and authorities allowed Romasanto an opportunity to explain his bloodlust. Speaking in his own defense, he claimed to be possessed every six months as a result of a curse, and he knew others who shared this predicament. This state, he told the court, made him feel "fantastic, powerful, exhilarating" and for its duration he was immune to death or injury.

Astonishingly Romasanto helped the court to locate the remains of his victims, and submitted to medical examinations, including a primitive psychological assessment. He was condemned to death in April 1853, but the sentence was commuted to life imprisonment through the intervention of a brilliant young defense lawyer, Manuel Figuera. However public outcry was such that the courts felt obliged to reinstate the death sentence and Romansanto was only spared as the result of a plea for clemency from the Queen of Spain.

Writing in *Fortean Times* (no.126, pp.40–44), Romano describes how Romasanto became a model, if eccentric, prisoner. Visitors peering into his cell would be surprised to see him wearing female clothing and making thread. At his trial, Romasanto had told the judge: "Were I to become a wolf, even you, a rational man, would be so terrified that you could not fire the gun, and even if you did, the bullets could never harm me." Today we can see beneath the lycanthropic trappings, the all-too-familiar ingredients of modern sociopathic serial killers. In Spain the legend of his ferocious conviction that his destiny was to be a werewolf still lingers on.

In search of ape-men

Wherever there are wastes and mountains, there are monsters – creatures that may be unknown to science but are quite familiar to the native inhabitants. They are described by people who have seen them as huge, hairy beings, half-men, half-apes, of supernatural intelligence and extremely elusive. Their giant footprints have been seen and photographed from the Himalayas to the mountains of North America, but not one of these creatures has ever been caught.

Everyone has heard about the Abominable Snowman or Yeti of the Himalayas, the manlike creature that lives high up in the snowy peaks. The local people know it well, and European and other visitors have seen it. A classic sighting was by the famous British mountaineer, Don Whillans, in the summer of 1970 at a height of 13,000 feet in the mountains of Nepal. One night, after he had spent the day photographing the tracks of some large, unknown animal in the snow, he saw in the bright moonlight the creature which might have made the tracks moving along a ridge opposite his tent. It was like an ape and moved on all fours.

A good account of the Yeti was given to Lord Hunt by the Abbot of Thyangboche Monastery

drove it off by blowing conch shells and bugles.

Despite innumerable reports by Sherpas and others, the evidence most acceptable to science for the existence of the Yeti is the footprints. On 8 November 1951 Eric Shipton, on one of his Everest expeditions with Michael Ward and a Sherpa, Sen Tensing, came across some remarkable tracks in the snow at an altitude of 18,000 feet. They were of a creature that walked like a man

Modern sightings of Yeti, Bigfoot and other 'manimals' perpetuate the traditional belief in 'wild men'. They were such popular characters that many coats of arms from the Middle Ages often feature male and female wildfolk as symbols of natural and ancestral strength. This pen and ink drawing, by H. Burgkmair, of a knight in combat with a wild man, dates from the beginning of the 16th century.

who had watched one playing in the snow outside his residence. It was about five feet tall, with grey hair. The other monks became very excited and

and, if it were of human proportions, would have stood about eight feet tall. The tracks continued for about a mile and disappeared on some ice.

An ice-pick gives the scale of one of the 'Yeti' footprints photographed by Eric Shipton in the Himalayas in 1951.

Many other Himalayan explorers, including the *Daily Mail* expedition of 1954, have recorded similar footprints; the most dramatic were those discovered in Sikkim in 1915 and reported by a forestry officer, Mr J. Gent. The prints were between 18 and 24 inches long. According to Gent's native informants, who identified them as belonging to one of a local race of giant wild men, the toes pointed in the opposite direction to that in which the creature was moving.

Similar to the Yeti are the hairy wild men of Soviet Central Asia, one of which was clearly seen in 1957 by a scientist from Leningrad University, A.G. Pronin. It was in the Pamir mountains, and Pronin, who saw it again a few days later, described it as reddish-grey, hairy, long-armed and of shambling gait. The local Kirghiz herdsmen had long known of the creature's existence, but neither they nor any of the Soviet expeditions dispatched to the region ever managed to catch one.

The notion of unknown giants and hairy wild men existing in the modern world is patently absurd, yet every year brings hundreds of reports from sincere people all over the world of sightings, encounters, giant spoors and other evidence of mysterious, man-like creatures. Palaeontologists tell us that similar creatures, supposedly long extinct, once roamed the earth. Perhaps, in remote corners, they roam it still. That is what many cryptozoologists believe, and the excitement of their quest is intensified by the idea that the quarry may be no ordinary animal but a human ancestor, a type of protoman, the much sought after "missing link".

Ivan Sanderson spent many years considering the depictions of wild men in the art of medieval Europe and earlier. Known as "woodhouses" or "woodwoses" or some other variation of the Anglo-Saxon *wudewasa,* meaning "wild man of the woods", their visual representation is ancient and universal and, as Sanderson notes, surprisingly consistent. Despite a hairy body the hands and feet are usually drawn hairless and manlike. Other details, like a belt or girdle, and crude weapons of wood, imply a simple culture and technology. Sanderson first discussed the idea that the image of the "wildman" may be the manifestation of a folk memory of the Neanderthal, in the anthropological magazine *Genus* (1967), and refined it over subsequent years. Writing in *Pursuit* (January 1981), he concluded that the *wudewasa* "are detailed and accurate descriptions of Neanderthaloids, probably of more than one type. They were familiar to the early artists because these shy, often solitary forest-dwellers were not exterminated by Cro-Magnon man, as children are taught today, but disappeared very gradually from western and central Europe over a long period. The evidence suggests that the Wudewasa were not organized into tribes, as was Cro-Magnon. They were less able to compete for the rich lands they once roamed, and chose to retreat to more remote regions where they could live peacefully, but with more difficulty, avoiding their noisy, aggressive, more 'civilized' cousins, much as their remnant does today." It was the spread of agriculture and the clearance of vast forested and wooded tracts which brought about the final dissolution of the Neanderthals, thought Sanderson, rather than deliberate massacre by more organized races. Anthropologists have observed that non-tribal peoples, once split into small relict groups and confined to limited and shrinking ter-

and anthropologist, Boris Porchnev, about sightings and traces of unknown "wild men" in modern Russia. Porchnev suggested that these might be survivors of the Neanderthal type. The idea proved popular in the Soviet Union, where evolutionism was one of the main supports of materialist philosophy. In 1958 the Soviet Academy of Sciences set up a commission to investigate the persistent rumours of *almas* or wild men in parts of Soviet Asia. Expeditions were sent to many of the likely areas, including the Pamir mountains of Central Asia, northern Siberia and the Caucasus, and researches were co-ordinated at a monthly seminar at the Charles Darwin Museum in Moscow. Reported sightings included one by a member of an expedition to the Pamirs in 1978, who described

Igor Bourtsev, the Russian 'snowman' hunter, compares his foot to a cast of a footprint found in August 1979 in the Gissar range of the Pamir-Altai mountains in Soviet Tadzhikistan.

ritories, soon suffer a progressive deterioration of their culture, fertility and numbers.

Bernard Heuvelmans published two large books on the evidence for pre-human or wildmen survivals in different parts of the world. The first, *L'homme de Neanderthal est toujours vivant* (1974), contains a long paper by the late Russian historian

a large, hairy creature jumping about upright among the rocks.

English anthropologist, Dr Myra Shackley of Leicester University, was reported in the *Daily Mail* (2 December 1980) as saying that in the course of expeditions to the Altai Mountains of Outer Mongolia she had found Neanderthal tools which the locals told her were made by the *almas.* "They now live in the mountains and we don't have any contact with them", said the Mongolians. "They don't interfere with us and we don't interfere with them." Dr Shackley knew of many reputable people who had seen the *almas,* the last encounter being in 1972 by a Russian doctor who had seen an entire *alma* family. "They live in caves, hunt for food, use stone tools and wear animal skins and furs", reported Dr Shackley. In her book-length consideration, *Wildmen* (1983), she concluded: "I cannot believe that Yetis and Almas are purely creatures of my imagination . . . imagination does not create unclassifiable footprints."

Earlier, in 1945, the English scientist W.C. Osman Hill, who became America's leading primatologist, suggested that the legendary *Nittaewo* people of Ceylon, said to be recently extinct, and also the *Orang pendek,* small hairy beings seen in the forests of Sumatra, might be modern apemen survivals. These have their equivalents in Malaysia in the form of the *Orang dalam* which, according to local reports, have the familiar characteristics of the unknown hairy giants in many lands, being from six to ten feet tall, having a foul smell and red eyes and leaving outsized footprints. The zoologist, Lord Medway, reported in the *Times* in 1960 that the natives of the central Borneo mountains know of a similar creature which he com-

This 16th-century woodcut shows a ruren, or 'like-a-man', said to be resident in the forests of Shandong province, northeast China.

pared to the Himalayan Yeti the "Abominable Snowman" whose appearances and doings first came to the attention of the European public in the nineteenth century. Heuvelmans' conclusion is that a form of Neanderthaler has survived throughout the wild places of Asia, from the Caucasus to Malaysia and Vietnam.

In 1979 a French anthropologist, Jacqueline Roumeguère Eberhardt, investigated reports that several types of "ape-men" or unknown primitives were inhabiting forests in Kenya. One type with a whitish skin was said to kill buffaloes, eating only their livers, and another wore a hide cloak, used a bow and arrow and cooked with fire. She never saw one herself, but stated that she was convinced from eye-witness sightings and other evidence that the beings existed.

The following year Heuvelmans published the second of his "ape-men" books, *Les bêtes humaines d'Afrique,* where he collected all the evidence of undiscovered primates or wild men in Africa, their types ranging from pygmies to supergorillas.

In common with such phenomena as UFOs, the Yeti has never yielded a single, undisputed, physical proof of its actual existence. Despite the eagerness of its pursuers over many years and several continents, there is no body, nor hair nor hide of one, nor even one satisfactory photograph. True, there are the footprints, but we know of many cases where footprints have appeared without, apparently, any physical agency (see UNREASONABLE FOOTPRINTS, p.237). Crypto-zoologists are in much the same position as ufologists with no physical relics for their faith. From time to time we hear exciting rumours of the sort of evidence which, if found, would settle all doubts; but so far these have remained only rumours.

We do not discount the possibility that giant primates may survive undiscovered, nor the possibility of extra-terrestrial spacecraft. Yet it still remains for the Yeti hunters, as for the ufologists, to demonstrate the reality of their quarry. Much has been said about the vastness and impenetrability of some of the earth's wildernesses, but in Scotland, where we hardly expect to find hidden giants or lost tribes, the evidence for the legendary Big Grey Man of Ben MacDhui in the Cairngorms, including some rare sightings, is of much the same quality as the evidence for the Himalayan Yeti. Thus we feel that in the great majority of cases the "hidden animals" theory is inadequate.

Although they may appear to witnesses as normal flesh-and-blood animals, there are certain things about Yetis (and their relations world-wide) which cast doubt on their physical reality, such as their unnatural elusiveness and their disregard for bullets. Their status seems similar to that of the

"thought-forms" of eastern mysticism, which are visible illusions created by the concentrated desires of a group or individual. Illusions of this sort are not always manifested consciously, but can arise spontaneously and unbidden in response to images, ideas or expectations formed in the human mind.

A clue to the nature of Yetis and *almas* as seen today may lie in the modern tendency to identify them as surviving Neanderthal or ape-men. In 1856, the same year that Darwin began writing *The Origin of Species,* fossilized human remains were dug up at Neanderthal in Germany. The biologist Thomas Huxley pronounced these remains to be ape-like, and reconstructed images were published of the "ape-man" as conventionally imagined at the time: brutal, hairy and shambling. Neanderthal man is now recognized as being within the range of modern human types, but the old image took root, and its influence can still be seen today in the "hairy ape" models of early humanity exhibited in museums of natural history. Between them, Darwin and the Neanderthal skull prompted the search for ape-men which has continued unsuccessfully to the present day. From the end of the nineteenth century, when people began seeing and thinking about Yetis, speculation has been growing about the possible survival of our pre-human ancestors in the form of hairy, apelike, wild men,

The well-preserved hands of what is, allegedly, a young ape-man, killed by villagers in eastern China in 1957. The palms are just under six inches long.

and it may be that the desire for such things has produced the corresponding apparitions or thought-forms. We note, for example, that the discovery of giant fossil teeth in China during the 1930s, which were said to have belonged to a man-like creature about twelve feet tall, anticipated the multiple reports in 1937 of giant footprints in the Himalayas.

The modern growth, or explosion, of the Yeti phenomenon is to some extent related to the frustrated desires of the evolutionists for relics of apelike human ancestors. There is of course much more to it than that. To be viable, a thought-form must reflect an archetype, or, as Rupert Sheldrake would put it, it must resonate with a morphogenetic field laid down in the past. As an archetypal form, the figure of the giant wild man among the rocks and forests is well established in human imagination. And if archaic forms can influence apparitions and thought-forms in the present, that might be the reason for the Yetis and Bigfoots sighted today. The *Gigantopithecus* of ancient China has often

been compared to the mountain giants of Chinese folklore, and Heuvelmans has stated his belief that the Himalayan Yeti is its close relation. *Meganthropus,* the Great Man of Java, as reconstructed from his teeth and jawbone, apparently prefigures the legendary giant forest dwellers of southeast Asia and Indonesia. In North America, Bigfoot has numerous ancient prototypes in the giants which have been excavated from ancient Indian mounds. (The records of these giants have been thoroughly suppressed by the archeologists; but that is a long and different story.) Our point is that the Yeti type shares a common characteristic with the other types of monsters and mystery creatures sighted today: they all represent apparent revivals of archaic, long extinct types which science has only revealed to us within the last two centuries. For ages after their physical disappearance from earth, the shades of atavistic creatures have continued to haunt their former regions and infiltrate the legends of the local people. Now, it seems, they are becoming more insistent.

The great American monster

In the United States and Canada, particularly among the Indians of the mountainous, forested areas of the West, native legends refer to manlike giants which leave footprints and seem related in other ways to the unknown hairy creatures of Asia. "Sasquatch" is one of the names the Canadian Indians give them, and it is commonly used by modern researchers together with the general term "Bigfoot", an allusion to their impressive tracks. These have been found in mud, dust and snow in parts of north California, Oregon, Washington State and elsewhere, one of the best examples being the set found in October 1969 at Bossburgh, Washington. It consisted of over a thousand prints, stretching for about half a mile, each print measuring about 18 inches in length. This implies that the two-legged creature that made them stood over 10 feet tall. The prints indicated that the right foot of the creature was crippled, but at one point it

stepped easily over a 43-inch-high fence. In his analysis of claimed Sasquatch footprints John Napier rates the Bossburgh examples among the best evidence for the creature's existence.

First-hand reports of encounters with the Sasquatch were made in the nineteenth century, mainly by hunters, loggers and prospectors. They even included stories of people who had been abducted by the hairy giants and of other people who had captured a specimen. These accounts, however, were generally classified as "tall tales from the woods", and it was not until the 1950s that rumours and sightings of the "American Yeti" began making headlines. Since then, reported sightings of monsters have proceeded thick and fast, together with waves of literature on the subject. There is now scarcely a state in the Union without its records of local Bigfoot sightings and giant tracks. Almost as odd as the phenomenon itself are the characters who chronicle it. Many of them are active as Bigfoot hunters in the field, vying with each other to obtain the valuable prize,

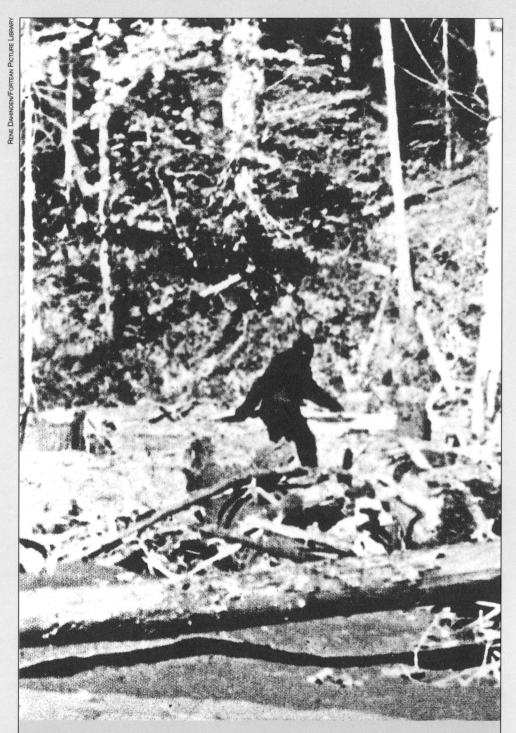

One of several frames from Roger Patterson's movie of a large hairy humanoid striding through Californian woods in 20 October 1967.

Rene Dahinden (left) holds a cast of a footprint found at Bluff Creek, California, by Roger Patterson after he had filmed his famous sequence of a Bigfoot there. Patterson (right) holds a cast of another footprint found at the same site in 1964.

the first physical or photographic proof of its existence. Among these author-adventurers are Jim McClarin, Roger Morgan, John Green, author of the trail-blazing *On the Track of Sasquatch* (1971), Dr Grover Krantz, a scientist who investigated the Bossburgh prints, the Irishman Peter Byrne, proprietor of the Bigfoot Information Center at Hood, Oregon, and Rene Dahinden, a veteran Swiss Maoist, who has spent much time in the courtroom suing or being sued by other researchers in respect of right to items of Bigfoot evidence. A conference of Bigfoot hunters and authors in May 1978 was marred by bad-tempered disputes among the participants. Happier events are the annual conferences held since 1988 by Don Keating and Marc DeWerth in Newcomerstown, Ohio.

As recently as August 1998, Wes Sumerlin, an experienced hunter, claimed to have found fresh Bigfoot tracks in the Blue Mountains of southeast Washington state. For fifty years, Sumerlin – who lived in the area – his wife Natalie, and his family had many experiences of Bigfoot in the Wenaha-

Tuscannon Wilderness Area, as recorded in Vance Orchard's book *Bigfoot of the Blues* (1992). Sumerlin first encountered Bigfoot tracks at the age of fourteen while taking a train of mules into the mountains. He had seen several specimens a number of times and had names for them such as "Big Jim", "Blue-back" (both males) and "Buckskin" (a female). He claims the Bigfoots migrate huge distances as he has seen tracks of one creature (identified by an injury or deformity to the foot) in Central Washington, British Columbia and California. One day he got to within fifty feet of Buckskin. "When she turned to look my way, she was real visible and so were her breasts, so I knew it was a female," Wes recalls. When asked if he thought Bigfoot was an animal, Wes replied: "No I think he's far more intelligent than other animals. He has a face, something like a human but it isn't exactly a human face either."

The sheer variety of reported "manimals" is demonstrated by *The Field Guide to Bigfoot, Yeti and Other Mystery Primates Worldwide* (1999), compiled by Loren Coleman and Patrick Huyghe, both experienced researchers. The book has a bias towards interpreting the phenomena as "undiscovered" species of primate, but it also includes such fantastic and folkloric entities as hairy dwarves, giants, creatures that are best described as aquatic apes, and the bizarre Chupacabras ("goatsucker") of Puerto Rico. While many writers and investigators have proceeded as if in no doubt that Bigfoot is a normal flesh-and-blood animal, with nothing but lack of a carcass preventing it from ranking among America's native fauna, others have been more circumspect.

In their book, *Bigfoot* (1967), B. Ann Slate and Alan Berry detail some of their telepathic experiences and other strange happenings during field researches into the mystery. There have been many reports of odd side effects to such researches, and connections have been made between Bigfoot and other phenomena, equally enigmatic, such as alleged UFO occupants and mysterious outbreaks of cattle mutilations. The first serious discussion of these and other such problems in relation to each other was in John Keel's *Strange Creatures from Time and Space* (1970). The Bigfoot investigations of Loren Coleman and Jerome Clark in Oklahoma, Ohio, Pennsylvania and other states (recorded in their *Creatures of the Outer Edge* (1978) have yielded good evidence of some form of link between Bigfoot, UFOs and other mysterious phenomena. In their summary Coleman and Clark list certain features of Bigfoot which recur in witnesses' accounts. It has red or luminous eyes and a foul smell; if shot at it is found to be invulnerable to bullets; it is shy and retiring but may kill animals; it can move at incredible speed, sometimes without leaving tracks, and where tracks *are* found they are of many different types and sizes. There is also a wide variation in the forms of the creatures reported and in the sounds they make. All these are features of Yetis and suchlike beings in other continents; and they are also the traditional attributes of phantoms and elementals. In seeking professional advice on the Bigfoot mystery, Coleman and Clark ask, "To whom shall we turn – the ufologist, the biologist, the psychologist or the demonologist?"

Ever since 1811 when the explorer, David Thompson, came across 14-inch tracks attributed to a Sasquatch, near Jasper, Alberta, many thousands of inexplicable footprints have been discovered; and continuing the Indian tradition that the Sasquatch is inclined to abduct human beings, several modern Americans have claimed that it has happened to them. The earliest case was in 1924: Albert Ostman, a lumberman, was camping opposite Vancouver Island when he was lifted up, sleeping bag and all, and carried some twenty-five miles to the lair of a Sasquatch family, consisting of Father, some eight feet tall, Mother, a foot shorter, and two children. They treated him well, and after six days he escaped. Fearing mockery he kept the experience to himself until 1955.

One of the most detailed (and earliest known) descriptions of an encounter with a Sasquatch took place in 1869. It comes from the weekly *Butte Record* (5 November 1870) although Janet and Colin Bord, in *Alien Animals* (1980), claim that the original source was a letter in an old Californian newspaper, the *Aurora Ledger* (16 October 1870). The creature was seen by a hunter camping in a forest below Orestimba Peak in northern California. Several times he had returned to camp to find that his belongings had been disturbed, so he lay in wait to catch the culprit. This is what he saw. "It was in the image of a man but it could not have been human. I was never so benumbed with astonishment before. The creature, whatever it was, stood fully five feet high, and disproportionately broad and square at the fore shoulders, with arms of great length. The legs were very short and the body long. The head was small compared with the rest of the creature, and appeared to be set on his shoulders without a neck. The whole was covered with dark brown and cinnamon coloured hair, quite long in some parts, that on the head standing in a shock and growing close down to the eyes, like a Digger Indian's." The creature gave a whistling sound and knocked the camp fire about with a stick. The hunter watched him for about fifteen minutes, until the visitor was joined by another, a female of his kind, and the two walked off together. He said that he could easily have shot it but did not care to do so.

There was an account in the *Seattle Times* (16 July 1918) of "mountain devils" attacking a prospector's shack at Mount St Helen's in the State of Washington. The devils were said to be members of a local race, intermediate between men and animals, with magical powers and the ability to make themselves invisible. In October 1940 the Chapman family of Ruby Creek, British Columbia, were approached by an eight-foot-tall, hairy male creature, which caused them to flee their house. It left behind it 16-inch footprints and an overturned barrel of salted fish. Many other such incidents and sightings are recorded in the books of Ivan T. Sanderson, John Green and other writers on the "Bigfoot" phenomenon. The evidence to date for the existence of these unknown giants in northwest America was soberly analysed in *Bigfoot*, a book of 1973 by the famous anthropologist Professor John Napier.

The most striking record ever made, or claimed, of the Great American Monster is the film shot by Roger Patterson while on a Sasquatch hunt at Bluff Creek, northern California, on 20 October

A report in the *New York Times* (30 June 1976) gives the experience of a logger, Jack Cochran, on 12 May 1974 in the Hood River National Forest, Oregon. At a distance of fifty yards he saw a "big, hairy thing" standing silently. Following his first, remarkable notion that it might be one of his fellow workers, he realized that the creature could only be the legendary Bigfoot. It finally walked away "gracefully, like an athlete" into the trees. Next day two other loggers of the same party were walking in the woods and disturbed the same or a similar creature. It ran away on two legs while they pursued it throwing rocks. Members of the Bigfoot Investigation Center at The Dalles, Oregon, later visited the site and found huge footprints with those of the loggers running alongside.

BERNARD HEUVELMANS

A composite photograph and a drawing of the unknown ape-like man – said to be a modern Neanderthal – studied in October 1968 by Dr Bernard Heuvelmans and Ivan T. Sanderson. The body of the 'Iceman' was being exhibited by Frank Hansen, a travelling showman in Minnesota, and the two cryptozoologists were convinced of its genuineness. Since then further study has been impossible (as Hansen has substituted a replica) and his claim that it was shot in Vietnam in recent times have not been verified.

1967. It shows at a distance of about 100 feet a hairy, manlike creature walking upright in full view of the camera. Experts of the time examined the film and found no flaws or evidence of fakery, but in 1999, with improved methods of analysis, suspicions of hoaxing emerged. A small object on the creature's body looks like the head of a zip-fastener to what may be a monkey suit.

We bear in mind a saying of the great anatomist, Sir Arthur Keith, that the only class of beings which are constantly seen but never present themselves at the dissecting table belongs to the world of spirits. In America the Bigfoot hunters are quite as active as the UFO and Loch Ness Monster people in the pursuit of evidence for the physical existence of their phenomenon; and they have had just the same degree of success or non-success – tracks, sightings, noises, strange feelings, mystical legends and above all, elusiveness. In July 1976, there was news in the American papers of a "secret expedition", organized by North American Wildlife Research, setting out to the wilds of British Columbia, where a "computer study" indi-cated that the Sasquatch was most likely to be located. Their destination was the spot where a fisherman had found tracks of the monster, and they intended to tranquillize one with a drugged dart, fit it up with a radio transmitter and then track its subsequent movements. But their plans were foiled by the creature's non-appearance.

Supporting our belief in the phenomenal reality that links so many of our sections is the following early Bigfoot record quoted by Warren Smith in *Strange Monsters and Madmen* from a diary shown to his friend, Brad Steiger, by the grandson of the man who wrote it, Mr Wyatt of Tennessee. Grandfather Wyatt, a woodsman in Humboldt County, wrote in his diary for 1888 that the local Indians were in contact with strange, hairy beings they called "crazy bears", which were brought down to earth from time to time by spacemen from UFOs in silvery, close-fitting outfits. The explanation, as Wyatt understood it, was that the space people were experimenting with stocking the earth with the animals they most liked to eat!

Wild people

In September 1731, a formidable little girl strode into a French village to become one of the nine specimens of "wild man" classified by Linnaeus as Homo sapiens ferus. A book of that name by Raüber in 1888 describes her first dramatic appearance: "A girl of nine or ten years, suffering from thirst, entered the village of Songy at dusk. The village is four or five leagues from Chalôns in Champagne. Her feet were naked, her body was covered with rags and skins of animals. Instead of a hat she wore a piece of bottle-gourd on her head. She carried a club in her hand, and when someone in the village set a dog at her she gave it such a heavy blow on the head that the animal fell over dead at her feet."

When finally captured and examined, she was found to have extra large thumbs, which was attributed to her Tarzan style of swinging from tree to tree. Several hot baths revealed that her skin was white. Some even identified her as an Eskimo. She was speechless, but she ran and swam wonderfully and caught and ate small animals, also raw fish and – appropriately for a French wild girl – frogs. A strange feature in the case was that, until her capture, she had had a wild companion, a young black woman, who continued to be seen in the neighbourhood but was never captured. She had quarrelled with this girl over an ornament they had found and had hit her head with her club. In later life, when she had learnt to talk, she could give no account of her previous existence, apart from some vague remembrance of a large water animal and of having twice crossed the sea. For one brief period of her life she had been taken in by a woman who had given her some clothes; before that she had been naked.

Captivity damaged the wild girl in health and spirit. The food she was given made her teeth fall out, she was often ill and became worse through the bleedings ordered by the doctors to weaken her savage nature. She was no idiot. She was taught to speak and behave like a civilized female of the time, and she finally gratified her benefactors by becoming a nun in a Paris convent.

The mystery of how two wild girls – one a Negress, the other apparently an Eskimo – could suddenly appear in eighteenth-century France has never been solved. Yet these are not isolated cases. Similar examples of *Homo sapiens ferus* have been recorded in every century and in every part of the world. Another, more famous, French wild child was caught in the woods of Caunes, in Aveyron, on 7 August 1800. As in all such cases his appearance, behaviour and diet were entirely animal-like, but under the care of Dr Itard – whose book, *The Wild Boy of Aveyron* was published in 1832 – the boy, Victor, eventually learnt to speak a little and lived on to the age of about forty. Several learned people who examined him thought he was an idiot, their evidence being his abnormal perception and love of nature. Dr Itard invented an early form of sign language to communicate with the boy and these events inspired François Truffaut's movie *L'Enfant Sauvage*.

A wild man of the sea is alluded to in Lady Camilla Gurdon's *Suffolk Folklore* "A curious story relating to Orford is told by Ralph of Coggeshall (abbot of the monastery there in the early part of the thirteenth century). Some fishermen on this coast (AD 1161) caught in their nets one stormy day a monster resembling a man in size and form, bald-headed, but with a long beard. It was taken to the Governor of Orford Castle, and kept there for some time, being fed on raw flesh and fish, which it 'pressed with its hand' before eating. The soldiers in the Castle used to torture the unhappy monster in divers fashions 'to make him speak'; and on one occasion, when it was taken to the sea to disport itself therein, it broke through a triple barrier of nets and escaped. Strange to say, not long afterwards, it returned of its own accord to its captivity; but at last, 'being wearied of living alone, it stole away to sea and was never more heard of'. A tradition of this monster, known as 'the wild man of Orford', still exists in the village."

Perhaps their visitor was a sea-lion-man or a were-seal or an old sea god or a teleported Finn or a lunatic fisherman. We are not happy with these or any other explanations for the repetitive wild man phenomenon, and we sympathize with

A 'horrible uncouth creature', who for some time had been haunting woods near Salisbury, Wiltshire, was reported in the *Illustrated Police News*, 24 March 1877, to have carried off a farmer's wife and to have dropped her only when shot at. He then disappeared.

The wild man in chains, supporting the arms of the Earl of Atholl, represents an actual wild man captured on the family estates by a 17th-century ancestor.

Linnaeus who, avoiding all explanations, dealt with the problem by classifying the Wild Man as a separate order, *Homo ferus*. However, there seems no reason to doubt the genuineness of this report. The incident would still have been a living memory at the time Abbot Ralph was writing, and the behaviour of the wild man was in character with others of his kind, as also was the uncomprehending way in which the creature was treated. When it comes to explanations, however, we are no wiser than the Orford people of the time.

The existence of wild people in the forests and waste places was commonly recognized throughout the Middle Ages. Called "woodwoses", they figure in Gothic carving and heraldic ornament. A supporter on the arms of the Earl of Atholl of the Murray family is a woodwose in chains; it commemorates the capture of a wild man among the rocks of Craigiebarns by a seventeenth-century Murray who was rewarded with the hand of the Atholl heiress and succession to the title. The wild or "green man" of the woods is frequently displayed on inn signs. At Sproughton in Suffolk the Wild Man Inn, built in the sixteenth century, was named after a wild man who terrified the builders. From the same county comes the well-known but inexplicable report by an old chronicler, William of Newburgh, of two children, a boy and a girl, greenish in colour and eating only beans, who suddenly appeared in a field near Woolpit, having apparently emerged from some underground workings there. Their story was that they came from a place called St Martin; they had been watching their father's sheep when they had heard a loud noise, and the next thing they knew was that they were mysteriously in the fields of Woolpit.

In the *American Weekly* (27 October 1935) is an account of a wild boy found naked in the El Salvador jungle. He was about five years old, lived off raw fruit and fish, and spent his nights in the trees to avoid predatory animals.

On 22 July 1724 a 'naked, brownish, black-haired creature' was seen in the woods near Hamelin and later caught. The creature turned out to be a savage boy of about twelve. He became docile, and was summoned from Hanover to the court of King George I in London. The boy refused all delicacies from the royal table, eating only raw meat and vegetables. He was sent to a family on a farm in Hertfordshire, where he spent many years roaming the countryside or lying before the fire – an amiable pet of the neighbourhood. His guardian had a brass collar made for him with the inscription 'Peter the Wild Boy, Broadway Farm, Berkhamstead.' He died at the age of about 72 in 1785 and was buried at Northchurch, Hertfordshire, where a plaque gives his history. Lord Monboddo, the early evolutionist, visited Peter at the farm in 1782 and pronounced him to be a fine specimen of unspoilt humanity.

Charles Fort was a great collector of wild man reports. In *Lo!* he quotes from the *New York Times* (19 January 1888) an account of five wild men and one wild girl who appeared in Connecticut at the beginning of that year. Fort claimed to have records of no less than ten wild men seen in England during the winter of 1904–05. One of them, of unknown origin, appeared naked in the streets of Cheadle, Cheshire, and was decently placed in a sack by a policeman and dragged off to the police station. Another carried a book with drawings and writings in an unknown script and speaking an unknown language himself. His case is reported in the *East Anglian Daily Times* (12 January 1905). A report in the *Chatham News* (10 January 1914), tells how a man was found running naked down Chatham High Street in bitterly cold weather. He was arrested, but like a true *homo ferus* could give no account of himself. He appeared suddenly, he was unknown, therefore he was declared insane.

Fort regarded these wild men appearances in much the same way as he regarded showers of fishes and frogs. Wild men, like falling fishes, must come from somewhere, and both these phenomena, so Fort suggested, were due to teleportation. His idea was that there was a relationship – as of one end of a tube to another – between places where people inexplicably vanish and places where "wild men" suddenly turn up. Thus, in every case of a strange appearance, one should look for another case of a strange disappearance.

One modern piece of evidence has since emerged to support Fort's view of the origin of wild men. In our HUMAN TELEPORTATION section (see p.6) reference is made to a young Brazilian, José Antonió da Silva in 1968. It is recorded that after being set down near Vitória, miles from the spot from which he had mysteriously vanished some four days earlier, his first impulse was to retire into the woods and to live off the wildlife.

Children raised by animals

Several mythologies embody the theme of human children cared for by animals. Best known are Romulus and Remus, the founders of Rome, who were suckled as infants by a wolf. The story was generally found credible, being backed by numerous reports of similar cases throughout history. But, by the nineteenth century – during which a sort of competition arose among scholarly and scientific people to see how much of popular lore and old history could be discredited – such reports were regarded as fables, amusing for children but too absurd for the attention of serious people.

Rudyard Kipling's idealized wolf-boy, Mowgli of *The Jungle Book*, made it seem that the motif was a fairy story. Yet at the same time as they were being rationally proved impossible, more and more cases of humans fostered by animals were reported, many were supported by good evidence and reliable witnesses. Finally, in 1920, the carefully documented history of the wolf children of Midnapore (see below) convinced all but the wilfully sceptical that children may indeed be nurtured by wild animals.

There are stories of children raised by wolves or bears, and less frequently by leopards, panthers, monkeys, antelopes, goats, pigs, cattle, sheep and other creatures. In virtually all cases where children were adopted as infants, they acquired (more or less permanently) the natures, habits, abilities and even some of the physical features of their animal guardians. There are few examples of such children becoming fully reconciled to human ways. The later acquisition of human speech has proved difficult in some cases and impossible in others, and the few who have managed to speak even a few words have invariably used them to express their preference for their old animal life above their present human one.

It is generally supposed that feral children have been stolen or found abandoned by a mother animal in milk and adopted by her. But their remarkable physical abilities, their speed or strength in the case of antelope or bear children, or the luminous, wolf-like eyes of, for example, the Midnapore children, suggest another and (even to us) rather fantastic theory; that some are truly the children of animal parents, but monstrosities, corresponding to the known monstrous births of

Tissa, the Monkey Boy of Ceylon (1973).

In this variation on the Romulus and Remus theme, a young boy is nurtured by a she-bear in 17th-century Poland.

Despite the evidence – or perhaps out of ignorance of it – many anthropologists are still unwilling to accept the phenomenon of the rearing of humans by animals. The phenomenon does indeed have many unexplained aspects, but they seem to prefer to believe that all animal children are idiots who have been found wandering near the animals supposed to have fostered them. Autistic children often have characteristics in common with those taken from animal homes. The French philosopher, Lévi-Strauss declared: "The majority of wild children are congenitally abnormal children who have been deliberately abandoned."

In his *Systema naturae* (1758), the great systematizer, Linnaeus, identified the wild man, *Homo sapiens ferus,* as a sub-species of humanity (see WILD PEOPLE, P.303). He characterized him as "four-footed, dumb and hairy", and cited as examples nine historical cases, among them the following.

Hunters, in a Lithuanian forest, saw two little boys among a group of bears. They caught one – he was about nine years old, strong, healthy and handsome – and took him to Warsaw where he became the pet of the royal family and the nobility. He could not be taught to speak or to give up his bearish nature, but he did learn to raise his eyes and arms to heaven when anyone uttered the name of Jesus. Several times he escaped to the woods, and was once seen exchanging affectionate hugs with a wild bear notorious for having killed two people. There seems to have been a rash of bear children in Lithuania at the time. This first case was in 1661, and there are two others recorded in Dr Connor's *History of Poland*. One child, captured in 1694, was seen by Connor

animal-like offspring to human mothers. Again, there may be a wild talent in all of us, an ability to grow more physically and mentally like other creatures around us.

himself, who found him unable to talk or walk upright, though he later acquired both arts imperfectly; another such captive had been inspected by a Dutch diplomat in Warsaw some years earlier.

It is strange that such a proverbially bad-tempered creature as the bear should be so tolerant of human cubs; yet it is credited with more adoptions than any other animal apart from the wolf. A case was reported in *The American Weekly* (5 September 1937). In his article titled "Raised by a She-bear that Stole Her When a Baby", George Maranz described his visit to a girl in a Turkish lunatic asylum who had just spent eight years with a bear family. One of a party of hunters near Mount Olympus had shot a she-bear and had then been violently attacked by a powerful little "wood spirit". Finally overcome, the spirit turned out to be a human child, though utterly bear-like in her voice, habits and physique. When Mr Maranz saw her, she was much the same as at her capture, though somewhat more docile, and starvation had made her accept cooked food.

In 1767, hunters from Fraumark, in lower Hungary, were pursuing a large bear when they noticed human footprints in the snow in a part of the mountains where they thought no humans had ever before penetrated. The prints were followed to a bear's den, and there was discovered a real Goldilocks, a girl of about eighteen, tall, healthy and brown-skinned. Her behaviour "was very crude", and when taken to an asylum she refused to eat anything but raw meat, roots and the bark of trees. Another case of a bear-boy occurred early in the seventeenth century in Denmark and, in 1897, a bear-girl of about three years old was found in India.

Anselm von Feuerbach, in his 1833 book on the mysterious foundling Kaspar Hauser, gives a sad account of a pig-girl seen by a Dr Horn. "He saw in the infirmary at Salzburg, but a few years ago, a girl of twenty-two years of age, and by no means ugly, who had been brought up in a hogsty among the hogs, and who had sat there for many years with her legs crossed. One of her legs was quite crooked, she grunted like a hog, and her gestures were brutishly unseemly in a human dress."

The first contemporary record of a wolf-boy is from Hesse, in 1341. The boy, taken from the wolves by hunters, ran on all fours and leapt prodigiously. He died from being forced to adopt civilized diet. Three years later in the same district another wolf-boy was captured and successfully educated, living on to the age of eighty. He said he had been adopted by wolves when three years old; they had fed him, sheltered him and taught him their ways, and he was very sorry to have been parted from them.

The majority of wolf-children recorded since the early nineteenth century have come from India, in most cases from the jungles of Bengal. The best documented of these is the history of the Midnapore children, written by their discoverer and subsequent guardian, The Revd J. Singh (*Wolf Children and Feral Man*, 1942) Singh was a missionary of the Midnapore Orphanage who made regular evangelical trips to the aboriginal tribes of his district. On one such expedition, in 1920, he came into contact with the inhabitants of a village who were terrified of two small ghosts with blazing eyes that apparently haunted a nearby wolf den. He took a party to investigate and from a tree observed the "ghosts" leaving the wolf den in the company of the wolves. Realizing that they were human, Singh ordered the den to be dug out. At the first strokes of the spade, two wolves fled into the jungle but the mother wolf held her ground and attacked the diggers. Before Singh could intervene, one of the men killed her with an arrow.

Inside the den they found a ball of cubs, two wolves and two little girls, clinging together. One girl was about one and a half years old, the other about eight. The wolf cubs were sold off by the Indians and the little girls dragged to the Orphanage. The younger died within a year, never speaking or walking upright; but the elder girl, lovingly cared for by Mrs Singh, survived her capture for nine years, during which she lost some of her animal nature and gradually learnt to stand, to eat civilized food and even to speak a few words.

From the 1970s come two cases of gazelle-boys. The *Sunday Times* (26 August 1973) described how "A Syrian 'gazelle-child', discovered by a local prince on a hunting party, was said to be capable of running at 50 mph with the gazelles. He also had superb eyesight and very acute hearing." The other case, reported in the London *Daily Mirror* (1 February 1971), told of a boy, discovered in the Spanish Sahara not far from Rio de Oro, who moved in leaps and bounds, although he was "not as fast or as graceful as his companions". Jean-Claude Armen, a distinguished anthropologist, reported to the Life Institute, Geneva: "I have watched him approach gazelles and lick their foreheads in a sign of recognition." A delightful book by Armen, *Gazelle Boy*, was published in 1974. At that time, despite attempts by American scientists to capture him, the boy was still at large. Armen gradually made friends with him and was able to watch as the boy danced and played with the gazelles. He thought it likely that the boy was from a nomadic tribe whose babies travel in baskets slung on a camel. He must have fallen from the basket and been suckled by a gazelle that had lost her fawn. How he had so quickly adapted to the mobility of gazelle life is a mystery.

Equally astonishing is the case of the ostrich boy, Sidi Mohamed, whose story, told by himself, is quoted by Armen from *Notes Africaines* (26 April 1945). At the age of five or six he wandered off from his North African family and after three days in the wild came upon an ostrich nest with chicks hatching. When the parent birds returned he stayed around until they became used to him, and for ten years he lived with them, learning to live off grass and to match their speed in running. At night he was sheltered by the two ostriches who each extended a wing over him. One day a party of ostrich hunters appeared on fast horses. For some hours the boy and the birds outran the hunters but finally they roped him and he was restored to his parents. It took him a long time to readapt to

human ways and he was always yearning for his old way of life among the ostriches.

The most recent case to arouse worldwide attention was the story of John Sseybunya from Uganda who claims that as a young child he lived with a colony of vervet monkeys. As a four-year-old John fled into the jungle after witnessing the brutal murder of his mother by his father. He was not heard of again until a year later when he was spotted accompanying the monkeys on their night-time raids on crops. Captured by local women, he was extremely malnourished but otherwise unharmed. The most persuasive evidence for the truth of his story is that as a young adult John possesses a level of communication with the animals that indicates a close and well-established relationship with them. His story was the subject of a BBC documentary in 1999. Today, as a young adult, John appears somewhat backward by usual standards, and no one has yet determined whether this is due to an inherent disability, to his simian sabbatical, or both. We suspect that if John had been younger when he joined the monkeys, he might never have readjusted to human society as well as he has done.

In Uganda, John Sseybunya plays with monkeys for a TV documentary about the year he spent with a monkey troop at the age of four.

We are struck by the similarities between children brought up by animals and children carried off by eagles and recovered from their nests (see AVIAN ABDUCTIONS, P.333). In both cases the authorities are inclined to say that it cannot really happen, but popular belief, supported by anecdotes from all ages and countries, insists that it does. This is the area that particularly interests us in this book, where archetypal themes of myth and legend break out of that category and merge into physical reality. This is where human imagination interacts with matter to create the world we experience.

11

Living Wonders

Living Wonders

Faithful dogs

Many are the stories of animals, usually dogs, so faithful to human companions that they will not be separated from them, even after death. Tribute was paid to this devotion by American lawyer George Graham Vest in a speech to a jury in 1855, which coined the phrase "man's best friend". Vest, who went on to serve as a senator for Missouri, said: "If fortune drives the master forth, an outcast in the world, friendless and homeless, the faithful dog asks no higher privilege than that of accompanying him, to guard him against danger, to fight against his enemies. And when the last scene of all comes, and death takes his master in its embrace and his body is laid away in the cold ground . . . there by the graveside will the noble dog be found, his head between his paws, his eyes sad . . . faithful and true even in death."

Loyal animals often gain reputations for saintliness and monuments are erected to them. One example is the granite stab beside the lonely waters of the Derwent Dam in Derbyshire, bearing this inscription:

In Commemoration Of The Devotion of Tip The Sheepdog Which Stayed By The Body Of Her Dead Master, Mr Joseph Tagg, On The Howden Moors For Fifteen Weeks From 12th December 1953 to 27th March 1954

It was erected by public subscription, a year after he event commemorated, on the death of the dog, Tip, who had become during the interval a popular national heroine. Tip's master, a retired gamekeeper, aged eighty-one, was found dead on the high Derbyshire moors fifteen weeks after they had both set off from their home at Bamford on one of their customary rambles over the Derwent Hills, where they had once lived and worked. Search parties had failed to discover them; frost and snow had covered the hills, and man and dog had long been presumed dead, when a couple of men rounding up sheep came across the body of Tip's master, with Tip, in piteous condition but still alive, beside it. Somehow, alone on the bleak winter moors, she had survived for three and a half months.

Tip's remaining year was spent in luxury and fame at the house of her old master's niece, who with difficulty protected her retirement from hosts of admiring visitors. In that time she was awarded the highest order of canine chivalry, and when she died a vast crowd attended the unveiling of her memorial. Thousands of pilgrims have since tramped along the banks of Derwent Dam to visit the shrine of the saintly pet.

There are a number of similar monuments about the world. At the English burial ground in Cephalonia, an island off the west coast of Greece, is the tomb of Captain Parker, who was shot and killed in 1848 by campaigners against British rule there. The Captain's little dog refused to move from beside its master's body, and thus became a local legend. On the tomb the dog is represented, still faithfully on guard.

In April 1805, a young man called Charles Gough took his dog on a tour of the Lake District. High up on Helvellyn he slipped on ice and

The sheepdog Tip, whose devotion in staying by his master's body on the Derbyshire moors for fifteen weeks in the winter of 1953–54 is commemorated by an inscribed stone at the scene of the incident.

fell, or collapsed from cold or even, some say, died a martyr to art while trying to paint a landscape. Frank Haley in the *North West Monthly* (January 1950), summarized inconclusively the various versions of the legend. Three months later Gough's skeletal remains were found by a shepherd, attracted to the spot by an emaciated dog, generally thought to have been a terrier, which was hovering round it. No one, apart from his own people, seemed to care much about the fate of

poor Gough, but his dog created a sensation. "A lasting monument in words this wonder merits well", wrote Wordsworth; and he provided that monument with his poem about Gough's dog, entitled "Fidelity". Sir Walter Scott added another poetic monument to the dog's loyalty, and Sir Edwin Landseer immortalized the creature in a painting. Finally, in 1890, a solid monument in the form of an inscribed plaque was affixed to the rock where Gough died. It is called the Gough Memorial, but the hero commemorated on it is, of course, Gough's faithful little dog.

With his sharp eye for curious items of natural history in newspapers and popular literature, Maurice Burton collected numerous anecdotes of dogs which have been faithful after death and printed a selection in his book *Just Like an Animal* (1978). They include, from *Komsomolskaya Pravda* (January 1977), the story of an Alsatian bitch which had haunted Moscow's Vnukovo airport for two years, waiting for the return of her master who was absent in Siberia. The animal would run up to aircraft as they landed, and no one could handle it. The newspaper finally traced the owner, who had simply abandoned the Alsatian at the airport because he had no veterinary certificate for it. The story in the press brought in several thousand letters from Russian dog-lovers offering to adopt it. A similar story involves a dog who died "of a broken heart" after spending five years on the quayside at Quebec from where its owner had sailed away.

The statue of the celebrated Greyfriars Bobby in Candlemakers' Row, Edinburgh. The Traill family kept an eating house near the scene of Bobby's vigil and provided him with regular dinners.

The most complete, archetypal form of this legend is presented in the case of "Greyfriars Bobby". This rough-looking canine saint was the companion of John Gray, or Auld Jock, a poor shepherd who died obscurely in Edinburgh in 1858. His identity was known only because his name was written on the flyleaf of his Bible, and the man who identified him together with the gravedigger were the only people to attend his funeral in Edinburgh's Greyfriars Churchyard. Bobby was there too and, despite the efforts of the gravedigger to drive him away and the "No Dogs" notice on the churchyard gate, he continued after the funeral and for fourteen years until his own death to haunt Auld Jock's grave, sheltering in a nearby tombstone. Every day at one o'clock, Bobby went to the Greyfriars Dining Room, a favourite haunt of Auld Jock, whose proprietor,

John Traill, knew Bobby and always had a good bowl of broth ready for him.

A crisis arose during the ninth year of Bobby's vigil, when he was arrested by the police as an unlicensed vagrant, a crime for which dogs could be sentenced to death. John Traill was also threatened by the law for having "harboured" him. The situation was saved by the intervention of Sir William Chambers, Lord Provost of Edinburgh, who paid for Bobby's licence and presented him with a collar with the inscription: "Greyfriars Bobby, from the Lord Provost. 1867. Licensed".

When Bobby died, the one and only canine Freeman of the City of Edinburgh, the *Scotsman* (17 January 1872) printed a respectful obituary. John Traill buried him in a flowerpot near his master at Greyfriars and, from then on, his cult flourished. A memorial in the shape of a red-granite

Winston the labrador stands, contentedly, in front of his thatched kennel at Bradford-on-Avon. Winston was thought to be keeping watch at the crossroads where his owners were killed but he turned out to be a fraud.

"Loyalty be damned – it's the thought of all those old bones down there"

McLachlan's cynical (literally 'doggish') view of the subject.

collection of other such anecdotes, in *Les Animaux Excentriques* (1913). "All Paris . . . has been to see a dog, which has stayed for several years on its master's grave in the cemetery of Les Innocents, resisting all attempts to remove it. Several times people have tried dragging it off and shutting it up at the other end of the town; but as soon as it could get away, it always returned to the post to which its lasting affection had assigned it, and there it remained even through the rigours of winter. The people of the neighbourhood, touched by its perseverance, would bring it food, but the poor animal seemed to eat only to prolong its grief and to show an example of heroic faithfulness."

We would not lightly give offence to devotees of the harmless, endearing cults of Tip, Greyfriars

drinking fountain, topped with Bobby's effigy in bronze, was erected by Baroness Burdett Coutts in Candlemakers' Row, near his graveyard. In 1924, a group, the "American Lovers of Bobby" erected a stone over his grave.

A similar story, from France, is no less touching. It is quoted by Henri Coupin, among a

Bobby and other loyal pets, but occasionally we have twinges of doubt. There are some clever dogs around. Recently an Edinburgh historian, Jim Gilhooley, claimed, in the Scottish *Daily Record* (24 May 1999), that two John Grays had died that week in 1858, and that Bobby's owner was the one buried in a pauper's grave at Newington, three miles from Greyfriars Churchyard. If Gilhooley is correct, Bobby spent fourteen years at the wrong grave, but this is unlikely to deter the many who continue to visit the famous scene of his vigil.

A story from Wiltshire prompts the heretical thought that perhaps some of these canine mourners were not so much saints as scroungers, having learnt the trick of gaining patronage and daily dinners. In 1971 Winston, a golden labrador and successful con-artist, turned up at Bradford-on-Avon, a small town near Bath. He stationed himself at a busy crossroads opposite the district hospital on the outskirts of the town, where he soon began to attract local attention. He would allow no one to touch him, nor would he leave the grass verge at the crossroads. By staring wistfully at passing cars, he managed to create the legend that he was a poor orphan whose owners had been killed in a car accident at that spot.

Winston's shameless exploitation of the Greyfriars Bobby image worked so well that for the next seven years he enjoyed a life of complete comfort and independence. Every day he strolled over to the hospital where the staff provided dinner. He was provided with a snugly thatched kennel in the hospital grounds, and another one, donated by anonymous admirers, situated in the hedge by the crossroads. There at Christmas time he would receive a flood of greetings cards and presents of food and other comforts. Throughout the year offerings of bones and such were brought him by local children and by increasing numbers of well-wishers from all over the world. As the leading local celebrity he enjoyed police protection, and his portly, dignified figure became familiar to television viewers.

Winston died at his home of old age on 17 October 1978 and, the following day, the *Bath Evening Chronicle* exposed his imposture. The story of his owners' death at the crossroads in a car crash was quite untrue. The facts were that the rascally dog had been sacked from his former post at a hunting establishment in Devon and had come to Bradford with a local inventor, Alex Moulton. From there he had moved to the home of a farmer, Mike Singer, before setting up as independent operator at his crossroads. Despite his exposure as a fraud, Winston's funeral at Claverton Dogs' Cemetery was a grand affair, with coffin, flowers, pallbearers, reporters, TV cameramen and a crowd of mourners. The cross over his grave was fashioned by a local blind carpenter. Donations from far and wide swelled his memorial fund which, reported the *Bath Chronicle* (23 October 1978), soon approached its £1000 target. Its object was to provide a blind person with a guide dog, Winston II.

As a postscript, here is a rare tale of a grave-haunting cat. According to reporter Barbara Jeffery, in an article in the *Sunday People* (20 October 1974), Mrs Bridget Wastie of Charlbury, Oxfordshire, was looking after a cat, Moggie, while its old mistress was in hospital. The old lady died, and the following night Moggie was missing. Two days later Mrs Wastie and her mother took the bus to attend the funeral at a village fifteen miles distant. This, in her own words, is what happened there. "Just as the coffin was being lowered into the grave I caught my mother's arm in amazement. For there was Moggie sitting on a gravestone, watching. Somehow she had come fifteen miles to a village she had never visited before to say goodbye to her old mistress."

Homing animals and owner-seeking pets

The 1963 Disney film, *The Incredible Journey*, in which two dogs and a cat travel for many miles and through many adventures in search of their owners, is constantly repeated in actual fact. Every year a fresh crop of incidents bears further witness to the ability of certain animals to make long, solitary journeys across unknown territory towards home. Some of the stories we have collected are so nearly incredible that we are inclined to agree with Charles Fort who pointed to it as an example of the magic that surrounds everyday life.

A case, described in the *Sunday Express* (22 July 1979) tells of Nick, the Alsatian bitch belonging to Doug Simpson of Selah, Washington. Nick had got lost while on a camping trip with Mr Simpson in the southern Arizona desert. For two weeks his master searched frantically for her before starting on the two-thousand-mile journey home. Four months later Nick turned up, bloody, battered and emaciated, at the family house in Selah. Somehow she had travelled alone through country described as "some of the roughest on earth", hundreds of miles across the scorching, waterless desert, across the Grand Canyon and through blizzards, icy rivers and snow-covered, 12,000-feet mountain ranges in Nevada and Oregon. Doug Simpson was away from home at

the time, but his parents recognized his dog and telephoned him at his work-place in Pennsylvania. He flew home immediately. When he walked into the house, Nick looked at him for a few moments, as if in reproach for leaving her behind, and then rose to give him a warm greeting. "I've been making a fuss of her ever since", said Doug.

There are several published collections of

In 1600 Henry Wriothesley, Earl of Southampton, was imprisoned in the Tower of London for involvement in the Essex conspiracy. His cat sought him out and climbed down the chimney.

homing pet anecdotes. Dr Rupert Sheldrake deals with this among other animal abilities in *Dogs That Know When Their Owners Are Coming Home* (1999) and there are summaries of homing cats and homing dogs by Paul Sieveking in *Fortean Times* (no. 61 and 70). One of our favourite cases is that of Micky the terrier, reported in the *Sunday People* (29 April 1979). His journey back to his old home was only five miles, but Micky was fifteen years old, blind and almost stone deaf. For three years since the death of his former master in King's Langley, Hertfordshire, he had lived at Hemel Hempstead with new owners, Mr and Mrs Philips. Over Easter Micky disappeared. The police were told, and they discovered him outside his old home which was now derelict. He was treated by a vet for a crushed paw, having apparently been run over during his trek, which took him across several main roads and through busy traffic.

Some odd cases of dogs finding their way home by means of transport are detailed in Edwin Arnold's book, *The Soul of The Beast* (1960). The most wonderful, or incredible, of such cases is that of a "well-bred collie" which was sent off by its owner, living near the small port of Inverkeithing in Scotland, to a friend in Calcutta. Some time after its arrival in India the dog disappeared, and a few months later it bounded into the house of its old master at Inverkeithing, showing great delight at being home again. Evidently it had stowed away at Calcutta on a ship bound for Dundee. There it had disembarked and proceeded on by a coastal vessel to Inverkeithing. It was suggested at the time that the collie had been attracted to the right vessel at Calcutta by the Scottish accents of the sailors!

Apart from dogs of all sorts, we have records of homing cats and pigeons, a frog, a duck, a hedgehog and a rabbit. Cats, despite the apparent indifference they often show their owners, turn out to be loyal and persistent creatures. They have been credited with solo treks of literally thousands of miles in search of old homes or human associates. In the autumn of 1977 fourteen-year-old Kirsten Hicks of Adelaide, Australia, left her pretty white Persian cat, Puss, with her grandparents, who lived over a thousand miles away on Queensland's Gold Coast, while she went abroad for a holiday. She returned to the sad news that Puss had gone missing. But the following autumn Puss arrived home, "footsore and with matted fur". The Sydney *Daily Mirror* (11 October 1978) reported that "He crossed rivers, sidestepped semitrailers and stalked the bush in an amazing 12-month trek".

We could go on for pages with similar accounts, variously authenticated. A cause for scepticism about some cases, is that people may be too impetuous in claiming to recognize a long-lost pet. Yet there are many cases which are as genuine as they are mysterious. One of the best authenticated, recounted by Dr Michael W. Fox in *Understanding Your Cat* (1974), is of a New York vet who left his cat in his home state while he went to take up a post in California 2500 miles away. Months later, an identical cat walked into his new house. Incredulously he examined the animal, and on the fourth vertebra of its tail he found the deformed bone growth which had marked his own cat as the result of a bite.

This brings us to the most mysterious part of the whole business. We know that many creatures have highly developed homing instincts, pigeons for example. But the cases which fascinate us above all others are those of animals making journeys to places where they have never been before, seeking not their homes but their owners. One epic feat, recounted in Joseph Wylder's book, *Psychic Pets* (1978) was performed by an American cat called Sugar, who walked from Gage, Oklahoma, where he had been left with some neighbours, to rejoin the Woods family who had moved to Anderson, California. The journey of no less than 1500 miles had taken him fourteen months, and he had never before been anywhere near his owners' new house. They recognized their cat by a slight deformity of his left hip joint. This is a particularly interesting case because it was personally investigated by the great ESP researcher, Dr J.B. Rhine, who went out to Oklahoma to observe Sugar and interview witnesses.

A case which became famous in the winter of 1914 was that of Prince, an Irish terrier, who manged to cross the English Channel in the early days of World War I to join his master in the trenches. In August 1914 Private Brown of the 1st North Staffordshire Regiment was sent over to France. On 27 September, his wife wrote with the news that their dog was missing. Private Brown wrote back: "I am sorry you have not found Prince and you are not likely to while he is over here with me. It is a very strange thing that I should have got him. A man brought him to me from the front trenches. I could not believe my eyes till I got off my horse and he made a great fuss of me. I believe he came over with some other troops." This case was investigated by the RSPCA and declared to be authentic.

Nor is it only dogs and cats that seem capable of these feats of miraculous loyalty. The case of an

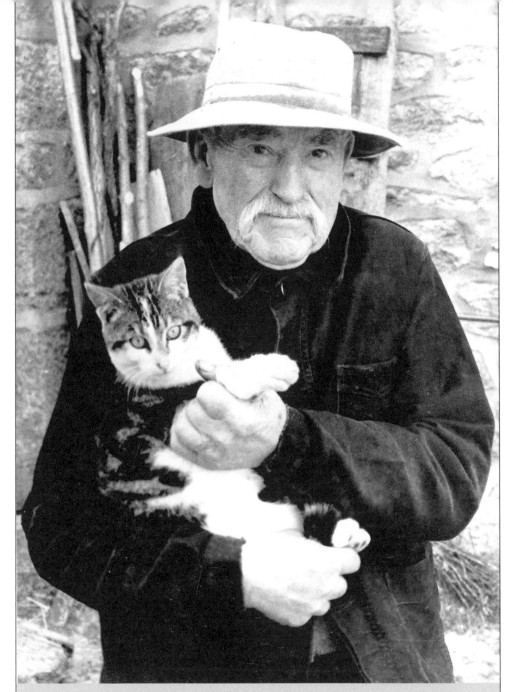

In the winter of early 1967 Minette followed her owner, Jean Pradel, home to La Ribière from Clermont-Ferrand, a journey of sixty-five miles. When she arrived, her claws were almost completely worn away.

owner-seeking pigeon was investigated by Dr Rhine with S.R. Feather. The pigeon belonged to a young West Virginia boy named Hugh Perkins. When Hugh fell ill and was rushed by his parents to a hospital 105 miles away, the pigeon

somehow traced him. "One dark, snowy night about a week later, the boy heard a fluttering at the window of his hospital room. Calling the nurse, he asked her to raise the window because there was a pigeon outside, and just to humour the lad, she did so. The pigeon came in. The boy recognized his pet bird and asked her to look for the number 167 on its leg, and when she did so she found the number as stated".

There have been many studies on the homing instinct of animals, especially pigeons. Do they navigate by landmarks, by the sun or stars, by terrestrial magnetic currents or by some other, more mysterious means? No single answer has been found to satisfy all the data, and in the cases of pets finding owners who have moved away there is no scientific theory at all. We suspect that the teleportation effect, triggered by intense longing by people for their pets or by animals for their owners, may be behind some of them. Most experiments that have been made, have been confined to investigating the homing instinct pure and simple. For instance, Dr Presch and Dr Lindenbaum in Germany took a number of cats varying distances from their homes and put each one in the centre of a maze with twenty-four exits. In each case the cat left the maze in the direction of its home. A similar experiment with dogs is described by Dr Bastian Schmid in his book, *Interviewing Animals* (1936). Dr Schmid arranged for a number of dogs to be taken from their homes in the back of a closed van and driven by a circuitous route to a spot miles away from their familiar territory. Every time this was done, the dog, on release, seemed temporarily confused, before resolutely trotting off in the direction of home. The same results have been obtained with homing pigeons. Dr Rupert Sheldrake in *Seven Experiments that Could Change the World* (1995) tells of pigeons, disorientated by rotating chambers and other means, that are able to fly back to their lofts. Even when the lofts were moved several miles away, they were still able to locate them. Sheldrake compares this to the ability of some animals to locate the new, unfamiliar homes of their owners.

We referred above to reports of a homing frog, a duck and a hedgehog. Details of the first two can be found in the "Homesick Pets" chapter of Frank Edwards's *Strange World* (1964). The case of the homing hedgehog was described in the *Sunday Express* (12 August 1979) based on an item in a Russian newspaper. The hedgehog was first found on a country road by a doctor at the Donetsk hospital. It had a broken paw, and the doctor, Nadezhda Ushakova, nursed it until it was fit. Then she gave it to her granddaughter who lived forty-eight miles away. At its new home it languished and would not eat, so the granddaughter wrote to say that she had set it free in the forest. Two months later, Dr Ushakova returned from work and found the same hedgehog sitting on her doorstep. Now, says the report, Soviet veterinary experts are investigating the homing instincts of hedgehogs.

We have just one story of a homing rabbit. White with red eyes, Robert was bought in 1978 for six-year-old Maud Cecil of Cambridge. He was a much-loved household pet until he grew too large and unruly, and Maud's mother decided to rehouse him in the walled garden. No sooner had she turned her back, than Robert disappeared. He was replaced with a look-alike rabbit but, later that year, there was a scratching at the gate, and Robert was back. Soon, however, his behaviour became worse and worse: he gnawed books, bounced heavily on beds at night and woke one overnight guest by trying to eat his moustache. Banished to the Suffolk house of Maud's grandmother, Mrs Margaret Hodson, he did not last long with her before she set him free in the wild half a mile away. Three days later she had Robert on her hands again. Robert was then taken back to Maud's house and put to live in the chicken-run. There before long he was discovered trying to rape the hens and, as a result of this misdemeanour, was taken to the Gogmagog Hills, about three miles out of Cambridge, and sent packing once more. This time two years passed before Maud and her mother heard a familiar scratching at the gate. Robert's final years were spent in a reinforced cage at Maud's grandmother's house, where he died in 1982 after losing a fight with a marauding rat.

Talking cats and dogs

An interview with a talking dog appeared in *Fate* magazine in July 1966. Clare Lambert went to interview Pepe, a tiny chihuahua, and his companion Mrs Genova. She had learnt about the talking dog from an article in a local trade newspaper, *Gas News*, the previous spring. Its front page had a photograph of Pepe talking to a gas fitter who had called to fix the boiler at the Genova family home in Torrence, California. He had been working in the basement boiler room, watched by Pepe, when the little dog suddenly said "I love you!" Unable to believe his ears, the fitter picked up the dog and watched his mouth open as he repeated "I love you" in a high-pitched, sing-song voice. The man was so delighted that he invited Pepe to visit the gas depot where his conversation made him a popular favourite.

Pepe was at home to receive Clare Lambert when she called, and he entertained her with other phrases from his vocabulary, including "I want you", "How are you?", "Not now", "Hello there" and "Ed Sullivan". Mrs Genova then told his story. The dog had been bought from local kennels, was less than two years old and was sensitive and fussy about his food. The first time she had heard him talking was in the back garden. "He was talking through the wire fence to his girl friend, Ranic. I distinctly heard the words, 'I love you-oo, I love you-oo, I need you-oo,' in a high singing voice and repeated over and over." These and his other phrases he had learnt from imitating Mrs Genova.

Clare Lambert described what happened when Mrs Genova picked him up for a chat. "A little singing sound starts in Pepe's throat as his muscles begin to move. In about six seconds he lifts his head high, opens his mouth wide and sings the words after her, repeating each phrase a couple of times. Pepe has a loud voice for so small an animal." Clare observed Pepe carefully: "I bent close to watch his throat muscles move and I saw his tongue turn towards the roof of his mouth as he made a conscious effort to form syllables. This tongue movement is most unusual. Dogs keep their tongue down on their lower jaw when emitting sounds." Pepe's "speech" was more like a combination of singing and talking: "With each phrase he goes up and down the scale rising three or more tones. It is difficult to describe. You have to hear it.

In 1951 Mrs Field of West Croydon, Surrey, was surprised when her 11-month-old puppy, Peter, said 'Mum' as he presented his bandaged paw for her attention. Later, when she offered him a dog biscuit, he said 'Please'. 'Please what?' she asked. 'Mum', he added.

Pepe is not a show-off. Indeed, he is a modest little animal and seldom speaks unless he is spoken to."

In Dallas, Texas, another talking dog, a Dobermann Pincher named Lancer, was interviewed for the *National Enquirer* (12 July 1977). Lancer was two years old with a large vocabulary, including the phrase naturally expected of pets, "I love you". According to his master, Mr Gerald Wright, "he can learn almost anything in a matter of minutes", and he is therefore useful to Mr Wright, who is president of a cosmetics company in Dallas, because he can charm the ladies at work by learning and speaking their names. There is no doubt that Lancer talks in a human manner, wrote Bud Gordon of the *Enquirer,* but "his voice sounds muddy, as though his mouth were stuffed with cotton".

A smooth-haired fox-terrier called Ben, belonging to Mr and Mrs Brissenden of Royston, Hertfordshire, was the subject of two articles in the *Daily Mirror* in August 1946. A *Mirror* reporter had visited Ben the previous day, and several times he had heard the little terrier say, clearly and distinctly, "I want one", evidently expressing desire for a cup of tea, a biscuit and other doggy treats. His voice was described as "dark brown" and "a rich baritone", low-pitched and authoritative. The reporter found it quite uncanny the way Ben used different tones of voice in making his requests, "from the wheedling note to the gruff, demanding one".

Contacted by the *Mirror,* two eminent veterinary surgeons, Professor W.C. Miller and Dr W. Wooldridge, went to Royston to examine the talking dog. To them he duly made his usual remark, "I want one . . . oh-h-h . . . I want one". Professor Miller observed: "In all my experience I have never heard a dog so nearly simulate the human voice." Dr Wooldridge added: "The most amazing thing is that Ben does actually use his mouth and, to some extent, his tongue, to formulate and control the words. He cuts his words clearly, and appears to use his tongue to change from one word to another." While the experts discussed his case in Mrs Brissenden's front room, Ben romped around them with a ball.

Some years ago a dog who could say "Beer please!" and other appropriate phrases helped retired actor, Ronald Shiner, keep the Porter Inn at Templecombe, Somerset. While in Australia there lived a truly remarkable dog whose spoken phrases included "Hello Mum" and "Here I am Mum" – and also, as the reporter primly put it, "a word often heard in masculine company and not

in the ladies' presence". Its speech, according to the London *Evening Standard* (17 January 1953), was "clear as a bell, and in an accent much nearer English than Australian".

A peculiar feature of this talking Australian fox-terrier was its background, which was ecclesiastical. Its owner was the Diocesan Registrar of Newcastle, New South Wales. There was cause for laughter, therefore, when Australian scientists advanced the conventional explanation for the animal's power of speech, that it was a "conditioned reflex", meaning that the dog had picked up its vulgar vocabulary from its environment. The London *Evening Standard* made a perceptive comment on this diagnosis: "This shows how stupid scientists can be. It is just conceivable that a Diocesan Registrar, on occasions of rare stress, might utter a word unfit for ladies to hear. But that he should be given, with such frequency as to condition a dog, to saying: 'Here I am Mum', surpasses belief. No man who called his mother 'Mum' could rise to even moderate eminence in the Anglican Church."

Of the various tales we have heard about talking cats the following is the most remarkable. In 1963 Mr and Mrs Deem of Hillside Acres, Florida, found an abandoned, starving male kitten near their home. They took it in, fed it and adopted it, calling it Whitey because of its colour. They had another tom cat, Blackie, with which Whitey was not always on good terms. A few months later, when Whitey was about six months old, he jumped onto the family bed and said, "Mama, I'm hungry." "What did you say?" asked Ruth Deem, and Whitey repeated, "I'm hungry". Mrs Deem said nothing to her husband but got up and fed the cat.

A few days later James Deem was stroking Whitey and telling him affectionately that he was a bad cat. "I am *not* a bad cat," said Whitey. "I want to go out." After that the cat spoke to the Deems quite frequently, at least once a day, often in a whining, self-pitying manner as though still aggrieved by its wretched infancy. Among its phrases were, "Why no one love me?", "I want to go home", "I want out", "I love Mama" and "He's bad", a reference to Blackie.

In January 1965 Whitey was interviewed at his new home, near Lake Hamilton, Florida, by Suzy Smith whose article, "In Search of the Talking Cat" appeared in the November issue of *Fate* magazine. Unfortunately Whitey had been ill and had not spoken for a while. Talking apart, he was a normal tom cat who liked to go out on prowls. On one of these outings he had been poisoned, temporarily inhibiting his speech. Suzy Smith wanted to find witnesses to the talking cat other than the Deems. Several neighbours claimed to have heard Whitey speaking, and two of them signed statements to that effect. A man who had looked after the cats while the Deems were away was another witness. On one occasion he had slapped at the cats with a newspaper to stop them fighting. When Ruth Deem returned home Whitey said, "Mama, he hit me". "What did he hit you with?" she asked. "Newspaper," he replied.

Suzy Smith discussed the case of Whitey with Dr Hornell Hart, a parapsychologist and Professor of Sociology at Florida Southern College. He produced three possible explanations: ventriloquism, misinterpretations of a cat's miaows, and "the development of a fad under which it becomes stylish for individuals to report having heard a cat make various remarks".

The "fad" explanation sounds rather like the theories of mass hysteria, psychic plague or group enchantment which are commonly applied to outbreaks of the abnormal. It is vague enough to

Murri, the German-speaking tomcat, whose vocabulary consisted of the words 'ja', 'nein' and 'Anna' which he pronounced distinctly. He would also sing along with nursery rhymes played on the piano. He made broadcasts and was exhibited at an international cat show in Vienna.

sound plausible, but Suzy Smith, having met several of the witnesses in the case, found no evidence of faddishness or hysteria among them, nor did she credit the suggestions of misheard miaows or ventriloquism. About a year after her visit, Whitey was heard to speak in the open air, well away from any member of the Deem family. One afternoon a neighbour, Joe Rhodes, saw the cat on a vacant lot near his trailer and went to pick him up to take him back to his owners. As he approached Whitey he distinctly heard the cat say, "You can't catch me!" And nor could he.

The Reverend Bennett Palmer, a close student of Whitey although he never heard him talk, compared him to another talking animal which fascinated psychical researchers in the mid-1930s (see Harry Price and R.S. Lambert, *The Haunting of Cashen's Gap*, 1936). This was a talking mongoose, or rather a disembodied voice claiming to be that of a mongoose called Gef, which haunted a house in the Isle of Man. Rustlings were heard and other evidence was given of a creature living in the attic or within the walls of the house, but nothing was ever clearly seen. Gef has been classified as a rare example of a talking poltergeist, and perhaps the voice speaking through Whitey was a similar phenomenon.

This reminds us of the old explanation of talking animals: that they were possessed by spirits or acting as mediums. Commenting on the limited speech of Ben, the talking dog of Royston, Dr E.J. Dingwall in *Peculiar People* (1950) compares it unfavourably with the powers of the black dog belonging to the mediaeval German magician, H.C. Agrippa. This omniscient animal could not only talk, but whispered the secrets of events all over the world into its master's ear.

SOVIET ZOO 'HAS TALKING ELEPHANT'

By RICHARD BEESTON in Moscow

Batyr, a 10-year-old Indian elephant at the Karaganda Zoo in Soviet Kazakhstan, can say phrases like "Batyr is good" and verbs like "drink" and "give," a Moscow newspaper reported yesterday. It said that a recording of its voice was heard recently on the Kazakh state radio.

"He just pushes his trunk into his mouth and starts talking," said the deputy director of the zoo, Mr Boris Kosinsky, He told a correspondent from the Young Communist League newspaper that it all began three years ago when a startled night watchman reported that he had heard the elephant talking to itself.

An unusual case of a talking elephant which appeared in the *Daily Telegraph*, 9 April 1980.

Calculating horses

The most famous case of a calculating animal is that of Clever Hans, a German horse at the beginning of the twentieth century. Hans was a young Russian stallion, acquired in 1900 by Wilhelm von Osten, who had long been obsessed by the idea that animals, if properly educated, could develop a degree of intelligence similar to that of humans. After several failures with other animals he discovered Hans, who turned out to be an ideal pupil.

sums; he knew how to read, and in music he could distinguish harmonious sounds from discords. He also had an extraordinary memory. He could tell the date of each day of the week. In short, his performance was up to the level of an intelligent fourteen-year-old schoolboy."

In response to the demands of an enthusiastic public, Clever Hans was submitted to inquiry by a committee set up for that purpose. It consisted of professors of psychology, physiology and zoology, some cavalry officers, a doctor, several veterinarians and a circus manager. For five weeks

Clever Hans undergoing a 'scientific examination' in mathematics from Professor C.G. Schillings.

Von Osten began with rows of up to nine skittles, calling out the number of skittles in the row, thus teaching the horse to recognize numbers and to associate them with the words, one, two, three, etc. Then he replaced the skittles with numbers written on a blackboard. When Hans was familiar with these, von Osten introduced him to elementary mathematics, and soon the horse was doing simple sums, followed by more advanced calculations involving square and cube roots. One of his early investigators, Professor Claparède, who spent several weeks putting Hans through his mathematical paces, wrote in the *Archives de psychologie de Genève* that Hans "not only knew how to do

they studied and questioned the horse, and did their best to catch von Osten out in some deceit. But even with his trainer out of the room Clever Hans continued to calculate and give answers with the same facility. The committee members then retired to write up their report, all stating that Hans had performed as well as had been claimed and that they had detected no trickery.

This positive result did not satisfy von Osten's critics, several of whom had stated in print that the pair were frauds. Among the accusers was an eminent academic, Oskar Pfungst of the Berlin School of Psychology. Although notably prejudiced in the matter, he was considered the most suitable person to conduct a new investigation of the wonder horse. Having done so, he published in 1908 a voluminous report in the form of a book, *Der kluge Hans* (Clever Hans), in which he dealt ruthlessly with all von Osten's claims. According to Pfungst, the horse knew nothing of figures or letters, was totally unable to count, read and reckon, and what skills he had were limited to recognizing slight, barely noticeable sounds or movements made by his trainer or by other people. The report was exactly what many, people wanted. It was widely acclaimed, and Hans and his owner became objects of public ridicule. Von Osten protested but few now took him seriously, and he died, an embittered man, the following year.

Hans, however, survived him and did much to restore his late master's reputation. Von Osten had willed him to a sympathetic business man, Karl Krall

Wilhelm von Osten, the brilliant animal trainer who undertook Hans's education at the beginning of the last century.

of Elberfeld. Krall had his own ideas on animal education. Unlike von Osten, who had been impulsive and irritable, he was endlessly patient with his pupil, and under his gentle tuition Hans's skills improved. Krall then added to his stable two further stallions, Muhamed and Zarif, and began to teach them. Muhamed in particular made rapid progress, learning addition and subtraction and the meaning of plus and minus signs all within two weeks. Zarif was almost as quick, and it took both

the horses only a few months to grasp the rudiments of mathematics, before moving on to spelling and sign language. In order to indicate numbers, they had been taught to tap out units with the right hoof and tens with the left. Krall devised a code sytem in which letters and sounds were similarly represented by a certain number of taps with each hoof. A full description of the method is given in Krall's book, *Denkende Tiere* (Thinking Animals) published in 1912.

After he had acquired and educated several more horses, including a Shetland pony, Hänschen, and a blind horse called Berto, Krall was ready to open his stables for inspection by scientists. Singly and in groups, distinguished professors from all over Europe converged on Elberfeld. Krall and his staff absented themselves, leaving the inspectors to work with the horses on their own, allowing them every opportunity to judge whether or not trickery was involved. They were unanimous in concluding that the criticisms brought by Pfungst against von Osten could not be applied to Krall's horses. To make sure that the animals were receiving no physical signals, the scientists arranged peep-hole tests, withdrawing from the stable to observe the horses through small glazed holes. Under these conditions the horses performed as well as ever.

Zarif, one of the calculating horses of Elberfeld, with his teacher, Karl Krall.

Calculating the square root of 1,874,161 was typical of the problems set by Professors Mackenzie of Genoa and Assagioli of Florence. The question was written on a blackboard, and the investigators then went out into the yard and peeped through chinks in the door of Muhamed's stable while he tapped with his hooves the correct answer – 1369. Questions to which the investigators did not know the answers were also put. A committee headed by Dr Haenel asked Muhamed to give the fourth root of 7,890,481. He quickly replied 53, which proved to be correct. Even the blind horse, Berto, who obviously could not receive visual signals, was able to solve more simple mathematical problems. Moreover, having learnt a sign language, the horses would sometimes make spontaneous comments. On one occasion, during a lengthy inquisition by Professor Claparède, Zarif suddenly stopped work and then tapped out the word "tired" followed by "pain in leg". He also told Krall when Hänschen was beaten by a groom.

Frank Edwards, in *Strangest of All* (1956) quotes Dr Schoeller and Dr Gehrke on a touching episode which they reported during their experiments with the horses. They asked Muhamed why he did not attempt speech instead of pawing with his hoof. The animal appeared to try to articulate. Then he tapped out the sentence, "I have not a good voice." Dr Gehrke tried to show him how he must open his mouth before speaking, and Muhamed showed he understood by signalling, "Open mouth". Human speech, however, was beyond him. Zarif was then asked how he communicated with Muhamed. "With mouth" he replied. "Why do you not tell us that with your mouth, Zarif?" asked the scientists. "Because I have no voice", signalled the stallion.

The tragic fate of the Elberfeld horses was to he called up for service on the battlefield in World War I. None of them survived.

Karl Krall's training methods had many followers, including several dog owners. Scientists, however, grew less interested in the phenomenon, for which they could find no acceptable explanation, and modern investigations of intelligent animals have mostly been left to researchers in ESP, telepathy and the like. In the case of the best known modern wonder horse, Lady, of Richmond, Virginia, our sources are newspaper and magazine articles rather than scientific reports.

Lady or Lady Wonder was a seedy-looking mare who lived for some thirty-three years in a ramshackle stable near the road between Richmond and Petersburg until her death in 1957. Her owners were Mr and Mrs C.D. Fonda, described as simple, God-fearing people, who had no interest in exploiting Lady. Despite their poverty, they consistently refused large offers from showmen and Hollywood agents. Their belief was that most animals could do much the same as Lady if only people bothered to teach them. In Lady's stable was a wooden contraption with a lettered keyboard, like a large typewriter. When Lady pressed one of the keys with her nose, the letter would stand up. In this way, Lady answered questions put to her by visitors.

Instead of plaguing her with mathematical questions, the people of Virginia treated Lady as a kind of oracle or wise woman. She was asked to predict the weather, the results of sporting events and the winners of elections, to locate lost property and to prescribe for ailments. On several occasions (details given in the *National Enquirer*, 31 October 1978) the Police Department engaged her to help them find missing people. In all these tasks she achieved a high rate of success. Inevitably, her legend became exaggerated, and many of the stories told about her cannot be authenticated, but she was examined in the course of her long career by scholars and scientists of many disciplines. Dr J.B. Rhine of Duke University describes in his book, *New World of the Mind* (1953), the studies of Lady made by himself and his wife between 1927 and 1929 and by other scientists in 1952 and 1953. He concluded that Lady had a remarkable ability to read people's minds.

In Lady's case there was never any suspicion of fraud. She could be seen operating her keyboard, unaided by any hint from her owners. Her messages made sense and, when relating to future events, were often proved correct. It is recorded that she accurately named Roosevelt and Truman as winners in their respective election campaigns, and gave other proofs of political foresight. It is also said that racecourse officials persuaded her owners to stop people from asking Lady to predict the results.

When it came to answering questions about people's private lives, Lady, like many sibyls before her, was often found to be too accurate and given to excessive honesty. Visitors attended by their wives, husbands or other intimate relations would ask for details of the early parts of their lives, and Lady would mention scandals or tragedies from the past which they had thought forgotten by everyone but themselves. Many people left her stable red-faced or in tears, and they would accuse her owners of dealing with the devil – forgetting that no one had asked them to consult the horse in the first place.

A problem for scientific researchers into the "clever animal" phenomenon is that any alternatives to straight-forward acceptance of the animal's powers – such as telepathy and demonic possession – are themselves unscientific. This problem was honestly faced by the greatest expert in animal intelligence of the period, Professor Ziegler of Stuttgart. After prolonged study of the Elberfeld horses he continued his work with a dog named Rolf. Finally he stated his complete belief in the animal's abilities: "Now that I have assured myself that the Elberfeld horses . . . are genuinely capable of reading and calculating, by their own reasoning powers, I consider it my duty as a scientist to support the claims made for these experiments by word and pen, although I do not disguise from myself the difficulty there is in making known to science discoveries which are in contradiction to accepted opinions."

There is no single theory of educated animals which accounts for all cases. The main contenders in the field are: that the animals genuinely think, calculate and communicate as claimed; that they are responding to signals from their trainers or others; that they read their questioners' minds; that they have mediumistic powers like oracles and relay messages and information from the spirit world. The first of these was forced on Ziegler, and many other scientific investigators, by their inability to account for the phenomena in any other way. But even those inclined to that theory have admitted doubts due to certain repeated anomalies in the animals' performances.

Several of the animals tested were found to have a higher rate of success with complicated mathematical questions involving cube roots and the like than with quite simple problems. It was often noticed by German investigators that the more intelligent the questioner, the better the animals did. Also, there is a repeated tendency in such animals to mix up their numbers, giving 15 for 51 etc. The horses would sometimes give a wrong answer to a question, and when asked a second question would reply with the correct response to the first. Eccentricities such as these have been cited by many writers as evidence that the animals were not their own agents and did not understand the meaning of their own communications.

Lady Wonder, the talking horse of Richmond, Virginia. By pressing the appropriate keys of her 'typewriter' with her nose she would answer questions, spell out messages, and foretell future events.

Since the theory of visible signals does not work in the case of the blind horse Berto, or of animals studied by "key-hole" methods, sceptics have fallen back on the notion of slight, unconscious sounds, such as produced by changes in onlookers' breathing rhythms or heart-beats, indicating to a trained animal the moment to stop counting. No doubt animals have sharper senses than most people, but one of the difficulties with the "slight signals" theory, is that it does not explain the cases of animals replying to spontaneous questions with previously unknown answers. Also, when the alleged signals are as slight as heart-beats, the theory begins to merge into one of its rivals, telepathy.

Trainers of clever animals for public show have often presented them as "psychic" mind-readers, thus confusing the issue. Most naturalists, or pet-owners, acknowledge some form of telepathy among animals, or between animals and people. In the cases described here, mental direction is the most attractive of general explanations. Again, however, it fails the "unknown answers" test. The advantage here passes to the spiritualists because, if an animal is acting as a spirit-medium, it matters not whether its questioner knows the answer to the problem he sets. Spiritualists compare the counting paw or hoof with which animals communicate to the swinging pendulum or rapping chair-leg at psychic seances. They point also to the trance-like state reported of many animals during their countings and calculations.

We ourselves are not specially addicted to any of these theories, although recognizing virtues in all of them. The actual function of many clever animals, such as Lady Wonder, has been similar to that of oracles, which no one has ever explained. Where modern scientists are as baffled as the ancients were by such things, we do not care to intrude with opinions.

Avian abductions

High on a desolate crag above Saint-Maurice in the French Alps, in 1950, a Swiss mountain guide found a child's skeleton. The remains were identified as those of a four-year-old boy who had vanished from a nearby village three years earlier. There was no way the child could have climbed there so it was widely agreed that he must have been carried to the ledge by a giant eagle.

Stories of giant birds kidnapping humans were already old when Herodotus heard one from the priests of Egypt. Such tales have been incorporated into the mythology and folklore of many nations – the abuction of Ganymede by Jupiter in the form of an eagle; Sindbad's *rukh*;the divine Garuda of the Hindus; and the tall tales of Ozark mountain men. However, as far as we can discover, no one has yet made any study or compilation of avian abductions and there is a great resistance among orthodox thinkers to such tales.

Most ornithologists believe that large birds, like eagles and condors, cannot carry more than their own weight (about twelve pounds), which limits their cargo to a small lamb – or possibly a new-born baby. There have been attempts to prove, scientifically, that stories of children borne aloft on eagles' wings are improbable, if not impossible. One such test of the weight-carrying abilities of various eagles was described in 1940 in *Nature* magazine. A tame golden eagle "was taken to an elevated platform and various weights were attached to its feet. It was then launched into the air. It was found that when each foot was loaded with a four-pound weight, the bird could hardly fly at all!"

On the other hand, all over the world woodsmen, mountaineers and farmers have maintained that large eagles will attack anything that moves, regardless of size, and in their frenzy often succeed in lifting animals forbidden by ornithologists. Lewis V. Cummings, in *I Was a Headhunter* (1941), says he once saw a great South American eagle carry off a half-grown deer which he reckoned weighed at least thirty-five pounds.

A famous case is reported by the French naturalist F.A. Pouchet in his encyclopaedia, *The Universe* (1870). The incident took place at Valais, in the French Alps, in 1838, where a five-year-old girl named Marie Delex, was playing with a friend on a mountainside. "All at once an eagle swooped down upon her and carried her away in spite of the cries and presence of her young friend. Some peasants, hearing the screams, hastened to the spot but sought in vain for the child; they found nothing but one of her shoes on the edge of a precipice. It was not until two months later that a shepherd discovered the corpse of Marie Delex, frightfully mutilated, and lying upon a rock half a league from where she had been borne off."

The fatal abduction in 1838 of Marie Delex by an Alpine eagle, illustrated some thirty years after the incident.

Not all cases end so tragically, but the survivors have their own problems dealing with the sudden, frightening and unwanted encounter, as the case of ten-year-old Marlon Lowe demonstrates. On the morning of 25 July 1977, he was playing in the yard of his home at Lawndale, Illinois. His parents and two friends working in the vicinity heard Marlon's terrified screams and they looked around to see two huge birds menacing the boy. As they watched, one swooped and fastening its talons into the boy's clothes carrying him for 25-30 feet at about three feet off the ground before dropping him. The witnesses said the dark birds were like "overgrown vultures" with curled beaks, white bands around their long necks and a wingspan of about eight feet.

From this photograph of an American Bald Eagle and its prey it seems that some eagles may be able to carry off creatures quite as large as a small child.

Ruth and Jake Lowe, Marlon's parents, both felt the birds resembled condors, an impression confirmed later when they looked through a wildlife book. A spokesman for the National Audubon Society told the media that the only known condors in the United States were confined to a dwindling colony in California – over 1500 miles away to the west. He suggested that the Lowes had mistakenly seen hawks, great horned owls, or even turkey vultures, which were better known in the Midwest. The local gamewardens showed little inclination to believe the Lowes, either, and they were put under pressure to change their story. When they stood by their testimony, it was suggested, crudely, that they were lying or that what they had really seen was simply the boy running along with the bird attacking his back.

The witnesses, however, reaffirmed their story to Jerry Coleman in 1977 and to his brother Loren in 1979. The Colemans discovered that the Lowe family had become embittered by the reactions of the local authorities and their neighbours. When the event was reported in the papers they began receiving anonymous notes and telephone calls and dead birds were left on their front porch. Worst affected was young Marlon who had to cope with nightmares as well as bullying at school. For weeks after the event, his naturally red hair grew a colourless grey at the roots; Ruth Lowe blamed the shock of the bird attack.

As if to confound the "experts" further, large unidentified birds continued to be seen in the skies of Illinois. The following year a farmer at Lincoln saw one snatch two piglets weighing about 20 lbs each; while a truck driver, ten miles from Lawndale, saw one try and fail to lift a large piglet.

Tales of baby-napping are more common than bird experts deem comfortable. Lee Wilson, writing in the London *Evening News* (4 November 1978), mentions three cases from the Middle East. In two of them, eagles carried away babies from riverbanks while their mothers washed clothes – one at Ainassia, southern Anatolia, in June 1937 and the other at Damascus, Syria, in February 1953. The third case was of a seven-year-old boy, in central Anatolia, who was abducted while foolishly trying to investigate an eyrie.

The problem of ascertaining the accuracy of such stories is a perennial one. In his *History of the*

Earth and Animated Nature (1774) Oliver Goldsmith observed how "Many marvellous tales are told of eagles, and there is scarcely a parish in Scotland, in which, if tradition be correct, they have not carried off a child. According to popular belief, an eagle transported one from the island of Harris to Skye, over a space of about twenty miles, but as even more wonderful events are as firmly believed, no confidence can be reposed in such accounts."

There are several legends of people using birds to make journeys through the air. One such incident is recorded in this 17th-century Turkish painting of a traveller, shipwrecked on a desert island, who escaped by hanging on to the legs of a large bird.

Fortunately, similar stories exist, from respectable sources, which are closer to us in time. For example, the following examples were sent to us by Dwight Whalen, a correspondent in the Niagara Falls area who loves trawling through local newspaper archives. In September 1885, a ten-year-old boy was pounced upon and carried across a road near Euphemia, Ontario, by what was described as the biggest bald eagle ever seen in the area. Five weeks later, another bald eagle carried off the two-year-old son of a farmer outside Montreal. Where the first boy was lucky to escape, the second was partly devoured by the eagle on the roof of a barn a mile away before an armed party could rescue him. More recently, in August 1924, near Chatham, also in Ontario, an eagle with a wingspan of eight feet managed to lift Fred Cunningham, aged fourteen, who weighed ninety-seven pounds. The lad's clothing gave way before he had travelled five feet in the air; in the continued struggle, the bird was forced against a fence and killed by men who came to Fred's aid.

When Roger Caras deals with such feathered felons in his book *Dangerous to Man* (1964) it is to express his conventional disbelief in them. However he does include a curious footnote referring to his correspondence with American naturalist Doug Storer over an incident in Norway in the 1930s. Caras writes: "Apparently a very large eagle attacked a very small seven-year-old girl and hit a powerful updraft at just the right moment. Mr Storer assembled an impressive collection of documents and his evidence would be difficult to refute." In fact the girl Svanhild Hansen was only four years old at the time and a full account of her

In his *Amazing But True Animals*, Doug Storer tells of the case of Svanhild Hansen, who as a four-year-old girl was playing in the yard of her parents' farm not far from Trondheim when she was snatched away by a huge eagle. She is seen here with her husband, a stuffed eagle and the dress she wore on that fateful day, complete with the rents made by her abductor's talons.

abduction and successful recovery – interpreted by the local community as a sign of God's providence – is in a Norwegian book entitled *Omerovet* (1960) by Steinar Hunnestad.

On 5 June 1932, little Svanhild was playing in the yard of her parents' farm in the village of Leka, not far from Trondheim, when the huge eagle swooped on her. The bird was unable to lift the girl to its eyrie but managed to transport her for more than a mile to the end of the valley where it dropped her on a high ledge. The rescuers, attracted to the location by the eagle's circling overhead, found the girl asleep, unharmed except for a tear-stained face and scratches.

For Caras and other naturalists this story is made more acceptable by the fact that the bird could have hit an updraught at the "right" moment. "It is all very startling," writes Caras, almost grudgingly, "but it would appear as if this is one case which must be accepted for the moment, at least." A similar qualification in print occurs in the third edition of Frank Lane's ever popular *Nature Parade* (1947). After stating the ornithologists' standard objection, Lane adds: "A correspondent wrote to me after reading this passage in the first edition of this book and gave evidence of how a young girl in Ireland was carried across the Kenmare river by a golden eagle and dropped on the other side. When she grew up she had a distinct limp as a result of her literally hair-raising experience."

Even as we swoop down and rescue these tales from obscurity, we are aware of another dimension – the significance they share with other archetypal phenomena. The image of the human soul borne aloft by an overwhelming force that is more than human in its vigour and precision is one that is expressed by poets and mystics the world over. As a symbol of transformation, abduction by a totemic animal has great magical significance in traditional societies, particularly for the initiation of shamans. A person subjected to mysterious levitation, by whatever agency, is considered to have displayed latent mediumistic or shamanic powers or to have been "selected" in some mysterious way.

In her study of Japanese shamanism, *The Catalpa Bow* (1975), Carmen Blacker refers to stories of children kidnapped by the *tengu,* mercurial beings, half hawks, half men, who haunt woods and mountaintops. The *tengu* take the form of golden eagles, carry off their chosen ones and rear them inside hollow trees until they are mysteriously returned to human society. According to Blacker, the *tengu*'s victims "return either as half-wits or as miraculous persons . . . to become renowned ascetics gifted with supernatural powers". No less prodigious, the lucky survivors in our stories are often set apart, as a result of their experience, by some distinguishing physical feature – Marlon Lowe's pale hair, for example, or the Irish girl's limp. They also frequently experience a sense of "transformation", of being different from others, that is clearly parallel to that of alien abductees (see ENCOUNTERS WITH ALIENS, p.137) and those who have experienced levitation or spontaneous flight (see LEVITATION AND SPONTANEOUS FLIGHT, p.81).

Animal councils and law courts

Observers ancient and modern are agreed that animals can communicate with each other both by sounds and by other more subtle means, but no one knows the nature or source of the impulse that makes birds in a flock execute simultaneous turns and manoeuvres in the air. Nor is anything known for certain about the mysterious phenomenon, rarely but regularly witnessed, of animal and bird assemblies where meetings are held for purposes apparently similar to those of human society – law-making, judgment or mourning of the dead. We are aware of the errors that can arise from interpreting animal behaviour in terms of our own, but there are so many reports from sober observers of animals acting together in a way which seems parallel to human customs that we leave readers to judge the matter as they will from the following few examples.

The Parliament or Tribunal of rooks is a much repeated classic of old-fashioned natural history books. M. Diarmid describes the proceedings thus in Cassell's *World of Wonders*: "In the spring months, when all the rooks are busy building nests or repairing old ones, certain evildoers invade their neighbours' store of sticks to save themselves the trouble of collecting materials in a more laborious and lawful way. But as often as offences of this kind are detected, a complaint is made to the proper quarter, and the delinquent bird tried and punished by his peers. Some veteran bird acts as chief justice, and from the bustle that goes forward,

كا باعله يوملر مياشك قايم ايدي لشكر جواد وسپاه خونخواد له زاغلم
شيجون ايوب كشودولشكرين خراب واشياندلن يباب ايندي
يا زوبيردي براودهد | سردشمان كرد چون خالص

in the Shetland Islands called *Corvus cornix*. They were studied by another naturalist, Dr Edmondson, who observed that the birds held regular assemblies, attended by deputies from distant parts of the islands. Sometimes the early arrivals have to wait several days for the late-comers, for the business may not begin until all are gathered. Mean-while, the prisoners among the rooks make no attempt to escape but quietly await judgment. What their crimes might be Dr Edmondson does not know, but he says that, when the proceedings are over, "judge, bar-risters, ushers, audience and all, fall upon the two or three prisoners at the bar, and beat them till they kill them."

From time to time eyewitness accounts of bird courts appear in local nature journals

From India comes this 16th-century illustration of a battle between owls and crows. The reported cause of it was that the crows objected to an owl being elected King of the Birds.

the cawing of some rooks and the silence of others, it is plain that the court proceeds upon system, though I can not subscribe to the startling opinion that they examine witnesses and empanel a jury. The presiding rook, who sits on a bough above all the others, is heard croaking last of all, and when sentence is pronounced, punishment follows very promptly. Either the culprit is seized and pecked most severely, or the nest containing the ill-gotten twigs is pounced upon and demolished."

G. Garratt in *Marvels of Instinct* (1862) refers to the remarkable rook tribunals held by a species

or in the popular press, the most prolific source we know of being the *Daily Mirror* letters column. On 19 June 1975, the *Mirror* printed an interesting letter from Mrs Rose Bridgett of Arnold, Nottinghamshire, about a crows' court she had seen one winter's day in a local field. The crows "had formed a perfect circle around the crow in the centre. I did not see any attack, but after the crows had flown away I went outside and picked up the crow which had been in the middle. It was dead but there were no visible signs of injury. I gave it to a taxidermist friend and it is now in a museum with a plaque stating that it was killed in a crows' court." The *Mirror's* comment on this was: "Presumably the crows put the 'fluence on the culprit and literally frightened it to death."

Another letter to the *Mirror* (13 April 1954), from naturalist L.W. Hayward, describes one of the tribunals of storks which, he said, are quite often observed in Germany: "There is a large meadow near the village of Oggersheim, on the Rhine, where storks assemble every autumn. On one of these occasions about fifty were observed forming a ring round one individual whose appearance bespoke great alarm. One of the party seemed to address the conclave by clapping its

well to learn this lesson." In the one modern account of a sparrow court we have on file (in a letter to the *Mirror*, 19 April 1954) the observer, Mr Wadsworth of London, intervened at the point where the sparrows, having with much chirping tried one of their number, were meting out punishment. Mr Wadsworth rescued the "defendant", who rose to his feet but made no effort to fly away. He took the frightened bird home and adopted it as a free-range pet. The sparrow rewarded him by returning to his house one day with a mate. Under Mr Wadsworth's protective eye the pair built a nest and raised young ones, the cock bird's previous unpleasantness with his tribe having presumably been forgotten.

There are even accounts of birds of one species trying an alien criminal. The letters page in the *Mirror*, (11 June 1975) quoted a reader's account of a circle of rooks sitting in judgment of a jackdaw, thought to be an egg-thief. At the end of the trial the rooks fell on the jackdaw and killed it. Another letter (22 September 1977) tells the remarkable story of crows apparently trying a fox. Early one summer morning Mrs Ruddy of Buckinghamshire was taking her dog for a walk when she heard a terrific cawing. "Looking through the hedge I saw a little fox sitting in a ring of crows. The fox had such a comical "Who, me?" look on its face. I wanted to see what would happen, but my dog barked and disturbed them."

Crows Court exacts the death penalty

National Park warden Richard Bell described this week to the Ryedale Natural History Society a crow court which was in session recently in Cropton Forest. It ended with one member of the colony being "sentenced" and put to death.

Mr Bell saw the crow court in a field about 100 yards away from his home at Sutherland Cottage.

He said: "I have read about and heard naturalists talk abour crow courts or crow parliaments. Usually they were with reference to rooks, as opposed to the carrion-crows I saw from my house. About six or seven of them were involved.

For about five minutes they were doing quite a lot of ritual and display, that sort of thing. Then they set about one of their number and killed him. As I went out, they flew away, leaving the dead bird behind.

"It was the first time that I had seen a crow court. I don't know why they set upon one of their number. I suppose it might have been something to do with territory. He might have been an intruder."

Mr Bell quoted the example of the crow court when Mrs Logan-Wood, the chairman of the Ryedale Natural History Society, asked members to report on unusual sightings. Mr

A recently witnessed Crow Court, as reported in the *Scarborough Mercury*.

wings for two or three minutes. This was followed by a second and a third and a fourth in regular succession, each like the first. At last they all joined in chorus and with one accord fell upon the culprit in the middle, and dispatched him in a few seconds."

Sparrows sometimes hold similar courts, writes Garratt, but they are more energetic and less formal than the rook and crow assemblies, and after a short, sharp punishment the criminal is soon re-admitted without rancour to sparrow society. He comments: "Many men would do

Other animals given to judicial proceedings, according to E.L. Arnold's *Soul of the Beast,* include a species of African monkey, which is said to "hold assizes in the forest for the trial of culprit, who are condemned and excommunicated". The old naturalist writer, Margrave, claimed to have been "a frequent witness of their assemblies and deliberations". Of the species called *ouarine* he wrote: "Every day, both morning and evening, the *ouarines* assemble in the woods to receive instructions. When all come together, one among the number takes the highest place on a tree, and makes a signal with his hand to the rest to sit round, in order to hearken. As soon as he sees them placed, he begins his discourse with so loud a voice, and yet in a manner so precipitate, that, to hear him at a distance, one would think the whole

Assemblies of animals for judicial or other purposes provide a common theme of folklore and fairy tales. This illustration by Griset of an assembly of mice appears to draw on reports of mice and rats which have been seen in conclave around their 'King'.

company were crying out at one time; however, during that time, one only is speaking, and all the rest observe the most profound silence. When this is done, he makes a sign with the hand for the rest to reply; and at that instant they raise their voices together, until by another signal of the hand they are enjoined silence. This they as readily obey; till at last the whole assembly break up, after hearing a repetition of the same preachment."

In the *Illustrated London News* (30 August 1952) Dr Maurice Burton told the story of a "turkey court" as described to him by a correspondent. One of the birds in a domestic flock was sick. The turkey hens formed a ring round the sick bird while the turkey cock, a short distance away, began his display. Puffed up, gobbling and rattling his wattles, he ran head down towards the group and, as he approached, the hens bowed their heads to the ground. The cock withdrew and then three times repeated the same performance. The third time, he charged through the circle of hens and dealt a blow with his beak on the sick bird in the centre. It fell, and the hens, one after the other, pecked it until it was dead.

Burton's belief is that the victims of bird courts in general are not being tried for wrong-doing, but that the birds are killing off one of their number which is sickly or diseased – as evidently was the case with the turkeys. This reminds us of Samuel Butler's imaginary state of Erewhon, where criminals were treated by doctors, while people who dared to fall ill were subject to punishment by law. It is a plausible explanation for many cases, but it could hardly apply to reports of birds of one species formally punishing a member of another.

Toad in the hole

The Great Exhibition of London, in 1862, contained a curious and controversial exhibit; a lump of coal from a colliery in Newport, Monmouthshire, and a frog. The frog, it was explained, was found in the heart of the coal, in a frog-shaped cavity that appeared to have been moulded around it. An irate Captain Frank Buckland wrote to the *Times*, accusing the directors of the Exhibition of "gross imposition" and calling for the frog and its prison to be "expelled". It was utterly impossible, he protested, for a frog to bear the heat and pressure necessary to form coal at depths of over 300 feet, to say nothing of the millions of years during which it must have lived so enclosed.

This outburst from Buckland, who later wrote *Curiosities of Nature* (1857–72), initiated a correspondence in the *Field* and other periodicals throughout 1862. Many more incidents came to light and several "specimens" were sent to the leading naturalists of the day, including Professor Richard Owen of the Natural History Museum who received so many that he appointed his wife to deal with them. While this was going on, workmen excavating a new cellar to a house in Stamford, Lincolnshire, found a toad in a cavity in solid stone seven-foot deep. The report in the *Stamford Mercury* (31 October 1862) concludes: "No fact can be more fully or certainly established by human evidence . . . let the sceptics on this subject say what they will."

Belief in the ability of toads to live encased in rock was popular for centuries though dismissed by the learned as a superstition of the countryside. The earliest first-hand story known to us is that of Ambroise Paré, chief surgeon to Henry III of France. "Being at my seat near the village of Meudon, and overlooking a quarryman whom I had set to break some very large and hard stones, in the middle of one we found a huge toad, full of life and without any visible aperture by which it could get there . . . The labourer told me it was not the first time he had met with a toad and the like creatures within huge blocks of stone."

An obvious way of testing whether toads can really endure long spells of solitary confinement without food or air is to seal them up in airtight cells. Quite a number of these cruel-sounding experiments have been performed. In 1825, Frank Buckland's father, William – then a professor of geology at Oxford – placed twelve toads in cells in two stone blocks, one of limestone, one of sandstone. He sealed them in with glass and putty, and buried them under a slate three feet down in his garden. A year later the toads in sandstone were found to be long dead. Most of the toads in limestone were alive – two had even put on weight. Buckland ascribed this to a crack in the glass, which possibly admitted small insects. He tried again, but all the toads died.

Buckland wasn't the first to try the experiment. In February 1771, the French naturalist, Herissant sealed three toads in plaster-lined cells in a block of fir-wood. Over three years later, in April 1774, the cells were opened in the presence of other scientists, and two of the toads were still alive. Herissant sealed up the two live toads again and presented the block of wood to the Academy of Sciences to open whenever they thought fit. He died soon after and the experiment was heard of no more. A similar experiment by another French naturalist was reported in the

An illustration from Gosse's *Romance of Natural History* of an incident commonly reported by quarrymen, the breaking open of a stone to reveal a long-immured but living toad, and its close-fitting hollow.

Times (23 September 1862); of the twenty toads that were encased in a block of plaster of Paris four were still alive twelve years later.

Animals other than frogs and toads are found in living tombs, though rather less frequently. The *Annual Register* of 1761 cites examples of snakes, crabs and lobsters from the classical writings of pioneering naturalists, including Francis Bacon. It also records the astonishing though apparently well-known information that the stones used to pave Toulon harbour were often broken to reveal "shellfish of exquisite taste"; and that in the hard stones quarried at Ancona on the Adriatic were to be found "small shellfish, quite alive and very palatable".

In February 1818, Dr E.D. Clarke, a geologist at Caius College, Cambridge, was present at the digging of a friend's chalk-pit in the hope of finding fossils. He was surprised when workmen found a layer of newts at 45 fathoms (275 feet). He thought they were fossils and had some broken out of a lump of chalk-stone. Placing them on a sheet of paper in the sunlight, he was astonished when three intact creatures began to move. Two of them died later; the third, when placed in water, "skipped and twisted about, as well as if it had never been torpid", so actively in fact that it escaped. Dr Clarke and his friend set about collecting specimens of all the species of newts in the area, but none resembled the recently revived ones: "They are of an entirely extinct species, never before known," wrote The Revd Richard Cobbold. "Dr Clarke took great delight in mentioning this." (Quoted by William Howitt, *History of the Supernatural*, 1863.) Howitt himself knew of a stone ball that had topped a gate-post of a mansion for hundreds of years. One day it fell and broke on the ground, revealing a live toad in its heart.

The phenomenon can be extended to creatures found in other material than stones and rocks. The *Memoires* of the French Academy of Sciences for 1719 reports that "in the foot of an elm, of the bigness of a pretty corpulent man, three or four foot above the root and exactly in the centre, has been found a live toad, middle-sized but lean and filling up the whole vacant space." The writer could only imagine that some spawn became lodged in the young tree, "by some very singular accident", and that the toad grew within the tree, living on its sap. It scuttled away as soon as the trunk was split open enough for it to fall out, so its limbs had certainly not atrophied from its supposed lifetime confinement.

Dr Robert Plot recorded several accounts in his *Natural History of Stafford-shire* (1686) of similar stories told to him by countryfolk. "Out of a great oak that grew at Lapley . . . there was a great toad sawn forth from the middle of the tree, in a place which when growing was 12 or 14 foot from the ground; the tree being sound and intire in all parts quite round, saving just where the toad lay, it was black and corrupted and crumbled away like sawdust." Plot's explanation was that an "agreeable dust" or airborne spawn, a concept also used to explain falls of frogs (see FALLS OF FROGS AND FISHES, p.17), had been wafted into a hollow high in the tree. When the toad hatched it could not escape and became slowly sealed up.

In another part of his book, Dr Plot tells of three field-mice – called "nursrows" in Stafford-shire dialect – found inside an oak tree near Biddulph "which being examin'd and found in all parts sound." Plot at first wonders if this was a

TO THE EDITOR OF THE TIMES.

Sir,—Your correspondent " P.," in last Friday's paper, demands the expulsion from the International Exhibition of a frog said to have been found alive embedded in coal. He also accuses the exhibitor of being an impostor, and attributes either credulity or inattention to the Commissioners, among whom he specially names Lord Granville. The only ground given for his conclusions is his own simple opinion that a frog could not have lived thousands of years so low down in the earth, and having over it such an enormous weight as it must have had if what is said of it be true. It is in my power, however, to show that your correspondent's opinion is wrong, and I shall be much obliged if you will allow me to do so.

1. My wife is prepared to state that she herself, many years ago, saw one of her father's workmen split open a piece of coal, and discover in the middle of it a moderate-sized frog or toad (she is not sure which) alive, and able to move, and she remembers distinctly the oval shape and smooth surface of the hollow where the animal had lain.

2. Samuel Goodwin, a stonemason, whom I myself have known these five-and-twenty years, and who is very trustworthy, states as follows :—" When I worked in the quarry at Kettlebrook, with Charles Alldridge, we sawed a stone through about four feet thick, quite solid, and in the middle was a toad about the size of my fist, and a hole about twice the size. We took it out, and it lived about half an hour, and then it died. We worked the stone, and it was used as a plinth stone in Birmingham Town-hall."

I trust this will induce " P." to apologize to the exhibitor of the frog, as well as to the Commissioners.

Yours respectfully,

JOHN SCOTT.

Lilleshall Coal Depôts, Great Western Railway, Paddington, Sept. 17.

One of several letters to the *Times*, in response to Captain Buckland's indignant demand for the expulsion of the embedded toad from the Great Exhibition of 1851.

"nursrow-tree". In the folklore of the farmhands of that county, a venerable tree (usually an oak, an ash or an elm) was drilled into and a living field-mouse was placed in the hole, which was then

This mummified toad was found by workmen who cracked open a flint nodule in a quarry at Lewes, East Sussex, in about 1900. Both toad and tomb are now in the Booth Museum in Hove.

plugged with a peg of the same wood. The branches of such trees were believed efficacious in curing swellings in cattle thought to be caused by the nocturnal biting of field-mice – the afflicted animal being whipped with the branch.

This custom was also referred to by Gilbert White in his *Natural History of Selborne* (1789). He describes a "shrew-ash", a gnarled old tree that stood near Selborne Church until "the late vicar stubb'd and burnt it", despite the pleas and remonstrances of the villagers. The cause of their lamentations was that a shrew had long ago been ceremonially sealed into its trunk; the branches being used to cure animals tormented by shrew-mice. Could the rustic magicians who buried mice within tree trunks be imitating the mysterious power in nature that encloses living animals in sealed cavities within trees and rocks?

In February 1861, J. Pemberton Bartlett, a parson living near Southampton, wrote to *The Zoologist* about a common toad that he recovered from a cavity in a 25-year-old fir tree. "I counted

the rings of the tree myself," he said, surmising that the young amphibian had crept into the hole which, in time, closed over. The naturalist W.H. Maxwell reported, in *The Field Book* (1833), that he once discovered a toad imprisoned in the bark, high up a mulberry tree. Although he offered no explanation of how the toad reached its high prison, he firmly believed that "as the tree increased in size there seems to be no reason why the toad should not in process of time become embedded in the tree itself."

Some reports of entombed creatures mention the lack of a mouth, as in the quite anomalous case of a number of frogs found in a gravel pit near Frederick, Oklahoma, during the 1920s. According to the report in the Dallas *Morning News* (9 August 1960), deep in the pit were found some clay balls, as hard as rock. These were broken open with sledgehammers and in them were frogs, some alive, some dead. Of the live frogs it was said, "their mouths had grown shut through the centuries. They were without pigmentation and so transparent one could see their hearts beating. Sudden exposure caused some of them to burst, but if quickly immersed in water they continued to live, some as long as a month." An odd feature of the case was that the balls of rock containing the frogs were found in the midst of the bones of mammoths and sabre-toothed tigers. Because of this association, scientists from the Smithsonian Institution concluded that the frogs in stones were contemporary with these extinct animals; their explanation of why the frogs were living is not recorded.

This association with ancient bones reminded us of a report sent to the journal of the Selborne Society, *Nature Notes*, in 1900, which referred to another ancient country belief that certain magical people and animals had toads embedded in their heads. The Vicar of North Moreton, Oxfordshire, wrote: "On July 20, while some repairs were being carried on in our church, a skeleton was discovered at a depth of about six feet under the pavement and in the skull a large yellow toad. The theory of the man who found it is that the creature was there in the man's lifetime and grew after his death!"

Stranger still is the story in the *Historia rerum anglicarum* (William of Newburgh, c.1198). It tells of the discovery by quarrymen of "a beautifully jointed stone . . . that is to say one formed from a fine conjunction of rocks". It was taken to the bishop, who had it opened "to see if within it lay concealed something mysterious". They found a toad with a gold chain round its neck. The bishop ordered the stone to be marked and then reburied in the quarry "for all eternity".

Details of the extraordinary case of a mummified marmoset discovered within the trunk of a birch tree at Bosham, West Sussex, are given, together with this picture of it, by Frank Buckland in the notes to his edition of Gilbert White's *Natural History of Selborne*. The tree had been cut down and taken to a carpenter's shop for stripping and sawing, in the course of which the strange find was made. The creature was presented to Buckland, who took it with him when he went to dine at Winchester with Bishop Wilberforce, the great opponent of Darwin and Huxley. At dinner Wilberforce started making jokes about the theory of human descent from monkeys, and Buckland added to the merriment by producing the dried marmoset from his pocket and introducing it as 'our Darwinian brother'.

How one swallow may make a winter

A favourite nineteenth-century topic of intellectual discussion and newspaper correspondence was the question of whether swallows occasionally hibernate. Orthodox ornithologists, who almost universally believe in the southward autumn migrations of swallows, swifts and martins from northern Europe and their return the following spring, are usually quite indignant should anyone dare to believe otherwise. Such authorities are usually surprised, and not a little embarrassed, to learn that the great founders of the modern natural sciences – Linnaeus, Buffon and Baron Cuvier – accepted without question the theory of hibernation. Cuvier in *Le règne animal* (1819) wrote: "It appears certain that swallows become torpid during winter, and even that they pass this season at the bottom of the water in the marshes."

The traditional form of belief in hibernating swallows was expressed in 1602 by Richard Carew in his *Survey of Cornwall*. "In the West parts of Cornwall during the winter season, swallows are found sitting in old deep tin works and holes of the seacliffs; but touching their lurking place, Olaus Magnus makes a far stranger report; for he saith, that in the North parts of the world, as summer weareth out, they clasp mouth to mouth, wing to wing, and leg to leg, and so after a sweet singing, fall down into certain great lakes or pools amongst the canes, from whence at the next spring they receive a new resurrection; and he addeth for proof hereof, that the fishermen, who make holes in the ice to dip up such fish with their nets as resort thither for breathing, do sometimes light on these swallows congealed in clods of a slimy substance, and that carrying them home to their stoves the warmth restoreth them to life and flight."

It is easy to dismiss this notion as based on poor observation of swallows swooping over ponds, marshes and the like as if preparing for a plunge into the depths. But it was not just a simple, rustic belief; men of science have claimed to witness the phenomenon. Dr Etmuller, cited in William Derham's *Physico-theology* (1714), was Professor of Botany and Anatomy at Leipzig, in the 1750s. He wrote: "I remember having found more than a

LIBER XX.

De mixtis Piscibus cum Hirundinibus.

CAP. XXI.

In the 16th century, Olaus Magnus recorded the popular belief that swallows sometimes hibernate on the beds of lakes and ponds, and illustrated it with this woodcut of fishermen dragging up a cluster of the birds in a net cast through a hole in the ice.

bushel would hold of Swallows closely clustered among the reeds of a fish-pond under the ice, all of them to appearance dead, but with the heart still pulsating." To this statement Derham adds a note of a meeting he attended of the Royal Society in February 1713, addressed by a Dr Colas, "a person very curious in these matters". Dr Colas said a common fishing practice in northern Europe was to break holes in the ice and draw the nets under it. Once, he saw "sixteen Swallows so drawn out of the Lake of Larnrodt, and about thirty out of the king's great pond in Rosneilen". At Schlefitten, near a house of the Earl of Dohna, he saw two Swallows just come out of the waters, that could scarcely stand, being wet and weak, with their wings hanging on the ground; and that he observed the Swallows to be often weak for some days after their appearance.

In the Academy at Uppsala, where Linnaeus reigned over the botany and medicine departments until his death in 1778, the submerged hibernation of the swallow was accepted as a fact. But his German colleagues were rather more sceptical – or scientific. For many years a reward was offered by a famous university of the bird's weight in silver for each swallow found under water and revivable in the prescribed manner. The prize was never claimed.

In addition to the belief that swallows were capable of sleeping on the bottom of ponds, there are many reports of swallows found hibernating in hollow trees, holes in cliffs and banks, up in attics, down in mines, etc. One of the best and earliest accounts comes from Peter Collinson, the friend and correspondent of Linnaeus, who reported to the Royal Society the following statement of a Monsieur Achard. He was travelling by barge down the Rhine to Rotterdam, at the end of March – about two weeks before the usual arrival of the sand martins – when, just below Basel, he saw an unusual sight. We quote from *Philosophical Transactions* (1763):

"I was surprised at seeing, near the top of the cliff, some boys tied to ropes, hanging down doing something . . . The waterman told us they were reaching the holes in the cliffs for Swallows or Martins, which took refuge in them, and remained there all the winter, until warm weather, and then they came abroad. The boys being let down by their comrades to the holes, put in a long rammer, with a screw at the end, such as is used to unload guns, and, twisting it about, drew out the birds. For a trifle I procured some of them. When I first had them, they seemed stiff and lifeless; I put one of them in my bosom, between my skin and shirt, and laid another on a board, the sun shining full and warm upon it, and one or two of my companions did the like. That in my bosom revived in about a quarter of an hour; feeling it move, I took it out to look at it; but perceiving it not sufficiently come to itself, I put it in again; in about another quarter, feeling it flutter pretty briskly, I took it out, and admired it. Being now perfectly recovered, before I was aware, it took its flight; the covering of the boat prevented me from seeing where it went."

The first modern compilation of records and legends of hibernating swallows was published by Philip Gosse in 1861 as a chapter in the second volume of his *Romance of Natural History*. Though not entirely sceptical, Gosse was unhappy about the anecdotal and second-hand nature of most of the evidence, and he wondered why the records of finds, "instead of increasing in frequency with the increase of scientific research and communication, strangely become more rare".

A number of Scottish accounts of hibernating birds was collected by Bishop Stanley in his *Familiar History of Birds* (1865). These include a group of five chimney swallows that were found huddled together on the roof-beam of a barn, in November 1826; a corncrake found in midwinter, when an Orkney crofter demolished a mud wall; and six swallows rescued from a hollow. The latter were taken "to a respectable person, by whom they were deposited in a desk, where they remained forgotten till the following spring." On hearing a fluttering in the desk, the man recovered the birds and managed to revive them.

Charles Dixon, the prolific writer of bird books, who was one of the few naturalists of his time to take the idea of avian hibernation seriously, includes this record among the many he listed in *The Migration of Birds* (1892). To it he adds another, from the *Edinburgh Journal* (viii), of three living but dormant corncrakes which were excavated from "a dung-heap that had long remained undisturbed" at Monaghan in Ireland. Dixon claimed that he could fill "scores of pages" with apparently well-authenticated instances of the hibernation of birds, and he called the refusal of his contemporaries to consider these records "most unwise and most unscientific".

Perhaps the most famous upholder of the belief was The Revd Gilbert White of Selborne in Hampshire. In the letters to Thomas Pennant and Daines Barrington which comprise his *Natural*

History of Selborne (1788) he returned again and again to the subject. The evidence for hibernation that seemed to him most compelling was that swallows would suddenly appear in his parish one fine spring day and then disappear for a while during a spell of bad weather. Similarly, in the autumn they would vanish, but a sunny day would see the return of a few individuals which he suspected of having temporarily re-emerged out of hibernation.

White also knew of a man who as schoolboy at Brighton had witnessed a cliff-fall during a winter storm which had exposed many hibernating swallows. A similar story was published in the *Zoologist* (1849, page 2590). In cutting away part of a rocky hill, situated between Hasting and St Leonard's, labourers had found an immense quantity of swallows within a cleft. "The birds were clinging together in large 'clots', and appeared to be dead, but were not frozen together, and the weather being rather warm for the season, nor were they at all putrid or decayed. . . The birds were found about ten feet from the surface of the rock facing the sea, and not very high up." Unfortunately, most of the birds were taken away and buried with the debris from the cliff.

We are impressed by a detail which recurs time and again in reports of hibernating swallows: that the torpid birds are found clinging together in "clots". In one of his poems the eighteenth-century Welsh bard, Iolo Morgannwg (alias Edward

Philip Henry Gosse (1810–88), the Victorian popularizer of natural history. Unlike Gilbert White, Gosse felt that the evidence was insufficient to support belief in hibernating swallows.

Williams), wrote the line: "And sleep the swallows in their cavern'd rocks", to which he added a footnote: "About the year 1768, the Author, with two or three more, found a great number of swallows, in a torpid state, clinging in clusters to each other by their bills, in a cave of the sea cliff near Dunraven Castle, in the county of Glamorgan." We have no further details of this discovery, but the belief in hibernating swallows was evidently part of Welsh traditional lore, for in a book called *The Bardic Museum* (1802) by Edward Jones, the swallow is listed among the "seven sleepers" recognized by the Druids, along with the dormouse and other hibernating animals. The clots or clusters formed by the sleeping birds are doubtless behind the Chinese legend that swallows in winter plunge beneath the water, cling together and turn into mussels.

W.L. McAtee, who wrote an article about hibernations of birds in the *Audubon* magazine (1950, vol. 52), was impressed by a case reported earlier in *Nature* magazine by observers of the highest repute, Sir John McNeill and Sir Henry Rawlinson. They stated that in Persia they had found hundreds of hibernating swallows in burrows. Their report – completely ignored at the time – has now been proved to have been largely accurate. The clinching evidence was provided by a whippoorwill, a kind of nightjar, which Professor E.C. Jaeger found hibernating in a hollow on a rock face in the Colorado Desert. That was in the winter of 1946, and the following winter Jaeger was able to observe, over a period of eighty-five days, a whippoorwill in the same hollow on the rock, and to prove that it was in a state of near-suspended animation and truly hibernating.

Maurice Burton, in a chapter on the hibernation of birds in his *Animal Legends* (1955), gives a fuller account of Jaeger's discovery, and comments that "he was merely confirming a deeply-founded suspicion". Indeed, one of the most respected of American ornithologists, Dr Elliot Coues, in the first part of his *Birds of the Colorado Valley* (1878) had cited over 250 references to hibernating swallows, stating his belief in the hibernation of several American bird species, notably the chimney swift. He showed that clusters of these birds sometimes spend the winter in hollow trees. Other reported American hibernators include swifts, swallows, martins, whippoorwills, ptarmigans and turkey vultures.

We may perhaps see the day when Gilbert White and the old school of naturalists are proved right by a new discovery of a clutch of hibernating swallows. We are concerned, however, by Gosse's observation, that these finds seem to be getting rarer. The same applies to several of the other phenomena described in this book – toads in stones and sea-serpent sightings, for example. On the other hand, many, of the monsters and weird creatures, written about in earlier chapters, are currently very much on the increase – at least, reports of them are. Perhaps the theories affect the evidence, as much as the other way round, and the decline in torpid swallows and stoned toads is nature's response to modern naturalists' refusal to believe in such things. Or perhaps, more prosaically, mechanical methods of earth-moving make it now more likely for such creatures to be squashed rather than observed.

12

Tail Pieces

Tail Pieces

Cats with wings

Many people do not believe in winged cats. It sounds too fantastic. But these seemingly impossible creatures do occasionally exist. There are several modern, authenticated examples of cats with wings, and even a few cases where such animals are said to be capable of making limited flights.

In the 1930s there was a winged cat on show at the old Oxford Zoo. Its wings were not mere ornaments but were used, according to the woman who discovered the animal, to gain height when leaping up from the ground. The *Daily Mirror* sent a Special Correspondent to Oxford to inspect it, and he reported (9 June 1933) as follows. "A few days ago neighbours of Mrs Hughes Griffiths of Summerstown, Oxford, saw a strange black and white cat prowling round their gardens. Last evening Mrs Hughes Griffiths saw the animal in a room of her stables. 'I saw it move from the ground to a beam – a considerable distance which I do not think it could have leaped-using its wings in a manner similar to that of a bird', she said to me. Mrs Hughes Griffiths at once telephoned to the Oxford Zoo, and Mr Frank Owen, the managing director, and Mr W.E. Sawyer, the curator, went to her house and captured the animal in a net. I carefully examined the cat tonight, and there is no doubt about the wings. They grow just in front of its hindquarters."

The Oxford Zoo is long defunct, and our inquiries have brought to light no other relic of its winged cat other than this one photograph (overleaf).

In *Strange Creatures from Time and Space* (1975) John Keel refers to three winged cats which appeared in Ontario, Canada, in 1966. Two of them were reported as having been shot near Montreal and near Ottawa, the third was said to be a large, black flying cat seen swooping down on terrified pets and farm animals at Alfred, Ontario in June 1966. On 24 June it was shot by Mr Jean J. Revers of Alfred as it sailed in, howling and screeching, to attack a local cat, "making gliding jumps of fifty or sixty feet – wings extended". The police were called, and Constable Argall later gave his description of the dead predator: "Its head resembled a cat's, but a pair of needle sharp fangs five eighths of an inch long protruded from the mouth. It had a cat's whiskers, tail and ears, and its eyes were dark, greenish and glassy. I never saw anything like it in my life."

The cat's measured wing-span was fourteen inches. It was buried in Mr Revers's garden, but a few days later it was dug up and sent for examination to Kemptville Agricultural School. The verdict of their veterinary laboratory was that it was an ordinary black cat with long growths of thick, matted black fur protruding from its back.

Whatever the nature of its wings, the fearful cat had been seen by many people in Alfred to fly

The winged cat of Oxford Zoo in 1933.

a foot or so above the ground after taking a leap; and the Oxford cat seems also to have used the flaps of fur on its back to assist flight. The Sheffield cat, illustrated opposite, could spread its wings, but we are not aware of any other cases of winged cats that actually flew. However, cats with wings – functioning or otherwise – have obvious value to showmen, and we have heard of lawsuits arising over disputed ownership.

Peter Dance tells a curious tale in his book, *Animal Fakes and Frauds* (1976). In the early 1960s he saw an advertisement for the sale of "Thomas Bessy, the Famous Winged Cat", together with a glass and mahogany showcase in which this stuffed oddity was mounted. It was said to be a nine-teenth-century specimen and to have belonged to a circus owner who exhibited it. There had been a dispute about possession. Its original owner went

to law to claim it back and won the case. The circus owner returned the cat in a box, but it was found to be dead on arrival home, and there was suspicion that it had been poisoned.

Dance says that he wrote to the London address given in the advertisement, but received no reply. About the same time of the Thomas Bessy advertisement another winged cat disap-peared. This second animal was also called Thomas (or Mitzi) and her story is told in John Keel's *Strange Creatures*.

In May 1959, fifteen-year-old Douglas Shelton was hunting in the hills near his home at Pinesville, West Virginia. His dog chased a cat which escaped up a tree. Douglas climbed after it, caught it and discovered that it had wings. These were boneless and furry but seemed to have gristle in them and felt gritty towards the body. The cat was a large

Persian with a tail like a squirrel. Douglas called it Thomas, a name it retained even though it later turned out to be a female. Thomas became a celebrity. Her picture was in many newspapers, and on 8 June 1959 she appeared with her owner on the New York television show *Today*. On her return to Pinesville, crowds of well-wishers journeyed through the West Virginia mountains to see and photograph her, paying a small sum to Douglas and his mother for the privilege. It was the biggest thing that had ever happened in Pinesville, and the town gained further notoriety when Thomas became involved in a law suit. A local woman, Mrs Hicks, claimed that Thomas was her cat and was really called Mitzi. She had been given to Mrs Hicks by a friend who bought her in a California pet store. The neighbours, said Mrs Hicks, well remembered Mitzi and her furry wings.

On 5 October 1959 Thomas/Mitzi was exhibited in court. But there was something different about her. She was wingless. Douglas

Shelton opened a box and displayed two large balls of fur. Thomas shed her wings in July, he said. Mrs Hicks denied that the cat was hers, and a confused judge awarded the animal to Douglas and compensated Mrs Hicks with one dollar for damages.

John Keel says that in 1966 he passed through Pinesville and made enquiries for Thomas/Mitzi but without success. She and her various owners were nowhere to be found. It was not long since Peter Dance had seen the advertisement for Thomas Bessy, the winged cat which had been exhibited and had also been the subject of a famous lawsuit. Were these two cats one and the same? And what has happened to it or them? If anyone should hear of another winged cat advertised for sale we should appreciate the information.

Yet another winged cat featured in the pages of *Weekend* (12 November 1980). This tortoiseshell cat, called Sandy, gained her wings when fully grown, but despite her impressive furry flaps she never flew. Sandy was exhibited at a carnival in

A tomcat called Sally which belonged to Mrs Roebuck of Attercliffe, Sheffield. This 1939 photograph shows Sally's two-foot wingspan which enabled him to make especially long leaps. Sally's markings are extremely close to the Oxford Zoo cat and it is possible that they were related.

This portrait of a winged cat appeared in the *Strand* magazine in November 1899. It belonged to a lady of Wiveliscombe, Somerset, to whom it had been given as a kitten.

Sutton-in-Ashfield, Nottinghamshire, in the 1950s, and is said to be remembered there still.

The only case we know of from recent years is the one seen by Rebecca Hough in Japan in May 1998. In a letter to *Fortean Times* (no.114, p.50) she reports how, while in the town of Kumamoto in Kyushu, she saw a cat with a "bumpy" back. "Then I realised it had weird growths – not fat or bones – but jutting-out fur-covered wing-like growths. In all other respects it seemed quite normal. The growths were triangular and covered in soft fluffy fur. They felt like the wings of a chicken."

Zoologist Dr Karl Shuker has carried out one of the few serious studies of the phenomenon. In *Fortean Times* (no.78, pp.32–33) he presents the novel theory that these cats might be suffering from an uncommon condition called feline cutaneous asthenia (FCA) which results in an elastic skin. In the normal course of FCA, the skin becomes extremely fragile and tears or sloughs off in time. The winged cats described above seem to be far more robust. Shuker also proposes that the earliest winged cat on record dates from 1868 when its skin was exhibited at a meeting of the Bombay Asiatic Society, the animal having been shot by one Alexander Gibson.

La GATA con ALAS

ES DISTINTA A TODOS
LOS EJEMPLARES DE
SU RAZA

LA PUBLICIDAD REALIZADA
POR "ALAS" TAMBIEN ES
DISTINTA Y ORIGINAL
PIDANOS IDEAS Y PRESUPUESTOS

EMPRESA ANUNCIADORA, S. A.
ALCALA, 32 - MADRID

An advertisement, in the Spanish daily paper *ABC*, announcing a forthcoming article about a cat with wings ('gata con alas') from Madrid named Angolina. The story duly appeared on 26 May 1950.

The winged cat which appeared in the yard of Banister Walton & Co., Trafford Park, Manchester, in the early 1970s and was resident there for several years.

Monkey chains

"When wolves cross a river, they follow one another directly in a line, the second holding the tail of the first in its mouth, the third that of the second, and so of the rest," (Abbé Pluché as quoted in Cassell's *World of Wonders*). We have searched in vain for witnesses' accounts of this performance and conclude either that the ancient Greek writers who reported it were testing our credulity, or that perhaps someone once trained captive wolves to hold each other's tails, like elephants at a circus, and that someone else saw the thing and garbled it in the retelling.

No one in modern times seems to have believed in the river-crossing wolf chain, but a similar belief, where the feat is attributed to monkeys, has proved more lasting.

An enduring feature of education in geography, until fairly recently, was the belief that the long-tailed monkeys of the South American jungles differed from their cousins in Africa and Asia in one important behavioural aspect arising from their extraordinarily prehensile tails. Generations of schoolchildren were presented with the charming picture of bands of resourceful monkeys crossing crocodile-infested rivers by forming themselves into a living bridge. Children's textbooks showed how one monkey would clutch a branch as anchor-man, while one after another the rest curled their tails around the monkey behind to form the next link in the chain, and when it was long enough they would swing to and fro until their momentum carried them out across the river. The monkey on the end would then grab a branch on the opposite bank, securing the chain while the old and young hurried across.

This example of collective intelligence and social organization was frequently and authoritatively cited, despite the doubts of no less a person than Alexander von Humboldt. He wrote, in his *Personal Narrative of Travels* (1852), that he believed the story had been invented by Europeans (probably as an instructive tale with which to admonish the natives) before passing into the traditions of the Mission Indians. However, the brothers H.M. and P.V.N. Myers, who explored the isthmus joining the two Americas in 1867–68, state in *Life and Nature under the Tropics* (1871) that, despite seeing "multitudes of these creatures, our observations convinced us that there was no foundation for the truth of the tale of the bridge-building monkeys.

In 1919 Professor E.W. Gudger wrote a short paper on the subject in *Natural History* (vol.19, no.2). He had reviewed the evidence with academicians and explorers attached to the American Museum of Natural History, and their opinion was that the monkey chain was a myth evolved from poor observations of the behaviour of individual monkeys, who were well known to dangle from branches by their tails or swing across gaps using liana vines. Further, Gudger doubted there would be enough room, where the dense jungle goes right up to the river's edge, for any living pendulum to work up a swing perpendicular to a river – unless they were dangling from a branch that already overhung the river.

The myth of the monkey chain, concluded Gudger, "attributes more collective intelligence to monkeys than they have ever been known to show". This sounds impressive, until one realizes the implication – that all other accounts would also be crediting the monkeys with more intelligence than they have ever been known to show – making impossible any appeal to an accumulating body of testimony. The same reasoning denies the collective testimony of UFO or Nessie witnesses by criticizing individual accounts in isolation.

But how did the story gain credence? Had anyone actually seen a monkey chain? In 1735, Antonio de Ulloa joined an expedition in the Panama region and wrote, in his *Voyage to South America* (1760), about "the different species of monkeys, skipping in troops from tree to tree, hanging from branches and in other places, six, eight or more of them linked together, in order to pass a river". De Ulloa admits that the phenomenon "will perhaps appear fictitious to those who have not actually seen it," but does not clarify

matters by stating specifically that he himself witnessed it. In fact it was de Ulloa's account that prompted Humboldt's refutation. Five years spent observing the monkeys convinced him that de Ulloa's assertion was "dubious".

However, Gudger located some earlier and more satisfying accounts. For example, Lionel Wafer was greatly amused by the antics of the monkeys which travelled through the trees alongside the party of the navigator, Captain Dampier, while he was crossing the American isthmus. He wrote: "To pass from top to top of high trees, whose branches are a little too far asunder for their leaping, they will sometimes hang down by one another's tails in a chain; and swinging in that manner, the lowermost catches hold of a bough of the other tree, and draws up the rest of them.' (*A New Voyage and Description of the Isthmus of America*, 1699).

But the earliest account is the best, originating with a Jesuit, José de Acosta, whose account was published in Spain in 1589, and later translated as *Naturall and Morall Historie of the East and West Indies* (1604). De Acosta states: "I did see in Capira one of these monkeys leape from one tree to another, which was on the other side of a river, making me much to wonder. They leape where they list, winding their tailes about a braunch to shake it; and when they will leape further than they can at once, they use a pretty devise, tying themselves by the tailes one of another, and by this meanes make as it were a chaine of many; then doe they launch themselves forth, and the first holpen by the force of the rest, takes holde where hee list, and so hangs to a bough, and so helpes all the rest, till they be gotten up". Gudger is certain that neither Wafer, de Ulloa, or Humboldt knew of this account, and claims it as the progenitor of the myth; and yet there is no sign here of a fable being spun for the edification of the ignorant.

The principal objection to the "myth" is that no such behaviour has been observed by contemporary naturalists – at least to their satisfaction. One of the most up-to-date accounts appeared in 1897, accompanied by the illustration we present here. It was signed by Charles Frederick Holder, whom Gudger acknowledged as a naturalist of high standing, but despite a search Gudger could find no corroboration of it in Holder's own books. This account is of an undated trip up the Amazon. Nightfall caught the party up a side stream where for safety's sake they anchored in midstream under trees which arched from bank to bank overhead. Just before dawn Holder was woken by a blow on

Illustration of Charles Holder's account of a monkey chain in Professor George Holmes's *Fourth Reader* (1897).

his face and caught a glimpse of a furry column swinging towards the far bank and pivoting from a branch of a tree on the opposite bank. It took him a few minutes to figure out what it was, and then: "The sight was so novel, the plan so daring, that I at once gave these queer bridge-makers my closest attention".

The monkey chain succeeded in securing itself on the farther bank after several tries, and Holder watched as the females, the young and old clambered across, until at last, startled by his sudden and irresistible laughter, the living bridge "dropped to pieces" and fled into the forest. Mrs Loudon, the author of a number of popular and well-respected natural history books, implies, in *The Entertaining Naturalist* (1867), that monkey-chain-type antics have been observed among the South American monkeys at London Zoo. But Gudger continues to maintain his objections on the grounds that no record of such behaviour has ever been reported in the *Proceedings* of the Zoological Society of London.

The only example we can find of creatures other than monkeys forming a living chain comes from a letter to *Animal and Zoo* magazine in about 1940 (our clipping is undated). In Africa, the writer saw an army of ants on the march, of the type that stop at no obstacle and devour everything in its path. A column of them was seen to cross a narrow ditch of water by means of an ant chain. It was formed by hundreds of the little creatures, holding on to each other, from bank to bank, while the rest swarmed across.

How rats steal eggs

A curiosity of animal behaviour that has always perplexed naturalists and is still not entirely explained is the ability of rats to take hold of hens' eggs and transport them considerable distances to their holes and dens. There was a debate on this in the old journal, *Nature Notes*, beginning in May 1898 when a contributor, Edmund Daubeny, reported that a labourer near his home in Market Weston, Norfolk, had discovered stores of unbroken eggs in rat holes. These were in a ditch about half a mile away from the nearest source of eggs at a local farm. How, asked Daubeny, had the rats carried them there?

Nature Notes readers replied with a variety of answers, and Daubeny summarized them in the September issue of the journal. The four most popular suggestions were: that the rats form a line and hand the eggs from one to another; that they roll them along the ground with noses and forepaws; that they hold them under their chins and hop along on their back legs; and finally the old story, that one rat lies on its back, clutching an egg to its stomach while another draws it along by the tail. Daubeny dismissed all these explanations and he was particularly hard on the last. He asked. "Is it likely that any animal would quietly submit to the ordeal of having its tail nipped and being rubbed the wrong way into the bargain?

A 19th-century Japanese fan painting by Satake Eikai showing rats carrying away a large egg by dragging one of their number by the tale. Though widely believed, there are no first-hand accounts of this method.

An engraving which shows three egg-carrying rats negotiating a step by delicately passing the egg one to another.

They would bump him terribly over rough ground, to the great danger of the egg; and how long would hair remain on his poor back, or the skin on his tail? . . . The theory lands us in endless difficulties, and I give it up."

Despite this rational dismissal, several correspondents repeated stories of rats being seen carrying off eggs, apparently by working out means of collaboration. One wrote that his neighbour in Derbyshire, "a truthful sort of person", had on two occasions in his youth seen a rat on its back, clutching an egg between its nose and paws and being carried by two others, one at each end. Another second-hand account, in the *Pall Mall Gazette* (quoted in E.L. Arnold's *Soul of the Beast*), told of a lady whose eggs were being stolen. "She hid up in her fowl house, and patiently waited till she saw a large rat run up a short ladder to a nest, and seize an egg between his paws. He then laid himself on his back, and held the egg on his chest. More rats appeared, and, forming themselves into a chain from the ground, they positively drew the rat with the egg down the ladder, passing it along from one to the other till it was safely below." A variation on this is given by the great rat authority, Rodwell, who tells how rats carry eggs up and down stairs. They pass them to each other, with their front paws when going downstairs and with their back legs when going up.

More recent observations tend to confirm the traditional account. In the 1980s a television programme which dismissed it as a fable prompted many viewers to respond with accounts of rats with eggs being dragged by the tail. Anthony Wootton in *Animal Folklore, Myth and Legend* (1986) says that he has literally dozens of such observations and that they are all much the same. "Essentially what happens, it seems, is that one rat lies on its back, clasping the egg (or whatever) between all four legs and paws, and is then dragged along by the tail, or sometimes the scruff of the neck, by the second; alternatively, the prone rat grasps the leader's tail in its teeth, thus making its passage slightly more comfortable, perhaps, in that it proceeds with the lie of the fur." The most amazing account came from a man who witnessed a line of four rats, each holding in its teeth the tail of the one in front while the last one lay on its back clutching an egg. When they had taken the egg to where they wanted it they all returned and took another, drawing it along in the same way and taking five eggs in all.

There are even accounts of one rat pulling another by slinging its tail over its shoulder and grasping it with its paws, like a man dragging a sled. Wootton says that he has seen a nineteenth-century ornament carved with this scene. Scientists are generally sceptical about all these stories (mainly because they are frightened of anthropomorphizing or attributing human-type reasoning to animals) and it is unfortunate that there are no authentic photographs of egg-stealing rats. Someone who could have taken one was Mark Atkinson, a farmer on the Somerset Mendips, who told John Michell that as a young man he had seen an egg-clutching rat being dragged along by another, but instead of running for his camera he fetched a shotgun and blew the vermin away.

Rat kings

In the case of MONKEY CHAINS (see p.357) the experts are divided on the credibility of the various accounts. In contrast, the story of the rat Kings is one of a peasant superstition that was verified, only to sink into obscurity. As curiosities go, the rat King seems even more obscure than most, even in its heyday it was hardly known outside Central Europe.

A rat King consists of a number of rats found with their tails inextricably tied together in a central knot. Another name for this fearful conglomeration is the Rat King's Throne. All the reports of rat Kings agree that black rats only are involved in these mysterious minglings; and one reason for the rarity of the phenomenon today might be the savage depletion of the black rat population by the hordes of brown rats that invaded Central Europe from the region of the Caspian Sea in the eighteenth century.

Most rat Kings have been found in continental Europe – none are known from Britain or the USA – and little has been written about rat Kings in English; most accounts have never been translated out of their French and German originals. The earliest depiction of a King dates to 1564, and there is a reference by Martin Luther to one in

The ground for the popular belief in rat Kings derives from the popular folk belief that each species of animal had its own society presided over by a king. The pioneer of cryptozoology, Conrad Gesner, wrote in 1555 of the belief that there were venerable rats who grew in size as they grew more ancient, and were tended by a pack who would

The earliest known illustration of a rat King from Johannes Sambucus' *Emblemata* (1564).

1524, so they must have been well known before that date. The naturalist, Alfred Brehm, collected stories of rat Kings, but when his *Thierleben* (1876–79) was translated into the multi-volume *Library of Natural History*, the editor, Richard Lydekker, saw fit to omit Brehm's pages on the subject.

steal food and fine velvet for their lord. No giant rat, imprisoned in splendour in a disused barn or cellar, was ever discovered, but as the original plague of black rats spread through Europe and ratting became a secure career for man and dog, the title of rat King was transferred to the occasional discovery of one of these tangled terrors of

This 1963 rat King was discovered at Rucphen, in North Brabant, Holland. The x-ray of its knotted tail proves it is a real tangle and not, as has been suggested, a matter of being glued together.

verminous vermicelli. Brehm gives a list of a few discoveries including a notable one at Altenburg composed of twenty-seven individuals. Usually a lesser number were found knotted, like the eight-fold rat King killed in a Düsseldorf abattoir in February 1880, and the seven-fold rat King found at Châteaudun in November 1889 and presented to the museum there.

Perhaps the most astonishing case of all occurred in Döllstedt, a German village near Gotha, in December 1822, when farmhands threshing grain investigated a squealing in the attic of their barn. Climbing up they found a hollow on the topside of the main beam full of rats which made no attempt to escape. The hollow was clean and, according to one account, lined with straw. The rats inside were apathetic and weak from hunger. When they were pushed out, they fell in two squeaking clusters to the floor below; one was composed of twenty-eight individuals and the other of fourteen. Villagers gathered to see the marvel, and later joined in its execution with flails. The rats were separated with great difficulty, and

a forester called to witness the strange discovery later testified that the skin on each tail was intact and "showed the impressions of the other tails, just like leather straps that had been plaited together for a long time."

The whole subject would have remained in the genre of "peasant superstitions" if a rat King had not been the subject of a legal squabble in 1774. A young man named Christian Kaiser, working in a mill at Lindenau, near Leipzig, discovered a group made up of sixteen rats, while ratting in the mill on 12 January. A few days later he travelled to the district office of the government of Saxony in Leipzig. He alleged that a local character, Johann Adam Fasshauer, had gained possession of the prodigy with the pretence that he wanted a painting done of it. Instead, Fasshauer put it on public exhibition and pocketed a tidy sum which, Kaiser claimed, rightfully belonged to his master. A tribunal took statements from all the witnesses, and then commissioned a doctor to examine the rat King, which he did in the Posthorn Inn at Lindenau and, despite Fasshauer's protests attempted to separate the rats. The doctor reported that it was "not one organism which is called a rat King but sixteen different rats of different size and colouration, and (in my opinion) different age and sex." They seemed undernourished, and fifteen of them "had their tails knotted together into a large knot in such a manner that most tails were completely in the knot except for one or two inches near their bodies". The tail of the sixteenth was twisted around the back of another rat.

Whereas the testimony of the forester of Döllstedt might have implied that a rat King could have been formed while the rats were still very young, their tails growing and locking into the configurations of the knot, the findings of the doctor at Lindenau showed the rat King was a fairly recent formation, its individuals being of different ages, sizes and so on. The doctor offered his theory that in excessively cold weather the rats huddle together for warmth, facing outwards for their mutual security. He had noted that their tails were dirty and speculated that urine and faeces from the ones in the upper circle had fallen onto the intertwined mass of tails and frozen solid. Brehm preferred his own theory – that huddling rats fall foul of a malady causing their tails to exude a fluid which then solidifies. Here is yet another curious case of a collector of stories going against the prevailing observations of his witnesses – which were that, apart from indentations from contact and pressure, the tails were apparently healthy.

Willy Ley, writing of his interest in rat Kings in *Galaxy* (October 1963), tried to find a modern case but could only come up with the ten-fold rat King found in the Westphalian village of Capelle in January 1907. It was quickly acquired by the Zoological Institute of the University of Göttingen, to the chagrin of their slower rivals in the Provincial Museum of Westphalia. The director of the Institute himself welcomed the celebrity, or celebrities, and personally conducted the examination. In answer to a professional query he confessed himself unable to account for the formation of the rat King. No modern zoologist claims to be any the wiser.

Our knowledge of the phenomenon has been greatly enlarged by the rat expert Martin Hart, who devotes a chapter to Kings in his *Rats* (1982), describing 57 discoveries between 1564 and 1963, including a ten-fold cluster of *Rattus brevicaudatus* (the only known exception to the black rat rule) in Java in March 1918. Hart's research led him to the discovery of a seven-fold King at Rucphen in Holland, in February 1963 (this being in the very year that Ley wrote of his failure to find a modern case). At Rucphen, a farmer, investigating a

A graphic illustration of a rat King from Henri Coupin's *Les animaux excentriques*.

squealing from a pile of bean sticks in his yard, saw a rat and killed it. As it would not budge when he tugged at it, he pulled away the sticks to reveal the six other black rats, which he also killed. They seemed to be of the same age and well fed. He offered the ratty tangle for study by veterinarians, resulting in a scientific description and a set of X-rays of the knotted tail showing fractures and calluses. This, wrote Hart, was final proof "that the tails had not grown together [but] had been knotted together for some considerable time."

Phenomena on the Internet

Readers wishing to extend their interests further will find many resources on the Internet. The following directory of Web addresses (URLs) only touches briefly on what is available. Many of our topics do not have any useful or related Web resources . . . yet; but most of the sites we list here provide comprehensive links to other sites and resource lists of their own and will serve as good starting points for further research.

The quality of information varies greatly, and covers the spectrum of interpretation from the completely credulous to the utterly sceptical. Remember Fort's advice: believe nothing absolutely and always seek more reliable evidence.

Readers wishing to pass on corrections, observations or personal stories may contact Bob Rickard by email at *rickard@forteantimes.com* or by post via our publisher Rough Guides.

Fort, forteanism and forteana

Fortean Times
www.forteantimes.com
A monthly "Journal of Strange Phenomena", founded in 1973 as a primary forum for news, discussion, links and archives to core and fringe forteana.

The Charles Fort Institute (CFI)
www.forteana.org
A charitable project to create an online museum, archive and library devoted to fortean topics and documentation. Site includes a biography of Fort.

International Fortean Organization (INFO)
www.research.umbc.edu/~frizzell/info
INFO was founded in 1965 as the natural successor to the original Fortean Society.

Mr X
www.resologist.net
Mr X has devoted years to checking Charles Fort's sources to provide a corrected text and commentary.

Enigmas
http://members.tripod.com/Dragonrest/enigmas.html
Marguerite Wolf's tribute pages of Charles Fort, with selections from his writings.

Strange Magazine

www.strangemag.com

Mark Chorvinsky's bi-annual magazine concentrates on investigating mainly American forteana.

The Anomalist

www.anomalist.com

A bi-monthly digest devoted to the mysteries of science, nature and history. Has a sampler of quotations from Fort.

Sourcebook Project

www.science-frontiers.com/sourcebk.htm

William R. Corliss is self-publishing a 25-volume collection of fortean data culled from scientific sources, with commentaries.

Fortean Picture Library (FPL)

(FPL) www.forteanpix.demon.co.uk
(eFPL) www.forteanpixonline.com

Along with its Internet branch (eFPL), the FPL aims to fund the preservation of visual documentation of forteana through commercial licensing.

Committee for the Scientific Investigation of Claims of the Paranormal (CSICOP)

www.csicop.org

The largest "skeptical" organization, founded by academicians to resist the "tide of superstition".

The Skeptic's Dictionary

http://skepdic.com

Dr Robert T. Carroll maintains this seriously sceptical yet essential guide to 338 topics of fortean interest.

Journal of Scientific Exploration (JSE)

www.jse.com

A fine forum for open-minded discussion of fortean topics in the scientific community.

Teleportation

Quantum Teleportation

http://info.uibk.ac.at/c/c7/c704/qo/photon/_teleport/
The experiments of physicist Charles H. Bennett's team.

Telekinesis and Psychokinesis

http://paranormal.about.com/culture/paranormal/msub20.html
Stephen Wagner's resources and links on "moving objects psychically at a distance".

Materialisation and Flight of Objects

http://moebius.psy.ed.ac.uk/spr.html
The archives of the Society for Psychical Research.

Strange Rains

Falls of Fishes

www.forteantimes.com/artic/106/sprats.html
Examples from Australia.

The Dundas Incident

www.resologist.net/art02.htm
Mr X on Charles Fort's own investigation of a fall of fish in Canada in 1926.

The Guyra Ghost

www.forteantimes.com/artic/116/guyra.html
Investigation of a stone-throwing poltergeist in New South Wales.

Red Rain

www.strangemag.com/redrain.html
A reference article by Mark Chorvinsky.

Weird Rains

http://members.tripod.com/Dragonrest/rains.html
Citations from the writings of Charles Fort.

Wild Talents

The Miracle Page
www.mcn.org/1/Miracles/
Contemporary reports of "miracles" from all over the world.

Wings of Fire
www.firewalking.org/
Firewalking for personal growth and development. Based in California.

Thoughtography
http://skepdic.com/pphotog.html
The Skeptic's Dictionary on the hypothesis of psychically imprinting images onto film.

Stigmata
http://crystalinks.com/stigmata.html
A general reference site.

Mystical Stigmata
www.newadvent.org/cathen/14294b.htm
The Catholic Encyclopedia site.

Levitation
http://skepdic.com/levitat.html
The Skeptic's Dictionary on levitation as an illusion or trick.

The Levitating Saint
www.crystalclarity.com/yogananda/chap7/chap7.html
Chapter 7 of *The Autobiography of a Yogi* by Paramahansa Yogananda

Incorrupt Bodies of Saints
http://members.aol.com/ccmail/incorruptbodies.html
A Catholic Community information site.

Incorruptible Bodies
http://skepdic.com/incorrupt.html
The Skeptic's Dictionary reviews natural methods of preservation.

The Madness of Crowds

Dancing Mania
http://neuroscience.about.com/library/pr/blpr991214b.htm
A recent article by Allan Sison on how medieval dance manias may have a neurological origin.

War of the Worlds
www.war-of-the-worlds.org
Everything you want to know about the original broadcast and related panics.

Steamshovel
www.steamshovelpress.com/
Kenn Thomas's site on modern conspiracy topics.

Conspiracies Galore!
www.solungen.hm.no/razor/conspir.htm
A good general links page of uncertain authorship.

Collective Hallucinations
http://skepdic.com/collective.html
The Skeptic's Dictionary investigates.

Major Apparitions of Jesus and Mary
www.apparitions.org
A Catholic chronology of over 100 vision sites from 1347 to the present with links.

The Chupacabra Page
www.princeton.edu/~accion/chupa.html
The original monitoring site, set up by Puerto Rican students at Princeton University.

The Watchman Fellowship
www.watchman.org/indxmenu.htm
A catalogue of over 1200 cults and groups with links.

The Good Folk

Fairy-related Links
www.faerielands.com/fairylinks/
A comprehensive resource on ancient and modern aspects of fairy-lore.

Fairies and their Kin
www.indigogroup.co.uk/edge/fairies.htm
Article by Bob Trubshaw from *At the Edge*, an excellent archive of new studies of mythology and folklore.

The Cottingley Fairies
www.lhup.edu/~dsimanek/cooper.htm
A near-definitive history by Joe Cooper.

Mysterious Lights
http://ufos.about.com/culture/ufos/library/weekly/ aa032999.htm
Background and links on "spooklights" and "earthlights" by Loy Lawhon.

Earth Lights
www.forteantimes.com/artic/103/earth.html
Paul Devereux on his investigations into transient light phenomena.

Cornish Fairies
www.gandolf.com/cornwall/fairies/index.shtml
A collections of texts about abductions and changelings.

Urban Legends
www.snopes.com
Probably the best archive of contemporary mythology and rumours on the Net.

Invisibles and other Assailants

CNI News
www.cninews.com/
Michael Lindemann's essential monthly digest of UFO-related news.

Magonia
www.magonia.demon.co.uk/
Home of the psycho-social school of British ufology.

Ultimate Ufologists WWW Page
http://ourworld.compuserve.com/homepages/ AndyPage/
Andy Page's general compendium of information and links for beginners.

UFO Folkore
www.qtm.net/~geibdan/framemst.html
General links on the subject of ufology as a cultural phenomenon.

The J. Allen Hynek Center for UFO Studies (CUFOS)
www.cufos.org
American ufology's serious face.

Alien Abductions
http://ufos.about.com/culture/ufos/
Background and links on UFOs and "alien abductions".

The Search for Extraterrestrial Intelligence (SETI)
http://setiathome.ssl.berkeley.edu/othersites.html
Comprehensive background and links page.

Mysterious Mutilators
http://skepdic.com/cattle.html
The Skeptic's Dictionary on cattle mutilation.

Spontaneous Human Combustion
http://skepdic.com/shc.html
Another investigation from The Skeptic's Dictionary.

The Haunted Planet

Hollow Earth
http://paranormal.about.com/culture/paranormal/
msub10.html
Stephen Wagner on "Hollow Earth" and Planets.

Haunted Highways
www.forteantimes.com/artic/104/belles.html
Sean Tudor on the "Bluebell Hill Ghosts".

The Ley Hunter
www.leyhunter.com
One of the most venerable and broad-minded of "Earth Mysteries" sites.

Anomalous Fossils
www.cremo.com
Michael Cremo's Forbidden Archeology site dedicated to "out-of-place" artifacts.

Noah's Ark
www.noahsarksearch.com
B.J. Corbin's expanding resource on historical and contemporary searches.

The Crop Circle Connector
www.marque.demon.co.uk/connector/connector.html
A wide range of links, photos, articles and resources.

Crop Circle Database
www.cropcircleresearch.com/database/
Interactive online catalogue of formations.

Signs and Portents

Coincidences
http://skepdic.com/jung.html
Skeptics Dictionary looks at Carl Jung, Synchronicity and the Collective Unconscious.

Cities in the Sky
www.resologist.net/art66.htm
Mr X on celestial and aerial mirages.

Images

Islamic simulacra
http://www.mcn.org/1/miracles/Allah2.html
Holy aubergines and other miraculous images.

Face on Mars
www.qtm.net/~geibdan/cydonia.html
Charting the belief in the "Face" and NASA's rephotography of the site.

Kirlian Photography
http://paranormal.about.com/culture/paranormal/
msub21kirlian.htm
Stephen Wagner's overview and resources.

The Turin Shroud
www.shroud.com
Barry M. Schwortz' comprehensive reference site.

Images that Weep and Bleed and apparently Move
www.mcn.org/1/Miracles/weeping.html
A Catholic devotional site.

Photos of Jesus
http://web.frontier.net/Apparitions/Ali.homepage.html
Sister Anna Ali's "visions" and messages.

Miraculous Photos
www.missionet.com/catholic/miracles/photos.html
A gallery of images for the faithful.

Monsters

International Society for Cryptozoology (ISC)
www.izoo.org/isc/
Evaluates the evidence for unverified animals.

The Cryptozoologist
www.lorencoleman.com
Loren Coleman's personal research archives.

In Search of Giant Squid
http://seawifs.gsfc.nasa.gov/squid.html
Smithsonian's National Museum of Natural History investigates the myth and the reality.

Zuiyo-maru Carcass
http://members.aol.com/paluxy2/plesios.htm
An analysis of the supposed plesiosaur carcass netted in 1977.

The Definitive Sea Serpent
www.strangemag.com/definitiveseaserpent.html
A comprehensive overview of the subject by Matthew Bille.

The Loch Ness Monster Research Society (LNMRS)
www.ness-monster.com
Everything you could possibly want to know.

The Legendary Champ
www.mountainmist.designspot.com/ Champsite.html
A balanced account and discussion of the Lake Champlain Monster.

Global Underwater Search Team
www.gust.st
Investigates lake-monster sightings in Norway, Sweden and Scotland.

Globsters
www.strangemag.com/globhome.html
Strange Magazine's Globster links and resources.

Werewolves
www.pitt.edu/~dash/werewolf.html
D.L. Ashliman translates historical narratives from Germany and Central Europe.

Black Dogs
www.indigogroup.co.uk/edge/bdogfl.htm
Bob Trubshaw discusses their role in British folklore (from *At the Edge*).

The Hairy Hominid Archives
www.ncf.carleton.ca/~bz050/HomePage.bf.html
Ben Roesch's "manimal" page.

Yetis, Almas and Wildmen
http://www.sonic.net/~anomaly/links/alkb0004.htm
Garth Haslam's link page.

Bigfoot Encounters
www.n2.net/prey/bigfoot
California sightings list.

Index

H

W

Y

Z